MUSIC ON RECORD 2

Big Bands

edited by Peter Gammond
and Raymond Horricks

MUSIC ON RECORD 2

Big Bands

edited by Peter Gammond
and Raymond Horricks

PSL Patrick Stephens, Cambridge

Title page *From an HMV advertisement for 'the pick of the dance bands' (Savoy Havana Band, Jack Hylton, Jan Garber, The Troubadours, Paul Whiteman and Nat Shilkret) in* The Melody Maker and British Metronome, *1927.*

First published 1981

British Library Cataloguing in Publication Data

Gammond, Peter
Music on record.
2: Big bands
1. Music—Discography
I. Title II. Horricks, Raymond
916.7899'12 ML156.2

ISBN 0 85059 495 2

Dedicated to
Jean Gibson, Anthony Wishaw, Peter Clayton and Richard Cole

Text photoset in 9 on 10 pt and 10 on 11 pt Plantin by Manuset Limited, Baldock, Herts. Printed and bound in Great Britain, on 100 gsm Fineblade coated cartridge, by The Garden City Press, Letchworth, Herts, for the publishers Patrick Stephens Limited, Bar Hill, Cambridge, CB3 8EL, England.

Contents

Introduction: The Sounds of Swing, by Peter Gammond 6

Contributors 8

'Scrapple from the Apple': **The Road to Swing and the Big Band era,** by Raymond Horricks 11

The British Bands, by Chris Ellis 38

The Bands and their LP recordings, by Burnett James and Peter Gammond 47

'Man, its hard!': The Big Band life, by Raymond Horricks 169

Bibliography 178

Introduction: The Sounds of Swing

by Peter Gammond

The music under consideration in this book, loosely known under such terms as swing, big band jazz, or even dance music, is, in essence, arranged or composed jazz and its offshoots and developments. It is not easy to decide where exactly such music takes over from improvised jazz for we can never be certain how much arrangement, even if unwritten, went into many early performances. Back in the ragtime days of the turn of the century orchestral arrangements were made and even printed, but this hardly comes under the present headings. As a tentative definition, jazz arrangement, which led to the swing era proper, has to be utilised when more than one of each instrument is involved. Thus one is aware of a degree of arrangement, if only by mutual agreement, in the early King Oliver bands where both Oliver and the young Louis Armstrong are heard playing quite involved breaks and solos in duet, surely at least in part 'by arrangement' if mainly through the instincts of collective improvisation. However, most people would keep those early Olivers in the category of improvised jazz.

The suddenness of jazz history, at least that part of it which we know, discounting the submerged part of the iceberg that made up its pre-history for three centuries, finds us plunging into early sophistication almost as soon as we are aware of jazz having an impact on popular music-making. The first jazz-orientated bands to employ instrumental sections probably did so simply to get a richer and more satisfying sound. In other words, there seems to have been no prophetic logic behind the history of big band jazz. Raymond Horricks advances his own interesting theories in his historical chapter, but some additional thoughts will not confuse the issue. All art forms tend to become more sophisticated and why should jazz be an exception? In all music, the folky element—which is almost, if not quite, the same thing as the improvisational element—soon becomes unfulfilling to the trained musician, but remains a vital spark; something to turn back to when the artifice itself becomes sterile. Improvisation is exciting when there is true inspiration behind it. In truth very few musicians are capable of improvising purposefully or interestingly, and the majority of the efforts we have to endure are nothing more than humdrum variations on chord sequences and melodies rather than the inspired and fresh creations that one always hopes for. For listener and player alike jazz could only become lastingly valuable once a grain of compositional organisation had been added. Most of the finest small group jazz on record has at least some degree of arranging in it—Armstrong's superb *West End blues*, for instance, or the recordings of Jelly Roll Morton's best period.

Jazz had the example of formal music all around it with bands of the kind that Sousa ran, theatre music and classical music. If it was to advance from the earthy innocence of its New Orleans days, it had to bring in the composer and the arranger. There is also a clear connection between popular music and jazz. If Tin Pan Alley took much of its styling and flavouring from jazz, it returned the debt by offering, as vehicles for jazz performance, music of growing complexity, shapeliness and harmonic interest. It is one thing to improvise on a 12-bar blues theme or *When the Saints go marching in*; quite another to do so on the songs of Gershwin. Thus swing and popular music went hand in hand. The adherents of improvised jazz will find what I am saying abhorrent. For my own tastes I find pleasure in all kinds of jazz, certainly not less in a good improvised session with inspired soloists than in the music of Duke Ellington where jazz has reached its organised peaks. Surely in the best jazz we simply demand that the spirit must be there, the true flight of fancy, but that it should be presented in a shapely and satisfying form. The best music of the swing era seems to satisfy both these demands.

Books must have some limitation put upon them. In considering big band music the most fascinating approach is through what went before, in the natural developments. Therefore we have considered some early groups and pioneers who came before the true and short-lived swing era of the 1930s. We have given less attention to what came after because it is more diffuse. Interestingly, the strongest link between the worlds of traditional and progressive jazz is swing, the big band sound, because it is a workable formula in both idioms. However, this is mainly a book built around the swing era and that is where our interest is concentrated.

The object of this *Music on Record* series is to open the way to various spheres of popular music through records. They are not discographies in the strict sense. We do not offer matrix numbers and complete biographies. The average record buyer today purchases LPs most of which are adequately supplied with their own historical data. We simply point the way (without striving for completeness) hoping that some guidance will be helpful amongst such a bewildering access of riches.

The appearance of entries in this book is dictated by the existence of LP recordings and many names are absent because they had no recorded representation in this form. The size and scope of entry is also largely dictated by LP representation, although other considerations play a part here. While fairly comprehensive lists of LPs are given (without regard to current availability, which is an extremely fluctuating situation anyway) no claim is made to completeness. This would need a book of twice the size of the present one.

Contributors

Peter Gammond was born in 1925 at Northwich, Cheshire, and was educated at the local grammar school and Wadham College, Oxford. After war service in the Royal Armoured Corps he joined the Decca Record Company in the early 1950s as musical editor of their jazz, popular and light music sleeves and publications and edited *The Decca Book of Jazz* (1958). Left Decca in 1960 to become a freelance writer. Edited *Audio Record Review* 1966-70 and then became Music Editor of the combined *Hi-Fi News & Record Review.* His wide ranging tastes in music are reflected in the titles of the books he has edited and written since 1958; including *Duke Ellington: his Life and Music* (1958), *Terms Used in Music* (1959), *101 Things* (with Peter Clayton) (1959, reprinted 1981), *A Guide to Popular Music* (with Clayton) (1960), *Jazz on Record* (1960), *Music on Record* (with Burnett James) (1962/4), *14 Miles on a Clear Night* (with Clayton) (1966), *Bluff Your Way in Music* (1966), *The Meaning and Magic of Music* (1969), *Your Own, Your Very Own* (music-hall) (1971), *One Man's Music* (1971), *Music Hall Songbook* (1975), *Musical Instruments in Colour* (1975), *Scott Joplin and the Ragtime Era* (1975), *The Illustrated Encyclopaedia of Opera* (1979), *The Magic Flute* (1979), *The Good Old Days* (1980) and *Music on Record 1: Brass Bands* (1980).

Raymond Horricks was born in 1933 at Withington and was educated at the Xaverian College, Manchester. From 1951 to 1953 he was first in France, then in Egypt, where he became a scriptwriter and broadcaster. Returning to London he worked (briefly) on the staffs of Decca (where he met Peter Gammond) and Pye Records; and for the past 20 years he has been an independent record producer of music ranging from Bach and Stravinsky to Frank Sinatra, stage musicals, brass and military bands, rock and modern jazz. This work has taken him to places as different as Berlin and the High Atlas in southern Morocco. He is the co-author, with Alun Morgan, of *Modern Jazz: A Survey of Developments Since 1939,* the first book on its subject; the author of *Count Basie and His Orchestra,* for which he received a fellowship; the editor and part-writer of *Jazzmen of Our Time* and the author of *The Jazz Century.* He has also written two monographs about Rudyard Kipling in India and about the Napoleonic period as well. In 1979/80 he collaborated with Peter Gammond on *The Music Goes Round and Round: A Cool Look at the Record Industry,* and their partnership has been continued with *Music on Record 1: Brass Bands,* before this present volume.

Chris Ellis was born in Shrewsbury. He sang with local bands as a teenager and, during the revivalist jazz era, he formed his own band with which he toured the Midlands and North Wales. In recent years he has sung and recorded with the Anglo-American Alliance and broadcast with the Alan Elsdon band. Writer of numerous articles on early jazz and dance music and of record sleeve notes, and a broadcaster and recitalist. Contributor to *Sinatra and the Great Song Stylists* (1972). An executive of EMI Records Repertoire Department for many years he has become well known amongst dance band enthusiasts as the expert archivist and editor of the popular historical series re-issued by World Records, especially the numerous albums in the Great British Dance Bands series.

Burnett James was born in 1919 at Winterbourne in Gloucestershire and was educated at preparatory school and the Nautical College, Pangbourne. In 1935 he was disabled by polio. After a long sojourn in Switzerland, he got married and returned to England to devote his life mainly to musical writing and criticism. Owing to his disability he came to music mainly through the gramophone, developing an interest in both classical music and jazz. He wrote poetry and drama reviews for *The Gramophone* from 1950 to 1955 and reviewed for *Gramophone Record Review* from 1955, becoming assistant editor from 1957. He is a prolific writer of sleeve-notes, and a broadcaster and lecturer. In the 1970s was joint editor of *Jazz Journal* with Sinclair Traill. Author of *Hi-Fi for Pleasure, Bix Beiderbecke* (1959), *Beethoven and Human Destiny* (1960), *Essays on Jazz* (1961), *Living Forwards*—an Autobiography (1961), *Music on Record* (with Peter Gammond) (4 Vols, 1962/4), *An Adventure in Music* (1967), *Brahms: a Critical Study* (1972), *Manuel de Falla* (1979). At present he is working on books on Wagner, Ravel and the great conductors.

'Scrapple from the Apple': The Road to Swing and the Big Band era

by Raymond Horricks

'When we started the band, the only purpose we had was to play music, and Gene Krupa, Teddy, Hampton, Jess, Hymie and the rest, they had a purpose. It was their life, it was important to them'.

— *Benny Goodman*

'Benny built himself a band playing musicians' music, but he didn't shoot over the heads of the people. It took the people time, but once they grasped the Goodman musical sermon, they easily understood, accepted and followed. Being a part of this band was the fulfilment of a dream for any young musician'.

— *Gene Krupa*

Mysteries are always annoying. And what is most annoying for followers of the big bands, be they jazz or dance, sweet or powerhouse, is that a very great mystery surrounds the real reasons for their origins. In other words, we know their phenomenon, and the full documentation of their existence, but not their own particular Book of Genesis. This immediately involves a would-be writer about them in the shoals and hazards of guesswork. After which he must stand out in the open: prepared to be sniped at. However, as Pascal once remarked, 'The last thing that we find in making a book is to know what we must put first'.

My own theory is that these bands developed as a result of changing patterns in social behaviour; especially with regard to dancing. These changes coincided with the invention of the saxophone family and a very different approach to certain other instruments, notably those comprising what we have come to label 'the rhythm section'. Until our present century pianofortes, acoustic guitars, double-basses and a wide variety of percussion had never before been used in the ways we now take for granted. But to nominate one specific moment in time and musical development when all of this happened; no, it's just not possible!

Until the late 18th century public dancing, for the more sophisticated western Europeans and their North American cousins, was a contrivedly genteel affair. This doesn't mean that all of their tempos were slow ones. But even the quicker sets were expected to be graceful, and the sound and the style of their music stayed suitably prim and proper, rather like the dress and expected, if not always actual, morals of the dancers. Many of the pieces played were borrowed from classical or court composers, while the orchestras or ensembles (one could hardly yet call them dance bands!) featured a plethora of strings, some sporadic woodwind and a delicate use of percussion, triangles and so on. The nearest thing to a hint of the sheer rhythmic drive of the greatest big bands over a century later would have been the occasional discreet tap-tap-tap on a military side-drum.

Well, all of this changed with the rise to fame of the truly amazing Johann Strauss. Strauss (1825-99) was a revolutionary both musically and socially—although as the darling of a final frantic flowering of the Austro-Hungarian Empire he would have been horrified to hear himself described as such. Nevertheless the fact remains: he was a natural swinger (in another book I felt compelled to call him the 19th century's Count Basie) and his output became a sociological foot-in-the-door. Today his Viennese waltzes might seem to progressive jazz and rock music enthusiasts just so much 'old hat', but one should not underestimate their impact at the time. They brought a new excitement into dancing—excitement and warmth and closer contact on the purely human level. Also, they knocked over a whole skittle-alley of class distinctions. Their popularity was universal; with a swirl and a flourish they were a source of pleasure to any couple who could afford a decent suit and a pretty frock. From quality dancing being the exclusive property of Europe's crowned heads, aristocrats and a few aspiring members of the bourgeoisie, Strauss' waltzes suddenly swept it to within everyone's hoped-for horizons. This in turn resulted in an enormous increase in the number of pay-at-the-door ballrooms—a name still used today by serious dancers to give dignity to what others call dance-halls and some refer to as mere 'hops'.

To return to the origins of the big bands though. Strauss continued to use mainly strings and the conventional classical woodwind instruments in orchestrating his outflow of waltzes. It is extremely unlikely that he would have appreciated the main melody line of one of his popular compositions being rendered by something so novel as a saxophone. And yet—and this is intriguing—Adolphe Sax was to enjoy an almost identical lifespan: born in 1814 and living until 1894.

Sax was a Belgian and underwent formal musical studies at the Brussels Conservatoire. As an inventor he has a number of claims to orchestral fame, including the development of the bass-clarinet and the standardisation (as regards pitch, etc) of most modern brass instruments. But it was to be with his saxophones that the Belgian made a more radical and far-reaching contribution to popular music. These were patented in Paris in 1846 and then launched simultaneously as a group of instruments: soprano, alto, tenor, baritone and bass. To begin with there was a lot of sniggering; and a quite genuine bewilderment on the part of all dedicated musicians. Obviously they were brilliant, but to what use other than with military bands could they be put? Moreover, just as the great Johann had no idea to where his revolution in dancing might lead, Sax had never thought of his new 'family' being further exploited except as an adjunct to the symphony orchestra. He certainly did not see it flying off as an important section of a 20th century dance band or as a vehicle for jazz improvisation. . . .

So the century wore on with, on the one hand, dancers growing eager for a wider variety of new steps and rhythms to augment the basic diet of waltzes, and then, as this one century became another, serious composers like Debussy and Ravel tentatively exploring the saxophone's potential within works of esoteric vision and imagination. They were considered 'very daring'. At this point in the history of big bands, attention abruptly switches to the United States of America: the New World and the fountain-head of all things bright and, well, if not aways beautiful, at least filled with opportunity.

John Philip Sousa (1854-1932) was a bandmaster *par excellence*, an instinctive patriot and a man with the burning ambition to write and so come to dominate his country's music, which, at the end of the 19th-century, he very largely did. In contrast to the sweet and sentimental songs of Stephen Foster, Sousa's music was clear and vigorous. He composed for the stage, the concert-platform, for human voices and, of course, for bands on the march, over one hundred marches, including the famous *Stars and Stripes forever*. He also availed himself of the improved instruments from Europe—standardised trumpets, trombones, horns, tubas—*and saxophones*, a move of particular significance. It's hardly surprising, in view of all this, that by the turn of the century Sousa's influence upon American music had become (briefly) all-pervasive. It had an effect upon the military establishments, upon what we now refer to as college bands, upon town bands large, medium-sized and small, but, more importantly to the early history of big bands, upon the Negro musicians—most of them ex-slaves—in New Orleans. It is important because it was here, in the colourful Crescent City of the old South, that a remarkable cross-fertilisation was to take place: a musical development directly leading on towards the first big bands which would play for people to dance to in the 1920s.

Sousa, quite unconsciously, had pointed the way for the black musicians at the same time that he himself was concentrating on America's white population. This initially by his use of the imported, standardised instruments, then by his showing how harmonies, likewise imported from Europe, could be adapted to underpin strong, new melody-lines, and finally by getting these same black players out and about on the march. Freedom had not dealt kindly with America's Negroes. It had taken them off the plantations and into the towns and cities, but racial prejudice and grinding poverty were still their natural lot. There were plenty of talented musicians in New Orleans—men who could handle trumpets, trombones, clarinets and so on as well as anyone, even if they had learned to play by ear. But circumstances had restricted their work to the bordellos and boozing-places of the city's 'red light' district, Storyville, until Sousa's example had persuaded them to take up their tools of trade and start walking in common with almost every other musician in America.

After 1900 it seemed as if New Orleans was forever on the march. Any excuse: marriages, funerals, picnics and, of course, Mardi Gras, the great carnival-time, and the bands would be out, with crowds thronging around them. Even the piano-players refused to be cheated of the fun. They had their keyboards set up on horse-drawn carts and so joined in with the rest of the musicians. String-basses were also heaved up on to the carts; but most of the bands preferred tubas for their rhythmic oompah. However, what had likewise occurred by 1900 was that these same black musicians were adding on their own refinements, creating the sounds and style we call ragtime and which would soon evolve into the music known as early jazz. As yet they didn't stray too far from Sousa's shapes and his form: the idea of theme-choruses with 'breaks' in between for solos, trios, etc, to help the arrangement along. But they brought in the rhythms (and often cross-rhythms) of their transported African heritage to give the basic beat an altogether different propulsion—a primitive version of what would later be referred to as 'swing'. Furthermore they allowed these African rhythmic ideas to affect the contours of their musical melody-lines; in other words, to shape or 'syncopate' the lines until one was into an area of virtually new composition, even if it was more often than not freely-improvised. All right, it was brash, it was novel and it put conventional European harmonies to a previously undreamt-of use; but it was also very exciting and quickly caught on with the public. Even Sousa himself was impressed when he heard some samples of it—and from this time on always included 'a little ragtime' in his concert repertoire.

It needs to be stressed here that there was still a fair way to go before the true era of the big bands, destined for their heyday in the late 1930s, early 40s. And this would come about as the result of quite a few purely technical changes: the rhythm sections moving their emphasis from two to four beats in the bar, for instance, and a switch away from the contrapuntal interweaving of the typical, freely improvising New Orleans frontline to well-drilled and arranged-for sections of instruments, with the saxophones at long last coming into their own, plus a few more social changes, again appertaining to dancing. Even so, New Orleans still has to be regarded as the fulcrum, from here on there are no more mysterious origins. We have the evidence, and with it plenty of documentation. The evolution of authentic jazz-music leads on to the big band era with a remarkable logicality and only time and the necessary experiments in between. (Although, one should add, once the big band era had been reached the diversification was considerable and only a half proportion of its leaders would feature jazz.)

In New Orleans itself all the legendary soloists became leaders of their own bands—Buddy Bolden, Freddie Keppard, Bunk Johnson, Kid Ory, Buddy Petit, Manuel Perez, Mutt Carey, Clarence Williams, Alphonse Picou, John Robichaux and George Lewis. However, their bands remained typical of the kind of early jazz that had grown up in the Crescent City. Three other New Orleans names are of much more importance to the big band story. The first is that of Joe 'King' Oliver (1885-1938) because he carried the musical testament far to the North and also because he served as John the Baptist to Louis Armstrong (1900-71), the one undeniably authentic genius to come out of early Southern jazz. Armstrong—like Oliver originally a cornetist—would later play with a big band (Fletcher Henderson's) and later still 'front' a couple of rather indifferent ones, Luis Russell's and Les Hite's. Moreover he spearheaded the move away from the cornet to the more brilliant-sounding trumpet. But his most significant contribution overall was to the nature of the jazz solo itself. Although continuing to improvise, Armstrong wrenched the soloist's melody-line out of its New Orleans counterpoint context and then isolated it as a virtuoso performance—at the same time imposing form and contour upon the line so that it had a whole new identity. Louis, or 'Satchmo' as he came to be known, could create more interesting ideas within the space of a few bars than most of his contemporaries could put together in half a dozen choruses, and it was his type of solo or 'classic break' that would become encapsulated as the variation on a given theme within the otherwise arranged material of the big bands.

Finally, the other New Orleans name to concern us is that of Ferdinand 'Jelly Roll' Morton (1885-1941). Joe Oliver and Louis Armstrong were the forceful cultural manifestation in America of transplanted black African roots. Morton was light-skinned, a Creole, and had started his career as a flashy-fingered pianist in some of the most notorious houses of Storyville. At one point he claimed to have 'invented' jazz and in general was so insufferably arrogant that on one occasion later even the mild-mannered Duke Ellington would be irritated into saying, 'Sure, Jelly Roll Morton has talent . . . talent for talking about Jelly Roll Morton!'. (Jelly's nickname is a reference not to music but to his alleged sexual prowess.) It was never his destiny to go on and lead a true big band. However, after the early years when jazz had relied for its thematic materials upon ideas built up often quite haphazardly 'in action' (rags, stomps, imported blues fragments and so on), it was Morton's great achievement that he gave the music its first substantial library of original compositions. Durable, well-worked out pieces such as *King Porter stomp, The Pearls, Milenburg joys, Wolverine blues, Shoe shiner's drag, Mournful serenade, Sweet mama, Grandpa's spells, Doctor Jazz* and (as yet another ego-trip!) *Mr. Jelly Lord.* Often these incorporated influences not previously associated with jazz—French and Spanish influences, even some Spanish-Cuban ideas, together with a more subtle variety of rhythmic feelings. No matter. They set the process of *deliberate* jazz composition in motion; and it is hardly surprising to find Gil Evans, still the most advanced arranger of jazz music through the 1970s and into the 80s, returning to a Jelly Roll composition *(King Porter stomp)* and experimenting with more than one arrangement of it. But this is running far ahead in the big band story . . ..

Morton was perhaps intuitive about the coming crash in New Orleans. He began to move around: up to Memphis, St Louis, Kansas City and then over to California, where he lived and worked from 1917 to 1922. He first recorded as a pianist in 1923 (in Richmond, Indiana); but not as a band leader until September 1926 (for RCA-Victor). Already though the word about him was getting around. His groups, the Red Hot Peppers, were becoming known as very organised affairs and, despite the recording overlap, they provide the music historian with an orchestral link between Southern jazz and the start of the big band era proper in New York, led by Fletcher Henderson and his first arranger, Don Redman. Oliver and Armstrong gave Henderson the necessary examples of a toe-tapping rhythmic propulsion for dancing and the classic 'hot' solo. Morton, although rarely using more than six or seven hand-picked musicians, demonstrated how jazz compositions could be arranged in a tight, integrated way—with opening thematic statements, clever variations, predetermined solo-lengths (the solos sometimes accompanied by other melody instruments) and then thematic recapitulation and climax. It only remained for a musician with the vision of Henderson and one with the originality of Don Redman to add more instruments and start drilling them into sections. Meanwhile the saxophone family was ready and waiting for them.

The jazz crash came to New Orleans in 1917, mainly due to wartime worries on the part of the US naval authorities and disease, drugs and the violent incidents in Storyville getting totally out of hand. Control of the district's worst excesses had been tried and failed; and there is a note of genuine regret in the final official statement given out by Mayor Martin Behrman of New Orleans: 'Pretermitting the pros and cons of legislative recognition of prostitution as a necessary evil in a seaport the size of New Orleans, our city government has believed that the situation could be administered more easily and satisfactorily by confining it within a prescribed area. Our experience has taught us that the reasons for this are unanswerable, but the Navy Department of the Federal Government has decided otherwise.' Louis Armstrong has testified to the amount of violence going on. 'Before they clamped down on Storyville there were an awful lot of killings going on,' he recalled. 'Mysterious ones too . . . Several sailors were all messed up—robbed and killed . . . Those prostitutes commenced to have their pimps hide somewheres around and either rob or bash their brains in—anything to get that money—and that's when the United States Navy started getting warm.' By 1917 Navy Secretary Daniels had had enough. He ordered the closing down of every bordello and drinking-den in the quarter. Hundreds of 'night birds' and their 'mackerels' and other vice-pushers were sent packing, which in turn meant the end of their employment for hordes of cooks, waiters, maids, butlers, dish-washers—and musicians—who had helped sustain the way of life in Storyville. This isn't the place for me to sit in judgement. I will simply state that Daniels' dramatic closing down of the area disseminated jazz-music in all directions; northwards to Chicago, then over to New York City—and eventually right around the world.

Southern jazzmen had been percolating through to and probing the North in small numbers over a period of years; often taking casual jobs with the various bands run by calliopist Fate Marable on the Mississippi riverboats, playing the odd gig in different towns and cities along the way and converting all the younger musicians who dropped by to hear them. But after 1917, in the mass exodus from New Orleans, things truly began to happen in the North. Chicago suddenly became the hottest place in the country, with 30 or more bands cashing in on what was about to be a national craze for dancing to jazz. With World War 1 over there was a general desire by almost everybody to 'live it up a little'. America was about to adjust to Scott

Fitzgerald's mad, magical early 1920s: the era of the cocktail party, cloche-hats, scandalously short skirts and a greater feeling of liberation altogether. Dancing was now made to fit this changing pattern of life. The polite polkas, mazurkas and even a lot of waltzes were simply thrown out of the window. Jazz became the new 'in'-thing to be danced to and wild steps like the Charleston and the Black Bottom were invented to make this possible.

It was also a period when jazz ceased to be exclusively black music. It would be a few years yet before any white player could hold his own with the New Orleans masters, Bix Beiderbecke being the notable and different exception. And the earliest and most important big bands in New York would likewise be black. Nevertheless, nothing creative can ever remain exactly the same; and an upsurge of white jazz was soon under way alongside that of the original Negro protagonists. It was a white band for instance, the Original Dixieland Jazz Band led by cornet-player Nick La Rocca, which first introduced 'live' jazz to British audiences in 1919. They had been booked to open at the London Hippodrome in a show called *Joy Bells*. But after one night the comedian, George Robey, threatened to quit. 'This dreadful noise!' he called their music; and so they were booked into a series of night-clubs, where they proved immensely successful. Their reputation was helped, of course, by their being on gramophone records by this time, having cut their first sides for RCA-Victor on February 26 1917. Such a loud, exciting 'noise' on disc might have seemed bizarre and offensive to Robey and others of the older generation. But it captivated the modern-minded and the young; while record companies could now expect to sell their wares to vast numbers of dancers even ahead of the bands making personal appearances. The early 1920s witnessed a boom for jazz on disc.

However, to return—briefly—to Chicago, because this was really the last stage before the birth of the big bands. History has come to give the then wide-open city on the shores of Lake Michigan a very special aura: namely its association with the years of Prohibition, bathtub gin, Al Capone, black armoured-cars with tommy-guns in violin cases, the St Valentine's Day massacre and, of course, jazz joints. And certainly the gangster element was real enough—and dangerous. Muggsy Spanier recalled as a youngster sneaking out from home and sitting on the kerb outside the Pekin Café, listening to the music. 'Sometimes the goings-on would get rough inside, then you'd hear the crash of forty-five calibre revolvers trying to fire with a beat. Before I knew it, I'd be running home as fast as my feet could take me.' And drummer George Wettling has since described what it was like to play *inside* the joints, when bass-players got used to hiding behind their instruments. 'We would see those rods come up—and duck. At the Triangle Club, the boss was shot in the stomach one night, but we kept on working. After that he walked sort of bent over!'

On other occasions, feeling in a sentimental mood, Al Capone would commandeer some joint and pay the musicians with five and ten-dollar bills just to let him hear his favourite tunes. And so the jazz there went on, right through until 1929 and the Wall Street slump. In fashionable Downtown Chicago one could hear well-organised white jazz from the Original Dixieland, now Jazz Band, the New Orleans Rhythm Kings and somewhat later, after being formed in Stockton, Ohio, the Wolverines with Bix Beiderbecke. But it was still in the black ghetto on the city's South Side that the most exciting sounds were being made. At the Royal Garden, at the Lincoln Gardens (each of which could hold up to a thousand people), at Dreamland and in clubs like the Sunset and the Apex, the exiles from New Orleans poured out their tough, lusty, uninhibited music which—when it bulked its way on to records—set the whole of America dancing to its powerful, nearly irresistible beat. There were never enough good bands to go round in the 1920s, but at the top of the heap in Chicago was King

Oliver's which remained there throughout the 'key' years. With Oliver playing lead cornet, the Dodds brothers, Johnny and Baby, on clarinet and drums, Honore Dutray on trombone, Lil Hardin, piano and, after 1922, Louis Armstrong on second cornet, they set the pace and they dictated the style.

Again to quote George Wettling: 'There was a painted canvas sign about two by four feet square hanging outside the Lincoln Gardens that read KING OLIVER AND HIS CREOLE JAZZ BAND. From the looks of the place on the outside one would never guess that on the inside was the hottest band ever to sit on a bandstand. But once you got through the crowded hallway into the café proper it was a sight to behold. The thing that hit your eye once you got into the hall was a big crystal ball that was made of small pieces of reflecting glass and hung over the centre of the dance floor. A couple of spotlights shone on the big ball as it turned and threw reflected spots of light all over the room and the dancers. Usually they'd dance the Bunny Hug to a slow blues tune like *London blues* or some other tune in a similar slow blues tempo, and how the dancers would grind away!

'If anyone ever looked good in front of a band it was Joe Oliver. He had a way of standing in front of Louie, Johnny, Baby and the other cats, that was too much. He and Louie had some breaks, they played together like I've never heard played since. Unless you were lucky enough to hear that band in the flesh you can't imagine how they played and what swing they got. After they would knock everybody out with about forty minutes of *High society*, Joe would look down at me and wink and then say, Hotter than a forty-five!'

The most obvious point in this account is the great impact which Oliver and Armstrong had on Wettling and other white youngsters from in and around Chicago. For these were well-educated youngsters, high school kids who were not only learning to play instruments, but also how to read music, (and an ability to sight-read would be crucial to the increased organisation and carefully arranged material of the big bands.) However, for the moment what these youngsters liked best about jazz was its being improvised, hot and black. They formed their own groups; to become the second-generation of Chicagoan jazz, modelling themselves on their New Orleans idols. (Some eventually even recorded with their idols, ie Muggsy Spanier with Sidney Bechet, and Jack Teagarden and Joe Sullivan with Louis Armstrong.) Leading figures alongside Wettling in his new development were the Austin High School 'gang', Jimmy McPartland, Frank Teschemacher, Bud Freeman and Jim Lannigan. Also the clarinetist Pee Wee Russell and a guitar-player who doubled on banjo, Eddie Condon. Of more importance to the story of the big bands though were those youngsters who merely flirted with jazz being played in Chicago. They would not have called it flirting at the time, of course. They appeared just as enthusiastic as their classmates. But they were not long for the format of small group jazz. They would master the improvised solo, and the basic pulsation, and then take these on, together with their reading and other musical abilities, to very different things. Leading luminaries in this particular direction were the Dorsey brothers, Tommy and Jimmy, the drummers Dave Tough and Gene Krupa; and also a boy in short trousers, 15 years old at the most, who one day sat in with the Austin High School gang and amazed everyone by playing 16 straight choruses of *Rose of the Rio Grande* on the clarinet. His name was Benjamin David Goodman.

New York, New York! No other title could have been more evocative for the recent film starring Robert De Niro and Liza Minelli about the big band life. (It is interesting too that Georgie Auld, stalwart sideman in several of the best big bands, coached the star in how to handle the tenor-saxophone and appear to be playing it, because Auld then *did* play it and also played the rather cynical band leader in the film!) Anyway, New York was *the* place—The Apple, as musicians called it—the cradle of big bands (and the graveyard for some)—the island (Manhattan) from which, following their initial formation, the successful ones sallied forth like teams of Roman gladiators on nationwide and eventually world tours.

To a casual visitor to New York City today who looks at all the *graffiti* and the piles of uncollected rubbish and who senses the tension and violence along the streets (in the 1950s the poet W.H. Auden always used to carry ten dollars in his wallet; to a desperate junky-turned-mugger then the price of a fix) the city can seem the biggest man-made failure in the whole of the western world. Well, to this same casual visitor it probably sounds hollow to say that once upon a time the place had its own genuine glamour, albeit a tawdry one. But for the big bands New York was an inescapable fact. If you didn't make it there, you didn't make it period. And certainly from the mid-1920s on it would all be, to borrow the title from Charlie Parker, *Scrapple from The Apple*....

Fletcher 'Smack' Henderson (1898-1952) was a gentlemanly figure, a gentle piano-player and the former 'house' accompanist (to Ethel Waters and others) at the Black Swan Recording Co, W.C. Handy's set-up—where, incidentally, he had been excellently placed to hear and assess the comparative abilities of the many musicians in New York City. He branched out on his own in 1923, forming a band to play at the Club Alabam; and his first choice as arranger, Don Redman (1900-64), was probably the most thoroughly-schooled music man then on the scene, a multi-instrumentalist (trumpet from the age of three, then all the saxophones) and a graduate from the Boston and Detroit Conservatories. Their essential expansion to what we now think of as a big band did not happen overnight. To begin with they settled for a line-up of three trumpets, trombone, three saxophones doubling clarinets and other woodwind, piano, banjo, tuba or string-bass and drums. But for the first time the men were organised into and rehearsed as sections, saxes against brass on a 'call and response' basis or with one section used to punctuate the melodic line of the other. Their rhythmic feeling was changing too, becoming tighter and more stream-lined although still in an essentially pound-along, 'swinging', two beats-to-the-bar accented style. Improvised solos were brief, hot and usually accompanied by unison or harmonised passages from one of the sections. Sometimes saxes and brass would be blocked in together by the arranger to make a choral effect. By and large though the 'call and response' technique predominated, and would continue to do so for the remainder of the big band era. (The most notable exceptions were within the Duke Ellington orchestra, and then later when Gil Evans began to arrange for Claude Thornhill. In both of these bands the writing was much more textural, and verging on tonal painting.)

Again, with Henderson one can pinpoint the true dawning of the saxophone age. Within New Orleans jazz, despite Sidney Bechet's predilection for the soprano of the family, Adolphe Sax's invention had lagged far behind the clarinet in popularity. Saxophones, especially the tenor and baritone, were considered far too unwieldy for good improvised solos, whereas all they lacked were the right exponents. And already in New York City the right exponents were hanging about in the wings, in particular Benny Carter on alto and the great Coleman Hawkins on tenor. Moreover Don Redman, himself a saxophone player, had discovered one vitally important ingredient whilst working on his initial arrangements. Three or even five clarinets scored as a section still sounded thin. Three or five varied saxophones not only afforded him more harmonic flexibility, in addition they could give him *impact*! Marked *double-forte* they produced a big, booting sound that could hold its own against any brass section.

Really this discovery was the point of no return. From now on bands would continue to feature the 'liquorice-stick', but principally as a solo instrument. Even the later clarinetist-band-leaders—Goodman, Artie Shaw, Buddy de Franco—never ever considered dispensing with saxophones. (Well, Shaw did once, but it didn't work out.) Other leaders as different as Duke Ellington and Glenn Miller would work on some subtle variations, ie clarinets interspersed with the saxophones, or sometimes saxophones and a flute. However, as the 1920s gave way to the 30s, none of these experiments and subtly sophisticated refinements prevented the instrumentation of a typical big band proceeding to its definitive, if not quite its final formation: three, four or five trumpets, two, three or four trombones, five saxes (two altos, two tenors and baritone, plus woodwind doubles), piano, guitar, string-bass and drums.

Just one other point about this 'classic' big band instrumentation. In the 1930s, during World War II and then on to our present day and those big bands still left, it has served both swinging and sweet-sounding (so-called 'Society') bands equally well. The hard-driving Goodman, Lunceford, Chick Webb, Count Basie, Woody Herman and Dizzy Gillespie bands in the one camp, and the silkier Guy Lombardos, Horace Heidts and Fred Warings in the other. Plus, of course, those who might be said to have occupied the middle ground: the Dorsey brothers, Miller, Charlie Barnet, Harry James and Les Brown. Paul Whiteman and Stan Kenton were special cases, because they dabbled with semi-symphonic instrumentations and often strayed far away from jazz or any other form of dance music. Yet in 1952 when Kenton reverted to a normal big band personnel he achieved the best recorded results of his entire career.

Again, this is letting the story run on to very near the end of the (main) big band era. For the moment (in 1923) we are still with Fletcher Henderson at the Club Alabam. His key personnel there consisted of Joe Smith and Howard Scott, trumpets, Charlie 'Big' Green (a favourite of 'Empress of the Blues' Bessie Smith) on trombone, Don Redman, alto-sax, Coleman Hawkins, tenor, Charlie Dixon, banjo, Bob Escudero on tuba and Kaiser Marshall, drums. Oh yes, and a violinist, Allie Ross, who fulfilled, in the words of critic John S. Wilson, 'the requirement of that day that every band had to have somebody in front of it waving a stick'. Fletcher did a few broadcasts (over station WHN); and musicians began dropping into the Alabam just to hear his soloists—especially Hawkins, whose rich and dramatic flights of the imagination via his tenor-saxophone turned on a whole new generation of youngsters to the instrument's potentialities.

It was Hawkins too who inadvertently caused the band to get its first big break. Singer Edith Wilson, one of the stars of the floor-show at the Alabam, asked to have the tenorman out in the spotlight to back her blues numbers. Hawkins was willing, but considered he should get extra money for it. The management said 'no'—and, adding insult to injury, told Henderson to fire this sideman with ideas above his station. It was one of the rare occasions when Fletcher actually lost his temper; and he promptly accepted a convenient offer to take the band over to the Roseland, a huge ballroom on the corner of 51st Street and Broadway. It was, one could claim, the moment when the first embryo big band 'went public'—and with the most tremendous consequences.

To begin with at the Roseland they had to share the twin bandstands with Sam Lanin's group, essentially polite in its sound, although it did include certain budding white jazz players like Red Nichols and Miff Mole. But the new black band soon set the place alight! So much so that Lanin had to try to play the same kind of way, otherwise the dancers just drifted away from him. And after 1924, when Henderson lured Louis Armstrong in to join him from Chicago, the white players recognised that it was a one-sided contest. In subsequent years other big bands would attempt to do battle at the Roseland: the Dorseys, the Casa Loma Orchestra, Vincent Lopez and Jean Goldkette. Not one of them ever managed to cut Henderson, who apart from occasional tours was to remain at this same ballroom for more than another decade. (In fact until Benny Goodman had been crowned 'The King of Swing' and Henderson was writing his arrangements!)

It had a lot to do with the marvellous musicians he picked, and Louis Armstrong is a perfect illustration of this. Again to quote John S. Wilson, 'his arrival had an electrifying effect on the Henderson band. It was made up almost entirely of Eastern musicians, men who had had little direct contact with the mainstream New Orleans tradition. Suddenly they found the finest flower of that tradition blowing lustily in their midst. It proved both a challenge and an education'. He goes on to say that Armstrong had brought with him a number by King Oliver called *Dippermouth blues*. 'Rechristened *Sugar foot stomp*, set in a framework by Redman and featuring some inspired playing by Armstrong, it became the prototype of the Henderson big band style with its mixture of driving beat, swinging ensembles and brilliant solo work.' And Fletcher's wife, Leora, confirms that when the band played *Sugar foot stomp* 'the crowd would go wild'.

Leora recalls too that often there would be as many musicians as dancers at the Roseland, just standing around, listening, learning. And if one player left the band there was always a queue to replace him—men of real calibre like Buster Bailey, Benny Carter, Bobby Stark, Rex Stewart, Jimmy Harrison and John Kirby. 'It was considered an honour to get in that band. It had the hardest book in the business, and many a musician just couldn't get to play those arrangements. Jimmy Harrison couldn't make it to begin with. Fletcher turned him away and he went out and studied before Fletcher would take him back. The same thing happened to Rex Stewart. They rehearsed 'most every night, and while there were drinkin' men in the band, I don't remember when any of them was ever drunk on the job.'

Even the young Duke Ellington came under Henderson's influence, and has described the band, during the 1920s, as 'the greatest dance band anyone had ever heard'. Ellington—a composer of genius—was destined to plough something of a lonely furrow through the history of big band music, only occasionally using the 'call and response' technique, preferring instead a more textural approach based upon the intensely individual sounds of his players. Nevertheless, he found it suited his writings to go along with the changes in instrumentation, the increased use of saxophones and so on, and he began to enlarge and expand his group along similar lines to Fletcher's.

Leora Henderson concludes on those heady pioneering days of the mid-1920s, before the hard times hit her husband and his life became a study in frustration. 'Around that time Paul Whiteman was called "The King of Jazz" and so people began calling Fletcher "The Coloured King of Jazz'. Whiteman would be playing all those novelties and semi-classical numbers and Fletcher would turn right around and swing them. I recall that Don Redman even did an arrangement of *Rhapsody in blue*, but later on they stopped the band from playing it.'

However, if Henderson was both 'King' and fountain-head of ideas at the Roseland, then there were also the copyists and some skilled disciples poised, Prometheus-like to take the Olympian fire and spread it far and wide—across the United States, to England, to Europe and eventually right around the world. They would be helped by radio and, of course, by records. From now on the big band story becomes one of proliferation, and gradually, as the 1920s progressed and various key sidemen left, Henderson had no more thunderbolts with which to eliminate his rivals.

After perfecting his reading, and beginning to develop his singing and clowning, Louis Armstrong had been the first to quit. Then in 1927 Redman also left to take over McKinney's Cotton Pickers. Fletcher began to do some of the arranging himself and hired Benny Carter to do the rest. Carter, born in 1907, and another multi-instrumentalist known as 'the cat with nine lives', also proved to be one of the greatest rehearsers of big bands, another important factor. Such men are often the unsung heroes of the big band years. Some (and not necessarily always arrangers) became virtually deputy-leaders, and students of the music cannot afford to ignore them. These include names like Sy Oliver with Jimmie Lunceford and later Tommy Dorsey; Willie Smith with Lunceford; Earl Warren and later Marshall Royal with Count Basie; Marshall Royal, earlier, with Les Hite and Lionel Hampton; Hilton Jefferson with Cab Calloway; Jimmy Mundy with Erskine Tate, Earl Hines and finally Benny Goodman (when Henderson became ill); Budd Johnson with Earl Hines; Jerry Gray with Artie Shaw; and not least Duke Ellington's help-mate, the diminutive 'Sweepea', Billy Strayhorn. Later still there would be some more of these interesting executive officers: for instance, Gil Evans with Claude Thornhill, transcribing the early, difficult be-bop themes for big band; the young, gifted and troublesome Gerry Mulligan with Gene Krupa; the largely misunderstood George Handy with Boyd Raeburn and undisguised be-boppers such as Gil Fuller and Tadd Dameron working for Dizzy Gillespie . . ..

Eventually though Benny Carter likewise left Henderson to form his own band. It was never a great success publicly, although destined to make some of the finest records of the early 1930s in association with English composer/arranger Spike Hughes. But its formation and struggle seemed to coincide with all sorts of interesting things happening in the exciting new world of the big bands. Duke Ellington had at last started to make it at New York's Cotton Club. In 1927 Jimmie Lunceford formed his first band in Memphis, Tennessee. And there were unusual rumours and rumblings coming from in and around Kansas City: the name most often mentioned being that of one Bennie Moten.

Meanwhile another important breakthrough was occurring on the largely white circuit due to the Midwestern Casa Loma Orchestra under the direction of guitarist Gene Gifford (1908-70). In the superficial sense its music was effete when compared with that of say, Duke Ellington, the good Lunceford, then later on Count Basie. And yet until the advent of Benny Goodman it was the nearest that white society dancers (apart from those slummers and a handful of genuine fans who made the pilgrimage to Harlem) ever came to appreciating black music. The Casa Loma Orchestra was white and looked respectable. But it played the same short, repetitive melodic phrases (or 'riffs') that Henderson's and the other black bands featured; while its beat was sufficiently fast and vigorous for those who wanted to try the Lindy Hop and other acrobatic dances. Gifford wasn't particularly interested in jazz soloists; for him the ensemble was what mattered most, and he had his brass players experiment with a wide variety of mutes and his saxophones double on flutes, oboe and bass-clarinet to give greater tonal colour. If anything his Achilles' heel lay in the quota of syrupy ballads he allowed the band to play; perhaps too in the crooning of vocalist Kenny Sargent. Because here he closed the 'swinging' doors and opened others leading to some of the worst excesses of sweet bands in the 1930s and 40s. As one swing fan later quipped: 'what does Guy Lombardo's drummer tell people he does for a living?'.

In fact, I have no quarrel with sweet bands of the calibre of Lombardo and his

Royal Canadians; nor should anyone else have. He gave good entertainment, played well for dancers and always achieved a high quality of musicianship. Both Louis Armstrong and Dizzy Gillespie admired him. Unfortunately, though, certain other leaders in this field (Kay Kyser, the self-styled 'Dean of the College of Musical Knowledge', and Horace Heidt to name but two) allowed their output to degenerate into mere 'Micky Mouse' music—without the redeeming showmanship of a Cab Calloway or the genuinely interesting novelty sounds of Spike Jones and his City Slickers. They brought down a lot of ridicule upon the big bands, and at a time when many more sincere groups were beginning to struggle.

Paul Whiteman (1890-1967), the other notably successful white band leader by the late 1920s and into the 30s, was almost exactly the opposite to Gene Gifford. Whereas the Casa Loma's musical director was proving to be precise, practical and very commercially-minded, albeit with little or no interest in jazz solos, Whiteman—a band leader since 1918—was crazy about jazz soloists and employed some of the best of them: Bix Beiderbecke, the Dorseys, Jack and Charlie Teagarden, Joe Venuti and Eddie Lang—plus several remarkable singers, Johnny Mercer and Hoagy Carmichael (both destined for future songwriting glories), The Rhythm Boys featuring the young Bing Crosby, and Mildred Bailey and even Billie Holiday. He was also a showman and, according to longtime *Metronome* editor George T. Simon, 'a great salesman—especially at selling himself to hotel managers, to radio sponsors and to anyone else who could do him and his band some good. He thought big, talked big and . . . acted big'. Simon illustrates his point well. 'When other bands eventually played at New York's Paramount Theatre for several weeks at a time and considered themselves fortunate to do so, Whiteman appeared there for two *years* at 12,500 dollars a week!' Oddly enough there was only one stipulation to this contract. The management thought Bing Crosby such a bad singer they insisted Whiteman did not give him a solo. (Two years later Bing was back at the Paramount—as the 'star' attraction.)

The trouble with Whiteman was that he had a personal ego second only to Jelly Roll Morton's. In 1924 he conducted the première of George Gershwin's *Rhapsody in blue* and afterwards never let anyone forget it. He was a good-hearted man, proud of his musicians and he paid them well. But he continuously surrounded their talents with pretentious, string-and-percussion-laden, semi-symphonic arrangements—and as such his music came to be a dirty word in the minds of genuine jazz fans, who considered he had smothered Beiderbecke and the other players. Those who liked their jazz in a big band format went off to listen elsewhere. For instance to Duke Ellington (born in 1899), and then to Jimmie Lunceford.

The Duke and his alumni were going from strength to strength. So much so that by 1932 they were able to leave the Cotton Club and in the following year embarked upon their first, highly successful European tour. They were broadcasting regularly, had made a film (*Check and Double Check* with Amos and Andy) and, more importantly, were into a very full recording programme based upon the leader's unique and dazzling abilities as a composer. The output from Ellington's pen over the years would run to literally hundreds of titles, including a good proportion of jazz masterpieces—*The mooche, Black and tan fantasy, Creole rhapsody, Reminiscing in tempo, Mood indigo, Sophisticated lady, Solitude, Daybreak express, In a sentimental mood, I got it bad and that ain't good, Stompy Jones, Rockin' in rhythm, Bojangles, Jack the bear* and *Harlem airshaft*. Not least the one which seemed to express it all as regards big bands: *It don't mean a thing if it ain't got that swing*. Moreover Ellington (like Count Basie) was destined to be a survivor. He would weave in and out of the big band era, always on the move, always writing, and leading an outstanding orchestra and recording with it until just a few days before his death in 1974. (His burial service in the Episcopal Cathedral Church of St John the Divine in New York City was attended by 10,000 people with thousands more in the street outside. 'A crowd', as Alistair Cooke wrote at the time, 'that ranged through the whole human colour scale, from the most purple black to the most pallid white, come there to honour the life and mourn the death of a man who had become supreme in an art that began in the brothels of New Orleans'.)

It would be ridiculous to attempt to summarise Ellington's music within a single chapter on the big bands in general. One could write a fat book just about his later, longer works: *Black, brown and beige*, *New world a' comin'*, *The tattooed bride*, the *Liberian suite* and *A tone parallel to Harlem*, and about his concerts of sacred music. Suffice it to say that by the early 1930s both his composing and the sound of his band had coalesced into an unmistakable identity. The Duke's melodic invention (based on tunes easily hummable) was invariably shaped by a most refined harmonic development, and yet these two essential elements seldom strayed far from—and were often overlaid by—a third key element, namely, black African roots. It was the latter which gave Ellington his rich, aggressive, 'jungly' effects; and, of course, his pounding, exotic rhythms and cross-rhythms.

No other band could satisfactorily reproduce his music, and this was because he continued to study the natural qualities (even the weaknesses) of his players and then

Duke Ellington and his Orchestra in the 1930s (William Morris Agency).

to write for the man behind the solo. As the personnel changed, so the Duke made use of each incoming 'voice'. The sleek, sensuous alto of Johnny Hodges; trumpeter Bubber Miley and trombonist Joe 'Tricky Sam' Nanton with their different plunger mutes; the fiery, brassier-sounding trumpet of Cootie Williams; Barney Bigard's fluid clarinet; Ben Webster's thundering tenor; the gurgly, vibrato-heavy baritone-sax of Harry Carney; and Jimmy Blanton, the first bass soloist of jazz. All were given leading roles in the Ellington canon. (Billy Strayhorn said: 'Ellington plays the piano, but his real instrument is his band.')

Jimmie Lunceford (1902-47), and a former student of Wilberforce J. Whiteman (Paul's dad), led an altogether different type of band. Ellington's was decidedly a band for listening to, always intriguing, often sensational. But it was not a great band for dancers, especially when they were getting into the new, freer expression of jive and the jitterbug-craze. Lunceford filled this particular vacuum. Although playing less-sophisticated material, it was generally acknowledged that his rhythm section was better than Duke's. (In fact, he had the hardest-driving rhythm section of any big band until the emergence of Count Basie's.) Furthermore, while still hinged upon the 'call and response' devices between the various sections, Lunceford's arrangers—Sy Oliver, pianist Ed Wilcox and later the young Gerald Wilson—whipped up these same sections into such a near-miracle of time and phrasing that even the Casa Loma Orchestra sounded slipshod by comparison. Naturally it all depended on quality musicianship, and Lunceford had hired some of the best; highly-disciplined men who were also creative jazz soloists. These included trumpeters Paul Webster and Eddie Tompkins; Trummy Young and Eddie Durham on trombones with the latter also playing solo guitar; saxists Willie Smith, Joe Thomas and Dan Grissom; and a sweep-all-along drummer, Jimmie Crawford.

Sy Oliver created a fresh kind of rhythm, still four beats to the bar, but with only two emphasised, and the slick showmanship became another hallmark. The trumpets, for instance, would throw their instruments in the air, clap their hands, catch the trumpets and carry on playing in perfect time! Anyway, it suited the dancers, and Lunceford would remain the favourite band up in Harlem and at other Negro ballrooms for many years, also selling a lot of records, of Will Hudson's *White heat* and *Jazznocracy* and Oliver's arrangements of *Swanee river, Four or five times, Organ grinder's swing* and *For dancers only*. (Oliver's most famous theme though, *Yes, indeed!*, was given the thumbs-down, either by Lunceford or American Decca. Later it became one of Tommy Dorsey's biggest hits.)

Lunceford's band might have gone on to be the most popular in the world had it not been for a single night in 1935—a single midsummer night at the Palomar Ballroom in Los Angeles—because on that night Benny Goodman made the most phenomenal breakthrough in the whole history of big band music. As name-tags go it changed the big band story in the story of 'Swing' . . .. Since our previous, brief glimpse of Goodman as a kid in short trousers astonishing the Austin High School gang much had happened to the prodigy clarinetist, most of it though out of the public eye and ear.

It has to be emphasised at this point how, during the earliest part of his career, Benny (born in 1909, and into a poor immigrant family) was actually advancing along two tangential courses, obviously still undecided as to where his real future lay. On the one hand, under the tuition and severe discipline of Franz Schoeppe, he was becoming a thoroughly-schooled soloist who would go on to perform and record Mozart's concerto and quintet for clarinet as well as works by Hindemith, Aaron Copland and Malcolm Arnold. (Schoeppe's discipline later became an underrated influence on the way Benny both ran and rehearsed his big band.) Meanwhile he continued to play jazz dates; but still without getting fully involved. He was an adept improviser and had developed a beautiful, clear tone, partly classical, partly descended from the jazz clarinetist Jimmie Noone. However, as John Hammond, his other important *éminence grise*, has described it: '[He] had the idea that real improvised jazz was uncommercial and that you had to have a compromise in order to sell any records. I'm pretty sure that Benny Goodman's musical tastes were those of a jazzman who was beaten and discouraged by the commercial life then prevailing at American radio stations, and the complete lack of appreciation anywhere for the great improvising jazz artist'. Goodman's own memories more or less confirm that this was his thinking at the time. 'Radio was just beginning to spread out, and it seemed to me that a musician's future was going to be tied up with it. I felt that I could work along and find a pretty secure living in that field . . . I guess I was in a kind of a bad groove mentally at that time, with not much desire other than to make money, keep the place going for my mother and the kids, and have as much fun as possible.'

Change and crystalisation came along from 1925 when the clarinetist took a job with Ben Pollack's band (ironically, sitting beside one of his future rivals, the trombonist Glenn Miller). Pollack played a mixture of jazz and straight dance music and it gave Goodman his first experience of working within a bigger group. More importantly it took him to New York—The Apple!—where on the strength of his abilities he immediately found himself in demand as a freelance player. He made many record dates, started to penetrate broadcasting (the media he was convinced would transform popular entertainment) and met and exchanged ideas with aspiring band leaders like the Dorseys. In 1929 he left Pollack to join Red Nichols who had the pit band for George Gershwin's musical *Strike Up The Band*, (Gene Krupa was the drummer). And in 1931 he conducted a pit band himself for a revue called *Free For All*. It closed after 15 performances.

1933 brought the final crystallisation a lot nearer. For that was when Goodman met and formed an association with John Hammond, the wealthy young enthusiast and record producer who seemed to know everything there was to know about jazz. Hammond turned Benny on to the best of black jazz in Harlem, to its greater excitement and also to some of the newer names who were worth watching. Fletcher Henderson had been struggling, too many good men had left him, but Ellington still prospered, so did Don Redman. Jimmie Lunceford had arrived in New York and there were promising big bands growing up around Cab Calloway (born 1907) and a little hunchbacked drummer, Chick Webb (1907-39). New soloists abounded, and some of them like trumpeter Roy Eldridge were very good indeed.

Not only was Goodman aroused by this music, it would be his destiny to become its St Christopher, carrying it in public, on record and over the airwaves to the largest audience ever to stop and listen to a big band. The world might call what he played 'Swing', but in reality it was Harlem's jazz, well-arranged, well-presented and presented by superlative musicians. 'Goodman played *blacker* than almost any white band—certainly any successful white band—had before', said Dan Morgenstern. Moreover he could take this black-sounding music where the black bands themselves were not yet allowed to go . . ..

The Benny Goodman big band went into rehearsals in 1934—with John Hammond as its main musical adviser and Willard Alexander of MCA as its prospective booking-agent. Hammond's activities were to prove crucial. As Nat Shapiro has indicated, he 'made full use of his encyclopaedic knowledge of who-was-who and what-was-what in even the most obscure corners of the jazz world. His most vital contribution to the band, aside from his infectious enthusiasm and his well-placed contacts in the talent agencies, record companies and other business citadels, was his almost unnerving ability to find for it the best musicians in the business. His getting Fletcher Henderson to write the arrangements, however, was, if not a stroke of genius, at least one of the luckiest things that ever happened to Goodman'.

In turn Benny used his own qualities of musicianship and his Schoeppe-like discipline to knock the band into shape. He always led from the front, sorting out each fresh arrangement for wrong notes, tempo, dynamics and so on, endlessly rehearsing, drilling the sections, controlling who took what solo and for how long. His manner was brusque but workmanlike. If a player did not fit in with the style of the band then he did not last two days. But ultimately the high standards paid off. So

Benny Goodman in the 1930s (RCA Records).

much so that when the band appeared in public George T. Simon would describe its overall togetherness as being 'close to perfection'. Also, it appeared an auspicious moment to be taking the necessary gamble in forming a band. To quote Nat Shapiro again: 'For the first time since the pre-crash days of 1929, there was a note of optimism in the air. Prohibition was over, the Roosevelt administration's initial efforts towards economic recovery were showing signs of success, and the depression-weary American public was ready for something new in the way of entertainment'.

But even for BG, the man who would be 'King of Swing', success did not come overnight. The band opened at Billie Rose's Musical Hall on Broadway and flopped. Then in May 1935, when Willard Alexander got them their first important hotel job (at the Grill Room in the Roosevelt Hotel, replacing Guy Lombardo) they flopped again. 'On opening night', Alexander recalls, 'they were given their two weeks notice!'. The worst was yet to come. Setting off on their first east-to-west tour in the summer of 1935 the initial response was pathetic, culminating in Denver, Colorado where, as Goodman later told Richard Gehman, 'I suffered just about the most humiliating experience of my entire life'. On opening night people started asking for their money back, and the manager would not let the band continue until they switched to playing waltzes.

As things turned out though, and fortunately for Benny, behind this initial public agony, the real seeds of his success story had been planted in other fields. One of the few people who had liked the band at Billie Rose's was a radio producer called Joe Bonime, and he managed to get Goodman 26 weeks on a programme sponsored by the National Biscuit Company, which in turn led to a good recording contract with RCA-Victor, plus coast-to-coast exposure via the airwaves. Goodman's belief in radio had been correct, and this was to prove of the utmost significance in California, where the different time zone had allowed all the younger people in the state to be either out of college or home from work to listen to the band. When Benny reached the West Coast at the end of his disastrous tour these same youngsters were waiting for him, queuing up, in fact.

Meanwhile, too, John Hammond had been finalising the personnel of the band. 'When it seemed to me that the band was making less of an impression than it should', he wrote afterwards in *Down Beat*, 'I took a trip to Chicago where Gene Krupa was imprisoned in Buddy Rogers' orchestra. It wasn't too difficult to persuade him to give in his notice to Buddy and join the *Let's Dance* programme in New York . . .. Gene's arrival marked a turning point in the Goodman organisation. Fletcher Henderson's arrangements began to take on excitement. It was about this time that Benny let Fletcher make arrangements of current pop tunes with a beat and irreverence he had never dared employ with his own band. I firmly believe that it was this approach to ballads that gave the Goodman band the style that made it conquer the nation . . ..' Also in Chicago Hammond found pianist Jess Stacy playing in a run-down saloon, and he hired Bunny Berigan to bolster the trumpet-section.

When the band arrived in California they were immediately encouraged by a good gig at Oakland. From here they moved on to the most famous of all West Coast ballrooms, the Palomar in Hollywood, opening on August 21. As Gene Krupa remembered it: 'We played the first couple of sets under wraps. We weren't getting much reaction, so Benny, I guess, decided to hell with playing it safe and we started playing numbers like Jelly Roll's *King Porter stomp*. Well, from then on we were in!'. In Benny's own words, 'I called out some of our big Fletcher arrangements and decided to let loose. The boys immediately got the idea. From the moment I kicked them off, they dug in with some of the best playing I'd heard since we left New York. And then boom! Everyone went wild. That first big roar from the crowd . . . one of the sweetest sounds I ever heard!'. Their impact upon the audience was truly amazing. People were milling around the bandstand, screaming for more. Within a week they were broadcasting from the Palomar, within six weeks Goodman was a national hero, within a year the band was an international sensation.

From California they moved back to Chicago. Booked into the Congress Hotel for three weeks, they eventually stayed for eight months. (After which the management closed the room and redecorated it. No one could possibly follow Benny!) And the first of their really big 'hit' records stemmed from this Chicago period. They had already cut a number of very fine sides: including the Fletcher Henderson arrangements of *Blue skies* and *Sometimes I'm happy*. But *Stompin' at the Savoy*, composed and arranged by Edgar Sampson (a saxophone player with Chick Webb's band) not only became a No 1 for Goodman, it changed the tastes of record-buyers. From this point on and until Swing declined in the 1940s Americans would buy more discs made by big bands than by any other kind of act or artist apart from Bing Crosby. To set the final seal on his triumphs now it only remained for Goodman to make it in New York, which he did from October 1936, after opening in the Manhattan Room at the Hotel Pennsylvania. Harry James joined the band at the Pennsylvania with another great trumpeter, the colourful, cigar-chewing Ziggy Elman. Together with Chris Griffin they blew up an absolute whirlwind. By the time Benny opened at the Paramount Theatre the fans were lining up for tickets at seven in the morning . . ..

'Nothing succeeds like success', is a cliché which might almost have been invented for Benny Goodman. He went on to become a millionaire, continuing to dominate the pyramid years of Swing and then quitting—apart from special engagements—while he was still at the top. He disbanded in the spring of 1944, just missing being overtaken in popularity by Woody Herman—but also when other factors, some economic, some musical, were starting to hit hard at the big bands. Right through to the end, however, he kept up the same standards of musicianship. The roll-call of those who passed through his band is a veritable Burke's Peerage of white Swing: Bunny Berigan, Harry James, Chris Griffin, Ziggy Elman, Lee Castle and Billy Butterfield, trumpets; Murray McEachern, Jack Lacey, Vernon Brown, Joe Harris, Lou McGarity and Cutty Cutshall, trombones; Toots Mondello, Hymie Schertzer and Skip Martin, alto-saxes; Arthur Rollini, Bud Freeman, Vido Musso, Babe Russin and Jerry Jerome, tenor-saxes; Jess Stacy, Frank Froeba, Johnny Guarnieri, Joe Bushkin and Mel Powell, piano; Allen Reuss, George Van Epps, Mike Bryan and Dave Barbour, guitar; Harry Goodman, Artie Bernstein and Clyde Lombardi, bass; and Krupa, Nick Fatool, Morey Feld and Dave Tough, drums. Then too there were the band's singers. For while continuing to render the latest popular tunes in a gutsy, jazz-flavoured, up-tempo style, the Goodman arranging team of Henderson and Sampson, Jimmy Mundy and later Eddie Sauter, grew adept at inserting what was called 'the vocal refrain', a middle chorus of words featuring some of the best voices of the day. Among the females were Helen Ward, Martha Tilton, Betty Van, Helen Forrest and the incredible Peggy Lee, and among the men, Dick Haymes and Art Lund, with trombonist Joe Harris also handling certain vocals. Soon this practice of 'refrain' choruses was taken up by nearly every other band and with some startling discoveries, ie one Francis Albert Sinatra who worked with both Harry James and Tommy Dorsey. (Although when Benny borrowed the young Ella Fitzgerald from Chick Webb's band for a record date, Webb's own label American Decca threatened to sue and the three sides had to be withdrawn.)

Finally, mention must be made of a pioneering contribution to the human side of the big band era. A Jew himself, Benny detested racial prejudice in any size, shape or form, so did John Hammond. They therefore took advantage of the band's fame and

Lionel Hampton (left) with Tommy Dorsey (RCA Records).

influence to have the clarinetist vary his programme by fronting small units which included Negro musicians. From within these Goodman trios, quartets and sextets the white world was given an opportunity to enjoy the talents of Teddy Wilson on piano, Cootie Williams, trumpet, Lionel Hampton ('stolen' by Hammond from the Les Hite orchestra) on vibes and Charlie Christian playing electric-guitar. Later still another Negro musician, drummer 'Big Sid' Catlett, enlivened the full Goodman band. It wasn't a total answer to the colour bar in America's places of entertainment, but it was another foot in the door. Its courage encouraged other band leaders to hire black soloists, notably Gene Krupa (with Roy Eldridge); Artie Shaw (Eldridge again and Billie Holiday); and Charlie Barnet (best-known for his 'hit' single *Skyliner*) who featured trumpeters Peanuts Holland, Howard McGhee and Clark Terry, trombonist Trummy Young and bassist Oscar Pettiford, plus of course the great Lena Horne. All of which can be seen to have led on to some genuinely multi-racial bands in the years following: the Miles Davis nine-piecer of 1949/50, Dizzy Gillespie's world-tour band of 1956/7 and in the 1970s the Thad Jones-Mel Lewis orchestra.

If one could pinpoint one specific occasion when Swing seemed to have become the most important thing in music, then it was probably the Goodman band's appearance at Carnegie Hall on the night of January 16 1938. Often at Benny's dances the dancers would stop and just stand by the bandstand listening to the musicians play, but to go and give a concert to a seated audience in New York's cultural holy-of-holies—now that was something else! However, it did happen, first, as the result of a suggestion by the publicist Wynn Nathanson, and then because the great Sol Hurok agreed to promote it. Benny had been scared stiff to begin with, but then he got down to making the idea work, based upon his own band and certain allied talent, ie, for the tribute to Duke Ellington he brought across Cootie Williams, Johnny Hodges and Harry Carney, while for the tribute to Bix Beiderbecke he decided to use Bobby Hackett. For the jam session some of Count Basie's men were co-opted, and there were featured spots for the Goodman Trio and Quartet—Martha Tilton was the solo singer.

Benny need not have had his preliminary worries. The occasion proved another monumental success and gave to Swing an ultimate respectability, its sounds, as *Metronome* put it, 'replacing Jack Barbirolli and his Philharmonic Cats, the regular band in that spot'. Irving Kolodin, who helped with some of the preparations, has described the almost magical atmosphere which prevailed that night. 'Inside, the hall vibrated. Seats had been gone for days, of course, but one of those last-minute rushes had set in, when all New York had decided that this was the place it wanted to be on the night of this particular January 16. The boxes were full of important squatters, and a jury-box had been erected on stage to care for the overflow. Tension tightened as the orchestra filed in, and it snapped with applause as Goodman, in tails, strode in, clarinet in hand, bowed, and counted off *Don't be that way*.'

Don't be that way, a new arrangement by Edgar Sampson, got off to a slightly shaky start, but halfway through Harry James' solo pulled in the first big applause of the evening. Then Gene Krupa played a drum-break which all-but lifted the roof. After this nothing could go wrong. The band, the jam session, the small groups, Martha Tilton's *Loch Lomond*, all drew wave after wave of cheering and clapping, and then to conclude it, the band again, piling one lift on top of another. Ziggy Elman launched forth on Jimmy Mundy's 'killer diller' *Swingtime in the Rockies* with such ferocity and pace that everyone thought the show must end with him, but it wasn't over yet. There were some more small group numbers before Krupa began tom-tomming in the beat for *Sing, sing, sing*, the climax originally intended. As Stanley Baron writes 'Gene and Benny alone together carried that number on and on, chorus after chorus, ecstatically. Then as the band came in on the tune again, Jess Stacy, who was relatively unknown at that time, meditatively plinked out some soft church music on piano. Benny gazed round at him in utter astonishment, laughing as he did so, and yells of happiness went sounding through the hall. Many who were there that evening remember Stacy's solo as one of the highlights of the show'. A show of many highlights. The idea of the big band concert had come to stay.

What of Benny Goodman's would-be rivals though, since his had now become the musical and financial yardstick of the whole big band era? Well, these were many and varied and many were very would-be indeed, but a select few were quite exceptionally good as well as being easily identifiable in style and for their sidemen. To write about each in only one or two sentences is extremely difficult, also unjust. However, a book is a book and has its own imposed length. Not surprisingly some of the best of the few were led by ex-Goodmanites. (After 1935, BG's Annus Mirabilis, his fans became in turn fans of every one of his players, making it that much easier for the more ambitious ones to branch out on their own.) Of these, Bunny Berigan drank himself to death in 1942, but not before he'd enjoyed a monster 'hit' with *I can't get started.* Ziggy Elman also enjoyed a successful single, *And the angels sing* (with BG), but preferred not to take a band out on the road and settled for a California residency. Gene Krupa (1909-73) left Goodman in 1938 and led a very good band for most of the 1940s. He made the extended drum solo a mandatory part of the big band repertoire, as well as propagating such diverse talents as saxist Charlie Ventura, the young arranger Gerry Mulligan and (with *Let me off uptown*) the exciting duo of Roy Eldridge and singer Anita O'Day. Harry James (born in 1916) left Goodman a year after Krupa and quickly prospered (with the canny BG owning a piece of the action until James could afford to buy him out). Harry could always pull the fans in with his virtuoso-style solos, and, in 1943, he became the envy of the world after his marriage to Betty Grable, but he has continued to front fine bands. (In 1951 the discerning Duke Ellington paid him an infuriating compliment by luring Willie Smith, Juan Tizol and Louis Bellson away from him!) However, James is another survivor, and so is the ubiquitous Lionel Hampton, last of the Goodman stalwarts to make it on his own. Born in 1909, 'Hamp' (whether playing vibes, two-finger piano or drums) is the very epitome of high-tension showmanship and drama. His bands don't so much swing as go on the rampage, and, in the 1940s, when those screaming tenor-players of his were on the go, Illinois Jacquet and Arnett Cobb . . . Wow!

Then, of course, there were 'the fabulous' Dorseys. Tommy (1905-56) had the more aggressive, genuinely beaty band of the two, in contrast with his own smooth, romantic trombone on ballads like *Marie* and *Song of India*. From 1939 he had the services of Sy Oliver, whose arrangements acted for him rather as Fletcher Henderson's had for Goodman. By the mid-1940s his trumpets were fired by the Negro, Charlie Shavers, while his drum-stool was occupied by the young Buddy Rich, a man soon to overtake even Gene Krupa and who is still, at the beginning of the 1980s, the finest drum technician in the world. Add the presence of Frank Sinatra, also probably the best vocal group around, The Pied Pipers, and one can understand the formula for Tommy's success. Several of his hits, *Well, git it* (featuring Shavers), *Opus 1* and *Yes, indeed!* are classics of their kind. Brother Jimmy (1904-57) although a fine jazz alto-saxist, led an altogether sweeter-sounding band, but in the early 1940s an equally popular one. His biggest hit, *Green eyes* in 1941, sold 90,000 copies in its first week of release, at a time when 20,000 was considered a best-seller.

A more direct challenge to Goodman was thrown down by the volatile Artie Shaw (born 1910), if only because Shaw himself was another brilliant clarinetist. His first important solo venture came in the summer of 1935, when he appeared at the Imperial Theatre in New York playing jazz in front of a string quartet. This first (good) use of strings with a beat caused a sensation and led to the formation of a band featuring strings, brass, rhythm section and one saxophone (Shaw's great friend, Tony Pastor). But, in 1937, the leader formed a more conventional big band: one that its acolytes could run against the bastion of BG, and did—helped by the enormous success of the band's *Begin the beguine* in 1938. ('He [Artie] lived to cut Benny and Benny to cut him. But they were both great musicians. Each was great in his own style', said Johnny Guarnieri.) The Shaw band *was* great, and in this writer's opinion it is still underrated, especially for its saxophone section under the influence of Georgie Auld. But in the end Shaw's own, dissatisfied personality told against him. He was the eternal searcher, forever breaking up and reforming his groups. BG, after hitting on a satisfactory style, had learned the additional value of continuity.

The case of Glenn Miller (1904-44) is rather special. One recognises that today, both in musical popularity and as a legendary figure, he has come to overshadow BG. (A

Artie Shaw (The Decca Record Co).

contributory factor to the latter being his tragic disappearance in an Air Force aeroplane over the English Channel during World War II.) But the truth is that Miller never really ran against Benny's band, not even with his choppy, novelty, semi-swing numbers like *In the mood, Little brown jug* and *American patrol*. What in fact happened was that from 1939, after two years of horrendous struggle, Miller emerged at the top of the heap of what I've so far referred to as 'sweet' bands, and his records of *Moonlight serenade* and *Sunrise serenade* immediately consolidated this position. From now on the Lombardos, Hal Kemp, Shep Fields (with his musical straw in a goldfish bowl!), Kay Kyser, Sonny Dunham, Fred Waring, Lawrence Welk, Vaughan Monroe and other leaders of sweet-style bands were no longer mentioned in the same breath as Miller, and the situation has remained unchanged since his death. Not even a good, workmanlike, semi-sweet, semi-swinging band of later vintage like Les Brown's has been able to build a comparable reputation.

For the one-time jazz trombonist had built up something unique, and a band sound and style that the public was ready for, took to—*and adored*. While working as the organiser of Englishman Ray Noble's first American band in 1935 Miller was coincidentally studying under Joseph Schillinger, and in the course of these studies he happened upon an unusual voicing of instruments—a clarinet lead over four saxophones. It was light, airy, beautifully smooth and yet it lent itself to a kind of muscular romanticism. The outcome was *Moonlight serenade*. The rest is show-business history.

As already mentioned, the band of Woody Herman (born 1913) peaked too late to challenge the 'King of Swing' with any degree of seriousness. Moreover, it peaked at a time when the band business itself was showing signs of wear and tear. But I honestly believe the Herman group of 1944-46 would have shredded Benny's crew,

Woody Herman (Verve Records).

and in all departments, except for the vocals. Until 1944 Woody had led what was billed as 'The band that plays the blues', a somewhat languid outfit, despite its one big hit *(Woodchoppers' ball)*. Then a whole new musicianship took over, younger players with an unprecedented fire, talent and the self-confidence to tackle almost anything. The rhythm section (Ralph Burns and then Tony Aless on piano, Billy Bauer, guitar, Chubby Jackson, bass, and Davey Tough playing his drums as never before) had perfect integration and the most phenomenal drive. Not even with Gene Krupa there could Goodman's band have matched their tempos. And yet Herman, with an intuitive nose for younger talent, found brass and reed players who did; trumpeters like the Candoli brothers, Pete and Conte, Ray Wetzel, Sonny Berman and 'the iron man', Conrad Gozzo; trombonist Bill Harris; and multi-saxist John La Porta and the roaring Flip Phillips on tenor. Also in Ralph Burns and Neal Hefti he found just the right arrangers to exploit this pool of talent. They revelled in the widening horizons of the players and began incorporating be-bop ideas and other fast, complex passages into their scores. If anyone doubts my word on all of this, then they have only to refer to Herman records of the period: *Caldonia, The good earth, Blowin' up a storm* and *Apple honey*. No wonder when Igor Stravinsky composed his one piece for jazz orchestra, the *Ebony concerto* of 1946, it was the Herman Herd who premiered it. Fortunately Woody too is still with us in the 1980s putting together Thundering Herds, because he loves to front a swinging band and to look for bright new soloists.

And the black bands meanwhile? Again, Ellington and Lunceford apart, there were some very good names to conjure with: veteran travellers like Noble Sissle, Jay MacShann (who first employed the young Charlie Parker) and the nearly-rhythm-and-blues outfit of Lucky Millinder; Earl Hines' band out of the Grand Terrace,

Chicago, featuring saxist Budd Johnson and Walter Fuller on lead trumpet; the Erskine Hawkins' group of *Tuxedo junction* fame and Andy Kirk and his 'Clouds of Joy', featuring tenorman Dick Wilson and the near-falsetto singing of Pha Terrell. Also until 1939, when the brave little giant died of spinal tuberculosis, there was still Chick Webb, still lording it up at Harlem's Savoy Ballroom together with the now rapidly maturing Ella Fitzgerald. Nobody dared take him on up there until the night of May 11 of 1937 when Benny Goodman tried. Four thousand people jammed inside, another 5,000 went crazy outside and New York's cops were all over the place. Benny played first and apparently made a good impression. But Chick came back at him and apparently nearly blew the walls out. 'I'll never forget that night', Gene Krupa recalled ruefully. 'He just cut me to ribbons—made me feel awfully small . . . That man was dynamite, he could reach the most amazing heights. When he really let go, you had a feeling that the entire atmosphere of the place was being charged!'

However, the one other and even more significant addition to the story at this point was the transfer from Kansas City to New York in the later 1930s of Count Basie. This was significant because, based upon The Apple, he would give to the big band era a new beat, a new approach to thematic materials and at the same time a galaxy of new and startling soloists the like of which no other band possessed apart from Duke Ellington's of 1940/41. In other words, an overall structure upon which to build for the future. In the 1930s 'Kaycee', as players called it, became an important place to jam, and a kind of jazz laboratory where many fresh ideas were tried. An average-sized city of the American Mid-west, a 'wide open' place dominated by booze racketeers and some corrupt politicians, Kaycee gained its prosperity through being at the centre of a vital network of rail, road and river routes, and it had some outstanding local musicians. (All the travelling bands loved to stop over there for jam sessions, sometimes with unexpected results. On one occasion Coleman Hawkins stayed so long, trying to beat the local tenormen, Lester Young, Herschel Evans and Ben Webster, that he wrecked his new Cadillac getting to the next night's job on time!)

But by far the most important idea to be developed in Kansas City was a new approach to the blues. The blues which was played faster and used as a launching pad for more varied flights of improvisation, their once-melancholy lines reshaped into brief, jumping figures or 'riffs'. Repeated several times, with minor but obvious alterations, these riffs became themes in themselves, later to be performed by sections of instruments scored in unison. Even the singers with the Kaycee bands had to go along with the blues being faster, happier and dominated by instrumental contours, singers like 'Big' Joe Turner and especially Jimmy Rushing, known as Mr Five-by-Five on account of his rotundity and because he could be heard several blocks away without a megaphone.

Bill 'Count' Basie was actually born in Red Bank, New Jersey (in 1904). However, he had worked as a pianist in and around Kansas City for a number of years before (in 1935) taking over the Bennie Moten band after the leader's sudden death. Basie then assembled some remarkable players. Oran 'Hot Lips' Page, Carl Smith and Buck Clayton on trumpets; Buster Smith (Charlie Parker's first idol) on alto-saxophone; Lester Young and Herschel Evans as his tenors; Jack Washington on baritone and Walter Page, bass. Also he sent for a drummer out of Chicago he had heard was 'playing like the wind' Jo Jones. Later, when John Hammond persuaded him to move East, Basie added the formidable Harry Edison to the trumpets, Dan Minor, Eddie Durham and later still Vic Dickenson and Dicky Wells on trombones; and he discovered Freddie Greene, the finest rhythm guitarist in jazz, playing in an obscure Greenwich Village club. With Jimmy Rushing taking care of the vocals, the band was ready to stun the musical world, and began to do so from its opening at New York's The Famous Door in late 1936. Since when, with multiple changes of personnel and on scores of gramophone records, it has continued to delight the world in general, *again though with no lowering of standards.*

After writing a full-length book about Basie it becomes doubly difficult for me to analyse his music within a few paragraphs. Let me begin by saying that Basie came to swing the blues with a verve and inherent spirit that became a marvel to every other band around, on the other hand, always tempering their magnitude of attack with qualities of precision and sensitivity. There's an obvious fire, but without exhibition—every man in the ensemble is on his toes, joining the fierce attack, but also helping the swing to be mellow and relaxed.

It was an amazing thing how this unique swing of Basie's grew up. Jo Jones, while lessening the force of his bass-drum beats, delivered a series of regulated stick-shots upon his otherwise foot-operated 'high hat' cymbal, creating a continuously shimmering effect, or else he laid a subtle, fluid beat on the top cymbal. Either way, he swept the ensemble along with apparent ease. Moreover, once the Basie rhythm section was fully formed, it seemed that certain Kansas City rhythmic patterns intermingled. The outcome was fresh and exciting, the rhythm men combining to produce a sure and steady, equally-accented 4/4 time, like 'a bouncing ball' as Jo Jones had described it. Anyway, it made for both heat and smoothness, propulsion and relaxation—with the ensemble able to swing over it as one man. In turn the ensemble players became capable of remarkable 'head' arrangements, that is, of building up spontaneous, unison riff-figures and gradually increasing the intensity and volume to create climaxes. Sections would often come together behind a soloist, selecting a basic blues phrase, then punching it out to inspire and urge him on. If he needed any urging—for Basie began pairing off soloists to make exciting contrasts, and this too has been a feature of all his later bands.

As for Basie himself, well, he plays like an additional section to the orchestra, sometimes alternating riffs with the ensemble, or cleaving open theme statements and inserting solitary piano chords where another band might have a trumpet stab. He leads from the piano, making it appear that every note he strikes is part of an informal cue to the other musicians. He uses technique for precision and timing, never for the merely decorative, and he places each note so carefully in relation to the rhythmic pattern that he swings from first to last. Also, when accompanying a soloist, the Count has something like a sixth sense for feeding him the right chords. He always has been—as Duke Ellington was—a supreme band pianist.

So what went wrong? With so much talent and enthusiasm around and a worldwide popularity to support it, why did the big band era come to an end? Certain critics maintain that Armageddon had been fought and lost by the end of 1946 when no less than eight top American bands broke up within the same few weeks. Other writers have taken a more cautious line, but agree that, by the mid-1940s, something was wrong and the band business went into a slow steady decline. If one is to go along with such a consensus, then it is not all that difficult to pinpoint the reasons. When the United States entered World War II in 1941 there was an immediate call for big bands to entertain the troops. However, these tended to be formed from *within* the armed forces (ie Glenn Miller's AAF band, and the naval groups led by Artie Shaw and Claude Thornhill). Being based on drafted sidemen they weakened and in some cases caused the break-up of 'name' bands on the home front. For those who kept going (Tommy Dorsey, Harry James, Ellington, Basie) there was first of all petrol rationing to contend with, then a 20 per cent tax slapped on entertainment and—shades of today?—the often outrageously greedy wage demands of the sidemen who were left. 'Some of them acted like spoiled brats', George T. Simon has written. 'I can remember one group of musicians in a top band cursing servicemen because they had to get up as early as noon to go out and play at a nearby camp.'

Another contributory factor was the advent of be-bop. To begin with bop was essentially the property of a small musical clique. It was difficult to play and even more difficult to score, especially for bigger bands. (There were the notable exceptions: Woody Herman's younger arrangers, Gil Fuller writing for Billy Eckstine's band, Fuller and Tadd Dameron for Dizzy Gillespie and Gil Evans with the post-war Claude Thornhill orchestra, the one featuring French horns and tuba.) As a result, be-bop continued to be performed mainly by small groups, quartets and quintets—which in turn suited many venues and booking agents because they were less expensive. One could go on. There was the disastrous recording ban imposed in 1942 by James Caesar Petrillo, the autocratic boss of America's Musicians Union. It was a ban only he wanted which went on for almost two years and kept innumerable potential big band hit records away from the public. During which time there was a noticeable switch of the public's attention towards Frank Sinatra and other former big band singers who were now stars in their own right. Finally too there was TV, the biggest stay-at-home entertainment of all time.

And yet . . . there are times when it is an advantage to be simplistic. The big band era didn't terminate in the 1940s. It merely changed. Otherwise how does one explain Herman and Basie being alive and well and still touring at the beginning of the 1980s? Likewise Ted Heath's band, Britain's finest and its only one ever to be accepted by American musicians on equal terms. It wasn't formed until after World War II; but Ted then kept it going for the next 20 years, taking in Carnegie Hall on

Stan Kenton in his dressing room at the Royal Albert Hall, London, 1956 (Fox Photos).

the way. Ellington and Kenton both carried on touring until their deaths in the 1970s. Buddy Rich goes on seemingly forever. Also in recent years we have seen the emergence of several of the best bands in the whole history of popular music led by Quincy Jones, Don Ellis, Clark Terry and, of course, Thad Jones and Mel Lewis—plus some very good ones in Europe: Harry Arnold, the Kenny Clarke/Francy Boland band, Kurt Edelhagen and, though disliked in some quarters, James Last.

No, the big band era didn't just stop, but its leading protagonists were forced to stop and take stock. By the mid-1940s there were too many of them competing for too few jobs, and some of them were charging too much money anyway. For those then prepared to take on the future it became a question not so much of belt-tightening, but of diversifying, taking their creative wares wherever the market-place happened to shift, going on TV spectaculars, touring the world, playing jazz festivals and so on. Buddy Rich on the Parkinson show? I didn't think it possible until I saw it! The next night he was playing Ronnie Scott's. But then Buddy is another of the great survivors. He went down equally well with both audiences, again, with no lowering of standards. Which is perhaps the lasting truth about the best bands. The music has always come out on top.

The British Bands

by Chris Ellis

What we now think of as The Dance Band Era lasted for roughly 45 years, from around 1912 to the late 1950s, give or take a year or so. During most of that period social dancing ranked with cinema going as one of the two or three most popular forms of mass entertainment. This is not the place for a treatise on the changes in customs and conventions wrought by the Great War. Suffice to say that the years 1914-1918 brought about a general loosening up of manners and morals and the freer mixing of class and sex on a social basis in turn led to an enormous boom in public dancing. Soon Hotel ballrooms and the night-clubs that were just starting to become a feature of London's entertainment scene were catering for this new phenomenon by employing bands to provide dance music for their patrons. Typical was the group that performed at Ciro's Club in Bond Street under the name of Ciro's Club Coon Orchestra. It consisted of banjo, banjoline, piano, bass and drums and the sound it produced was still very close to ragtime. The end of the War in 1918, far from signalling a return to pre 1914 standards, seemed instead to accelerate the speed with which the old patterns were being broken down as the survivors of the holocaust returned, hungry for entertainment to help them to blot out the memories of those four dreadful years.

It also meant that travel was no longer restricted by wartime conditions and thus it came about that in April 1919, The Original Dixieland Jazz Band from New Orleans, via Chicago and New York arrived in London to give Britain a first hand taste of real jazz music. We are not concerned here with the story of this remarkable quintet or the controversies that still exist as to its exact place in jazz history. What is beyond dispute is that they were the first jazz band to make records (in 1917) and because of the enormous commercial success of these records were, more than any other artists, responsible for the amazingly rapid spread of jazz throughout the civilised world. The ODJB instrumentation of cornet (Nick La Rocca) clarinet (Larry Shields) trombone (Emile Christian) piano (J. Russell Robinson, later replaced by Londoner Billy Jones) and drums (Tony Sharbaro) became, with the usual addition of bass and banjo or guitar, the standard Dixieland-Style jazz line-up still in use to the present day. During their British stay, which lasted for over a year, they appeared in night-clubs such as The Embassy and Rector's and also, more significantly, at the newly opened Hammersmith Palais de Danse, an enormous dance hall converted from a roller skating rink, which was designed to bring social dancing to the masses at moderate cost. Its success led to the opening of similar venues throughout Britain and soon every town of any size had at least one public dance hall ranging from the primitive to the plush. And, of course, with the proliferation of dance halls came the need for dance bands to play in them and countless groups were soon being formed to meet the demand. Often these would be of semi-professional status, working only in their own home districts and a visit from a nationally known 'name' band would be an eagerly awaited event. Among the earliest of the bands that sprang up in the wake of the ODJB was an outfit calling itself The Darnswells led by the brothers Sid and Harry Roy. Later in the decade this developed into The (Chrichton) Lyricals and finally, in the 1930s, blossomed into the famous Harry Roy Orchestra.

When the ODJB went home they proved to have been merely the spearhead of an American invasion which continued unabated until a dispute between the British and American musician's unions put a stop to this almost exclusively one way traffic in 1933—a situation that was to continue until the late 1940s. Among the major American bands which came to Britain were those of Paul Specht, Paul Whiteman, Hal Kemp, Ted Lewis and Abe Lyman, not forgetting such lesser groups as The Original Capitol Orchestra and The Southern Rag and Jazz Band. Many individual Americans, too, found work with British Orchestras. For example, trombonist Ellis Jackson with Billy Cotton, trumpeter Sylvester Ahola and clarinetist Danny Polo with Ambrose, while The Savoy Orpheans and The Savoy Havana Bands in their early days contained almost as many American musicians as it did British. A surprisingly large number of well known 'British' band leaders were of Transatlantic origin, among them Roy Fox, Carroll Gibbons, Jay Whidden, Van Phillips, Al and Ray Starita, Teddy Brown, Jack Harris, Billy Bissett, George Fisher, Howard Jacobs, Teddy Joyce, Charlie Kunz, Hal Swain, Joe Orlando, Don Parker and Bert Ralton.

Ironically, while the ODJB were enjoying their British success they were already becoming outmoded in their homeland. Art Hickman, a band leader from San Francisco, had introduced what was to become the most characteristic sound in dance music—the saxophone. The earliest Hickman recordings, made in September 1919, reveal for the first time the basic shape and instrumentation of the modern dance band consisting of trumpet, trombone, two saxophones, violin, bass, banjo and drum. Through the years this would often be modified by the addition of extra brass or reeds so that, for example, in place of one trumpet one might have a 'trumpet section' of two, three or four, but size was the only major variant throughout the rest of the era. The already larger size of Hickman's orchestra also meant that, whereas the ODJB had played without written music from memorised 'head' arrangements flavoured with a certain amount of improvisation, written arrangements now became a necessity. Hard on the heels of Art Hickman came another West Coast band leader who was soon to be the first international star of the dance band world. His name was Paul Whiteman.

Back in London in 1920, one of the most popular resorts for dancing was The Queen's Hall Roof. The precise instrumentation of its resident band seems to be a matter for conjecture but it is known that it included a black American clarinetist by the name of Ed Jenkins and a young Lancastrian who had been playing the piano in Concert Parties, pit orchestras and the like since around 1905. His name was Jack Hylton and many years later he told how Monsieur Henri, Manager of the venue, had played the first Paul Whiteman records to the band and of the furore they caused. 'I boldly said, "It seems to me they are playing from music", which monstrous assertion focused quite a lot of uncomplimentary attention on me.' Fortunately, Jenkins (who seems to have been the only other 'schooled' musician in the orchestra) agreed with this opinion, whereupon Hylton promptly offered to copy the arrangements from the records and adapt them to the existing instrumentation, persuading Monsieur Henri that the addition of a trumpet would be essential. In this way Jack Hylton became the first known British dance band arranger. In May 1921 the 'Queen's Dance Orchestra' began recording for HMV using trumpet, trombone, clarinet/alto saxophone, violin, piano, banjo and drums. Each man was paid £5 per session. Hylton felt that he should be paid an extra 10 shillings for his arrangements but, when the others disagreed, he suggested that he should instead be given credit on the record labels. 'To my astonishment they didn't seem to realise the significance of this idea and, to my great glee, quite off-handedly agreed to it, so from that time onwards the records came out as 'The Queen's Dance Orchestra' directed by Jack Hylton. I had thereby promoted myself as the band's titular head.' Hylton also shrewdly managed to take over the band's recording contract so that when he later left the Queen's Hall he was able to continue on HMV as Jack Hylton and his Orchestra. The first major British dance orchestra had been born.

But even during his Queen's Hall days, Jack Hylton's ambitions were leading him away from being a mere band leader towards his eventual emergence in the 1940s as a theatrical impresario. As a foretaste of things to come, he instigated cabaret at the Queen's Hall, booking such stars as Jack Buchanan, Beatrice Lillie and the Trix Sisters. He also saw the possibilities inherent in presenting dance bands as theatre attractions. After a break-in date at the Bedford Theatre, Camden Town the Hylton Orchestra played for 36 weeks at The Alhambra Theatre in Leicester Square and by 1924 they were established as a top of the bill theatre attraction, remaining basically a 'show' band until they disbanded in 1940. Hylton also quickly saw the commercial sense of having a second orchestra to play some of the many dates that were being offered to him and so he formed The Metro-Gnomes, under the ostensible leadership of his wife, singer Ennis Parks. From this in turn grew a booking agency which supplied orchestras for such major venues as The Kit-Cat Club, the Piccadilly Hotel, the Café de Paris, The Ambassador's Club and others. The Kit-Cat Club band was led by American Al Starita while his brother Ray led at the Piccadilly, but the recording contracts for both these very successful outfits were with Jack Hylton. It was Hylton, too, who took his by now 14 strong Orchestra (two trumpets, trombone, four reeds, three violins, piano, bass, banjo, drums) on a wildly successful five-month Continental tour from October 1928 to March 1929, appearing in France, Germany and Italy and recording in the latter two. The Orchestra continued to make regular Continental jaunts for several years, though an attempt to conquer America in 1936 foundered due to the afore-mentioned dispute between the British and American Musicians Unions.

Musically, the Hylton band followed fairly closely in the footsteps of Paul Whiteman's Orchestra. In 1927 sax/vocal/arranger Billy Ternent joined the organisation and soon became deputy leader and principal arranger, proving to have a great flair for producing arrangements in a pastiche of the American's style, including the somewhat pretentious 'Concert' arrangements of popular tunes that had become a Whiteman feature following the enormous success of the 1924 *Rhapsody in Blue* commissioned by Whiteman from the young George Gershwin. Whatever their artistic merits, such pieces as *Handsome Gigolo* and *When the white Elder tree blooms again* required great technical and musical skill from their players and it is to Hylton's credit that he always ensured that his Orchestras never contained less than top-flight men who handled with ease the varied demands that membership of Britain's No 1 show band placed on them.

In 1922, when the dance band era was just beginning to get into its stride, came the birth of British radio. The honour of being the first British dance band to broadcast went to the almost forgotten Marius B. Winter, but on October 3 1923 listeners heard a programme by The Savoy Orpheans and an important chapter in dance band history had begun. By the end of the decade the wireless had overtaken the gramophone as the most important means of spreading the fame of the best British talent throughout the country. The Savoy Orpheans were the first, but by no means the last band to become a household name through their regular radio appearances. There had been a resident dance band at the Savoy Hotel since the early days of the war, but it was of a similar type to Ciro's Club Coon Orchestra. In 1920 a Belgian named William F. de Mornys became Entertainment Manager of the Savoy, Berkeley and Claridges Hotels. In 1921 he met an American saxophonist named Bert Ralton, who had been leading a band in Havana, Cuba and the result was The New York Havana Band playing at the Savoy Hotel, which eventually evolved into the famous Savoy Havana Band. In 1923 de Mornys added a second band, the Savoy Orpheans, led by Debroy Somers. Both bands contained large American contingents throughout their lives which lasted effectively until 1927 when de Mornys left the Savoy. As the bands had been under contract to him rather than to the Hotel they also left and though attempts were made to continue them their great days were over and they soon disbanded. In 1931 a new band named The Savoy Hotel Orpheans was formed under the direct aegis of the hotel itself. Their co-leaders were two Americans who were veterans of the original Orpheans, pianist Carroll Gibbons and alto sax Howard Jacobs, both of whom had started their British careers at the Berkeley Hotel in 1924 with the Boston Orchestra. Gibbons joined the original Orpheans in 1925 and remained with them until 1928 when he left to become leader of HMV's house-band, the New Mayfair Orchestra. By 1932 he was in sole charge of the new Orchestra and remained there, a brilliant pianist and a much loved personality, until his death in 1954.

In 1926 the first broadcasting orchestra per se was formed under the name of the (original) London Radio Dance Band, led by Sid Firman, one of three band-leading brothers (the others were John and Bert). It consisted of trumpet, trombone, two reeds, violin, piano, banjo, bass and drums and lasted until early 1928 when its place was taken by the slightly larger band of Jack Payne, who had been resident at and a regular-broadcaster from the Hotel Cecil, practically next door to the BBC's Savoy Hill studios since 1925. Payne's outfit now became known as Jack Payne and his BBC Dance Orchestra and by the time he left to go into Variety in early 1932 it had increased in size to 16 pieces and became nationally famous. The replacement for Jack Payne was The New BBC Dance Orchestra directed by Henry Hall who, since 1924, had been leading an excellent little band at The Gleneagles Hotel, Scotland, showplace of the London Midland and Scottish Railways Hotel chain, for whom he had eventually become Musical Director. His had been the first band to broadcast regularly from outside London. His quiet charm soon made him a favourite with listeners and today he is one of the best remembered of all band leaders of the era. Since the BBC Dance Orchestra's regular transmissions were at 5.15, tea-time for the average family, the Corporation's musical policy firmly forbade the use of any material that was considered to be too jazzy, or sophisticated, musically or otherwise, for a family audience and also perforce meant the inclusion in the programmes of quite a lot of comedy and items intended specifically for children to enjoy. In this way Henry Hall's name became closely associated with such pieces as *The Teddy Bear's Picnic* and *Butterflies in the rain.* However, when they did get the chance the Orchestra could play first rate dance music, a fact which they proved when they in turn left the BBC for the wider field of Variety. By this time Henry Hall was a household name, aided by a very popular 1935 film *Music Hath Charms* that had been built around the Orchestra and also by a series of broadcasts that he had started and which he was to continue for many years after he ceased to lead the BBC Dance Orchestra called Henry Hall's Guest Night. When the Orchestra made their last broadcast on September 25 1937 they were not replaced and never again was the BBC to have its own Dance Orchestra as such.

Concurrently with having their own Dance Orchestra and lasting right through the era, the BBC also broadcast a great amount of dance music by other bands, many from top London night spots on a regular basis. Lew Stone, for example, had a regular programme in the 1930s at 10.30 on Tuesday evenings. By the 1930s too, much dance music was being transmitted from the commercial radio stations, Radio Luxembourg, Radio Normandie, etc, so British and Continental listeners had plenty of choice.

Today it is, of course, largely through the medium of the gramophone records that were made and sold in large quantities throughout the era that we can hear how the dance bands sounded. In the early 1920s HMV and Columbia were the dominant recording companies and Parlophone arrived in 1924 to joint them. There were numerous smaller companies such as ACO Scala and Imperial which also produced dance records but, with few exceptions, the major labels had the major names. The Great Depression of the late 1920s and early 30s caused the death of most of the small fry and in 1931 HMV and Columbia (who had already absorbed Parlophone) amalgamated to form EMI Records whose only real competition throughout the 1930s and 40s came from Decca Records, a late entry in the field (1928) who surprisingly managed to ride the slump and build up a very fine catalogue. Because of the Depression, records from the early 1930s tend to be scarcer than those of either earlier or later times. As well as making records of their contract artists the bigger record companies also had what were known as 'house' bands which existed only for recording purposes. At Decca the first 'house' band leader was Phillip Lewis; at Columbia, Van Phillips, at Zonophone, Bert Firman; while HMV, from 1928 onwards, employed first Carroll Gibbons and, succeeding him on Gibbon's recommendation in 1929, a young arranger named Ray Noble to lead what was described as The New Mayfair Dance Orchestra. Despite the fact that 'house' bands tended to be used to record the tunes that were left over after the big stars such as Jack Hylton and Ambrose had had their choice, Noble's superbly polished and original arranging style plus a talent for writing superb tunes, eg *The very thought of You*, etc, soon turned the New Mayfair into a best selling proposition not merely in Britain but also in America where, up till then, British bands had meant very little. Eventually interest grew to a point where HMV started labelling the records as by Ray Noble and his Orchestra. The quality of the Noble output is still something to be marvelled at. He had, of course, one major advantage in that he could use the cream of Britain's musicians for his recording and in fact his personnel were usually drawn largely from the ranks of the Ambrose and Lew Stone orchestras, two of the very first bands of the time. He also often availed himself of the services of Lew Stone's vocalist, Al Bowlly, around whom there has grown in recent years a posthumous cult, though at the time he was rated no higher than Sam Browne, Les Allen, Pat O'Malley or many of the 'crooners', male and female, who had become an essential feature of the dance bands since the microphone came into general use in the late 1920s. It is somewhat ironical that Ray Noble, who (apart from a short engagement, using Lew Stone's band, in Holland) had never led a dance band in public should have been invited to go to America in 1934 (taking Bowlly with him) to lead a specially formed orchestra of star American musicians at the fashionable Rainbow Roof in New York and should thereby have become the only British dance band leader to make a truly international 'name'.

It was, as we have noted, the quality of Noble's arrangements that was the real key to his success. Other outstanding British arrangers included Lew Stone, whose tasteful and original work helped first Ambrose and then Roy Fox on the road to stardom before he became the leader of one of Britain's best bands in his own right. Sid Phillips brought a very individual style to the Ambrose band of the 1930s with his arranging and also such striking compositions as *Cotton Picker's Congregation* and

Hick Stomp. Later in the 1940s and 50s, Phillips, a brilliant clarinetist, was to lead his own small Dixieland-styled unit with great success. Paul Fenhoulet with Carroll Gibbons and later The Skyrockets, George Evans with Geraldo and Stan Bowsher are just a few of the many arrangers whose flair and imagination contributed far more to the dance band years than they are generally given credit for. Bowsher was an amazing individual who, besides making arrangements for the very individual Harry Roy Orchestra also worked for a publishing firm, turning out as many as half a dozen arrangements of a current popular song, each tailored to the style of a particular band. (Harry Roy made a speciality of ragtime numbers styled to feature the two pianos of Ivor Moreton and Dave Kaye against tight punchy brass and with a rather Dixieland feel to the drumming of Joe Daniels and Nat Temple's soaring clarinet.) Most bands apart from the big-timers, worked from what were known as publishers' 'stocks', arrangements that could be bought ready made and varied to suit a wide variety of instrumental combinations. The inspiration throughout came, of course, from America, but the best British bands managed to add a distinctive touch of their own and could hold up their heads against their Transatlantic counterparts remarkably well. Most bands at one time or another copied specific American arrangements, particularly of jazz or swing style instrumentals, a few literally went in for carbon copying, for example, Maurice Winnick adopted not merely the Guy Lombardo style but even his signature tune, *The Sweetest Music This Side of Heaven*, and for some time in the 1930s Billy Ternent copied the trademarks of Hal Kemp. A few provincial orchestras, among them those of Leslie Jeffries from Glasgow, Bertini and Larry Brennan from Blackpool, Herman Darewski from Bridlington and Billy Merrin and his Commanders from Nottingham, made a greater or lesser national reputation but most major bands were based in London, from which they would venture forth every now and again on tours of ballrooms and variety theatres attracting large audiences eager to see these heroes of radio and records in person. In London's West End alone there were, in 1938, some 40 venues (not counting theatres) where dance music could be heard, ranging from Brian Lawrence's spritely Quartet at The Lansdowne Restaurant, Berkeley Square to The Savoy Hotel which had the orchestras of both Carroll Gibbons and Geraldo to delight their patrons, and from the exclusive Ciro's Club in Orange Street featuring Jack Harris's Orchestra which was for members only, 'Evening Dress Essential', to The Astoria Ballroom, Charing Cross Road where the bands of Joe Loss and Jack White could be enjoyed by anyone who could afford 1/6d from 3-6pm or 2/6d for evenings, 'Evening Dress Optional'. Concerning what was being danced, the foxtrot, the one step and the waltz were the staple fare in 1920. By the 1930s and remaining constant from then onwards, the basic ballroom dances had become the quickstep, the slow foxtrot and the slow waltz (as distinct from the earlier Viennese or 'quick' waltz). In the mid-20s the Charleston had a short-lived vogue and it's successor, the black bottom, vanished even more quickly. The tango kept a tenuous hold throughout but the rumba and beguine were considered by most to be far too exotic and overtly sexy and found little favour outside the more sophisticated venues and the ranks of the ballroom dancing cultists, whose world of competitions, Gold Medals, yards of tulle and complicated footwork requiring plenty of space to execute to good effect was somewhat apart from that of the masses who were content to shuffle happily around on crowded floors concerned only that they should not look too conspicuous. Many still remembered songs with such titles as *The Varsity Drag* or *The Breakaway* which were actually written for show routines and never played as individual ballroom dances per se, but were used as foxtrots. Such 'novelty' dances as 'The Lambeth Walk' or 'The Palais Glide' were regarded as 'party' dances and were usually of a type that could be danced in groups rather than by couples. They were mainly played at the big popular priced dance halls (or Palais de Danses, as many of them were termed—colloquially 'The Palais') to give those people without partners of their own a chance to join in the fun. Few of them ever found their way into the smarter venues. The energetic acrobatics of The Lindy or Jitterbug which erupted in America concurrently with the Swing craze in the mid-30s found no favour until the arrival in Britain of thousands of American troops during World War II brought them a belated popularity, though the more spectacular steps were soon eliminated and the whole style was eventually emasculated into the 'jive' that was to be the hold-over from the dance band era into the age of rock 'n' roll.

A few bands particularly from the 1930s onwards were of a somewhat specialist nature, such as Geraldo's Gaucho Tango Orchestra and the rumba bands of Edmundo Ros and Don Marino Barretto, all of which made a feature of Latin-American style music, generally somewhat watered down. Even these, when playing for dancers, had to play a high proportion of basically straight dance music given a Latin flavour by the exotic rhythm instruments (such as maracas and claves and the extensive use of flutes, accordions and marimbas in lieu of the more conventional dance band line-up). For the dedicated ballroom dancer there was, usually on record only, the 'strict-tempo' dance band as epitomised by Victor Silvester and his Ballroom Orchestra whose records sold in their hundreds of thousands from the mid-30s onwards. Everything in these records was subordinated to the correct tempo for the particular dance that was being played. The 'Orchestra' consisted of two pianos, saxophone doubling clarinet and any other necessary reeds, violin, guitar, bass and drums. The melody was played straight without any distracting variations that might take the dancers' minds off their footwork and the result makes dull listening today. At least until the later years of the dance band era, Britain had few jazz or swing bands working on a regular basis. It should be noted at this point that records of the period often give a misleading impression as to what their makers actually played on the bandstand. Britain produced plenty of musicians whose ability to play 'hot' could stand comparison with their American counterparts but, with few exceptions, they got little chance to display their talents except at after hours informed 'jam-sessions' at places like the 'Bag o' nails' in Kingly Street or 'The Palm Beach' in Frith Street and on a few record sessions aimed at the jazz market. Some hotel and club dance orchestras worked without brass instruments (to keep the volume down to a level that would not be too distracting for the patrons who had only come to dine and gossip) and were augmented for recording purposes. Phillipine born Fed Elizalde led an interesting band modelled on the New York jazz style of 'Red' Nichols, Miff Mole and The California Ramblers and containing several one-time members of the latter band, at the Savoy Hotel during 1927-8 but complaints from both the hotel patrons and listeners to the regular BBC broadcasts from the ballroom brought the experiment to a premature end. On records the bands of Spike Hughes and Madame Tussaud's Dance Orchestra led by Stanley Barnett made some interesting music, somewhat in the style of Duke Ellington. But only the small groups led by trumpeter/vocalist Nat Gonella (a self-avowed disciple of Louis Armstrong whose playing had previously added sparkle to the bands of Billy Cotton, Roy Fox and Lew Stone, and drummer Joe Daniels, formerly of Harry Roy's band, whose records were labelled as Joe Daniels and his Hot-Shots in Drumnasticks), gained any large following in pre-World War II days and they worked mostly as stage acts in Variety.

The outbreak of World War II in September 1939 brought a lot of changes to the dance band scene. After the first few months the public demand for entertainment reached a new peak but at the same time many of the younger dance band musicians were being called up for military service. Some band-leaders like Jack Hylton disbanded rather than face the constant problem brought about by wartime conditions, of which the replacing of musicians was only one. Others struggled along sometimes not even sure from week to week what instruments they would be using, let alone who would be playing them. Several 'all-girls' bands were formed, that of Ivy Benson having a particularly big success.

Inevitably much of the individuality that had so distinguished the best bands slowly disappeared. The so-called 'Glenn Miller sound', easily adaptable for 'Sweet' or 'Swing' style, boosted by hit records and two enormously popular films featuring the Glenn Miller Orchestra, gained an ever increasing stranglehold as the war ground on and it soon became almost impossible to tell whether you were listening to Joe Loss, Geraldo or Carroll Gibbons, until maybe a recognisable singer such as Dorothy Carless with Geraldo, or a few bars of unmistakable Gibbons piano revealed the answer. Many of the musicians who joined the Armed Forces were seconded for service with the various entertainment units and soon each of the Services had its own dance bands and because they had the pick of the very best players such orchestras as The Squadronaires and the No 1 Ballroom Centre Dance Orchestra, or 'Skyrockets' as they were generally known, from the Air Force set very high standards and also played a far higher proportion of 'Swing' than any of their predecessors. Both these orchestras continued as civilian bands for many years after the war ended alongside the older established ones, but by now, right in the forefront, was Geraldo and the ever popular Joe Loss, the Palais de Danse leader par excellence since he became a name band leader at The Astoria Ballroom in 1930 at the tender age of 21. Today Joe Loss remains as the only surviving full-time band leader from the great days and he is as busy as ever.

Ted Heath in concert (The Decca Record Co).

For several years after the war ended in 1945 the dancing craze continued apparently unabated. Though the bands of Roy Fox, Jack Harris, Henry Hall and many others were missing from the scene old favourites such as Harry Roy and Carroll Gibbons continued to draw the crowds along with newer names like Lou Praeger and Ken Macintosh. Ted Heath, one of Britain's finest trombonists from right back to the early 1920s formed a big band playing advanced 'Swing' music and even made a success in America. At home, however, his following was as much dependent on the charm and talent of his vocalists, Dickie Valentine, Lita Roza and Dennis Lotis, singing the usual current commercial dance tunes and novelty numbers, as it was on such fine instrumentals as *Hot Toddy*. But, by the early 1950s, the public was at last beginning to desert the dance floors. Also, the costs of running a big band had escalated to an uneconomical degree. Everything from the price of band uniforms to bed and breakfast at a provincial hotel was becoming more and more expensive. Musicians' wages too were going up and the final coup-de-grâce for the dance band era arrived when, in the mid-50s, the youth of Britain found themselves some new idols from America in the shapes firstly of Bill Haley and his Comets and then of Elvis Presley. Rock and Roll had arrived and, to the young at least, the dance bands suddenly sounded hopelessly old-fashioned.

Within a few years it was all over. A few survived—old-timer Billy Cotton, who had progressed from Palais to Variety, made a successful transition into television by exploiting the comedy talents in the band and his own ebullient Cockney personality, but his orchestra was no longer really a dance band. Jack Jackson and Jack Payne became radio disc jockeys. Many of the best musicians found employment as 'studio' men in the various recording studios. Many more just quietly faded into retirement. In the quarter of a century or so since the dance band era came to its end there have been persistent rumours of a revival, but if such an unlikely thing were to happen it could be like the ragtime revival of the late 1970s, a short lived craze. Let those of us who still love the sound of the dance bands of yesteryear treasure our memories and be grateful for the gramophone records that enable us to recapture at least some part of those happy times when dancing or listening nightly to the bands was almost a way of life.

The Bands and their LP recordings

by Burnett James and Peter Gammond

Whilst every effort has been made to ensure that the numbers in these listings are as accurate as possible, errors may occur. The authors would be pleased to hear from readers who can provide any additional, relevant information. While mainly keeping to records that are currently available, a large number of deleted items are included—indicated by (d)—which carry repertoire of exceptional interest. Dates in brackets (68) indicate approximate year of issue.

The following abbreviations are used in the text: as—alto-sax; b—banjo; bar—baritone; cl—clarinet; d—drums; g—guitar; fl—flute; p—piano; t—trumpet; tb—trombone; ts—tenor sax; vln—violin; vo—vocalist; xyl—xylophone.

Bert Ambrose

(b London, 1897; d London, June 12 1971)
Studied first in London then went to America for further study of music and violin. Played in theatre and symphony orchestras in New York, then in 1917 was appointed Musical Director of the Club de Vingt and led a band at the Palais Royal. Was brought back to London by Luigi to play at the Embassy Club in 1920. Returned to New York in 1922 to work at the Clover Gardens, then came back to London to open with a new band at the Embassy late 1922, and began his recording career. Left the Embassy Club in 1927 to form a band at the Mayfair Hotel with mixed British and American musicians [Joe Crossman (ts), Sydney Lipton (vln), Ted Heath (tb), later Max Bacon (d)] which became one of the top British dance bands of the period. In late 1933 Ambrose returned to the Embassy Club and continued popular broadcasts and recordings, the resident 11-piece band being augmented for radio and records. Chief arrangers/composers were Sid Phillips (bar, cl) and Bert Barnes (p). The style mixed 'sweet' dance band music with 'hot' numbers, the latter strongly Ellington-based, under the influence of Phillips. Like Ellington, Ambrose featured a notable trombone trio [Lew Davis, Ted Heath, Tony Thorpe; later Davis, Eric Breeze, Les Carew] and a number of prominent British [Max Goldberg, Tommy McQuater (t), Davis (tb), Billy Amstell (ts), Dick Ball, Tiny Winters (b), Bacon (d)] and American [Danny Polo (as, cl)] musicians, and vocalists Vera Lynn, Sam Browne, Elsie Carlisle and Evelyn Dall. At various times later band leaders Lew Stone, Stanley Black, George Melachrino and George Shearing also worked for him. Continued working through 1940s and 1950s and ended career in field of musical and theatrical management. Generally regarded as best British dance/swing band of 1930s, the only real rival in dual roles being Lew Stone. Appeared in film *Soft Lights and Sweet Music* (1935).

Selected LP recordings

Ambrose and his Orchestra—World Records SHB21 (2) (74). *Without you, sweetheart* (1928); *I'm Riding to Glory* (1928); *If I had You* (1930); *Singapore Sorrows* (1928); *Moanin' for You* (1930); *A Japanese Dream* (1930); *'Leven-thirty Saturday Night* (1930); *Cryin' for the Carolines* (1930); *The 'free and easy'* (1930); *Stardust* (1931); *Half Caste Woman* (1931); *Blue Again* (1931); *Moonlight Saving Time* (1931); *Blue turning grey over you* (1930); *Good Evenin'* (1930); *Bye Bye Blues* (1930); *Yes, yes (my baby says yes)* (1931); *They didn't believe me* (1931); *Whistling in the Dark* (1931); *I'm thru' with love* (1931); *No Hum* (1931); *I Don't Know Why (I Just Do)* (1931); *You rascal you*

Bert Ambrose (World Records).

(1931); *Dancing in the Dark* (1932); *Soft Lights and Sweet Music* (1932); *When Yuba plays the Rumba on the Tuba* (1932); *Isn't it Romantic* (1932); *Puleeze, Mister Hemingway* (1932); *Old Man of the Mountain* (1932); *Too Many Tears* (1932); *Is I in love? I is* (1932); *Let's put out the Lights* (1932).

Saturday Night—Decca DDV5003/4 (77). *Embassy Stomp; Down the Old Ox Road; Night Ride; Caravan; Tick Tock Town; A Latin from Manhattan; Dames; It's a Sin to Tell a Lie; Lulu's Back in Town; Lazybones; Lady of Madrid; Chasing Shadows; On the Good Ship Lollipop; Wagon Wheels; Cotton Pickers' Congregation: etc.* (1935-39.)

Also:

Hors d'oeuvres (1935-37)—Decca LF1105 (53) (d); (A) London LB-706.

The Best of Ambrose and his Orchestra (1928-32)—Music for Pleasure MFP1128 (d).

The Bands That Matter (1933-39)—Decca 'Eclipse' ECM2044 (d).

Ambrose and his Orchestra—MGM CD-2 (55) (d); (A) MGM 3350.

Latin America after dark—MGM CC-2 (57) (d); (A) MGM 3478.

London Jazz Scene—the 30s (with Lew Stone)—Decca 'Ace of Clubs' ACL1103 (62) (d).

A Tribute to Cole Porter—Decca 'Ace of Clubs' ACL1186 (64).

Champagne Cocktail—Decca 'Ace of Clubs' ACL1246 (68).

Ambrose and his Orchestra (1928-32)—(A) Monmouth-Evergreen MES7032.

The Best of Ambrose and his Orchestra at the Mayfair Hotel, London, 1928-32—Music for Pleasure MFP-1258 (d).

Louis Armstrong

(b New Orleans, July 4 1900; d New York, August 6 1971)

Much of the history of Louis Armstrong and his tremendous influence on jazz history lies outside the scope of this book, but some of his activities had a very important bearing on the development of big band jazz and the styling of music in the swing era. Much of his own early development was in organised groups rather than in the areas of improvised New Orleans jazz and even some of his small jazz group recordings suggest carefully considered patterns of playing rather than spontaneous improvisation. Armstrong's big, broad cornet and trumpet style with its controlled vibrato was essentially the kind of playing that the swing trumpeters aimed for and there is little doubt that Armstrong enjoyed playing above instrumental sections and organised backgrounds rather than mixing in a free-for-all. Even his later All-Star recordings suggest this. Having learned to play the trumpet in a New Orleans waifs home he joined Kid Ory's band in 1917, replacing King Oliver. From 1918 he played in various New Orleans clubs and on river-boats. In 1922 he was asked to join King Oliver's famous and successful Creole Jazz Band in Chicago and it was in the carefully planned cornet duets and breaks with Oliver that we can see the early pattern of the arranged instrumental section emerging. Big band jazz was already developing elsewhere

Right *Louis Armstrong at the Empress Hall, London, 1956* (Daily Express).

and bands like Fletcher Henderson's were shaping the future in the early 1920s. At the end of 1924 Armstrong joined the Henderson band and what was already a very lively ensemble was given an increased vitality by the addition of his swinging trumpet style in the year that he stayed with the band. Throughout the 1920s Armstrong was very much involved in the big band scene that preceded the true swing era of the 1930s. He played and recorded with the band led by Erskine Tate at the Vendome Theatre in 1926 and at the end of the year joined the Carroll Dickerson band with which he made recordings under his own name and eventually took over, leading it at the Savoy Ballroom in 1928. From 1929 he was making a fine series of big band recordings with the Luis Russell Orchestra (many as Louis Armstrong and his orchestra) and throughout the 1930s with the bands of Les Hite, Charlie Gains, Chick Webb, Jimmy Dorsey, the Casa Loma Orchestra, as well as with Russell and his own bands. There were also swing sessions in the 1940s. Certainly Armstrong's influence in this field must be reckoned as an important part of his overall influence on jazz.

Selected LP recordings

Louis Armstrong V.S.O.P., Vol.1—CBS 62470 (76). (Hot Five recordings 1925/26).

Louis Armstrong V.S.O.P., Vol.2—CBS 62471 (76). (Hot Fives, Sevens & Stompers, 1926-27).

Louis Armstrong V.S.O.P., Vol.3—CBS 62472 (76). (Hot Sevens & Fives, 1927-28).

Louis Armstrong V.S.O.P., Vol.4—CBS 62473 (76). *Savoyager's Stomp* (1928) (with Carroll Dickerson's Orchestra); (plus Savoy Ballroom Five 1928).

Louis Armstrong V.S.O.P., Vol.5—CBS 62474 (76). *Ain't misbehavin'* (1929); *Black and Blue* (1929); *That Rhythm Man* (1929); *Sweet Savannah Sue* (1929); *Some of these Days* (1929); *When you're Smiling* (1929); *After You've Gone* (1929) (with Carroll Dickerson's Orchestra); *I ain't got Nobody* (1929); *Dallas Blues* (1929) (with Luis Russell's Orchestra); (plus Savoy Ballroom Five & small groups, 1929).

Louis Armstrong V.S.O.P., Vol.6—CBS 62475 (76). *St. Louis Blues* (1929); *Rockin' Chair* (1929); *Song of the Islands* (1930); *Bessie couldn't help it* (1930); *Blue turning grey over you* (1930); *Dear Old Southland* (1930) (with Orchestra (Luis Russell's Orchestra)); *My Sweet* (1930); *I can't believe that You're in Love with Me* (1930); *Indian Cradle Song* (1930); *Exactly like You* (1930); *Dinah* (1930); *Tiger Rag* (1930) (with 'Cocoanut Grove' orchestra); *I'm a Ding Dong Daddy* (1930); *I'm in the Market for You* (1930); *Confessin'* (1930); *If I could be with you* (1930) (with Sebastian New Cotton Club Orchestra (Les Hite's Orchestra)).

Louis Armstrong V.S.O.P., Vol.7—CBS 62476 (76). *Body and Soul* (1930); *Memories of You* (1930); *You're Lucky to Me* (1930); *Sweethearts on Parade* (1930); *You're Drivin' Me Crazy* (1930); *The Peanut Vendor* (1930); *Just a Gigolo* (1931); *Shine* (1931) (with Les Hite's Orchestra); *Walkin' my Baby Back Home* (1931); *I Surrender, Dear* (1931); *When it's Sleepy Time down South* (1931); *Little Joe* (1931); *You Rascal, You* (1931); *Them There Eyes* (1931); *When Your Lover Has Gone* (1931) (with Zilmer Randolph's Orchestra).

Louis Armstrong V.S.O.P., Vol.8—CBS 62477 (76). *Lazy River* (1931); *Georgia on my Mind* (1931); *Chinatown, my Chinatown* (1931); *I got Rhythm* (1931); *Wrap your Troubles in Dreams* (1931); *Star Dust* (1931); *You can depend on me* (1931); *The Lonesome Road* (1931); *Between the Devil and the Deep Blue Sea* (1931); *Kickin' the Gong Around* (1931); *Home* (1931); *All of Me* (1931); *Love, you Funny Thing* (1931); *New Tiger Rag* (1931); *Keepin' out of Mischief Now* (1932); *Lawd, You Made The Night Too Long* (1932) (with Zilmer Randolph's Orchestra).

All the above issued in four double albums CBS 88001/2/3/4 as listed (76).

Also (big band recordings only):

Louis Armstrong Classics (1935-41)—Brunswick LA8528 (52) (d).

Laughin' Louie (1933)—HMV DLP1036 (54) (d).

Louis Armstrong (1929-31)—Philips BBL7046 (55) (d).

Louis Armstrong Orchestra (1932-33)—HMV DLP1105 (55) (d).

Louis Armstrong Story, Vol.6 (1930-33)—Philips BBL7218 (58) (d).

Jazz Classics (1935-41)—Decca 'Ace of Hearts' AH7 (61) (d); (A) Decca DL8284).

Satchmo Style (1929-30)—Parlophone PMC7045 (68) (d).

Louis and the Big Bands (1928-30)—Parlophone PMC7074 (69) (d).

Swing that Music (1935-44)—Coral CP1, CRLM1020 (74).

Satchmo's Greatest, Vol.3—(F) RCA

731.050.
Louis Armstrong and his Orchestra—(F) Blue Ace BA-3603.
Louis Armstrong Favorites—(A) Columbia CL-854.
Louis Armstrong: Rare Items—(A) Decca DL-79225.
A Rare Batch of Satch (1930s)—(A) RCA LPM-2322.
See also under Fletcher Henderson.

Gus Arnheim

(b Philadelphia, September 11 1897; d Los Angeles, January 19 1955)
Leader of successful dance and session band during 1920s and 1930s. After playing in cafés and theatres in Chicago teamed with Abe Lyman to form Syncopated Five. Accompanist to Sophie Tucker, then rejoined Lyman in 1927. Formed his own band and toured Europe and America before settling as resident band at the Cocoanut Grove for extended runs. Backed Bing Crosby and Rhythm Boys in 1931 and in the same year made nationwide impact on the *Lucky Strike* radio show, and in 1934 again backed Bing Crosby. In 1936/7 featured arrangements by Budd Johnson. Several jazz clarinetists (Woody Herman, Joe Dixon, Irving Fazola) worked with Arnheim, and in 1937 Stan Kenton worked with him and did arrangements. Continued to lead a band through the 1940s on the west coast, but then retired. Returned to music business in 1954, doing various television sessions. Arnheim was also a popular song writer, among his successes being *Sweet and Lovely, I Cried for You, I'm Gonna Get You* etc. Appeared in a number of movies, including *Puttin' on the Ritz, The Street Girl, Cuban Love Song.*

Selected LP recordings
From the Cocoanut Grove, 1932—(A) Sunbeam HB-394 (74).
The Young Bing Crosby (9 tracks)—RCA RD-27075; (A) RCA LX-995.

Charlie Barnet

(b New York, October 26 1913)
The son of wealthy parents, he had a solid education, musical as well as general. By 16 he was leading a band on Atlantic liners and later played in and around New York. Formed a 'society' band in 1933, playing in various top New York hotels; also featuring Dixieland type music. Went into films in 1935 with bit-parts. In 1936 he formed a new band featuring the modern style vocal group The Modernaires and playing good style swing arrangements. Formed new band again in 1938, this time with marked success, playing at Famous Door Club in New York and the Palomar ballroom in Los Angeles. A lifelong admirer of Duke Ellington, Barnet's music was always strongly Ellington-based. A competent alto and tenor player who featured himself well but not exclusively; also led reed section on soprano sax with distinctive effect. Billy May (qv,) played trumpet with Barnet for a time and

Gus Arnheim and his Orchestra (Music Corporation of America).

did a number of successful arrangements. Vocalists in 1940s included Lena Horne and Kay Starr, and in 1949 he hired Maynard Ferguson and promoted his high note trumpet to fame. Appeared in several films during 1940s, and when big band scene declined organized smaller groups. Went to the West Coast in late 1950s where he continued actively at intervals. Chief claims to fame—bands of 1938-52 playing a good jazz-swing style with notable if not always big name soloists, though 1946/47 bands contained several famous players [Clark Terry, Al Killian, Jimmy Nottingham (t), Bud Shank (ts), Barney Kessel (g), Claude Williamson (p)].

Selected LP recordings

Some Like it Hot—(A) Swing Era LP-1002. *Night Song* (1939); *Some Like It Hot* (1939); *I Never Knew* (1939); *Ebony Rhapsody* (1939); *The Last Jump* (1939); *Cuban Boogie Woogie* (1939); *Reminiscing* (1940); *No Name Jive, Parts 1 & 2* (1940); *Buffy Boy* (1940); *Merry-go-round* (1941); *Ponce de Leon* (1941); *Little Dip* (1941); *Dark Bayou* (1946); *All The Things You Are* (1949); *Durango* (1952).

Charlie Barnet and his Orchestra—(A) Bandstand BS-7123. *Make Believe Ballroom* (1936); *What's New* (1939); *Love grows on the White Oak Tree* (1939); *Between 18th and 19th on Chestnut Street* (1939); *Clap hands, here comes Charlie* (1939); *720 in the Book* (1940); *Flying Home* (1940); *No Name Jive* (1940); *The Sergeant was shy* (1940); *Ring dem Bells* (1940); *Southern Fried* (1940); *Nowhere* (1940); *He's a Latin from Staten Island* (1940); *The Captain and his men* (1941); *Birmingham Breakdown* (1941).

Skyliner (1942-46)—Decca 'Ace of Hearts' AH157 (67) (d). *Pow-wow* (1942); *I like to Riff* (1942); *Baby, won't you Please Come Home* (1942); *Washington Whirligig* (1942); *Madame Butterball* (1945); *Andy's Boogie* (1946); *The Moose* (1946); *Things ain't what they used to be* (1946); *Smiles* (1942); *Cement Mixer* (1946); *Drop me off at Harlem* (1944); *Skyliner* (1944).

The Big Band Sound of Charlie Barnet—Polydor 'Verve' 2317 060 (64) (d). *Bunny; Atlantic Hop; Power Steering; Blue Lou; Jubilee Jump; Moods; Budandy; Southern Fried; Charleston Alley; The Gal from Joe's; Rockin' in rhythm; Pompton Turnpike; Cherokee; Skyliner.* (1946-47.)

Bebop Spoken Here—EMI 'One Up' OU2008; Bovema 5C 052 80054 (70). *Cu-ba; Overtime; Charlie's other Aunt; Bebop Spoken Here; Claude Reigns; Easy Living; O'Henry; Really.* (1949, coupled with Goodman.)

Charlie Barnet (RCA Records).

Classics in Jazz—Capitol LCT6018 (55) (d); (A) Capitol T-624. *Eugipelliv* (1949); *Lonely Street* (1949); *Cu-ba* (1949); *Charlie's other Aunt* (1949); *O'Henry* (1949); *Portrait of Edward Kennedy Ellington* (1949); *Over the Rainbow* (1949); *Pan Americana* (1949); *Claude Reigns* (1949); *Spain* (1950).

Also:

Dance Session—Columbia 33C9024 (56) (d); (A) Verve 2007.

Jive! Jive! Jive!—HMV CLP1143 (57) (d).

Cherokee (1958)—Top Rank 35/037 (59) (d); World Records T141 (d); (A) Everest BR5008, (S) 1008.

Charlie's Choice—(A) Camden 389.

A Tribute to Harry James—Eros ERL50014, (S) ERLS50014 (61) (d).

Charlie Barnet Big Band—1967—Vocalion LAE-L604, (S) SEA-L604 (67) (d); (A) Credo W1056.

Lonely Street—(A) Verve MGV-2040.

Hop on the Skyliner (1942-45)—Brunswick LAT8094 (d); (A) Decca DL8098.

Charlie Barnet Orchestra, Vol.1 (1939-41)—RCA RD-7965 (d); (A) RCA LPV-551 (68).

Charlie Barnet Orchestra, Vol.2—RCA RD-8088 (d); (A) RCA LPV-567 (69).
Jazz Oasis—(A) RCA T1403.
Silver Star Swing Series—EMI (Int) PC07840 (75).
Charlie Barnet & Orchestra (Broadcasts 1940 & 1945)—Aircheck 5 (76).
Duke's Ideas, Vol.1 (1939-41)—(F) RCA PM-42041 (77).
In Disco Order, Vol.1—Ajax 104 (77).
In Disco Order, Vol.2—Ajax 106 (77).
Charlie Barnet 1945-47, Vol.1—First Heard FH12 (77).
Charlie Barnet 1944-47, Vol.2—First Heard FH17 (77).
Skyliner (with Billy May)—Pye 'Golden Hour' GH868 (77).
Swing Street, Vol.3—Columbia 33SX1511; (A) Epic SW6042/3.
Charlie Barnet plays Duke Ellington—(A) RCA LPT-3062.
Charlie Barnet and his Orchestra (1939-41)—(A) Sounds of Swing LP-103.
Swingin' on Nothin' (1939-41)—(A) Big Band Archives LP-1209.
Rhapsody in Barnet (1940-47)—(A) Swing Era LP-1019.
Big Band 1967—(A) Vault S-9004.
Charlie Barnet 1936-37, Vol.2—Ajax 106 (79).
Charlie Barnet 1942-43, Vol. 16—Ajax 140 (79).
Charlie Barnet 1944, Vol.17—Ajax 147 (79).
Charlie Barnet, Vol.18—Ajax 155 (79).
Charlie Barnet—Bright Orange BO76 (79).
Dance Date—Swinghouse SWH6 (79).
On Stage—Bright Orange BO719 (79).

Count Basie

(b Red Bank, New Jersey, August 21 1904) Began his career playing piano in New York and touring with road shows. In 1927 he found himself in Kansas City without employment and worked as theatre organist until he joined Walter Page's Blue Devils in 1928, and then Bennie Moten (qv). With Moten until his death in 1935. Led group in 1936 with Lester Young (ts) and famous rhythm section [Walter Page (b), Jo Jones (d)] and blues singer Jimmy Rushing. Brought to Chicago, then New York by John Hammond and established reputation with full band at the Savoy Ballroom and the Famous Door. This band [Buck Clayton, Harry Edison, Ed Lewis (t), Dicky Wells (tb), Lester Young, Herschel Evans (ts), Earl Warren, Tab Smith (as), Buddy Tate (ts), with Freddy Green (g) added to rhythm section of Page and Jones] rivalled Ellington and Lunceford (qv) in popularity with its forthright swinging style. Vocals shared by Rushing and Helen Humes. Basie continued to front big band through 1940s with other star players. Economic pressures led to reduction to small group in 1950, [Clark Terry (t), Buddy de Franco (cl), Wardell Gray (ts)], but reformed full band in 1952 using similar style but modern sound and approach [Joe Newman, Thad Jones (t), Henry Coker, Al Grey (tb), Paul Quinichette, Eddie 'Lockjaw' Davis (ts), Frank Foster (ts), Frank Wess (ts, fl) Joe Williams (vo)] with arrangements by Ernie Wilkins, Neal Hefti, Johnny Mandel and band members Foster and Wess. Continued to front major band up to the present. Distinctive band pianist with deceptively simple and economical style. Frequent appearances at Montreux and Nice festivals in Europe, often featuring arrangements by Bill Holman. Prolific recording career from 1930s onwards; appearances in films and on radio and television and as

Count Basie.

backing for singers [Sarah Vaughan, Ella Fitzgerald, Sammy Davis, Tony Bennett, Frank Sinatra and Billy Eckstine].

Selected LP recordings

Swinging at the Daisy Chain—Coral CP75, CRLM1052 (75). *Honeysuckle Rose* (1937); *Pennies from Heaven* (1937); *Swinging at the Daisy Chain* (1937); *Roseland Shuffle* (1937); *Boo hoo* (1937); *The Glory of Love* (1937); *Smarty* (1937): *One o'clock Jump* (1937); *Listen my children and you shall hear* (1937); *Our Love was Meant To Be* (1937); *I keep Remembering* (1937); *Let me dream* (1937).

You can depend on Basie—Coral CP76, CRLM1053 (75). *Now will you be good* (1938); *Swinging the Blues* (1938); *London Bridge is falling down* (1938); *Dark Rapture* (1938); *Panassié Stomp* (1938); *My Heart belongs to Daddy* (1939); *Sing for your Supper* (1939); *You can depend on me* (1939); *Blame it on my Last Affair* (1939); *Jive at Five* (1939); *Thursday* (1939); *Oh, Lady be Good* (1939).

Jumpin' at the Woodside—Decca 'Ace of Hearts' AH111 (66) (d); Coral CP-106 (d); CRLM1066 (74); (A) Brunswick 54012. *Jumpin' at the Woodside* (1938); *Every Tub* (1938); *Out the Window* (1937); *Shorty George* (1938); *Time Out* (1937); *Doggin' around* (1938); *Texas Shuffle* (1938); *Blue and Sentimental* (1938); *Cherokee* (1939); *Topsy* (1937); *John's Idea* (1937).

Lester Young Memorial Album, Vol.1—Fontana TFL5064 (59) (d); (A) Epic LG3167. *Pound Cake* (1939); *Rock-a-bye Basie* (1939); *Riff Interlude* (1939); *Shoe Shine Swing* (1936); *Clap hands, here comes Charlie* (1939); *Taxi War Dance* (1939); *Ham 'n' eggs* (1939); *Lester leaps in* (1939); *Dickie's Dream* (1939); *Blow Top* (1940); *Broadway* (1940); *Boogie Woogie* (1936).

Lester Young Memorial Album, Vol.2—Fontana TFL5065 (59) (d); (A) Epic LG3168. *Easy does it* (1940); *Lady be Good* (1936); *Jump for me* (1939); *Hollywood Jump* (1939); *Louisiana* (1940); *Moten Swing* (1940); *Tickle-toe* (1940); *Twelfth Street Rag* (1939); *Let me see* (1940); *I never knew* (1940); *Song of the Islands* (1939); *I left my Baby* (1939).

(Two albums above as (A) Epic LN-6031/2; (F) CBS Epic 66212 (2).)

Kansas City Jazz—Coral CP39; (A) Decca DL-8044. *Good Morning Blues* (1937); *Doggin' around* (1937). (With tracks by Andy Kirk, Hot Lips Page, etc.)

Count Basie—Queen Disc 015 (76). *Fare thee, Honey, fare thee well* (1939) (quartet); *What's your Number* (1940); *Draftin' Blues* (1940); *Rockin' the Blues* (1904); *It's Square but it Rocks* (1941); *You Lied To Me* (1941); *Wiggle Woogie* (1941); *Music Makers* (1941); *9.20 Special* (1941); *H & J* (1941); *Feedin' the Bean* (1941); *Goin' to Chicago* (1941); *You Betcha Life* (1941); *Down, Down, Down* (1941); *King Joe* (1941).

The Second Big Band Sound—Polydor Verve 2317 074 (73). *New Basie Blues; Sure Thing; Why Not; Fancy Meeting You; Jive at Five; No Name; Redhead; Every Tub; Jack and Jill; Bread; There's a Small Hotel; Hob Nail Boogie; Basie Talks; Paradise Squat; Bunny; Tippin' on the Q.T.* (1952.)

The Kid from Red Bank, Vol.1—Polydor 2682 033 (2) (74); (A) Roulette 42015. *Whirlybird; Splanky; For Lena and Lennie; Blues in Hoss' Flat; The Deacon; The Wiggle Walk; Vine Street Rumble; Rare Butterfly; Swinging at the Waldorf; Pensive Miss; Bag-a-bones; Back to the Apple; The Swizzle; Quince; Kansas City Shout; Summer Frost; Easy Money; Cute; TV Time; Meeting Time; Katy-do; A Little Tempo, Please; The Elder; Rat Race.* (1957-62, from previous LPs.)

A Night at Count Basie's—Pye PPL 11005 (57) (d); Vanguard VRS8508 (d). *Indiana; More than One for my Baby; Too Marvellous for Words; Sent for you Yesterday; Perdido; I Want a Little Girl; Please don't talk about me when I'm gone; Canadian Sunset.* (1956.)

The Big Band Sound of Count Basie—Polydor Metro 2356 063 (74) (d) (A) Pablo 2310 756. *April in Paris; I'm Walkin'; Squeeze Me; St. Louis Blues; St. Thomas; Hey Jim; Shiny Stockings; Watermelon Man; Makin' Whoopee; Frankie and Johnny; It's only a Paper Moon; One o'clock Jump.* (1950s-60s.)

The Atomic Mr. Basie—Columbia 33SX1084 (58); (S) SCX3265; Vogue CVR36012; (A) Roulette (S) R52003. *The Kid from Red Bank; Duet; After Supper; Flight of the Foo Birds; Double-O; Teddy the Toad; Whirlybird; Midnite Blue; Splanky; Fantail; Li'l Darlin'.* (1957.)

Chairman of the Board—Columbia 33SX1224, (S) SCX3304 (60); (A) Roulette R52032, (S) SR52032. *Blues in Hoss's Flat; HRH; Segue in C; Kansas City Shout; Speaking of Sounds; TV Time; Who, me?; The Deacon; Half Moon Street; Mutt and Jeff.* (1957-58.)

The Atomic Mr. Basie and **Chairman of the Board** reissued in one album—Vogue VJD517 (76) as **The Atomic Mr. Chairman.)**

The Best of Basie—Polydor Roulette 2682 047; (A) Roulette RE-118 (2). *Jumpin' at the Woodside; Broadway; Lester leaps in; Blue and Sentimental; Shorty George; Jive at Five; Red Bank Boogie; Down for Double; Rock-a-bye Basie; Swingin' the Blues; Topsy; Taps Miller; Out of the Window; Every Tub; Doggin' around; 9.20 Special; Texas Shuffle; Dickie's Dream; Time Out; Tickle toe; Avenue 'C'; The Kid from Red Bank; Splanky; Whirlybird; Li'l Darlin'; Flight of the Foo Birds; One o'clock Jump.* (1957-61. Taken from previous LPs **The Count Basie Story**, etc.)

Live in London—1966—Extreme Rarities LP1006 (74) (d). *All of me; Flight of the Foo Birds; The Midnight Sun Never Sets; Blues for Eileen; Jumpin' at the Woodside; April in Paris; I needs to be beed with; Whirly Bird; Lil' Darlin'; One o'clock Jump.* (1966.)

Basic Basie—Polydor 2384 010; BASF BMPS19-20724-2, BAP5007 (74), *Idaho; Blues in my Heart; I Don't Stand a ghost of a Chance with you; Red Roses for a Blue Lady; Moonglow; Ma, he's making eyes at me; M-Squad; Sweet Lorraine; Ain't Misbehavin'; Don't worry 'bout me; As Long as I Live; I've got the world on a string.* (1969.)

Also:

Basie's Best (1937-38)—Brunswick LA8589 (53) (d); (A) Brunswick BL-58019.

Lester Leaps In (with Basie)—(A) Epic LG-3107.

Count Basie and his Orchestra (1937-39)—Brunswick LAT8028 (54) (d); (A) Decca DL-8049; (T) 78049.

Count Basie and his Orchestra—MGM MG25015 (54) (d).

The Count—Columbia 33S1054 (55) (d).

The Old Count and the New Count—Philips BBR8036 (55) (d).

Dance Session—Columbia 33CX10007 (55) (d); (A) Clef MGC-626.

Count Basie Swings and Joe William Sings—Columbia 33CX10026 (55) (d); (A) Verve MGV-8063.

Dance Session No.2—Columbia 33CX10044 (55) (d); (A) Clef MGC-647.

Basie Roars Again—(A) Verve 8018 (55) (d).

King of Swing—(A) Verve 8104 (55) (d).

Basie's back in town—Philips BBL7141 (57) (d); (A) Epic LN-3169.

April in Paris—Columbia 33CX10088 (57) (d); HMV Encore ENC153 (63); (A) Verve MGV-8012.

The Count—(A) Verve MGV-8070.

Blues by Basie—Philips BBL7190 (57) (d); (A) Columbia CL-901.

Basie at Newport—Columbia 33CX10110 (58) (d); (A) Verve MGV-8243 & 6024; (F) 711.044.

Basie in London—(A) Verve MGV-8199.

Basie plays Hefti—Columbia 33SX1135 (58) (d); (A) Roulette 52011, (S) S-52011.

One o'clock Jump—Fontana TFL5046 (58) (d); (A) Columbia CL-997.

Swing along with Basie—Columbia 33SX1151 (59) (d); (A) Roulette R-52018.

Sing a Song of Basie—(A) ABC 223 (58).

The Count—Camden CDN-120 (59) (d); (A) Camden CAL-395.

Basie Swings, Tony Bennett Sings—Columbia 33SX1174, (S) SCX3278 (59) (d).

Memories Ad-lib—Columbia 33SX1175, (S) SCX3280 (59) (d); (A) Roulette 52021, (S) S-52021.

One More Time—Music of Quincy Jones—Columbia 33SX1183, (S) SCX3284 (60) (d); (A) Roulette 52024, (S) S-52024.

The Best of Basie—(A) Roulette 52081, (S) S-52081.

The Best of Basie, Vol.2—(A) Roulette 52089, (S) S-52089.

Breakfast Dance and Barbecue—Columbia 33SX1209, (S) SCX3294; (A) Roulette 52028, (S) S-52028.

Count Basie Classics (1940-46)—Fontana TFL5077 (60) (d); (A) Columbia CL-754.

Basie Rides Again—(A) Verve 8108.

Basie's Basement (1947-49)—Camden CDN-145 (60) (d); (A) Camden CAL-497.

Dance along with Basie—Columbia 33SX1264, (S) SCX3333 (60) (d).

Not Now, I'll Tell You When—Columbia 33SX1293, (S) SCX3356 (61) (d); (A) Roulette 52044, (S) S-52044.

Band of Distinction—HMV CLP1428 (61) (d); (A) Verve 8103.

Count Basie—Billy Eckstine—Columbia 33SX1202, (S) SCX3290 (61) (d); (A) Roulette 42017.

The Count Basie Story, Vol. 1 & 2 (1960)—Columbia 33SX1316/7, (S) SCX3372/3 (61) (d); (A) Roulette RB-1 (2), (S) SRB-1(2).

String along with Basie—Columbia 33SX1332, (S) SCX3383 (61) (d); (A) Roulette 52021, (S) S-52051.

Kansas City Suite (Benny Carter)—Columbia 33SX1347, (S) SCX3393 (61) (d); (A) Roulette 52056, (S) S-52056; Roulette 124 (2); Vogue VJD-569.
Basie at Birdland—Columbia 33SX1404, (S) SCX3433 (62) (d); (A) Roulette 52065, (S) S-52065; Vogue VJD568.
The Best of Count Basie—(A) Decca DX-170, (S) DXS-170 (2).
Echoes of an Era: Basie Years—(A) Roulette 102 (2).
Basie's Best (1943-45)—(A) Harmony HS-11247 (60).
The Legend—Columbia 33SX1496, (S) SCX3471 (63); (d); (A) Roulette 52086, (S) S-52086.
Echoes of an Era: Basie Vocal Years—(A) Roulette 107 (2).
On My Way and Shoutin' Again—Verve VLP9031, (S) SVLP9031 (63) (d); (A) Verve 8511, (S) 68511.
Lil' Ol' Groovemaker—Verve VLP9051, (S) SVLP9031 (63) (d); (A) Verve 8549, (S) 68549.
Count Basie in Kansas City—(A) RCA LPV-514 (65).
Basie at Newport with Joe Williams—(A) Verve 8560, (S) S-8560 (63).
Back to Basie and Blues—(A) Roulette 52093, (S) S-52093.
Basie—(A) Roulette 52003, (S) S-52003.
Basie/Eckstine Inc—(A) Roulette 52029, (S) S-52029.
Basie Land—(A) Verve 8597, (S) 68597 (64).
Count Basie—(A) Metro 516, (S) S-516 (65).
Easin' It—(A) Roulette 52106, (S) S-52106; Roulette 124 (2).
The Essential Count Basie—(A) Verve 8407, (S) 68407.
Fantail—(A) Roulette 42009.
Count Basie's Greatest—(A) Verve 2016, (S) 62016.
Hits of the 50s & 60s—(A) Reprise 6070, (S) 9-6070.
More Hits—(A) Verve 8563, (S) 68563 (63).
Count Basie in Sweden—(A) Roulette 52099, (S) S-52099.
Just the Blues (with Joe Williams)—(A) Roulette 52054, (S) S-52054
Basie Picks the Winners—(A) Verve 8616, (S) 68616 (65).
Pop Goes Basie—(A) Reprise 6153, (S) S-6153 (65).
The Swinging Count—(A) Verve 8090.
Verve's Choice Best—(A) 8596, (S) 68596 (64).
The World of Count Basie—(A) Roulette 52111/3 (3), (S) S-52111/3.
Blues I Love To Sing (with J. Rushing)—Decca 'Ace of Hearts' AH119 (66) (d); (F) MCA 510 062.
Basie captures the Happiest Millionaire—Decca SH8347 (67) (d); (A) Coliseum 51003 (68).
Basie meets Bond—Sunset SLS50183 (70) (d); (A) Solid 18032 (68).
Afrique (1970)—Philips 6369 408 (72) (d); (A) Fly 10138.
Bing 'n' Basie—Pye 'Daybreak' DAL2001 (73).
On the Sunny Side of the Street—Polydor 2317 048 (73).
Basie's in the Bag—MCA MUPS300 (73) (d).
Jazz at the Santa Monica Civic '72—Pablo 2625 701 (3) (74).
Super Chief—CBS 67205 (74).
Early Count—(SW) Jazz Panorama LP-23.
Rock-a-bye Basie—Pye Vogue VJD503 (74).
Basie meets Ellington—Embassy EMB31055 (74).
Have a Nice Day (1971)—Polydor 2932 002, Daybreak DAL2008 (74) (d); (A) Daybreak 2005 (71).
High Voltage (1970)—BASF BMPS19/20744; BAP5006 (74) (d).
The Count swings out (1937-38)—(F) MCA 510 061 (74).
At the Savoy Ballroom, 1937 (broadcasts)—Sagapan PAN6903 (74).
Count Basie (1944-46) (broadcasts)—Sagapan PAN6932 (75).
The Live Big Band Sound of Count Basie—Verve 2317 084 (75).
The Count at the Chatterbox 1937—(A) Jazz Archives JA-16 (75).
V-Discs (1944-45)—(A) Jazz Society AA-505 (75).
William and the Famous Door (broadcasts 1937-38)—DJM DJML053 (75).
Basie's Best—Pye 'Ember' CJS849 (75).
Basie Double—Vogue VJD509 (2) (75).
Basie's Beat (1963)—Verve 2352 098 (75); (A) Verve V-8687.
Stompin' at the Savoy (1937 broadcasts)—(D) Collector's Classics CC-8.
Basie on the Air (1937-38) (broadcasts)—(D) Collector's Classics CC-9.
Basie Live—DJM DJB26068 (76).

Count Basie (1939-41)—Queen Disc 015 (76).
Featuring Lester Young (1943-45) (broadcasts)—Swing Treasury 101 (76).
Swing Music from the Southland Café, Boston (1940)—(D) Collector's Classics CC-11.
Basie Big Band (1975)—Pablo 2310 756 (76).
Blues by Basie (1942)—(Sw) Tax M-8025 (76).
Count Basie and Joe Williams (1955)—Verve 2317 111 (76).
Hall of Fame—Black Lion BLPS20155 (76).
The Board of Directors (W. Mills Bros)—Music for Pleasure MFP50255 (76); Anchor ABCL5070 (A) Dot 25838 (68).
The Jitters (1939-41)—(Sw) Tax M-8027 (77).
Count Basie Orchestra—(F) Jazz Anthology JA5147 (77).
Basie Straight Ahead—(A) Dot DL-25902 (69) (77).
Count Basie on Broadway—Music for Pleasure MFP50319 (77); (A) Command 40004, (S) S-905 (67).
I Told You So—Pablo 2310 767 (77); (A) ditto.
Prime Time—Pablo 2310 797 (77); (A) ditto.
The Lester Young Story, Vol.1—CBS 88223 (2) (77); (A) Columbia.
The Lester Young Story, Vol.3—CBS 88266 (2) (78); (A).
Count Basie's Big Band (1976)—Pablo 2308 207 (77).
Sixteen Men Swinging—Verve 2632 068 (2) (78).
Jumpin' at the Woodside—Pye 'Golden Hour' GH873 (78).
Joe Williams and Count Basie—Vogue VJD553 (2) (78).
Basie plays Quincy Jones and Neal Hefti—Vogue VJD5581 (2) (78).
On the Road—Pablo 2312 112 (80).
The Best of Count Basie—Pablo 2310 852 (80).
Café Society Uptown 1941, Vol.1—(F) Jazz United JU4.
Café Society Uptown 1941, Vol.2—(F) Jazz United JU5.
Count Basie, Vol.1 (1947)—(F) RCA 731.111.
Count Basie, Vol.2—(F) RCA 730.608.
Count Basie, Vol.3—(F) RCA 741.042.
The Count and Lester Young—(F) Verve 711.044.
Count Basie in Kansas City—(A) RCA LPV-514 (65).
Basie's in the Bag—(A) Brunswick 754127.
Retrospective Sessions (1962 & 1969)—(A) Impulse IA-9351 (2).
Ain't It the Truth—Black Lion BLM51009 (81).
I Got Rhythm—Affinity AFF48 (81).

Louis Bellson

(b Rock Falls, Illinois, July 26 1924)
Outstanding jazz drummer. Played in early days first with Ted Fio Rito then Benny Goodman, either side of the World War II. With Tommy Dorsey (qv) 1947-49. Twice highly effective drummer with Duke Ellington (1951-53, 1965); his compositions *Skin Deep* and *The Hawk Talks* became Ellington features. Formed several big bands and had biggest success with the band featuring his wife, singer Pearl Bailey, and then on Johnny Carson television show in early 1970s. Still active as drummer and leader of forceful, driving big bands.

Selected LP recordings

Louis Bellson—Columbia 33C9017 (55) (d); (A) Verve 8137.
Louis Bellson—Columbia 33CX10083 (57) (d); (A) Verve 8186.
Drumorama—Columbia 33C9040 (58) (d); (A) Verve 8193.
Louis Bellson at the Flamingo—Columbia 33CX10142 (59) (d); (A) Verve 8256.
Flying Hickory—Columbia 33CX10141 (59) (d).
The Brilliant Bellson Sound—HMV CLP1343 (60) (d); (A) Norg MGV-2123.
The Dynamic Drums of Louis Bellson (1968)—Columbia 'Studio Two' (S) TW0322 (70).
Conversations/Drum Spectacular—Parlophone PCS7151 (72) (d).
The Mighty Two (with Jean Krupa)—Roulette LDM30124 (74).
Big Bands (1964) (with Mills Blue Rhythm)—Polydor (S) 2344 048 (75) (d).
Louis Bellson—(F) Barclay 920 061 (75).
The Louis Bellson Explosion (1975)—Polydor Pablo 2310 755 (76).
King of the Drums—CBS 52736 (76).
Thunderbird—(A) Impulse AS9107 (77).

With Bellson Big Band Jazz from the Summit—Vogue VJD564 (2) (79).
Jam—Polydor Pablo 2310 838 (79).

Bunny Berigan

(b Hilbert, Wisconsin, November 2 1908; d New York, June 2 1942)
One of the leading white jazz trumpet players, notable for his range of tone and dynamics and driving yet polished style with big bands. Famous solos during short stays (1935) with Benny Goodman (qv) and 1940 Tommy Dorsey (qv). Spent much time as session and studio musician. First major job with Hal Kemp (qv) and did stint with the Dorsey Brothers. Formed his first big band in 1937 [Sonny Lee, Ray Coniff (tb), Joe Dixon (cl), Georgie Auld (ts), Joe Bushkin (p), Hank Wayland (b), George Wettling, Buddy Rich (d)]. Forced to disband after financial failure in 1940, but managed to reform in 1941. Excessive drinking undermined his health and he collapsed and died in New York after returning to work too soon after attack of pneumonia. Berigan's bands were never as polished and sophisticated as those of Goodman or Dorsey; but played good sturdy music in a mixture of Dixieland and swing styles popular at the time. Underrated as both player and leader for many years, but quality of musicianship realised in recent years. His theme number, *I Can't Get Started,* demonstrates the range of his instrumental skill and the sensitivity of his phrasing.

Selected LP recordings

Bunny Berigan, Vol.1 (1934-38)—(F) RCA FXM1 7172 (76). *Blue Moon* (1934); *Plantation Moods* (1934); *Down t'Uncle Bill's* (1934); *Troubled* (1934); *Swanee River* (1937); *All God's chillun got Rhythm* (1937); *Mahogany Hall Stomp* (1937); *I Can't Get Started* (1937); *The Prisoner's Song* (1937); *Caravan* (1937); *Study in Brown* (1937); *Mama, I wanna make Rhythm* (1937); *Black Bottom* (1937); *Trees* (1937); *Can't help lovin' that man* (1937); *Never felt better, never had less* (1938).
Bunny Berigan: his Trumpet and Orchestra—RCA LSA-3018; (A) RCA LPV-581. *Mahogany Hall, Stomp* (1937); *I Can't Get Started* (1937); *The Prisoner's Song* (1937); *Can't help lovin' that man* (1937); *Livery Stable Blues* (1938); *Jelly Roll Blues* (1938); *In a Mist* (1938); *Flashes* (1938); *Davenport Blues* (1938); *Candlelight* (1938); *In the Dark* (1938); *Walkin' the Dog* (1938); *Peg o' my heart* (1939).
Great Dance Bands of the Thirties—(A) RCA LPM-2078 (60). *'Cause my baby says it's so* (1937); *Swanee River* (1937); *Frankie and Johnny* (1937); *Trees* (1937); *I Can't Get Started* (1937); *The Prisoner's Song* (1937); *Caravan* (1937); *Black Bottom* (1937); *Never felt better, never had less* (1938); *The Wearin' o' the Green* (1938); *Jelly Roll Blues* (1938).
Through the Years 1936-42—(A) Jazz Archive JA-19 (74). *I Can't Get Started* (1936); *Notre Dame Victory March* (1936); *The Jazzeroo* (1936); *Body and Soul* (1936); *Ride, Red, Ride* (1936); *Mr. Ghost goes to Town* (1936); *Sweet Varsity Sue* (1938); *Study in Brown* (1938); *Downstream* (1938); *Black Bottom* (1938); *Sugarfoot Stomp* (1939); *I'm Confessin'* (1942); *Contact* (with Jimmy Dorsey's Orchestra) (1940); *East of the Sun* (with Tommy Dorsey's Orchestra) (1940); *Ad lib Blues* (Jam session) (1940).
Also:
Berigan Plays Again—HMV DLP1018 (53) (d); (A) RCA LPT-1003.
Bunny Berigan and his Orchestra (1937) (with other orchestras)—Columbia 33SX1491 (55).
Take it, Bunny—Philips BBL7086 (56) (d); Columbia 33SX1491 (63) (d); (A) Epic LG3109 or 16006.
Bunny (1937-39)—Camden CDN159 (61) (d); (A) Camden CAL-550.
Bunny Berigan and his Orchestra (1936-38) (mainly broadcasts)—(A) Collectors Classics CC-15 (74).
Down by the Old Mill Stream (1936-39) (live recordings)—(A) Jazz Archive JA-11 (74).
Shanghai Shuffle—CBS DJM DJB26078 (76) (d).
Bunny Berigan and his Orchestra (1936-38)—Alamac QSR2414 (76).
Bunny Berigan, Vol.1—(A) Shoestring SS-100 (77).
Bunny Berigan, Vol.2—(A) Shoestring SS-101 (77).

Les Brown

(b Reinerton, Pennsylvania, March 14 1912)
Began career leading dance band at Duje University in 1935. In 1938 formed big band to play at Hotel Edison, New York. Soon established reputation as leader of major dance band of 1930s, 1940s and on to 1970s,

as 'Les Brown and His Band of Renown'. Particular association with Bob Hope from 1947 on. Also featured on Steve Allen's television show on Sunday nights from 1950. Survived the vicissitudes of big band economic slump and continued in business when others succumbed. Versatile musicianship in area between jazz, dance band and session/show band enabled Brown to outlast the bad years and the changing fashions which he embraced without making any of them an issue. Featured good musicians including Billy Butterfield (t), Dave Pell (ts, cl) etc. Among vocalists were Doris Day in 1940s.

Selected LP recordings

The Les Brown Orchestra—Vogue-Coral LVC10002 (55) (d).
Les Brown at the Hollywood Palladium—Vogue-Coral LVA9001/2 (55) (d); (A) Coral CX-1 (2) or CRL-57000/1 (2).
Les Brown Band—Vogue-Coral LVC10017 (55) (d).
Les Brown Band—Vogue-Coral LVC10033 (55) (d).
Sentimental Journey—(A) Columbia CL-649.
Les Brown plays Lerner & Loewe—(A) Columbia CL-1594.
Your Dance Date with Les Brown—(A) Columbia CL-6123.
That Sound of Renown—Vogue-Coral LVA9019 (56) (d); (A) Coral CRL-57030.
Les Brown Band of Renown—Vogue-Coral LVA9026 (57) (d); (A) Coral 57051.
Les Brown Band of Renown—Vogue-Coral LVA9043 (57) (d); (A) Coral 57058.
Les Brown All Stars—(A) Capitol T-659.
Brown's in Town—Capitol T746 (57) (d); (A) T-746.
Dancer's Choice—Capitol T812 (57) (d); (A) T-812.
Composer's Holiday—Capitol T886, (S) ST886 (58) (d); (A) ditto.
Love Letters in the Sand—Vogue-Coral LVA9084 (58) (d); (A) Coral 57165.
Dance to 'South Pacific'—Capitol T1060 (59) (d); (A) T-1060 (58).
The Les Brown Story—Capitol T1174, (S) ST1174 (59) (d); (A) Capitol T-1174.
Swing Song Book—Vogue-Coral LVA9113 (60) (d); (A) Coral CRL-57311.
Greatest Hits—Pye 'Golden Hour' GH812 (70) (d).
One Night Stand (1945)—(A) Joyce JLP1008 (74) (d).
The Greatest—(A) Halcyon HL-7100 (58).
You're My Everything—(A) Coral CRL-56046.
A Mellow Bit of Rhythm (1937-40)—(A) Big Band Archives LP-2201 (2) (74).
Les Brown and Orchestra (1944-46) (broadcasts)—London HMP5039 (78).
Les Brown and Orchestra, 1949, Vol.1—London HMP5054 (79).
Les Brown and Orchestra, 1949, Vol.2—London HMP5059 (79).
Les Brown's in Town—(A) Decca DL-4607.
The 1943 Band—Fanfare 30-130.

Willie Bryant

(b New Orleans, August 30 1908; d Los Angeles, February 9 1964)
Grew up in Chicago and was reported to have invented the dance known as the 'Shim Sham' in 1928 at the Alhambra Theatre, New York. Later led a band after the departure of Lucky Millinder (qv) to lead the Mills' Blue Rhythm Band (qv). Worked in vaudeville and with Bessie Smith, then led a big band from 1934 [Ben Webster (ts), Teddy Wilson (p), Cozy Cole (d); later Taft Jordan (t), Benny Carter (t, as, cl)] until 1938. Thereafter worked as solo act in general entertainment and MC for Apollo Theatre. After World War II led another good band; then concentrated on successful career as disc jockey and MC in California.

Selected LP recordings

Willie Bryant and his Orchestra—(F) RCA FXM1 7084 (75).
Throwin' Stones at the Sun (1935); *It's over because we're through* (1935); *A Viper's Moan* (1935); *Chimes at the Meeting* (1935); *Rigmarole* (1935); *'Long about Midnight* (1935); *The Sheik* (1935); *Jerry the Junker* (1935); *The voice of Old Man River* (1935); *Steak and Potatoes* (1935); *Long gone* (1935); *Liza* (1935); *Mary had a Little Lamb* (1936); *I like Bananas* (1936); *Cross Patch* (1936); *I'm grateful to you* (1936).
Also:
Willie Bryant and his Orchestra—(F) RCA 430.584.
Willy Bryant and his Orchestra (1936) (coupled with Teddy Hill (1937))—(G) RCA LPM-10116.

California Ramblers

Also known as the Golden Gate Orchestra

(with other pseudonyms for recording) the original group was founded in 1921 by impresario and manager Ed W. Kirkeby, as a fairly straight dance band. But the presence of a number of jazz stars, principally Jimmy and Tommy Dorsey, Red Nichols and later Chelsea Quealey (t), and Adrian Rollini (xly, bs-s) soon caught the attention of other musicians. Played first at the Post Lodge, New York, then settled in 1925 at the California Ramblers Inn which became a meeting place for jazzmen and their fans. After several members had left for London to join Fred Elizalde, and Kirkeby had reorganized the band, it disbanded in 1929 but was briefly re-formed by Adrian Rollini to work a brief stint at Hunter Island Inn. Recorded regularly for various labels between 1923 and 1929. Name used for recording 1935/36 by a spin-off group from Adrian Rollini's band, sometimes under title Little Ramblers, a name also used in the previous decade when a smaller group was in action. All the music is firmly rooted in the white New York style.

Selected LP recordings

Flapper Party—VJM Halcyon HAL8 (73). *Ev'rything is Hotsy Totsy now* (1925); *Sweet Georgia Brown* (1925); *I'm gonna Charleston back to Charleston* (1925); *Show me the way to go home* (1925); *No Foolin'* (1926); *The Girl Friend* (1926); *Ya Gotta Know How To Love* (1926); *Stockholm Stomp* (1926); *We love the College Girls* (1927); *Yes she do—no she don't* (1927); *Vo-do-do-de-o Blues* (1927); *Nothin' does does like it used to do-do do* (1927); *Make my cot where the cot-cot-cotton grows* (1927); *Mine—all mine* (1927); *Singapore Sorrows* (1928); *The Pay-off* (1928).

Also:

The Roaring Twenties—London 'Origins of Jazz' AL3516 (54) (d); (A) Riverside.

Tommy and Jimmy Dorsey with the California Ramblers—London 'Origins of Jazz' AL3545 (55) (d); (A) Riverside.

New York Jazz of the Roaring Twenties—London 'Origins of Jazz' AL3562 (57) (d); (A) Riverside.

Jazz of the Roaring Twenties—(A) Riverside RLP12-801 (61).

Miss Annabelle Lee (1925-27)—(A) Biograph BLP-12020.

Hallelujah! Here comes the California Ramblers (1925-29)—(A) Biograph BLP-12021.

California Ramblers, Vol.1 (1925-27)—(A) The Old Masters TOM-20.

Cab Calloway

(b Rochester, New York, December 25 1907) Most famous as 'King of the Hi-De-Ho' with strongly featured 'scat' singing and showmanship; but leader of excellent band with many top jazz soloists [Doc Cheatham, Dizzy Gillespie, Jonah Jones (t), Tyree Glenn, Quentin Jackson, Claude Jones (tb), Illinois Jacquet, Chu Berry, Ben Webster (ts), Hilton Jefferson (as), Milt Hinton (b), Cozy Cole (d)] at various times. Began career touring with roadshows in vaudeville with sister Blanche. Led various groups until he took over The Missourians and went under his own name to the Cotton Club in 1931. Appeared with band in many films, including *Big Broadcast of 1932, The Singing Kid* (1936), *Stormy Weather* (1943) and *St Louis Blues* (1958). Part of Sportin' Life in Gershwin's *Porgy and Bess* was written for him. He did not appear in original production but took it up in 1952 and toured widely; soon became especially associated with the role. The all black version of *Hello Dolly* in the 1960s featured Calloway. Author or co-author of many hit songs, including (most famous) *Minnie the Moocher, The Scat Song, The Jumpin' Jive, Peck-a-Doodle-Doo, Hi-de-ho Man, Rhapsody in Rhumba, Geechy Joe.*

Selected LP recordings

The Beginning—(A) Bandstand BS-7124 (75). *Gotta Darn Good Reason* (1930); *Is that Religion?* (1930); *Minnie the Moocher* (1931); *Doin' the Rumba* (1931); *Old Yazoo* (1932); *Beale Street Mama* (1932); *Hot Water* (1932); *Harlem Hospitality* (1933); *Harlem Camp Meeting* (1933); *Zah Zuh Zah* (1933); *'Long about Midnight* (1934); *Moon Glow* (1934); *Jitterbug* (1934); *Hotcha Razz-ma-tazz* (1934).

Cab Calloway and his Orchestra 1932—(D) Collector's Classics CC-20 (75). *Strange as it seems; This time it's love; Hot Toddy; I've got the World on a String; Harlem Holiday; Dixie Doorway; Wah-dee-dah; Sweet Rhythm; Beale Street Mama; That's what I Hate about Love; The Man from Harlem; I gotta Right to Sing the Blues; My Sunday Gal; Eadie was a Lady; Gotta Go Places and Do Things; Hot Water* (1932.)

A Night at the Savoy—(Sw) Tax M-8006

(74). *Nagasaki* (1935); *F.D.R. Jones* (1938); *Ebony Silhouette* (1941); *Special Delivery* (1941.) (With tracks by Redman, Henderson & Wilson.)

Penguin Swing (Chu Berry featured with Cab Calloway)—(A) Jazz Archives JA-8 (74). *Bugle Blues* (1937); *Rustle of Swing* (1938); *Three Swings and Out* (1938); *Penguin Swing* (1938); *Trylon Swing* (1939); *Calling all bars* (1940); *The Lone Arranger* (1940); *Who's Yehoodi* (1940); *Bye Bye Blues* (1940); *Sunset* (1940); *Cupid's Nightmare* (1940); *Hot Air* (1940); *Hep Cat Love Song* (1941); *Jonah joins the Cab* (1941); *Geechee Joe* (1941); *Special Delivery* (1941). [Chu Berry joined the band in 1937, Dizzy Gillespie in 1940, Jonah Jones in 1941.]

Cab, Ella and Chick—(A) Bandstand BS-7125 (75). *That man is here again* (1937); *Swing, Swing, Swing* (1937); *She's tall, she's tan, she's terrific* (1937); *Azure* (1938); *Shout Shout, Shout* (1938); *The Ghost of Smoky Joe* (1939); *Floogie Walk* (1939). (With tracks by Chick Webb.)

Also:

Collector's Items 1922-30—Historical Jazz HLP-11.

Cab Calloway's Orchestra (1930-32) (with Noble Sissle)—(G) Swingfan.

Blues—(A) Vocali on 73820.

The King of Hi-De-Ho—Decca 'Ace of Hearts' AH106 (66) (d); (A) Brunswick BL-58010.

The Man from Harlem (1930-32)—(Sw) Jazz Panorama JPLP-22.

Cab Calloway 1940 (also Erskine Hawkins) —(Sw) Jazz Panorama LP-16.

Cotton Club Orchestra 1933-4—(F) RCA FXM1 7125 (75); (G) RCA LPM10120.

Sixteen Classics—(F) CBS 62950; (A) Epic LN-3265.

Swinging Forties, 1939-45—(A) CAR439 (74).

Cab Calloway (3 Vols)—(A) Jazum 20, 29 & 45 (with Basie).

Awful Natural '49 (with Lucky Millinder) —(F) RCA PM42030 (77).

Calloway '68—(A) PIP 6801 (68).

Benny Carter

(b New York, August 8 1907)

One of the three top alto-sax players in jazz, Carter is also masterful on clarinet and trumpet, as well as being an outstanding arranger. Worked early with June Clark and Earl Hines (qv), later with Fletcher and Horace Henderson (qv) and Chick Webb. Took over leadership of McKinney's Cotton Pickers in 1931 before forming his own band in 1932. Did much arranging for all top bands, notably Duke Ellington, Fletcher Henderson, McKinney's Cotton Pickers, Teddy Hill and Benny Goodman. Came to Europe in 1935, in between 1936 and 1938 was staff arranger for Henry Hall and the BBC Dance Orchestra. After returning to US Carter formed new bands but never on a permanent basis. Did his best work free-lancing and arranging in television, radio and shows as well as jazz fields. Versatile musician in every sense, Carter continues to blow elegant alto and front groups at jazz festivals. Generally regarded as one of the outstanding jazz musicians of all time, he ranked as altoist with Johny Hodges and Charlie Parker, and as arranger with any of the best.

Selected LP recordings

Ridin' in Rhythm—World Records SHB42 (2) (79). *Swing it; Synthetic Love; Six Bells Stampede; Love, you're not the one for me; Devil's Holiday; Lonesome Nights; Symphony in Riffs; Blue Lou.* (1933). (Coupled with tracks by Fletcher Henderson, Coleman Hawkins, Duke Ellington, etc.)

Benny Carter and his Orchestra—(F) RCA 741.073. *All of me; The Very Thought of You; Cocktails for Two; Taking my time* (all 1940); *Cuddle up, huddle up; Babalu; There I've said it again; Midnight; My Favourite Blues; What a Difference a Day Made; Sunday; Back Bay Boogie.* (All 1941.)

The Chocolate Dandies 1928-33—Parlophone PMC7038. *Cherry* (1928); *Paducah* (1928); *Stardust* (1928); *Birmingham Breakdown* (1928); *Four or five times* (1928); *That's how I feel today* (1929); *Six or seven times* (1929); *Goodbye Blues* (1930); *Cloudy Skies* (1930); *Got another sweetie now* (1930); *Bugle Call Rag* (1930); *Dee Blues* (1930); *Blue Interlude* (1933); *I never knew* (1933); *Once upon a time* (1933); *Krazy Kapers* (1933). (1928 tracks directed by Don Redman.)

Swingin' at Maida Vale—Decca LK4221 (58); ACL1167 (64) (d). *Swingin' at Maida Vale; Nightfall; I've got two lips; There'll be some changes made; If only I could read your mind; Gin and Jive; Accent on Swing; Just a Mood; Royal Garden Blues; When Lights are Low; Waltzin' the Blues; When Day is*

Done. (London, 1936.)

Benny Carter/Metronome All Stars—Queen-Disc Q009 (75). *Who's sorry now; Co-ed; Prelude to a Kiss; Back Bay Boogie; I got it bad; Patience and Fortitude; I surrender, dear; Stompin' at the Savoy* (1945): *King Porter Stomp* (1940); *All-Star Strut* (1940); *Royal Flush* (1941); *Dear old Southland* (1941); *I got Rhythm* (1942); *Sweet Lorraine* (1946); *Nat meets June* (1946).

Benny Carter, Vol.1 (1939-44)—(F) RCA HOL6426 (78). *Lady be Good* (1939); *Liebestraum* (1939); *My Heart has Wings* (1939); *Big wig in the wig wam* (1939); *Melancholy Lullaby* (1939); *Honeysuckle Rose* (1940); *Stardust* (1940); *I used to love you* (1943); *Rose Room* (1943); *Sweet Georgia Brown* (1943); *Swanee River* (1944); *All of me* (1944); *Fish Fry* (1944); *Jubilee Jump* (1944); *Sleep* (1944); *Ill Wind* (1944).

Also:

The Benny Carter Orchestra—Columbia 33C9002 (55) (d).

Aspects—London LTZ-15169 (59) (d); (A) United Artists LP-4017.

Swingin' the Twenties—Vogue LAC12225 (59) (d); (A) Contemporary M-3561, (S) S-7561 (63).

Further Definitions—HMV CLP1624, (S) CSD1480 (63); World Records ST864; (A) Impulse AS12 & IMPL8037.

Dynamic Hit Sounds (1946)—Ember CJS802 (63).

Additions to Further Definitions—Impulse AS9116; (A) ditto.

Big Band Bounce—(G) Bovema 5C 052 80850; SM11057.

Melancholy Benny 1939-40—(Sw) Tax M-8004 (74).

Benny Carter in Hollywood 1943-46—(A) Jazz Society AA-502 (74).

Chocolate Dandies 1926-30—(A) Historical Jazz HLP-16.

The Fabulous Benny Carter—(A) Audio Lab 1505.

Casa Loma Orchestra

Originally from Detroit where it worked as the Orange Blossom Band. In 1928 band leader and impresario, Jean Goldkette, arranged a booking at the Casa Loma Hotel in Toronto. The engagement did not last; the hotel went bankrupt, but the band stayed together and went on tour under name Casa Loma Orchestra. In 1929 it became a self-governing, independent body registered as Casa Loma Orchestra, Inc, with saxophonist Glen Gray (Knoblaugh) as president and tenor player Pat Davis as secretary and treasurer. The personnel remained stable, with only a minimum of inevitable changes; there were few big names but one or two like Bobby Jones (t) and Pee Wee Hunt (tb) were in among the sections which gradually achieved a strong identity and outstanding polish and musical discipline. The band's style and presence was largely the work of the outstanding arranger Gene Gifford, who also played banjo and guitar. Often criticised for stiff and mechanical playing, in fact the Casa Loma played an early 'swing' style long before 'swing' was invented and Goodman and Dorsey had hit the headlines. Ironically, the Casa Loma was criticised for precisely those faults of formalism and stylisation that were to be levelled at the entire swing movement a decade later. Began prolific recording career, sometimes under pseudonyms, in 1930, while playing regularly at the Glen Island Casino, New York and Essex House. The Casa Loma strongly influenced British band leader Lew Stone who featured Gifford's 'hot' numbers *Blue Jazz* and *White Jazz* as well as adopting the general style. Other arrangers to work for the Casa Loma included Bill Challis, Bill Raunch and Sonny Durham who also played trumpet and trombone in the brass section.

Selected LP recordings

Curtain Call Series, Vol.3 (with Lombardo, Morgan & J. Dorsey)—Brunswick LA8695 (53) (d).

Five Feet of Swing (with Crosby, Dorsey Brothers, J. Dorsey & Webb)—Brunswick LAT8037 (54) (d); (A) Decca DL8045.

Smoke Rings—(A) Decca DL-8750 & 10" DL-5089.

Casa Loma in Hi-Fi—Capitol LCT6128 (57) (d); (A) Capitol W-747.

Sounds of the great Casa Loma Bands—Capitol LCT6178 (59) (d); EMI SM1588 (75); (A) Capitol T-1022.

The Greatest—(G) Electrola 1C 052 80231.

On the Air 1934—(A) Extreme Rarities ER-1005 (74).

Glen Gray and the Casa Loma (1934-38) —(G) Swingfan 1024.

Casa Loma Orchestra (1934-38)—(G) Brunswick 87.534.

The Swing Tonic (Glen Gray and his Orchestra) (1938-46)—(A) Swing Era LP-1018.

Glen Gray and the original Casa Loma Orchestra (1930-36)—(A) Bandstand BS-7126.
Glen Gray: Casa Loma Orchestra (2 Vols)—(A) Jazum 32 & 33.
Casa Loma Orchestra (1944)—(A) Joyce LP-1017 (75).
Glen Gray and his Casa Loma Orchestra (broadcasts)—London HMG-5028 (78).
Glen Gray and his Casa Loma Orchestra 1939-40 (broadcasts)—London HMP-5043 (79).
Glen Gray and his Casa Loma Orchestra 1943-46 (broadcasts)—London HMP-5050 (79).
Great recordings—(A) Harmony HL-7045.
Great Jazz of 1930 (5 tracks)—(A) The Old Masters TOM-4.
Hoagy Carmichael Songs—(A) Coral CRL-56006.
Sounds of the Great Casa Loma Bands, Vol.2—(A) Capitol T-1067.
Solo Spotlight—(A) Capitol T-1234.
Please, Mr. Gray—(A) Capitol T-1506.
Sounds of the great Casa Loma Band—(A) Capitol T-1588.
Greatest Hits—(A) Decca DL-75016.

Charleston Chasers

Name given to house band and recording units of American Columbia during latter half of the 1920s. Two separate groups, one led by Red Nichols, one by Benny Goodman, included collectively most of the top white jazz musicians of the period. [Phil Napoleon, Charlie Teagarden (t); Jack Teagarden (tb, vo), Miff Mole, Tommy Dorsey (tb), Jimmy Dorsey (as, cl), Fud Livingston (ts, cl), Larry Binyon, Babe Russin (ts), Arthur Schutt, Frank Signorelli (p), Joe Tarto, Harry Goodman (b), Dave Tough, Stan King, Gene Krupa (d)]. Clarence Williams's wife, Eva Taylor, an outstanding jazz singer, took a number of vocals. Recorded regularly from around 1927, but most famous session was the last, on February 9 1931, which produced the classic Goodman/Teagarden *Basin Street Blues* and *Beale Street Blues.*

Selected LP recordings

Classic Jazz Treasures, Vol.3—Philips BBL7433 (60) (d). *Mississippi Mud; My gal Sal; Farewell Blues; Wabash Blues; Davenport Blues; After you've gone; Sugar Foot Strut; Imagination; Delerium; Five Pennies; Someday, Sweetheart; Feelin' no pain.* (1925-8).
Also:
The Charleston Chasers (1925-28)—VJM VLP26 (74) (d).
The Charleston Chasers (1929-31)—VJM VLP44.
See also under Benny Goodman, Phil Napoleon and Red Nichols.

Kenny Clarke

(b Pittsburgh, January 9 1914)
Important figure in the be-bop phase of the 1940s, helping to establish the new style of drumming that moved away from the regular beat of the swing era. Began career in the 1930s with the Leroy Bradley Band. Joined Roy Eldridge in 1935 then played in St Louis with Jeter Pillars, with Edgar Hayes in 1937-38, Claude Hopkins in 1938 and with Teddy Hill in 1939-40, the band with which he first played at the famous Minton's Club in the 1940s. It was here that he joined such players as Charlie Christian, Charlie Parker, Dizzy Gillespie and Thelonious Monk in formulating the modern jazz style that changed the face of jazz in the 1940s. Before the war he also played with Benny Carter and Red Allen in the older style and led his own band in New York. After war service he played with various bop groups, notably with Dizzy Gillespie 1946-48, and visited Europe. Became a founder member of the Modern Jazz Quartet 1952-55. Settled in France in 1956, working with various jazz groups and playing at the Blue Note 1961-67. From the late 1960s onwards he has been the co-leader of one of the most important European bands with Belgian pianist Francy Boland.

Selected LP recordings

All Smiles—Polydor 583727 (70) (d). *Let's Face the Music and dance; I'm all smiles; You stepped out of a dream; I'm glad there is you; Get out of town; By Strauss; When your lover has gone; Gloria; Sweet and Lovely; High School Cadets.* (1968.)

Latin Kaleidoscope—BASF BMP29685-7; BAP5015; (74) (d); (A) Prestige S-7760 (69). *Latin Kaleidoscope*—suite; *Cuban Fever*—suite (1968).

At Her Majesty's Pleasure—Polydor 'Black Lion' 2460 131 (75). *Pentonville; Wormwood Scrubs; Doing Time; Broadmoor; Holloway; Reprieve; Going Straight.* (1969.)

Off Limits—Polydor 2310 147 (71) (d). *Wintersong; Astrorama; Osaka Calling; Our kind of Sabi; Sakara; Exorcisme; Endosmose.* (1970.)

More Smiles—BASF BMPS-15-29746; BAP5014 (74) (d). *Johnny One-Note; Lullaby of the Leaves; Bei dir war es immer so schön; My Favourite Things; Just in Time; All Through the Night; November Girl; My heart belongs to Daddy; Love for Sale.* (1971.)

Also:

Jazz is Universal—London HA-K8085 (63); (A) Atlantic 1401.

Now Hear our Meaning (1965)—CBS BPG62567, (S) SPBG6257 (66) (d); (A) Columbia CL-2314; (S) CS-2314.

The Best of the Clarke-Boland Big Band—BASF (S) BAB9003 (74).

Change of Scenes—Polydor (S) 2304 034 (75).

Second—Polydor 'Black Lion' (S) BLP30109 (76).

Fire, Heat, Soul and Guts—(A) Prestige 7634.

Kenny Clarke—Francy Boland Big Band—(A) Atlantic 1404, (S) S-1404 (63).

The Big Band—(A) Prestige S-7699.

Volcano—(A) Polydor 244501.

Larry Clinton

(b Brooklyn, New York, August 17 1909)

He made his name as an arranger and composer who was adept at recasting classical melodies for jazz and popular usage. Worked initially as assistant of Ferde Grofe in early 1930s, then arranged for Isham Jones, the Dorseys, Bunny Berigan and others, providing original compositions as well as arrangements. He formed his own big band in 1937 and achieved considerable success, especially through recordings for Victor. The band featured good musicians and some jazz luminaries [Toots Mandello (as) and Babe Russin (ts)] and was notable for excellent team work. It had several hits, including *Dipsy Doodle* and later *Deep Purple.* Continued band leading until military service in World War II; afterwards resumed but without much success and subsequently went into record and music publishing business.

Selected LP recordings

Larry Clinton in Hi-Fi—RCA RC-24003 (57) (d); (A) RCA LPM-1342.

Larry Clinton and his Orchestra (1937-41)—(A) Swing Era LP-1006.

Larry Clinton and his Orchestra (1939-41)—(A) Bandstand BS-7102.

Larry Clinton and his Orchestra, Vol.2 (1937-38)—(A) Bandstand BS-7109.

Larry Clinton and his Orchestra (1937-38) (broadcasts)—London HMP5045 (78).

This is Larry Clinton—(A) RCA VPM-6085 (2).

Dance Date with Larry Clinton—(A) Camden CAL-434.

Music for Tired Golfers—(A) MGM E-3567.

Larry Clinton Plays for Dancing—(A) Tops L-920.

Calypso Medodies for Dancing—(A) MGM E-3541.

Coon-Sanders Orchestra

Group formed immediately after World War I by two American soldiers recently demobbed—Carleton A. Coon (February 5 1894-May 4 1932) and Joe L. Sanders (October 15 1896-May 15 1965) who met in Kansas City (some say Chicago). Band played first as Coon-Sanders Original Nighthawk Orchestra and built rapid reputation for combined musicianship and showmanship. Played in 1924 and 1926 at the Blackhawk Restaurant in Chicago and achieved their own show on NBC radio. Went to Hotel New Yorker in 1931 and to College Inn of Hotel Sherman in Chicago in 1932 where Carleton Coon died suddenly following an abscess on a tooth. Joe Sanders continued to lead the band for a time, but had to re-organize before a new phase could begin at the Blackhawk, and thereafter Sanders continued in the music business for many years.

Selected LP recordings

Coon-Sanders Nighthawks-Radio's Aces—RCA RD-7697 (d); LSA-3068; (A) LPV-511.

Coon-Sanders Orchestra—(A) The Old Masters TOM32/33.

Billy Cotton

(b Westminster, England, 1899; d London, March 25 1969)

Typical British show band, often deceptive in the way of excellent musicianship, both 'sweet' and jazz biased, is frequently undervalued due to a general taste for fooling and putting over the act. Billy Cotton himself was a natural showman of the type found on

Billy Cotton (from a 1951 sheet music cover) (Macmelodies Ltd).

fairgrounds and in circuses as well as theatres—vulgar, brash, ebullient, always good humoured and always in complete command of material. In later years the Billy Cotton Showcase brought huge popularity, especially on television; but in the earlier years band was noted for professional quality of good dance music with capable players and worthy vocalists. Among his personnel in 1930s were Teddy Foster (t, vo), Joe Ferrie (tb) and Sydney Lipton (vln). Vocalist Alan Breeze stayed with Cotton through several decades. Despite the demise of many dance bands, Billy Cotton, who began as an Army drummer, played at London's Astoria Ballroom and Ciro's in the 1920s, and flirted with becoming a racing driver, kept his show on the road and a going concern until his death at the age of 70.

Selected LP recordings

Billy Cotton and his Band—World Records SH141 (77). *New Tiger Rag* (1930); *Why did she fall for the leader of the band?* (1936); *Dancing with my shadow* (1935); *Bessie couldn't help it* (1930); *The Tattooed Lady* (1934); *St. Louis Blues* (1934); *What a difference a day made* (1935); *Avalon* (1933); *Nobody loves a fairy when she's forty* (1934); *Hyde Park Corner* (1933); *Truckin'* (1935); *Shine* (1936); *They all start whistling Mary* (1932); *After you've gone* (1936); *She was only somebody's daughter* (1932); *I'll never say 'never again' again* (1935).

Also:

Soldiers of the Queen—Decca LF1124 (53) (d).

Wakey Wakey—Decca LF1185 (54) (d).

Billy Cotton Band Show—Decca Ace of Clubs ACL1041 (60) (d).

Let's All Join In—Pye Ember SE8011 (65).

The World of Billy Cotton—Decca (S) SPA19 (69).

The World of Billy Cotton, Vol.2—Decca (S) SPA128 (71).

Billy Cotton and his Band—EMI SH141 (71).

Billy Cotton Band Show—Philips SBL-7030 (72).

Bob Crosby

(b Spokane Wash, August 23 1913)

Younger brother of Bing Crosby. Made his first impression with Anson Weeks Orchestra in 1933/34. Joined the Dorsey Brothers' Orchestra in 1934. His first experience of band leading came when he took over the former Ben Pollack (qv) band in association with Gil Rodin. The band [Yank Lawson (t), Matty Matlock (cl), Eddie Miller (ts), Nappy Lamare (g) and Ray Bauduc (d)] contained the nucleus of the later famous Crosby bands. Residency with Ruth Etting show on radio; subsequently developed an individual style rooted in Dixieland, with arrangements by Deane Kincaide, Matlock and featured bass player, Bob Haggart. Later groups included major jazz stars [Billy Butterfield, Muggsy Spanier (t), Irving Fazola (cl), Bob Zurke, Jess Stacy and Joe Sullivan (p), and vocalists Kay Weber, Teddy Grace and Doris Day to supplement Crosby himself]. Usual (for the period) 'band within a band', The Bob Cats emphasized Dixieland style. Successful residency at the Black Hawk restaurant, 1938/39, and then standing in for Benny Goodman on the Camel Caravan led to repeat engagement. The Crosby band lasted, with intermissions, until 1942 with, latterly, arrangements by Jimmy Mundy and Paul Weston. Later Crosby became featured in films and band leading either side of World War II, including radio work with Jack Benny and others, and later still on television. Always maintained a Dixieland/jazz affiliation and latterly organised groups relating back to Bob Cats style. Crosby appeared in a number of films between 1940 and 1959, including *The Road to Bali* (1952) and *Five Pennies* (1959).

Selected LP recordings

Come on and Hear, Vol.1—Coral CP109 (74). *South Rampart Street Parade* (1937); *Dixieland Shuffle* (1936); *Who's sorry now* (1937)*; *Savoy Blues* (1936); *Coquette* (1937)*; *Gin Mill Blues* (1937); *Royal Garden Blues* (1936); *I hear you talking* (1938)*; *Squeeze me* (1937); *Fidgety Feet* (1937)*; *Call me a Taxi* (1938)*; *Dogtown Blues* (1937). (*Bob Cats & small groups.)

Come on and Hear, Vol.2—Coral CP110 (74). *Yancey Special* (1938); *Mournin' Blues* (1939)*; *Big Noise from Winnetka* (1938)*; *Milk Cow Blues* (1938); *The Love Nest* (1939)* *I'm prayin' humble* (1938); *Till we meet again* (1939)*; *Honky Tonk Train Blues* (1938); *Jazz me Blues* (1940)*; *Feather your Nest* (1939)*; *All by myself* (1940)*; *Diga Diga Doo* (1938). (*Bob Cats & small groups.)

Bob Crosby and his Orchestra-1936—Decca London HMG5021 (77). *Summertime; 'Tain't no use; Here comes your Pappy; The Way You Look Tonight; Ol' Man Mose; Fidgety Feet; Bye Bye, Baby; Sing, Baby, Sing; I'm putting all my eggs in one basket; It's the Gypsy in me; What's the Name of that Song; There goes my attraction; Savoy Blues* (Taken from radio broadcasts.)

Five Feet of Swing—Brunswick LAT8037 (55) (d); (A) Decca DL8045. *South Rampart Street Parade* (1937); *Dogtown Blues* (1937). (With tracks by Dorsey Brothers, Jimmy Dorsey, Chick Webb, Glen Gray.)

Bob Crosby Orchestra 1936-1956—Vogue Coral LVA9045 (57) (d); (A) Coral CRL57089. *Come back, sweet Papa; The Old Spinning Wheel; I'm prayin' humble; Smokey Mary; Ja Da; Sugar Foot Stomp; That Eccentric Rag; Original Dixieland One-step; Tin Roof Blues; Rose Room; Echo in the Cavern; At the Jazz Band Ball* (1936-56.)

Also:

Greatest Hits—(A) Decca DL-74856.

Bob Crosby's Greatest Hits—London HA-D2293, (S) SAH-D6105 (60) (d); (A) Dot DLP3278.

Dance Date (1938-51) (A) Sounds of Swing LP-109 (74).

South Rampart Street Parade—MCA MCFM2578 (74) (d).

Doin' the Big Apple (1936-40)—(A) Bandstand BS-7111.

Bob Crosby and his Orchestra (1936-42)—(A) Bandstand BS-7121.

Bob Crosby and his Orchestra—(A) Jazum 5.

Bob Crosby and his Orchestra (1940 broadcasts)—(A) Aircheck 17 (76).

Stomp Off, Let's Go (1937-42)—Decca 'Ace of Hearts' AH29 (62) (d).

Bob Crosby and his Orchestra (1936-39) (Musak transcriptions, World and Standard trans & Decca releases)—(A) Jazum 48 & 49 (76).

Bob Cats:

Big Noise from Winnetka (1938-42)—MCA MCFM2695 (75).

Orchestra & Bob Cats (1936-42)—(G) Swingfan 1016.

Bob Crosby 1935, Vol.1—Ajax 144 (79).

Bob Crosby 1935, Vol.2—Ajax 151 (79).

Bob Crosby 1936-7, Vol.3—Ajax 159 (79).

Bob Crosby (1940)—Aircheck 17 (79).

Bob Crosby and his Orchestra (1935-6)—Rarities 41 (79).

Bob Crosby and his Orchestra—Joker SM3243 (79).

Bob Crosby Plays—Circle CLP1 (79).

Bob Crosby and his Orchestra (1946)—Jazz Anthology JA5142 (79).

John Dankworth

(b Highams Park, Essex, September 20 1927)

With his brilliant and versatile wife, singer Cleo Laine, he is one of the major talents in contemporary British popular music. Studied briefly at the Royal Academy of Music in 1944. Formed the Johnny Dankworth Seven which achieved widespread recognition, and later led big bands with success. He has written a great deal of music, for concert, radio, television and films, much of it designed specifically for Cleo Laine's huge talent. Like Ellington he has based a suite on Shakespeare, with jazz settings of lyrics, another on Dickens. Original work in films particularly good. In everything he and Miss Laine do there is a truly individual, genuinely creative impulse, reflected in band work, notably during the 1960s. In recent years Johnny Dankworth and Cleo Laine have run educational and co-operative music courses and demonstrations at their home in Buckinghamshire, known as Wavendon All-Plan Music.

Selected LP recordings

Full Circle—Philips 6308 122 (72). *Eleven Plus; Academy One: The Italian Girl; Grow*

your own; Earthman; Schmaltz Waltz; Triple Portrait; You are too beautiful; Family Joy. (1970-72.)
The Big Band Sound—Polydor Roulette 2934 021 (73). *African Waltz; Specs Yellow; New Forest; String of Camels; Curtain Up; Moanin'; S.O. Blues; Desperate Dan; Dauphine Blues; Winter Wail; Chano; Sack O' Woe.* (1960s—from earlier Columbia LPs.)
Jazz Routes—Columbia 33SX1280, (S) SCX3347 (60) (d); (A) Roulette R-52096. *Tribute to Chauncey; Slo Twain; Sunflower; Dauphine Blues; Honest-dew Melon; Joe and Lol's Blues; International; Kool Kate; New Forest; Specs Yellow; Desperate Dan.* (1960.)
Also:
Shakespeare and All That Jazz—(A) Fontana 27531.
The Vintage Years—Parlophone PMC1076 (58) (d).
London to Newport (1959)—Top Rank 30/019 (60) (d).
London to Newport (1959)—Top Rank 30/020 (59) (d).
Lifeline—Philips 6308 169 (73) (d).
Movies 'n' Men (1974)—RCA SF8405 (75) (d).
Curtain Up—Columbia 33SX1572 (63).
From Seven On—HMV Encore ENC165.
Five Steps to Dankworth—Parlophone PMC1043; (A) Verve 20006 (61).
What the Dickens—Fontana TL5203; (A) Fontana 27525 (64).
Zodiac Variations—Fontana TL5229; (A) Fontana 27543 (65).
Million Dollar Collection—Fontana TL5445.
Johnny Dankworth Orchestra (mid-1950s)—Big Band LPS2703 (75.)

Sam Donahue

(b Detroit, March 8 1918; d Reno, Nevada, March 22 1974)
Powerful tenor player and leader who worked in Detroit in the 1930s with a youth band and later joined Gene Krupa. He had brief stints with Harry James and Benny Goodman before re-forming own band which played at the Glen Island Casino, New Rochelle, New York. During World War II served in US Navy and took over Navy Band on the discharge of Artie Shaw in 1943. Widespread success in US and Europe with Navy Band. Formed fine civilian band in 1946 with good soloists and strong arrangements featuring his own tenor. After brief recall to US military service in 1951, Donahue briefly joined Tommy Dorsey, but formed his own band once more in 1953. In 1954 took over lead of the Billy May (qv) band under ownership of Ray Anthony. In 1960 he worked with Stan Kenton, and later fronted the 'Tommy Dorsey Orchestra'. Continued to work through the 1960s, leading band at the Playboy Club, New York, and later led a band at Reno until his death from cancer in 1974.

Selected LP recordings

Sam Donahue Orchestra (1945-47)—Capitol LCT6019 (55) (d).
Sam Donahue-Navy Band 1945—Jazz Society AA507 (74) (d).
Sam Donahue's Navy Band, Vol.2—Hep HEP5 (75) (d); (77).
Convoy—Hep HEP2 (74) (d); (77).
Young Moderns In Love—(A) Capitol T-613.
Sam Donahue—(A) Capitol T-626.

The Dorsey Brothers

Jimmy (qv) and Tommy (qv) Dorsey established themselves as outstanding white players in the early 1920s, working with various name bands of the period and recording widely. They formed joint recording groups from 1928 onwards. In 1934 they formed a permanent band playing good, sophisticated jazz-based music as forerunners of the 'swing' style (though the term had not yet achieved general currency), with arrangements often by Glenn Miller (qv). Jimmy (as, cl) and Tommy (tb, occasional t) were supported by excellent musicians, including Bunny Berigan and Manny Klein (t), Eddie Lang (g), Fud Livingston (as, cl), Stanley King (d) and Mildred Bailey (vo). But an inveterate habit of quarrelling (they were very different in temperament and approach) led to a final break in 1935 which lasted for ten years. Both formed orchestras of their own, with considerable success. They rejoined forces to make the film *The Fabulous Dorseys*, a typical piece of Hollywood hokum, and in 1953 were finally reconciled when Jimmy joined Tommy's band and remained there until Tommy's death in 1956, as 'The Tommy Dorsey Orchestra Featuring Jimmy Dorsey'. The Dorsey Brothers Orchestra itself refers to the 1934-35 aggregation, which achieved a distinctive style and played much good music in a recognizably white New York style, based on the trombone playing of Tommy and the alto sax and clarinet of Jimmy plus good ensemble work and solos by Berigan and others.

Selected LP recordings

The Young Dorsey Brothers 1928-30—World Records SHB67 (2). *Mary Ann* (1928); *Persian Rug* (1928); *Coquette* (1928); *The Yale Blues* (1928); *My Melancholy Baby* (1928); *Indian Cradle Song* (1928); *That's my Mammy* (1928); *Dixie Dawn* (1928); *Evening Star* (1928); *Forgettin' You* (1928); *Was it a Dream?* (1928); *Round Evening* (1928); *Out of the Dawn* (1928); *Sally of my Dreams* (1928); *Cross Roads* (1928); *She's funny that way* (1928); *I can make most anything* (1928); *Let's do it* (1929)*; *The Spell of the Blues* (1929)*; *My kinda love* (1929)*; *Mean to me* (1929); *Button up your Overcoat* (1929); *I'll never ask for more* (1929); *Lover, come back to me* (1929); *Am I blue?* (1929); *Baby, oh where can you be* (1929); *Breakaway* (1929); *Singin' in the Rain* (1929); *Your mother and mine* (1929); *Maybe, who knows* (1929); *Can this be love?* (1930); *Fine and Dandy* (1930). (*Vocals by Bing Crosby; arr Glenn Miller.)

Five Feet of Swing—Brunswick LAT8037 (55) (d). *Solitude* (1935); *Weary Blues* (1935). (With tracks by Bob Crosby, Jimmy Dorsey, Chick Webb & Glen Gray.)

Dorsey Brothers Orchestra—Brunswick LAT8256 (58) (d); (A) Decca DL-8631. *St. Louis Blues* (1934); *Milenberg Joys* (1934); *Stop, Look and Listen* (1934); *Honeysuckle Rose* (1934); *Tailspin* (1935); *Dippermouth* (1935); *Eccentric* (1935); *By Heck* (1934); *Basin Street Blues* (1934); *Dese, Dem, Dose* (1935); *Weary Blues* (1935). (Reissued as *The Fabulous Dorseys*, Coral CP27 (75).

Also:

The Fabulous Dorseys Play Dixieland Jazz (1934-35)—Coral CP-27 (d); CRLM1027 (74); (A) Decca DL-8631.

Sweet and Hot (1934-35)—(A) Sunbeam HB-301 (74).

Bring back the Good Times—(G) MCA COPS7443 D1/2 (75).

Tenderly—(A) Decca DL-8217.

Dixieland Jazz—Brunswick LA5254 (52) (d); (A) Decca DL-6016.

Spotlight on the Dorsey Brothers—(A) Design DLP-147.

Jimmy Dorsey with the Tommy Dorsey Orchestra:

The Fabulous Dorseys in Hi-Fi, Vol.1—(A) Columbia CL-1190.

Sentimental and Swinging—(A) Columbia CL-1240.

The Golden Era, Vol.4—(A) Colpix CP-436.

Last Moments of Greatness, Vol.3—(A) Urania UJ-1215.

Jimmy Dorsey

(b Shenandoah, February 29 1904; d New York, June 12 1957)

Elder brother of Tommy and like him played in early years with various bands, including the California Ramblers, Jean Goldkette etc, and also with Paul Whiteman (qv) and Ted Lewis (qv). After break with Tommy he took over the Dorsey Brothers band and became immediately successful. Recorded regularly for Decca, at least once with Louis Armstrong, between 1935 and 1946, mixing swing style numbers with ballads and standards featuring vocalists Kay Weber, Ray Eberle and Helen O'Connell. The band [Shorty Sherock (t), Sonny Lee (tb), Babe Russin, Skeets Herfurt (ts), Joe Lippman (p) and Ray McKinley (d)] gave excellent support to Jimmy's own distinctive alto sax and clarinet playing, and had good ensemble, in arrangements by a number of gifted men, including Larry Clinton, Bobby van Epps,

Jimmy Dorsey (Pye Records).

Toots Camarta and Joe Lippman. Like other bands of the time it featured Dixieland numbers by a small group from time to time. Jimmy appeared in several films and, after Tommy's death, he took over the band they both led, but was forced to give up because of ill health and died of cancer the following year. Though never quite attaining the celebrity 'name' of Tommy during the 1930s and 1940s, Jimmy maintained a strong popular following with records and on radio, notably with Bing Crosby's Kraft Music Hall broadcasts.

Selected LP recordings

Jimmy Dorsey and his Orchestra-1935—Decca London HMG5022 (76). *Dorsey Stomp; Top hat, white tie and tails; You are my Lucky Star; The Peanut Vendor; Cheek to Cheek; Tap Dancers' Nightmare; Three Little Words; It never dawned on me; No Strings; Beebe; East of the Sun; Wolverine Blues.* (Taken from radio broadcasts.)

Five Feet of Swing—Brunswick LAT8037 (55) (d). *Song of the Volga Boatmen* (1938); *I cried for you* (1938). (With tracks by Bob Crosby, Dorsey Brothers, Chick Webb, Glen Gray.)

Dixie by Dorsey—Columbia 33S1026; (A) Columbia CL-608. *Jazz me Blues; Panama; Tin Roof Blues; High Society; Struttin' with some Barbecue; Chimes Blues; Muskrat Ramble; South Rampart Street Parade* (1949). (Original Dorseyland Jazz Band—small group.)

The Fabulous Jimmy Dorsey—HMV CLP1132 (57) (d). *Contrasts; Jay Dee's Boogie Woogie; Mambo en Sax; Maria Elena; Speak Low; It's the Dreamer in me; June Night; Amapola; Just Swinging'; Sophisticated Swing; No one ever lost more; So Rare; Contrasts.*

Jimmy Dorsey and his Orchestra 1944-1947—First Heard 1974 (75). *Perdido; I got Rhythm; One o'clock Jump; Sackhouse Stomp; King Porter Stomp; Sunset Strip; Grand Central getaway; Take it Easy; Parade of the Milk Bottle Tops; Perdido.*

Also:

Jimmy Dorsey's Greatest Hits (dir Lee Castle)—Fontana TFL5057 (59) (d).

The Great Jimmy Dorsey—Decca 'Ace of Hearts' AH114 (66) d MCA COPS7449/1-2. (A) Decca DL-8609.

Contrasts (1939-1940s)—(A) Big Band Archives LP-1203 (74).

Latin American Favorites—(A) Decca DL-8153.

Jimmy Dorsey and his Orchestra (1949)—(A) Big Band Archives LP-1216.

Jimmy Dorsey and his Orchestra (1935-41)—(A) Bandstand BS-7104.

Jimmy Dorsey and his Orchestra (1935-40)—(A) Bandstand BS-7120.

Jimmy Dorsey and his Orchestra (1935-41)—(G) Swingfan 1007.

In Disco Order Vol.1—(Sw) Ajax 103 (77).

Silver Swing Series, 1940-46—(G) EMI PC07839 (75).

Jimmy Dorsey and his Orchestra (late 1930s)—Golden Era 15011 (75).

Jimmy Dorsey & His Orchestra (1939-40) (broadcasts)—London HMP5042 (79).

Remember Jimmy—(A) Decca DL-4248.

Jimmy Dorsey's Greatest Hits—(A) Decca DL-4853.

Latin American Favorites—(A) Decca DL-8153.

The Great Jimmy Dorsey—(A) Decca DL-8609.

So Rare—(A) Dot DLP-3437.

Jimmy Dorsey and his Orchestra—(A) Lion L-70063.

The Fabulous Jimmy Dorsey—(A) Frat F-1008.

Jimmy Dorsey Vols.1-10—Ajax 103/114/117/118/124/128/134/141/148/156 (79).

Tommy Dorsey

(b Shenandoah, November 19 1905; d Greenwich, Connecticut, November 26 1956)

Younger brother of Jimmy (qv) with whom he formed the Dorsey Brothers Orchestra (qv). In early years played with various bands, including the California Ramblers (qv), Jean Goldkette (qv), Roger Wolfe Kahn (qv), Vincent Lopez, Nat Shilkret etc, and did much freelance recording. In those days, especially on trumpet, played a forceful gutsy style later abandoned mostly for the smooth legato manner which earned him the title 'The Sentimental Gentleman of Swing', largely on account of his way with his signature tune *I'm Getting Sentimental Over You*, and his masterly technique and breath control which became dubbed 'the endless pipe'. After break with Jimmy formed his own band from the nucleus of Joe Haymes's group and through the late 1930s and the 1940s rivalled Benny Goodman and Artie Shaw (qv) as the most popular swing band leader. This band [Bunny Berigan, Pee Wee

Tommy Dorsey (RCA Records).

Irwin, Max Kaminsky (t), Bud Freeman (ts), Joe Dixon (cl) and Dave Tough (d)] recorded extensively for Victor and had many hits. Like other big swing bands Dorsey also featured a small group from within the ranks, known as the Clambake Seven, which played in a more direct jazz style and showed that Tommy himself could still remember how hot trombone should sound. He held a number of lucrative hotel residencies and appeared on many radio shows, using arrangements by Deane Kincaide, Sy Oliver, Bill Finegan and others, and featuring vocalists Joe Stafford, Dick Haymes and the important group, the Pied-Pipers. Most famous vocalist during 1940-42 was the young Frank Sinatra who has always claimed that he learnt his sense of time and phrasing from listening to Tommy's trombone. In 1942 the band was enlarged with a string section and moved still farther away from its jazz origins, but continued to hold its popularity. He appeared in several films, featuring himself in *A Song is Born* in 1948. Later sidemen included Yank Lawson, Charlie Shavers, Ziggy Elman (t), Babe Russin (ts), Joe Bushkin (p), Buddy Rich (d) and Buddy de Franco (cl). Maintained position as outstanding band through the high tide of 'swing' and through the difficult later years by sound musicianship and smooth, but not devitalized, sound.

Selected LP recordings

The Best of Tommy Dorsey, Vol.4 (1935-37)—RCA FXM1 7098 (75). *Weary Blues* (1935); *I'm Getting Sentimental Over You* (1935); *The Music goes 'Round and Around* (1935)*; *The day I Let You Get Away* (1935)*; *Rhythm Saved the World* (1935)*; *Royal Garden Blues* (1936); *Stardust* (1936); *Ja Da* (1936); *At the Codfish Ball* (1936)*; *That's a-plenty* (1936); *After you've gone* (1936); *Maple Leaf Rag* (1936); *Melody in F* (1937); *Song of India* (1937); *Marie* (1937); *Beale Street Blues* (1937). (*Clambake Seven.)

Tommy Dorsey-Vol.2—RCA DPM2042 (2) (74). *Weary Blues* (1935); *The Music goes 'Round and Around* (1935)*; *Royal Garden Blues* (1936); *After you've gone* (1936); *That's* *a-plenty* (1936); *Stardust* (1936); *Ja-Da* (1936); *Humoresque* (1937); *Mr. Ghost goes to Town* (1937); *Blue Danube* (1937); *Beale Street Blues* (1937); *Nola* (1937); *The Sheik of Araby* (1937); *Barcarolle* (1937); *Night and Day* (1937); *I may be wrong* (1937); *Little White Lies* [Just a Simple Melody] (1937); *Dipsy Doodle* (1937); *Tea for Two* (1939); *Lonesome Road* [Parts 1 & 2] (1939); *Come rain, come shine* (1946); *Deep River* (1941); *Swing High* (1940); *Not so quiet please* (1942); *On the Alamo* (1942); *Mandy, Make up your Mind* (1942); *Chicago* (1945); *There's Good Blues Tonight* (1946); *After Hour Stuff* (1945); *At Sundown* (1946); *Trombonology* (1946.) (*Clambake Seven.)

Tommy Dorsey 1942-1946—First Heard 1973-4. *Ciribiribin; I'm satisfied; Sweet and Lovely; Somebody loves me; Easy Street; It could happen to you; When I get it (Love Department); Blue Lou* (1944)*; *Theme* (1942); *Dinah* (1942); *Chicago* (1943); *The Minor goes A-mugging* (1944); *Hawaiian War Chant* (1945); *Midriff* (1945); *Swing High* (1945); *'Tain't me* (1945); *Tico Tico* (1946); *Closing Theme* (1946). (Side 1 has Tommy Dorsey fronting the Harry James Orchestra (owing to the indisposition of James) for a broadcast from the Casino Gardens Ballroom, Ocean Park in 1944. Side 2 is the Dorsey Band 1942-45). (*Clambake Seven.)

The Best of Tommy Dorsey, Vol.6—(G) CA FXM1 7284 (76). *Mary had a little Lamb* (1936); *San Francisco* (1936); *Keepin' out of Mischief Now* (1936); *The Milkman's Matinee* (1937); *Twilight in Turkey* (1937); *Rollin' Home* (1937); *Smoke Gets in your Eyes* (1937); *The Big Apple* (1937); *Little White Lies* (1937); *Music, maestro, please* (1938); *I'll See You in My Dreams* (1938); *You Must Have Been a Beautiful Baby* (1938); *Hawaiian War Chant* (1938); *Milenberg Joys* (1939); *Blue Moon* (1939); *By the River Sainte Marie* (1939).

Also:

In a Sentimental Mood—Brunswick LA8610 (53) (d); (A) Decca DL-5448 (d); 8218.

Tenderly—Brunswick LA8640 (54) (d); (A) Decca DL-5449 (d), 8217.

Your Invitation to Dance—(A) Decca DL-5452 (d).

Tommy Dorsey Orchestra—HMV DLP1123 (56) (d).

The Fabulous Dorseys in Hi-Fi—Philips BBL7295 (58) (d); (A) Columbia C2L-8 (2) (58).

Tommy Dorsey Arrangements in Hi-Fi—Brunswick LAT8282, (S) STA3007 (59) (d).

Tea for Two Cha Cha Chas—Brunswick LAT8286, (S) STA3009 (59) (d).

The Swinging Era—Brunswick LAT8311, (S) STA3020 (60) (d).

Tommy Dorsey's Greatest Band, No.1—Top Rank 35/026 (6) (d); (A) 20th Century Fox TCF101 (3157).

Tommy Dorsey's Greatest Band, No.2—Top Rank 35/027 (60) (d); (A) 20th Century Fox TCF102 (3158).

More Tea for Two Cha Cha Chas—Brunswick LAT8323 (60) (d).

It Takes Two To—Brunswick LAT8353 (60) (d).

Dance Party—Decca 'Ace of Hearts' AH15 (61) (d); (A) Vocalion 3613 (58).

Easy does it (1937-50)—(A) Swing Era LP1003 (74) (d).

In the Tommy Dorsey Mood—Decca 'Ace of Hearts' AH101 (66) (d).

In a Sentimental Mood—Decca 'Ace of Hearts' AH138 (67) (d); (A) Decca DL-8227.

Tommy and his Orchestra—RCA DPM2026 (2).

Tommy Dorsey at the Fat Man's (1946-48)—Hep HEP-9 (77).

Yes, Indeed (1935-44)—(A) RCA LPM-1229 (d).

The Beat of the Big Bands—CBS Embassy EMB31016.

The Best of Tommy Dorsey, Vol.1 (1937-41)—(F) RCA 731.129; (A) RCA LPM-1432 (d).

The Best of Tommy Dorsey, Vol.3—(F) RCA 741.079.

The Best of Tommy Dorsey, Vol.5—(F) RCA FXM1-7171.

The Best of Tommy Dorsey—(G) RCA INTS-5017 (80).

That Sentimental Gentleman (broadcasts)—(A) RCA LPM-6003 (2).

It Feels So Good—Golden Era GE15020 (76) (d).

Tommy Dorsey Orchestra 1935-39—(A) Sunbeam SB-201 (74).

Tommy Dorsey, Vol.1—RCA DPM-2026 (2); (A) RCA AXM2-5521 (76).

This is Tommy Dorsey—(A) RCA VPM-6038 (2).

Tommy Dorsey, Vol.7 (1938-41)—(F) RCA PM-42036 (77).

Tommy Dorsey 1950-52 (unissued

items)—First Time 1519 (74).
Tommy Dorsey's Dance Party—(A) Vocalion VL-3613.
Swing High (1939-50)—(A) Sounds of Swing LP-106.
Swing Out (1936-39)—(A) Bandstand BS-7116.
Tommy Dorsey (V-discs, 1945)—(A) Joyce 1022 (76).
I'm Getting Sentimental Over You—Pye 'Golden Hour' GH870 (78).
Hawaiian War Chant—(A) RCA LPM-1234.
Tribute to Dorsey, Vols. 1 & 2—(A) RCA LPM-1432/3 (2).
Frankie and Tommy—RCA SD1000; (A) RCA LPM-1569.
Dedicated to You—(A) Camden CAL-800, (S) S-800.
Making Big Band History—First Heard FH1003 (81).

Billy Eckstine

(b Pittsburgh, Pennsylvania July 8 1914.)
Best known as band vocalist, beginning with Earl Hines band (qv), 1939-43, then formed a big band with tenor saxist Budd Johnson in 1944 which became an important ingredient in the growth and spread of 'bebop'. Band particularly important because of the presence of some of the great modernists of the period [Dizzy Gillespie (t), Charlie Parker (as), Lucky Thompson, Dexter Gordon (ts), later Kenny Dorham, Fats Navarro, Miles Davis, Howard McGhee (t) and Art Blakey (d)]. Fine arrangements by Tadd Dameron, Budd Johnson and Dizzy Gillespie, and early vocal prowess of Sarah Vaughan. The band broke up in 1947, due to the usual economic problems, and from then on Eckstine was featured largely as solo turn in which role he had an enormous success.

Selected LP recordings

Greatest Hits—Polydor 2353 071. *I Apologise; Love Me or Leave Me; St. Louis Blues; Here comes the Blues; Life Is Just a Bowl of Cherries; Tenderly; Taking a Chance on Love; Everything I have is yours; How High the Moon; Laura; You're Driving me Crazy; No one but you; I left my hat in Haiti; As long as I live.* (1947-54.)
Also:
Eckstine's Big Sixteen (1950s)—HMV Encore ENC203 (66) (d).
Billy Eckstine and his Orchestra—(1945) Spotlite 100.

Billy Eckstine (Fosters Agency Ltd).

Fred Elizalde

(b Manila, December 12 1907; d Madrid, January 16 1979)
Studied with his brother Manuel at Standford University, California, and later at Cambridge, where they formed a group known as Fred Elizalde and his Cambridge Undergraduates in 1926. Coming down from Cambridge, Fred Elizalde raided the California Ramblers (qv) for four musicians [Chelsea Quealey (t), Bobby Davis (as), Adrian Rollini (bs s) and Jack Rusen (p)] and opened at the Savoy Hotel, London in January 1928. Through 1928 and 1929 the Elizalde band continued at the Savoy interspersed with tours of Europe. In 1929 the Americans went home and Elizalde went to Madrid and subsequently made his home in Paris where he continued his studies with Ravel and others, as well as (previously) with Ernst Bloch and Ernesto Haelffter. After the early excursion into jazz Elizalde spent his life playing and composing concert music, in which he had considerable success. During the Savoy Hotel years, Elizalde ran two

Fred Elizalde.

groups, one 'hot', one 'sweet', and recorded prolifically with both.

Selected LP recordings

Jazz at the Savoy—Decca LF1277 (57) (d). *Arkansas* (1928); *Dixie* (1928); *Hurricane* (1927); *Sugar Step* (1928); *Somebody Stole my Gal* (1928); *The Darktown Strutters' Ball* (1928); *Clarinet Marmalade* (1927); *Sugar* (1928); *Stomp your Feet* (1927); *Tiger Rag* (1928).

An Evening at the Savoy—Decca DDV5011/12 (78). *Stomp your Feet* (1927); *Rhythm Step* (1927); *Tweet, Tweet* (1927); *Clarinet Marmalade* (1927); *Don't Bring me Posies* (1927); *Barbara* (1927); *Dancing Tambourine* (1927); *Diane* (1928); *Under the Moon* (1928); *Sugar* (1928); *Calling me Home* (1928); *You can't have my sugar for tea* (1928); *Arkansas* (1928); *Sugar Step* (1928); *How long has this been going on* (1928); *Tea-time* (1928); *Here I am Broken-hearted* (1928); *Smile* (1928); *Dance, little Lady* (1928); *Room with a View* (1928); *The Darktown Strutters' Ball* (1928); *Somebody Stole my Gal* (1928); *Chopinata* (1928); *Gypsy Sweetheart* (1928); *Blue Baby* (1928); *Coquette* (1928); *Just Imagine* (1929); *Wherever you are* (1929); *Laughing Marionette* (1929); *Crazy Rhythm* (1929); *Misery Farm* (1929); *I'm sorry, Sally* (1929).

Jazz at the Savoy—The 20s—Decca 'Ace of Clubs' ACL1102 (62) (d). *Arkansas Blues; Dixie; She's a great, great girl; Hurricane; Sugar Step; Siam Blues; Somebody Stole my Gal; The Darktown Strutters' Ball: Clarinet Marmalade; Allah's Holiday; Sugar; Stomp your Feet; Vamp till Ready; Tiger Rag* (1927-28).

Edward Kennedy 'Duke' Ellington

(b Washington DC, April 29 1899; d New York, May 23 1974)

One of the most important figures not only in jazz but in the whole of contemporary American music, as genuine composer and not as performer only. After first studying art he turned exclusively to music. Played piano in and around Washington then joined Wilbur Sweatman's Jazz Band in 1920, then played with Elmer Snowden's Orchestra. Began to record with his own band in 1926, known as The Washingtonians. Made the first evolutions of his personal style while leading his band at the Kentucky Club (formerly the Hollywood Club). Individual members of that band, notably trumpeter Bubber Miley and trombonist Joe 'Tricky Sam' Nanton, greatly influenced his music, forming at an early stage the 'growl' or 'jungle' idiom which became a leading feature of his work. Miley also had a hand in several of the early Ellington classics, like *Black and Tan Fantasy, East St. Louis Toodle-oo, Creole Love Call* etc. Miley did not originate the 'growl' style (the credit for that probably lies with Johnny Dunn). Miley learnt it first from King Oliver (qv) who he first heard while working with Mamie Smith's band in the early 1920s. But Miley's playing, supported first by Charlie Irvis and then, decisively, by Nanton's, soon established Ellington's special 'hallmark'.

In 1927 Ellington accepted an engagement at the Cotton Club in Harlem, after King Oliver had turned it down. It was a major turning point; thereafter his fortunes rose while Oliver's declined. During the Cotton Club years, the Ellington band reached its first full maturity, its personnel stable. Miley left in 1928, to be replaced by 'Cootie' Williams. In the same year Johnny Hodges (as) joined and remained a major voice in the band, with a break in the 1950s when he tried his hand at band leading on his own, until his death in 1970. Harry Carney (bar) joined in 1926 and remained without a break through the band's entire history, dying shortly after Ellington. The creole styled clarinet of Barney Bigard was another distinctive voice for more than 20 years. Arthur Whetsol (t) and Sonny Greer (d) remained from the earliest days at the Kentucky Club, and Wellman Braud (b) laid down a solid New Orleans beat until the mid-1930s.

As Ellington's style grew and matured, so did the constitution of the band. A third trombone, Lawrence Brown, was added to the existing duo of Nanton and Puerto Rican valve trombonist, Juan Tizol, to make one of the great trios; a fourth saxophone was brought in with the return of the original, pre-Hodges, soloist Otto Hardwick, and later Duke began to use a tenor saxophone, Ben Webster, who, after sitting in as guest on various occasions, became a regular member. The second great period came in 1940, which many still consider the highest peak of all. As well as the established members, the late Jimmy Blanton brought for a couple of years a wholly new conception of bass playing which markedly influenced the sound and rhythmic subtlety of the band. A whole series of miniature masterpieces came from these years, made possible in great part by a stable and permanent personnel. Cootie Williams left to join Benny Goodman in 1940; he was replaced by Ray Nance (t, vln).

For many years Ellington's own piano playing was not widely featured. As a performer he tended to be modest and self-effacing (although he did make one or two solo records). But from about the mid-1950s onwards he began to feature his own playing more, and from then on established himself as one of the most imaginative and resourceful of all jazz pianists, in a style rooted in Harlem 'stride', not only taking a more prominent part with the band but also extending his activities as a solo player. This was sometimes with musicians outside his own band, and sometimes with those of a decidedly 'modernist' persuasion—Charlie Mingus, Max Roach, John Coltrane, Ray Brown etc.

The Ellington band visited England in 1933 and made a great impression, although on stage he tended to feature more 'show business' material (as he obviously had to *in situ* at the Cotton Club) than the more striking and original 'serious' compositions on which his reputation among jazz enthusiasts, who knew his work only from records, was primarily based. Though this bias caused some disappointment among the 'purists', it served as a reminder that any band has to earn its living either out on the road or in an economically viable 'residency'.

Because of the dispute between the Musicians' Unions in England and America, the Ellington band was not heard again in England until 1958, although it had been to Europe and Ellington himself, with Ray Nance and singer Kay Davis, had visited London in 1948. By 1958 many changes had taken place; a number of familiar names were missing from the ranks. In their place were men who were to dominate Ellington's music for the next decade or so [Harold Baker, Cat Anderson, Clark Terry (t); Quentin Jackson (tb); Paul Gonsalves (ts); Jimmy Hamilton (ts, cl); Russell Procope (as, cl) and Sam Woodyard (d)]. Most of these were familiar from records, and stalwarts like Johnny Hodges, Harry Carney and Ray Nance were there from the old days, and of course the band remained 100 per cent Ellington.

Early and mid-1950 was a difficult time for big bands, and Ellington was one of the very few to keep on going and in continuing existence (even Count Basie was obliged to front a small group for a time). Ellington, however, survived all the vicissitudes and retained his place as the top band leader for more than half a century, which was an achievement in itself. And he kept it going despite all the difficulties and economic strains, first and foremost so that he could have the right instrument at hand for the performance of his compositions. Ellington was always a composer above all, his band a composer's band and not, like virtually all others, an arrangers' band. It is a significant difference in kind.

As a composer Duke Ellington was a romantic impressionist, primarily of mood and locality, whose aim it always was to portray in music the life, the feelings and aspirations, the sufferings and sorrows, the joys and vivacity of his people, the black Americans. In this he was remarkably successful, developing through the years a music style and idiom of great range and flexibility, rooted in the basic jazz idiom and using always the true language of jazz, while at the same time enormously extending both.

The 'Afro' elements were always prominent, beyond the obviously exotic 'jungle' style for which he was famous. Rather than being always simple and direct, these elements were creatively integrated into a musical idiom of much outward sophistication. Pieces like *Echoes of the Jungle, Jungle Nights in Harlem, Ko-Ko*, refer not so much to the African in Africa as to the American city Negro conscious of his racial background and inheritance.

He was also a notable portraitist in music, whether of individuals or types—numbers like *Bojangles, Portrait of Bert Williams, Portrait of The Lion* (Willie Smith), *Jack the Bear* (a sporting house character) catch to perfection the characteristic quirks and essential nature of their subjects, revealing another aspect of the strongly visual nature of much of his music, a legacy no doubt of his early training in art. He was also a lifelong and dedicated admirer of beautiful women, and they too left an effect on his music, as in *Sophisticated Lady, Lady of the Lavender Mist, Golden Cress,* and more extensively, *The Perfume Suite*; also the charming *Satin Doll*, a prime example of Duke's gift for writing genuine popular tunes of high quality.

Duke Ellington (Central Press Photos).

Largely because of the physical restrictions of the 78 rpm record, most of Ellington's early music was cast in the short form designed to accommodate that technical necessity. Sometimes he ventures beyond, as in *Creole Rhapsody* (1931) and *Reminiscing in Tempo* (1935); but for the most part, recognizing the essential part played by recording in circulating his work, he astutely adapted himself to practical requirement. But later he began to expand, not only because of the introduction of the LP record (several of his 'extended' works appeared before the LP era, including *Black, Brown and Beige*) but because that was the way his genius was leading him, and also to a lesser extent because of the introduction of jazz to Carnegie Hall and other places usually reserved for concert music, which made 'concert jazz' both practical and fashionable.

There is, however, a certain amount of confusion about Ellington's 'extended compositions'. Most of these are in reality suites of short pieces linked by a common subject, as in the fine Shakespeare suite *Such Sweet Thunder*. It is not surprising, in view of his earlier work, that the suite form that he most frequently adopted suited his particular gifts best. True musical development, in the stricter sense, usually associated with extended composition was not a notable feature of Ellington's music: the habit of composing the comparatively short genre of mood pieces became ingrained early, partly out of necessity, partly because it was inherent in his specific talent, and for the most part remained dominant. That he could work on a larger canvas is demonstrated by one or two works that break the more familiar mould, notably the *Tone Parallel to Harlem* (1951) which really does deserve the description 'extended' and is a memorable achievement. Thus Ellington's forte as a composer remained the short or shortish tone poem, either on its own or as part of a group or 'suite' linked by a common subject, in the general line of *Black, Brown and Beige*. (The 'extended' version of 1958 made selected sections longer but still did not contain much in the way of thematic development but brought in the great gospel singer Mahalia Jackson to sing *Come Sunday* and add a version of the 23rd Psalm). The same is true of later works such as the *Far East Suite*, the *New Orleans Suite* (1970) and others of a similar nature.

The collaborative aspect of Ellington's composing methods has been noted with members of the band contributing in more than an incidental way to the finished work. In 1939 this took a step further when the young pianist and composer, Billy Strayhorn, joined the organisation. Strayhorn, while modelling himself on Ellington, brought an individual touch to the general output, contributing many characteristic numbers. Ellington and Strayhorn had a great natural sympathy and understanding, and the relationship between the two soon became difficult to define precisely. Strayhorn remained part of Ellington's music until his death from cancer in 1967. But the master mind and guiding hand remained Duke's own, as it was for well over half a century.

Selected LP recordings

The Duke in Harlem—Decca 'Ace of Hearts' AH47 (63) (d) (A) Decca 79241 (69). *The Creeper* (1926); *Immigration Blues* (1926); *Song of the Cotton Field* (1927); *Red Hot Band* (1927); *Doin' the Frog* (1927); *Jubilee Stomp* (1928); *Black and Blue* (1929); *Jungle Jamboree* (1929); *Cincinnati Daddy* (1929); *Jungle Blues* (1930); *Maori* (1930); *Admiration* (1930.) (Recordings made just before and during the Cotton Club period.)

Cotton Club Days—Decca 'Ace of Hearts' AH23 (62) (d). *Cotton Club Stomp* (1930); *Harlem Flat Blues* (1929); *Wall Street Wail* (1929); *Doing the Voom Voom* (1929); *Rent Party Blues* (1929); *Jolly Wog* (1929); *Black and Tan Fantasy* (1927); *East St. Louis Toodle-oo* (1927); *Goin' Nuts* (1929); *Home again Blues* (1930); *Paducah* (1929); *Birmingham Breakdown* (1927).

Cotton Club Days, Vol.2—Decca 'Ace of Hearts' AH89 (65) (d). *Tiger Rag* (1929); *Louisiana* (1928); *Take it Easy* (1928); *Black Beauty* (1928); *Accordion Joe* (1930); *When You're Smiling* (1930); *Runnin' Wild* (1930); *The Wang-Wang Blues* (1930); *Oklahoma Stomp* (1929); *Six or seven times* (1929); *Double Check Stomp* (1930); *Creole Rhapsody* (1931).

Cotton Club Days, Vol.3—Decca 'Ace of Hearts' AH166 (68) (d). *East St. Louis Toodle-oo* (1926); *Birmingham Breakdown* (1926); *Song of the Cotton Field* (1927); *Soliloquy* (1927); *Yellow Dog Blues* (1928); *Tishomingo Blues* (1928); *Awful Sad* (1928); *Jazz Convulsions* (1929); *Mood Indigo* (1930); *Rockin' Chair* (1931); *Twelfth Street Rag* (1931); *Is that Religion* (1931).

Hot from Harlem (1927-30)—World Records SHB58 (2) (78). *What can a poor fellow do?* (1927); *Black and Tan Fantasy* (1927); *Chicago Stomp Down* (1927); *Sweet Mama* (1928); *Stack o' Lee Blues* (1928); *Bugle Call Rag* (1928); *Take it Easy* (1928); *Jubilee Stomp* (1928); *Harlem Twist (East St. Louis Toodle-oo)* (1928); *Diga Diga Doo* (1928); *Doin' the new Low-down* (1928); *Black Beauty* (1928); *Swampy River* (1928); *The Mooche* (1928); *Move Over* (1928); *Hot and Bothered* (1928); *The Blues with a Feeling* (1928); *Goin' to Town* (1928); *Misty Morning* (1928); *Jungle Jamboree* (1929); *Snake Hip Dance* (1929); *Lazy Duke* (1929); *Blues of the Vagabond* (1929); *Syncopated Shuffle* (1929); *Big House Blues* (1930); *Rocky Mountain Blues* (1930); *Ring dem Bells* (1930); *Three Little Words* (1930); *Old Man Blues* (1930); *Sweet Chariot* (1930); *Mood Indigo* (1930); *I Can't Realise You Love Me* (1930); *I'm so in love with you* (1930); *Rockin' in Rhythm* (1930).

Toodle-oo—Vocalion VLP4 (74). *East St. Louis Toodle-oo* (1927); *Birmingham Breakdown* (1927); *Immigration Blues* (1926); *The Creeper* (1926) (2 takes); *New Orleans Low-down* (1927); *Song of the Cotton Field* (1927); *Birmingham Breakdown* (1927) (2nd take); *East St. Louis Toodle-oo* (1927) (2nd take); *Black and Tan Fantasy* (1927); *Soliloquy* (1927); *Red Hot Band* (1927); *Doin' the Frog* (1927); *Take it Easy* (1927); *Jubilee Stomp* (1927).

Rare Duke Ellington Masterpieces—VJM VLP9 (66) (d). *Hottentot; Move Over; Jubilee Stomp; Misty Morning; Who said 'it's tight like that'; East St. Louis Toodle-oo; Hot and Bothered; The Mooche; Take it Easy; Saratoga Swing; Doin' the Voom-Voom; Saturday Night Function.* (1928-29.) (From the Cameo and Romeo labels.)

Duke Ellington-The Perfect Era—(D) Collector's Classics CC4 (74). *East St. Louis Toodle-oo* (1928); *Jubilee Stomp* (1928); *Take it Easy* (1928); *Hot and Bothered* (1928); *The Mooche* (1928); *Move Over* (1928); *Hottentot* (1928); *Misty Mornin'* (1928); *Saratoga Swing* (1928); *Who said 'it's tight like that'* (1928); *Doin' the Voom-Voom* (1929); *Saturday Night Function* (1929); *St. James Infirmary* (1930); *When You're Smiling*

(1930); *Rent Party Blues* (1930); *Jungle Blues* (1930).

All that Jazz—Decca Dream DJL-MD28020 (2). *Rockin' in Rhythm* (1937); *Tootin' Through the Roof* (1940); *Carnival in Caroline* (1938); *Little Red Cottage by the Sea* (1939); *Every Day: Lost in Meditation*; etc. (Mainly taken from broadcasts, some previously issued on Ember CJS840.)

At the Cotton Club 1937-38—(Sw) Tax M-8001 (74) (d). *I'm Slappin' Seventh Avenue* (1937); *Swingtime in Honolulu* (1937); *You gave me the gate* (1938); *Watermelon Man* (1938); *Love in Swingtime* (1938); *When my sugar walks down the street* (1938); *If you were in my place* (1938); *Skrontch* (1938); *Chatter Box* (1937); *Prologue to Black and Tan Fantasy* (1937); *Please Forgive Me* (1938); *Alabamy Home* (b); *All God's chillun got Rhythm* (1937); *I've got to be a rug-cutter* (1937); *The New Birmingham Breakdown* (1937); *Scattin' at the Kit-Kat* (1937).

Braggin' in Brass—(Sw) Tax M-8010 (74). *Braggin' in Brass* (1938); *You can't run away from love tonight* (1937); *The lady who couldn't be kissed* (1937); *It's Swell of You* (1937); *Mood Indigo* (1936) (solo); *Solitude* (1936) (solo); *Mighty like the Blues* (1938); *Lost in Meditation* (1938); *Smorgasbord and Schnapps* (1939); *Carnival in Caroline* (1938); *Solid Old Man* (1939); *T.T. on Toast* (1938); *Bouncing Buoyancy* (1939); *Sophisticated Lady* (1936) (solo); *In a Sentimental Mood* (1936) (solo); *I Never Felt This Way Before* (1939); *A Lonely Co-ed* (1939); *Braggin' in Brass* (1938).

Ridin' in Rhythm—World Records SHB42 (2). *Merry-go-round* (1933); *Sophisticated Lady* (1933); *I've got the world on a string* (1933); *Down a Carolina Lane* (1933). (Coupled with tracks by Fletcher Henderson, Coleman Hawkins, Benny Carter, etc.)

Cotton Club Stomp 1937-39—(Sw) Tax M-8012 (74) (d). *Cotton Club Stomp* (1939); *In a Mizz* (1939); *Lambeth Walk* (1938); *La De Doody Do* (1938); *The Stevedore's Serenade* (1938); *Country Gal* (1939); *Killin' Myself* (1939); *Your Love has Faded* (1939); *Doin' the Voom Voom* (1939); *You Can Count on Me* (1939); *A Blues Serenade* (1938); *Old Plantation* (1937); *Jubilesta* (1937); *Lady in Blue* (1939); *Hip Chic* (1938); *There's a Lull in my Life* (1937).

In Hollywood/On the Air—Max MLP1001 (74). *Lightinin'; Rockin' in Rhythm; Stormy Weather; Bugle Call Rag; Lightnin'* (from Paramount 'Bundle of Blues' 1933), (with Ivie Anderson): *The Laborers; A Triangle (Dance-Jealousy-Big City blues); A Hymn of Sorrow; Harlem Rhythm* (from Paramount short, 1934) (with Billie Holliday); *An Interview in Stockholm* (with Duke Ellington) (1939); *Serenade to Sweden; Rockin' in Rhythm; Cottage by the Sea* (Stockholm, 1939); *Sepia Panorama; Concerto for Cootie* (Chicago, 1940).

Duke Ellington at the Cotton Club 1938, Vol.1—(A) Jazz Archive JA-12. *Dinah; If You Were in My Place; Oh, Babe; Maybe Someday; Downtown Uproar; You went to my head; Harmony in Harlem; At your Beck and Call; The Gal from Joe's; Riding on a Blue Note; If Dreams Come True; Birmingham Breakdown; Blue Room.* (All unissued live recordings.)

Duke Ellington at the Cotton Club 1938, Vol.2—(A) Jazz Archive JA-13. *If Dreams Come True; Harmony in Harlem; Three Blind Mice; On the Sunny Side of the Street; Dinah's in a Jam**; *If Dreams Come True; Echoes of Harlem; It's the Dreamer in me; Ev'ry Day; Lost in Meditation; Prelude in C sharp minor; Rockin' in Rhythm.* (All, except*, unissued live recordings.)

The Jimmy Blanton Years—Queen-disc Q007 (75). *Ko-Ko; Blue Goose; So far so good; Cotton Tail; Concerto for Cootie; Jack the Bear; Boy Meets Horn; The Sergeant was shy; Ring dem Bells* (1940); *Chelsea Bridge; Bakiff; Jive Rhapsody; Jumpin' Punkins; Frankie and Johnny; Take the 'A' Train* (1941).

At his Very Best—RCA RD-27133 (59) (d); LSA3071 (73); (A) LPM-1715 (59). *Jack the Bear* (1940); *Concerto for Cootie* (1940); *Harlem Air-shaft* (1940); *Across the Track Blues* (1940); *Chloe* (1940); *Royal Garden Blues* (1946); *Warm Valley* (1940); *Ko-Ko* (1940); *Black, Brown and Beige* (1944); *Creole Love Call* (1927); *Transblucency* (1946).

In a Mellotone—RCA RD-27134 (59) (d), LSA3069; (A) LPM-1364 (59). *Take the 'A' Train* (1940); *A Portrait of Bert Williams* (1940); *Main Stem* (1942); *Just A-settin' and A-rockin'* (1941); *I got it bad and that ain't good* (1941)*; *Perdido* (1942); *Blue Serge* (1940); *The Flaming Sword* (1940); *In a Mellotone* (1940); *Cotton Tail* (1940); *I don't know what kind of Blues I got* (1941)†; *Rumpus in Richmond* (1940); *All too soon* (1940); *Sepia Panorama* (1940); *Rocks in my Bed* (1941)*; *What am I here for?* (1942).

(Vocals by *Ivie Anderson, †Herb Jeffries.)

Johnny Come Lately—RCA RD-7888 (d); (A) RCA LPV-541 (67). *The 'C' Jam Blues* (1942); *Moon Mist* (1942); *I Don't Mind* (1942)*; *Someone* (1942)*; *Johnny Come Lately* (1942); *Hayfoot, Strawfoot* (1942)*; *A Slip of the Lip* (1942); *Sherman Shuffle* (1942); *I ain't got nothin' but the blues* (1944)†; *Mood to be Wooed* (1945); *Kissing Bug* (1945)**; *Everything But You* (1945); *Riff Staccato* (1945)‡ *Prelude to a Kiss* (1945); *Caravan* (1945); *It don't mean a thing if it ain't got that swing* (1945)***. (Vocals by *Ivie Anderson, †Al Hibbler & Kay Davis, **Joya Sherrill, ‡Ray Nance, ***Joya Sherrill & Kay Davis.)

Duke Ellington and his Orchestra—HMV DLP1070 (55) (d). *Black, Brown and Beige*-suite (1944); *Perfume Suite* (1945).

Duke Ellington—World Records R12 (d); Ember 3327 (61). *Overture to a Jam Session; Jam-a-ditty (Concerto for 4 jazz horns); The Beautiful Indians (Hiawatha/Minnehaha); Happy-go-lucky Local; Blue Skies; Diminuendo in Blue; Magenta Haze; Golden Feather; Sultry Sunset; Flippant Fury.* (1946). (Reissued on RCA Prestige PR24029 (2) with *Tulip or Turnip* and *It shouldn't happen to a dream* added; Record 2-piano solos & duets.)

Mood Ellington—Philips BBR8044 (55); (A) Columbia CL-6024 (d). *On a Turquoise Cloud* (1947); *New York City Blues* (1947); *Golden Cress* (1947); *Three Cent Stomp* (1947); *Hy'a Sue* (1947); *Lady of the Lavender Mist* (1947); *The Clothed Woman* (1947); *Progressive Gavotte* (1947).

Duke Ellington's Liberian Suite—Philips BBR8060 (55) (d); Columbia CL-6073. *Liberian Suite* (1947).

Duke Ellington—Philips BBL-7287; CBS 62686. *Liberian Suite* (1947); *A Tone Parallel to Harlem* (1951); (A) Columbia CL-848 (d).

Duke Ellington 1945—Queen-disc Q006 (75). *How blue can you get (Ultra blue); Tear Drops in the Rain; Time on my Hands; Ko-Ko; Honeysuckle Rose; Perdido; Air-conditioned Jungle; Waitin' for the train to come in; I'd do it all over again; If I Loved You; Fancy Dan; Homesick, that's all; Blues on the Double; Caravan.* (1945 broadcasts.)

Ellington in Concert—World Records T160 (62) (d). *How High the Moon; Brown Betty; Don't be so mean to baby; Humoresque; Dancers in Love; Creole Love Call; Don't Blame Me; Limehouse Blues; Blue Skies (Trumpet no end).* (Dec 1948.)

Ellington in Concert, Vol.2—World Records T195 (62) (d). *She wouldn't be moved; Paradise; Tootin' Through the Roof; Lady of the Lavender Mist; Suddenly it Jumped; Medley; The Tattooed Bride.* (Dec 1948.)

The Duke—Edward Kennedy Ellington 1899-1974—CBS 88077 (2) (74) (d). *Hy'a Sue; Lady of the Lavender Mist; Women; Golden Cress; It's Mad, Mad, Mad; You Gotta Crawl Before You Walk; Kitty; Brown Penny; Maybe I should change my ways; Boogie Bop Blues; Sultry Serenade; Stomp, Look and Listen; Air-conditioned Jungle; Three Cent Stomp; Progressive Gavotte; Take Love Easy; I can't believe that you're in love with me; How High the Moon; Singin' in the Rain; Don't get around much any more; I Could Get a Man; On a Turquoise Cloud.* (1947.)

The World of Duke Ellington, Vol.1—CBS 88128 (2) (75). *The Clothed Woman* (1947); *New York City Blues* (1947); *Let's go Blues* (1948); *Creole Love Call* (1948); *The Greatest there is* (1948); *Snibor* (1948); *Joog, Joog* (1949); *Good Woman Blues* (1949); *On the Sunny Side of the Street* (1949); *B sharp Boston* (1949); *Build that Railroad* (1950); *Love you madly* (1950); *Great Times* (1950); *Fancy Dan* (1951); *The Hawk Talks* (1951); *VIP's Boogie* (1951); *Jam with Sam* (1951); *Monologue* (1951); *Ting-a-ling* (1951); *Eighth Veil* (1951).

The Golden Duke—RCA Prestige PR24029 (2) (74) (d). *Jam-a-ditty; Diminuendo in Blue; Magenta Haze; Blue Skies; The Beautiful Indians (Hiawatha/Minnehaha); Overture to a Jam Session; Flippant Fury; Golden Feather; Tulip or Turnip; It shouldn't happen to a dream; Sultry Sunset; Happy-go-lucky Local.* (1946.) (Coupled with piano solos and duets.)

Pretty Woman—RCA RD7942; (A) RCA LPV-553 (68). *My Honey's Lovin' Arms; Pretty Woman; Midriff; Esquire Swank; Just Squeeze Me; Memphis Blues; I'm just a lucky so and so; St. Louis Blues; A-gathering in a Clearing; I let a song go out of my heart; Back home again in Indiana; Long, Strong and Consecutive; Tonk; Drawing Room Blues; Hey Baby; Beale Street Blues.* (1945-46.)

Duke Ellington's Greatest Hits—CBS-Realm RM52550; CBS64692; (A) Columbia CS-9629. *Satin Doll* (1958); *Don't get around much anymore* (1947); *Do nothing till you hear from me* (1947); *Take the 'A' Train* (1956);

Solitude (1957); *C Jam Blues; Mood Indigo* (1957); *I'm Beginning to See the Light; Prelude to a Kiss* (1957); *Perdido.*

The Indispensable Duke Ellington, Vol.1—RCA RD-27258 (62); (A) RCA LPM6009-1 (61). *Morning Glory* (1940); *Don't get around much anymore* (1940); *Bojangles* (1940); *Pitter Panther Patter* (1940); *Mr. J.B. Blues* (1940); *Raincheck* (1941); *Chelsea Bridge* (1941); *I didn't know about you* (1944); *Carnegie Blues* (1945); *Blue Cellophane* (1945); *Black and Tan Fantasy* (1945); *Mood Indigo* (1945.)

The Indispensable Duke Ellington, Vol.2—RCA RD-27259 (62); (A) RCA LPM6009-2 (61). *Sophisticated Lady* (1945); *Black Beauty* (1945); *The Perfume Suite* (1945); *Things ain't what they used to be* (1945); *Rockabye River* (1946); *Suddenly it Jumped* (1946); *Blue is the Night* (1946); *Just you, just me* (1946); *Swamp Fire* (1946.)

Duke Ellington and his Orchestra—(A) Big Band Archive LP1217 (74). *Riff 'n' Drill; Rugged Romeo; Passion Flower; Tip Toe Topic; Rockabye River; Sono; Jennie; Blue Abandon; The Jeep is Jumpin'; A-gatherin' in a Clearin'; A Flower is a Lonesome Thing; Suddenly it Jumped; In a Jam; Blue is the Night; Moon Mist; Suburbanite* (1946.)

Ellington Masterpieces—Columbia 33SX1022 (54); CBS 63838; (A) Columbia CL-825. *Mood Indigo; Sophisticated Lady; The Tattooed Bride; Solitude.* (Dec 1950.)

Primping for the Prom—(F) CBS 62993. *Primping for the Prom* (1952); *B sharp Boston* (1949); *Cop Out* (1958); *Walkin' and Singin' Blues* (1958); *Suburban Beauty* (1956); *Jingle Bells* (1962); *Asphalt Jungle Twist* (1961); *I can't believe that you're in love with me* (1947); *Progressive Gavotte* (1947); *Boogie Bop Blues* (1947.)

Duke Ellington 1953-54—World Records T708 (d); Capitol T1602 (63) (d). *Warm Valley* (1953); *Rockin' in Rhythm* (1954); *Prelude to a Kiss* (1953); *Satin Doll* (1953); *Caravan* (1954); *Flamingo* (1953); *In a Sentimental Mood* (1953); *Black and Tan Fantasy* (1953); *Passion Flower* (1953); *Bakiff* (1954).

Band Call—World Records TP86; (A) Capitol T-795. *12th Street Rag* (1954); *Isle of Capri* (1954); *Chile Bowl* (1954); *All Day Long* (1954); *Bunny Hop Mambo* (1954); *Satin Doll* (1953); *If I Give My Heart To You* (1954); *Blue Jean Beguine* (1953); *Echo Tango* (1954); *Band Call* (1954); *Blue Moon* (1953); *Smile* (1954).

Ellington Showcase—World Records T309, Capitol T679 (56) (d). *Harlem Airshaft* (1955); *Serious Serenade* (1955); *Clarinet Melodrama* (1955); *Blossom* (1953); *Theme for Trambeam* (1955); *Gonna Tan Your Hide* (1954); *Falling like a Raindrop* (1954); *La Virgen de la Macarena* (1955); *Don't ever say goodbye* (1953); *Big Drag* (1953).

Duke Ellington Seattle Concert—RCA (A) LJM-1002. *Skin Deep; Sultry Serenade: Sophisticated Lady; Perdido; Caravan; Harlem Suite; The Hawk Talks; Ellington Medley; Jam with Sam.* (March 1952).

Ellington Up Town—Philips BBL7003 (55); BBL 7443 (61) (d); (A) Columbia CCL-830; ML-4639. *A Tone Parallel to Harlem* (1951); *Take the 'A' Train* (1952); *Perdido* (1952); *The Mooche* (1952); *Skin Deep* (1952).

The Great Big Bands, Vol.1—Capitol T20808 (d). *Harlem Airshaft* (1955); *Stormy Weather* (1953); *Band Call* (1954); *Clarinet Melodrama* (1955); *Liza* (1953); *My Old Flame* (1953); *Frivolous Banta* (1954); *Things ain't what they used to be* (1953); *Cocktails for Two* (1953); *Three Little Words* (1953); *Ultra De Luxe* (1953); *I can't give you anything but love* (1953); *C Jam Blues* (1954).

Cottontail—Parlophone PMC1136 (61); London LTZ-N15078 (57) (d); Ember CJS-813; Polydor 54515 (d); (A) Bethlehem BPC-6005. *Summertime; Laura; I Can't Get Started; My Funny Valentine; Cottontail; Daydream; Deep Purple; Indian Summer; Everything but You; Frustration; Blues;* (1956) (Issued previously as Duke Ellington Presents.)

At the Bal Masqué—Philips BBL7315 (60), (d) (S) SBBL (61) (d), CBS63513; (A) Columbia CL1282; (S) CS8098. *Alice Blue Gown; Who's Afraid of the Big Bad Wolf; Got a Date with an Angel; Poor Butterfly; Spooky Takes a Holiday; The Peanut Vendor; Satin Doll; Lady in Red; Indian Love Call; The Donkey Serenade; Gypsy Love Song; Laugh, Clown, Laugh.* (1959.)

Ellington Jazz Party—Philips (S) SBBL516 & BBL7324 (A) Columbia CL1323, (S) JCS8127 (60) (d); CBS67285. *Malletoba Spank; Toot Suite; U.M.M.G.; All Of Me; Tymperturbably Blues; Hello, Little Girl.* (1959.) (With Dizzy Gillespie.)

Historically Speaking—The Duke—London LTZ-N15029 (56); Parlophone

PMC1116 (60); *Ember CJS-809; **Polydor 2941 202; ***CBS82108 (A) Bethlehem BCP-60. *East St. Louis Toodle-oo; Creole Love Call; Stompy Jones; The Jeep is Jumpin'; Jack the Bear; In a Mellow Tone; Ko-Ko; Midriff; Stomp, Look and Listen; Unbooted Character; Lonesome Lullaby; Upper Manhattan Medical Group.* (February 1956.) [Re-issued as *Stomp, Look and Listen, **The Big Band Sound of Duke Ellington and ***The Bethlehem Years, Vol.1.]

Duke Ellington and the Buck Clayton All-Stars at Newport—Philips BBL7152; (A) Columbia CL-933. *Take the 'A' Train; Sophisticated Lady; I got it bad and that ain't good; Skin Deep.* (July 1956.)

Ellington '55—Capitol LCT6008 (54); (A) Capitol W521 (d). *Rockin' in Rhythm; Black and Tan Fantasy; Stompin' at the Savoy; In the Mood; One o'clock Jump; Honeysuckle Rose; Flying Home; Happy-go-lucky Local.* (1953-54.)

Ellington at Newport—Philips BBL7133 (57) (d) (S) SBBL526 (59); CBS65113 (F) 63531; (A) Columbia CL934, (S) CS-8648. *Newport Jazz Festival Suite; Jeep's Blues; Diminuendo and Crescendo in Blue* (July 1956.)

Such Sweet Thunder—Philips BBL7203 (57) CBS Realm 52421; (A) Columbia JCL-1033, (S) CS-8091. *Such Sweet Thunder; Sonnet for Caesar; Sonnet to Hank Cinq; Lady Mac; Sonnet in Search of a Moor; The Telecasters; Up and Down, Up and Down; Sonnet for Sister Kate; The Star-crossed Lovers; Madness in Great Ones; Half the Fun; Circle of Fourths.* (1956-57.)

Solitude—Philips BBL7229 (58) (d), (S) SBBL532 (60) (d); (A) Columbia CL-1085. *Solitude; Where or when?; Mood Indigo; Autumn Leaves; The Sky Fell Down; Prelude to a Kiss; Willow, Weep For Me; Tenderly; Dancing in the Dark.* (1957.)

Duke Ellington—Columbia 33CX10055. *Hi'ya; Snibor; Texas Blues; The Happy One; Duke's Jam; Night Walk; You got it coming.* (1956.)

Duke Ellington—Columbia 33CX10098. *Meet Mr. Rabbit; Duke's in Bed; Just Squeeze Me; Confab with Rab; Ah Oodie Oobie; Ballad for Very Sad and Very Tired Lotus Eaters; It had to be you; Black and Tan Fantasy; Take the 'A' Train.* (1956.)

A Drum is a Woman—Philips BBL7179 (57) (d); (A) Columbia JCL951; CBS 65185. *A Drum is a Woman; Rhythm Pum Te Dum; What else can you do with a drum; You Better Know It; Madam Zajj; Ballet of the Flying Saucers; Zajj's Dream; Rhumbop; Carribee Joe; Finale. New Orleans; Hey, Buddy Bolden; Carribee Joe; Congo Square.* (Late 1956.)

Duke Ellington and his Orchestra featuring Mahalia Jackson—Philips BBL7251 (58) (d) (S) SBBL506 (59) (d); CBS 63363; (A) Columbia CL1162, (S) JCS8015. *Black, Brown and Beige.* (Feb 1958.)

The Ellington Suites—Pablo 2335 743 (Polydor) (76); (A) 2310 762. *The Queen's Suite* (1959); *The Goutelas Suite* (1971); *The Uwis Suite* (1972).

Festival Session—Philips BBL7355, (S) SBBL556 (60) (d); CBS 64063; (A) Columbia CL1400, (S) CS8200. *Perdido; Copout Extension; Dual Fuel, Parts 1-3; Idiom '59, Parts 1-3; Things ain't what they used to be; Launching Pad.* (1959.)

Blues in Orbit—Philips BBL7381, (S) SBBL567 (61) (d); (A) Columbia CL-1445. *Three J's Blues; Smada; Pie Eye's Blues; Sweet and Pungent; C Jam Blues; In a Mellow Tone; Blues in Blueprint; The Swingers get the Blues too; The Swingers Jump; Blues in Orbit; Villes Ville is the Place, man.* (1959.)

The Nutcracker Suite—Philips BBL7418 (61), (S) SBBL594 (61) (d); CBS BPG62030; (A) Columbia CL-1541. *Overture; Toot Toot Tootie Toot; Peanut Brittle Brigade; Sugar Rum Cherry; Entr'acte; The Volga Vouty; Chinoiserie; Danse of the Floreadores; Arabesque Cookie.* (1960.)

(Coupled with *Peer Gynt Suites* Nos 1 & 2 (selections)—CBS 61899; (A) CBS Odyssey 321-60252 (68).)

Duke Ellington's Concert of Sacred Music—RCA RD7811, (S) SF-7811; LSP-3582; (A) LSP-3582. *In the beginning God; Tell me it's the Truth; Come Sunday; The Lord's Prayer; Come Sunday; Will You Be There? Ain't But The One; New World A-coming; David danced before the Lord with all his might.* (1966.)

The Popular Duke Ellington—RCA SF-7835; LSA3072; INTS5006 (80); (A) LSP-3576 (66). *Take the 'A' Train; I got it bad (and that ain't good); Perdido; Mood Indigo; Black and Tan Fantasy; The Twitch; Solitude; Do nothin' till you hear from me; The Mooche; Sophisticated Lady; Creole Love call.* (1966.)

The Far East Suite—RCA RD-7894, (S) SF-7894 (d); LSA3063; (A) LPM3782, (S) LSP-3782 (67). *Tourist Point Of View; Bluebird of Delhi; Isfahan; Depk; Mount*

Harissa; Blue Pepper; Agra; Amad; Ad lib on Nippon. (1967.)

Duke Ellington Souvenirs—Reprise 64021 (5 LPs). *Harlem Suite; Mary Poppins*—highlights; *Big Band Signature Tunes; So Little Time* (and other popular songs); *Afro-bossa;* etc (1962-64).

Second Sacred Concert—United Artists UAD60007-8; (A) Fantasy 8407/8; Prestige 24045 (2). *Praise God; Supreme Being; Heaven; Something about Believing; Almighty God; The Shepherd; It's Freedom; Meditation; The Biggest and Busiest Intersection; T.G.T.T.; Don't get down on your knees to pray until you have forgiven everyone; Father Forgive; Praise God and Dance.* (1968.)

The Second Big Band Sound—Polydor Verve 2317 073. *The Old Circus Train Turn-around Blues; All Too Soon; Diminuendo and Crescendo in Blue; Blow by Blow; Trombonio-Bustoso-issimo; Rose of the Rio Grande; La Plus Belle Africaine; West Indian Pancake.* (Antibes Jazz Festival, 1966.)

And His Mother Called Him Bill—RCA (S) SF7964 (d); LSA3073; (A) RCA LPM-3906; (S) LSP-3906 (68). *Snibor; Boo-dah; Blood Count; U.M.M.G.; Charpoy; After All; The Intimacy of the Blues; Raincheck; Day Dream; Rock Skippin' at the Blue Note; All Day Long; Lotus Blossom.* (1968.)

Soul Call—Verve VLP9197, (S) SVLP9197; (A) Verve V.8701. *La Plus Belle Africaine; West Indian Pancake; Soul Call; Skin Deep; Jam with Sam.* (1966-Antibes Jazz Festival.)

Yale Concert—Fantasy 9433 (74) (d); (A) same. *The Little Purple Flower; Put-tin; A Chromatic Love Affair; Boola, Boola; Warm Valley; Drag; Salome; Swamp Goo; Up-jump; Take the 'A' Train.* (1968.)

New Orleans Suite—Atlantic 2400 135, K40209, K50403; (A) Atlantic S-1580. *Blues for New Orleans; Bourbon Street Jingling Jollies; Portrait of Louis Armstrong; Thanks for the Beautiful Land on the Delta; Portrait of Welman Braud; Second Line; Portrait of Sidney Bechet; Aristocracy à la Jean Lafitte; Portrait of Mahalia Jackson.* (1970.)

Latin American Suite—Fantasy 8419 (74); (A) same. *Oclupaca; Chico Cuadradino; Eque; Tina; The Sleeping Lady and the Giant Who Watches Over Her; Latin American Sunshine; Brasilliance.* (1970.)

The English Concert—United Artists UAD60032/3 (73) (d); Sunset SLD507/8 (2) (77). *Togo Brava Suite; C-Jam blues; Happy Reunion; Addi; Lotus Blossom; Cotton Tail; Checkered Hat; La Plus Belle Africaine; In a Mellow Tone; I got it bad; Goof (Retrospect-ion); Soul Flute* (1971.)

Third Sacred Concert-The Majesty of God—RCA SF-8406. *The Lord's Prayer; My Love; Is God a Three-letter Word for Love; The Brotherhood; Hallelujah; Every man prays in his own language; Ain't Nobody Nowhere Nothin' without God; The Majesty of God.* (1973.)

Eastbourne Performance—RCA SF-8447 (75). *The Piano Player; Creole Love Call; Don't you know I care; I can't get started. New York, New York; Pitter Panther Patter; How High the Moon; Basin Street Blues; Tiger Rag; Woods; Meditation.* (1973.) (Last recorded concert.)

Collections

The Ellington Era, 1927-1940, Vol.2—CBS BRG66302/1-3; (A) Columbia C3L-39 (3) (66). *Down in our Alley Blues* (1927); *Take it Easy* (1928); *Move Over* (1928); *Goin' to Town* (1928); *Misty Morning* (1929); *Syncopated Shuffle* (1929); *Beggar's Blues* (1929); *Flaming Youth* (1929); *Rent Party Blues* (1930); *Sweet Chariot* (1930); *Baby, when you ain't there* (1932); *Jazz Cocktail* (1932); *Rose Room* (1932); *Swing Low* (1932); *Creole Love Call* (1932); *Jive Stomp* (1933); *In the Shade of the Old Apple Tree* (1933); *I'm Satisfied* (1933); *Sumpin' about Rhythm* (1934); *In a Sentimental Mood* (1935); *Truckin'* (1935); *Showboat Shuffle* (1935); *No Greater Love* (1936); *Reminiscin' in Tempo* (1935); *Kissin' my Baby Goodnight* (1936); *Uptown Downbeat* (1936); *Exposition Swing* (1936); *Azure* (1937); *All God's chillun got Rhythm* (1937); *Dusk on the Desert* (1937); *Stepping into Swing Society* (1938); *Pyramid* (1938); *A Gypsy without a Song* (1938); *Dinah's in a Jam* (1938); *Buffet Flat* (1938); *Old King Dooji* (1938); *Pussy Willow* (1939); *Something To Live For* (1939); *Way Low* (1939); *I'm checkin' out, goodbye* (1939); *Serenade to Sweden* (1939); *Little Posey* (1939); *Weely* (1939); *Tootin' Through the Roof* (1939).

The Ellington Era, 1927-1940, Vol.1—CBS BPG62178/9/80; (A) Columbia C3L27; CBS66307 (3).

Complete Duke Ellington—Vol.1 (1928-30)—CBS S67264; Vol.2 (1928-30)—CBS S68275; Vol.3 (1930-32)—CBS 88000; Vol.4 (1932)—CBS 88035; Vol.5 (1932-33)—CBS 88092; Vol.6 (1933-36)—CBS 88137; Vol.7

Duke Ellington and his Orchestra in the 1920s.

(1936-37)—CBS 88140; Vol.8 (1936-37)—CBS 88185; Vol.9 (1937)—CBS 88210.

Complete Works—Vol.1—RCA 731.043; Vol.2—RCA 741-028; Vol.3—RCA 741.029; Vol.4—RCA 741.039; Vol.5—RCA 741.048; Vol.6—RCA 741.068; Vol.7—RCA 741.085; Vol.8—RCA 741.114; Vol.9—RCA FPM1 7002; Vol.10—RCA FPM1 7047; Vol.11 (1940)—RCA FXM1 7072; Vol.12 (1940)—RCA FXM1 7094; Vol.13 (1940)—RCA FXM1 7133; Vol.14 (1941)—RCA FXM1 7134; Vol.15 (1941)—RCA FXM1 7135; Vol.16—RCA FXM1 7201; Vol.17—RCA FXM1 7274; Vol.18—RCA RXM1 7301; Vol.19—RCA FXM1 7302; Vol.20 FXM 7303. Also boxed as Vols.1-5—RCA Duke 1; Vols.6-10—RCA Duke 2; Vols.11-15—RCA Duke 3; Vols.16-20—RCA Duke 4.

The Complete Duke Ellington, Vol.1—CBS 67264 (76). *I'm gonna hang around my sugar* (1925); *Trombone Blues* (1925); *Georgia Grind* (1926); *Parlor Social Stomp* (1926); *East St. Louis Toodle-oo* (1927); *Hop Head* (1927); *Down in our Alley Blues* (1927); *What can a poor fellow do* (1927); *Black and Tan Fantasy* (2 takes) (1927); *Chicago Stomp Down* (1927); *Sweet Mama* (1928); *Stack o'Lee Blues* (1928); *Bugle Call Rag* (1928); *Take it Easy* (1928); *Jubilee Stomp* (1928); *Harlem Twist* (1928); *East St. Louis Toodle-oo* (1928); *Jubilee Stomp* (1928); *Take it Easy* (1928); *Diga Diga Do* (1928); *Doin' the New*

Low Down (1928); *Black Beauty* (1928); *Swampy River* (1928); *The Mooche* (1928); *Hot and Bothered* (1928); *Move Over* (1928); *The Mooche* (1928).

The Complete Duke Ellington, Vol.2—CBS 68275 (76). *The Mooche* (1928); *Move Over* (1928); *Hit Me in the Nose Blues* (1928); *It's All Coming Home to You* (1928); *Hottentot* (1928); *Misty Mornin'* (1928); *The Blues with a Feelin'* (1928); *Goin' to Town* (1928); *Misty Mornin'* (1928); *Saratoga Swing* (1928); *Who said 'it's tight like that'* (1928); *He just don't appeal to me* (1928); *Freeze and Melt* (1929); *Mississippi Moan* (1929); *I Must Have That Man* (1929); *That Rhythm Man* (1929); *Beggar's Blues* (1929); *Saturday Night Function* (1929); *Jungle Jamboree* (1929); *Snake Hip Dance* (1929); *Doin' the Voom Voom* (1929); *Flaming Youth* (1929); *Saturday Night Function* (1929); *Lazy Duke* (1929); *Blues of the Vagabond* (1929); *Syncopated Shuffle* (1929); *St. James Infirmary* (1930); *When You're Smiling* (1930); *Rent Party Blues* (1930).

The Complete Duke Ellington, Vol.3—CBS 88000 (76). *Jungle Blues* (1930); *The Mooche* (1930); *Ragamuffin' Romeo* (1930); *East St. Louis Toodle-oo* (1930); *Sweet Mama* (1930); *Double Check Stomp* (1930); *Hot and Bothered* (1930); *Black and Tan Fantasy* (1930); *Big House Blues* (1930); *Rocky Mountain Blues* (1930); *Ring dem Bells* (1930); *Three Little Words* (1930); *Old Man Blues* (1930); *Sweet Chariot* (1930); *Mood Indigo* (1930); *Rockin' in Rhythm* (1930); *I'm so in love with you* (1903); *I can't realize you love me* (1930); *Them There Eyes* (1931); *Rockin' Chair* (1931); *I'm so in love with you* (1931); *Rockin' Chair* (1931); *Moon over Dixie* (1932); *It don't mean a thing* (1932); *Lazy Rhapsody* (1932); *Blue Tune* (1932).

The Complete Duke Ellington, Vol.4—CBS 88035 (76). *Baby, when you ain't there* (1932); *St. Louis Blues* (1932); *Creole Love Call* (1932); *Rose Room* (1932); *The Sheik of Araby* (1932); *Swampy River* (1932); *Fast and Furious* (1932); *Best Wishes* (1932); *Slippery Horn* (1932); *Blue Ramble* (1932); *Clouds in my Heart* (1932); *Blue Mood* (1932); *Ducky Wucky* (1932); *Jazz Cocktail* (1932); *Lightnin'* (1932); *Stars* (1932); *Swing Low* (1932); *Baby* (1932); *Any time, any day, anywhere* (1932).

The Complete Duke Ellington, Vol.5—CBS 88082 (76). *Any Time, Any Day, Anywhere* (1932); *Delta Bound* (1932); *Diga Diga Doo* (1932) (w Mills Brothers); *I can't give you anything but love* (1932) (w Ethel Walters); *Porgy* (1932) (w Ethel Waters); *I Must Have That Man* (1933) (w Adelaide Hall); *Baby* (1933) (w Adelaide Hall); *Eerie Moan* (1933); *Merry-go-round* (1933); *Sophisticated Lady* (1933); *I've got the World on a String* (1933); *Down a Carolina Lane* (1933); *Slippery Horn* (1933); *Drop me off at Harlem* (1933); *Blackbirds Medley, Parts 1 & 2* (1933); *Happy as the Day is Long* (1933); *Raisin' the Rent* (1933); *Get Yourself a New Broom* (1933); *Bundle of Blues* (1933); *Sophisticated Lady* (1933); *Stormy Weather* (1933); *I'm Satisfied* (1933); *Jive Stomp* (1933).

The Complete Duke Ellington, Vol.6—CBS 88137 (76). *Harlem Speaks* (1933); *In the Shade of the Old Apple Tree* (1933); *Solitude* (1934); *Saddest Tale* (1934); *Moonglow* (1934); *Sumpin' about Rhythm* (1934); *Admiration* (1935); *Farewell Blues* (1935); *Let's have a Jubilee* (1935); *Porto Rican Chaos* (1935); *Margie* (1935); *Moonlight Fiesta* (1935); *Tough Truckin'* (sextet) (1935); *Indigo Echoes* (sextet) (1935); *In a Sentimental Mood* (1935); *Showboat Shuffle* (1935); *Merry-go-round* (1935); *Admiration* (1935); *Cotton* (1935); *Truckin'* (1935); *Accent on Youth* (1935); *Reminiscing in Tempo, Parts 1-4* (1935); *I don't know why I love you so* (1936); *Dinah Lou* (1936).

The Complete Duke Ellington, Vol.7—CBS 88140 (76). *Isn't love the strangest thing* (1936); *No greater love* (1936); *Clarinet Lament* (1936); *Echoes of Harlem* (1936); *Love is like a Cigarette* (1936); *Kissin' my Baby Goodnight* (1936); *Oh, Babe!; Maybe Someday* (1936); *Shoe Shine Boy* (1936); *It was a sad night in Harlem* (1936); *Trumpet in Spades* (1936); *Yearning for Love* (1936); *In a Jam* (1936); *Exposition Swing* (1936); *Uptown Beat* (1936); *Rexatious* (1936); *Lazy Man's Shuffle* (1936); *Clouds in my Heart* (1936); *Frolic Sam* (1936); *Caravan* (1936); *Stompy Jones* (1936); *Scattin' at the Cotton Club* (1936); *Black Butterfly* (1936); *Mood Indigo/Solitude* (1936); *Sophisticated Lady/In a Sentimental Mood* (1936); *The new Birmingham Breakdown* (1937); *Scattin' at the Kit Kat* (1937).

Also:

Premiered by Ellington (1953)—Capitol LC6616 (53) (d).

Ellington's Greatest (1945)—HMV DLP1007 (53) (d); (A) RCA LPT-1004.

Highlights of the Great 1940-41 Band—HMV DLP1034 (54) (d).
The Duke plays Ellington (piano solos) (1953)—Capitol LC6670 (54) (d); (A) Capitol T477.
Jazz Cocktail (1932-36) (w Ivie Anderson)—Columbia 33S1044 (54) (d).
Duke Ellington's Coronets (small group) (1951)—Vogue LDE035 (55) (d); (A) Mercer LP-1005.
Duke Ellington and his famous Orchestra, Vol.1—Coral LRA10027 (55) (d); (A) Brunswick BL-54007.
Duke Ellington and his famous Orchestra, Vol.2—Coral LRA10028 (55) (d); (A) Brunswick BL-54007.
Blue Light (1935-38)—Philips BBR8086 (56) (d); (A) Columbia CL663 (d).
Saturday Night Function (1927-29)—HMV DLP1094 (55) (d).
The Duke 1926—London 'Origins of Jazz' AL3551 (56) (d); (A) Riverside RPL-1065; (F).
Duke Ellington Sidemen (1938-40)—Philips BBL7163 (57) (d); (A) Encore 22005.
A Blues Serenade (1937-39)—HMV DLP1172 (58) (d).
Newport 1948 (with Gerry Mulligan)—Philips BBL7279, (S) SBBL526 (58) (d); (A) Columbia CL1245, (S) CS-8072.
The Cosmic Scene (Spacemen)—Philips BBL7287 (58) (d); (A) Columbia CL-1198; CBS 64703.
Anatomy of a Murder (soundtrack 1959)—Philips BBL7338 (59) (d); (S) SBBL514 (61); (A) Columbia CL1360, (S) CS8166; CBS 63939.
Back to Back (with Johnny Hodges) (1959) —HMV CLP1316 (60) (d); (A) Verve MGV-8317; Polydor 2682 005 (d).
Side by Side (with Johnny Hodges) (1959) —HMV CLP1372 (61) (d); (A) Verve MGV-8345; Polydor 2682 005 (d).
Duke Ellington at the Cotton Club (1929-31)—Camden CDN-119 (59) (d); (A) Camden CAL-459 (d).
Jungle Jamboree (1927-30)—Parlophone PMC1154 (61) (d).
The Music of Duke Ellington (1928-49)—(A) Columbia CCL-558.
The Duke and his Men (1940-42)—(A) RCA LPM-1092.
Early Duke—(Sw) Jazz Panorama LP-12.
Duke Ellington, Rare and Unissued Masters—(It) Discriminate Collectors FDC-1003.
The Ellington Era, Vol.1 (1927-40)—CBS BPG62178/9/80; (A) Columbia C3L-27 (3); CBS 66307 (3).
Money Jungle (with Mingus & Roach) (1962)—United Artists ULP-1039; (A) United Artists UAL-14017, (S) UAS-5632; Solid 18022.
Piano in the Foreground—CBS BPG62204; (A) Columbia CL-2029; CBS 67252.
It's Duke Ellington—Ember EMB-3327; (A) Allegro LP-3074.
Fargo, 7th November 1940—Palm Club (S) 30 (3).
Afro-Bossa—Reprise R6069 (63); (A) R6069.
Daybreak Express—(A) RCA LPV-506.
Jumpin' Punkins—(A) RCA LPV-517 (65).
Music from 'Mary Poppins' (1965)—Reprise R6141; (A) R6141.
Duke Ellington—(Sw) Tax (S) LP-9.
Rockin' in Rhythm (1928-30)—Parlophone PMC1184 (64) (d); (A) Decca DL-79247.
The Duke, Big Band and Small—(C) International Association of Jazz Record Collectors IAJRC11.
Midnight in Paris—CBS BPG62120 (63) (d); (A) Columbia CL-1907.
Will the Big Bands Ever Come Back?—Reprise R6168; (A) Reprise R6168 & 54064.
Ellington '65—Reprise R6122; (A) Reprise R6122.
Ellington '66—Reprise R6154; (A) Reprise R6154 (65).
Concert in the Virgin Islands (1965)—Reprise R6185; (A) Reprise R6185.
Francis A. & Edward K. (w Sinatra)—Reprise FS-1024; (A) Reprise FS-1024.
Greatest Hits (1963)—Reprise R6234; (A) Reprise R6234 (67).
Hits of the 60s (1965)—Reprise R6122; (A) Reprise R6122 (64).
Duke Ellington (1943 Concert)—Saga 6902 (74).
Duke Ellington in Europe, Vol.1 (1965)—Jazz Classics JC-124 (74).
Duke Ellington, Vol.2 (1941-48)—Saga 6926 (74).
The Best of Duke Ellington (1953-54)—Capitol T1602; (A) T1602 or SM1602 (61).
A Date with 1945—Jazz Classics JC-122 (74).
Duke Ellington 1943-46 (broadcasts)—Jazz Society AA-501 (74) (d).
The Symphonic Ellington (1963)—Reprise R-6097; (A) R6097.

Peer Gynt, Suites 1 & 2/**Suite Thursday**—Philips BBL7470, (S) SBBL618 (61); (A) Columbia CL-1597; CBS BPG-62056.

Blue Rose (with Rosemary Clooney)—Philips BBL-7090; (A) Columbia CL-872.

The Big Sound—Columbia 33CX10136; (A) Verve MGV-8271 as Johnny come lately.

The Duke is on the Air (1950 broadcasts)—Aircheck 4 (74); (1952)—Aircheck 3.

Treasury of Jazz No.10—Duke Ellington—(F) RCA 130.280.

Piano in the Background—Philips BBL7460, (S) SBBL611 (61).

Ella Fitzgerald sings the Duke Ellington Songbook, Vol.1—HMV CLP1213/4; (A) Verve 64008-1/2.

Ella Fitzgerald sings the Duke Ellington Songbook, Vol.2—HMV CLP1227/8; (A) Verve 64009-1/2.

The Duke Ella's Way (excerpts)—Verve VLP-9149; 2683 059 (75).

Treasury of Jazz, No.31—Duke Ellington—(F) RCA 430.616.

The Duke Steps Out (1927-32)—RCA RD-7731.

Paris Blues—HMV CLP1499 (61).

Ellington Sidemen—HMV DLP1025 (55).

Duke Ellington and the Ellingtonians (small groups) (1950-51)—Vogue VJD525 (2) (76).

Great Ellingtonians—World Records T479/80 (2).

Johnny Hodges and the Ellington All-Stars—Columbia 33CX10098; (A) Verve MGV-8203 as *Duke's in bed.*

Duke Ellington meets Coleman Hawkins—HMV CLP1644, (S) CSD1494 (63); (A) Impulse IMPL 8018; (S) S-26.

Dance to the Duke—(A) Capitol T-637; in UK as EPs.

The Bethlehem Years, Vol.1—CBS 82108 (77).

Duke Ellington—CBS 'Epic' 24203.

Film Soundtrack, Vol.1—Storyville SLP702 (77).

The Music of Ellington—(A) CSP CCL-558.

This is Duke Ellington—(A) RCA VPM-6042 (2).

The Age of Duke Ellington and his Orchestra (1927-66)—Sunday Times STM1/2/3 & 4)—RCA PL42086 (3).

Duke Ellington and his Orchestra/ Johnny Hodges and his Orchestra—Storyville SLP243.

Duke's Big Four (1973) (Quartet)—Pablo 2310 703 (74); (A) same.

Collectors' Items (broadcasts)—DJM DJD28035 (2) (77).

English Concert (1971)—Sunset SDL507/8 (2) (77).

At Carnegie Hall (1948)—Ember EMBD2001 (2) (78); (A) JA-5140/1.

All That Jazz (1937-40) (live & broadcasts)—DJM DJLMD-8020 (2) (76).

The Best of Duke Ellington and his Orchestra—Pablo 2310 845 (80).

At Southland 1940—Collector's Classics CC-16.

Radio Transcriptions, Vols.1-5—London HMP5033/7 (78).

Up in Duke's Workshop (1969-72)—Pablo 2310 815 (79); (A) ditto.

Unknown Session (1960) (studio)—CBS 82819 (79); (A) Columbia JC-35342.

My People (original cast) (1955). Stateside SL10073; (A) Contact 1; Fly 10112.

Ellington on the Air—Pye Ember CJS-840 (73) (d).

The Great Paris Concert—Atlantic K60004 (2) (74); (A) Atlantic 2-304 (2).

Jazz at the Plaza (1958)—CBS 65779 (74); (A) Columbia C-32471.

The Best of Duke Ellington (1942-46)—Festival 130 (74).

New York Jazz 1928-33—(A) Historical HLP-19.

Ellingtonia-Revaluations—Impulse AS-9258-2 (2) (74).

My People (1963)—Philips 6369 400.

Horizons of Jazz—(F) CBS 52976.

Daybreak Express—(A) RCA LPM-506 (64).

Pure Gold (1966)—(A) RCA ANL1-2811.

Afro-Eurasian Eclipse (1971 concert)—(A) Fantasy 9498.

At Tanglewood (with Boston Pops Orchestra) (1965)—(A) Camden CAL-7052.

For Always—(A) Stanyan 10105.

First Time (with Count Basie) (1961)—(A) Columbia CS-8515 (62).

The Washington D.C. Amory Concerts (1955)—(A) Jazz Guild 1002 (76).

The Intimate Duke Ellington—Pablo 2310 787 (77).

In Harlem—(Sw) Jazz Panorama LP-17.

The Integrale Works—3 Vols—(F) RCA 731.043, 741.028, 741.029.

Duke Ellington (1928-31)—(Sw) Jazz Panorama LP-6.

Battle Royal—The Duke meets the Count—Philips BBL7528, (S) SBBL857

(62).
The Golden Duke—(A) RCA Prestige PR24029 (74).
The Legendary Duke Ellington—Pye Ember CJS852 (75).
Duke Ellington Band Shorts (1929-35) (Sound tracks)—(A) Biograph BLP-M-2 (80).
Duke Ellington and his famous Orchestra, Vol.1 (1932-8)—(G) Swingfan 1001.
Duke Ellington (1926-31)—(N) Raretone RTE23000.
Duke Ellington (1932-37)—(N) Raretone RTE23001.
Duke Ellington (1937)—(N) Raretone RTE23002.
Duke Ellington (1938)—(N) Raretone RTE23003.
Duke Ellington (1939)—(N) Raretone RTE23004.
Recollections of the Big Band Era (1962-63)—Atlantic SD1665 (75).
The Art of Duke Ellington (1963)—Atlantic ATL60 044 (2) (75).
Jazz Spectrum, Vol.17—(F) Verve 2355 020.
Hot in Harlem (1928-29)—(F) MCA 510 017 (74); (A) Decca 79241 (69).
A Date with Duke, Vol.1 (Live recordings 1945)—(A) Fairmount FA1001.
A Date with Duke, Vol.2 (1945)—(A) Fairmount FA1002.
A Date with Duke, Vol.3 (1945)—(A) Fairmount FA1003.
A Date with Duke, Vol.4 (1945)—(A) Fairmount FA1004.
A Date with Duke, Vol.5 (1945)—(A) Fairmount FA1007.
A Date with Duke, Vol.6 (1945)—(A) Fairmount FA1008.
A Date with Duke, Vol.7 (1945)—(A) Fairmount FA1009.
A Date with Duke, Vol.8 (1945)—(A) Fairmount FA1010.
Duke Ellington—27th March 1959 (broadcasts)—(A) Fairmount LPM107.
Souvenirs (a 5 record-set made up of the 7 previously released Reprise albums of the 1960s)—Warner K64021 (5) (76).
Early Ellington (1926-28)—(A) Everest Archives 221.
The Early Years (1926-28)—(A) Everest Archives 249.
Ellington Indigos (1957)—(A) Columbia CS-8053.
Fantasies—(A) Harmony 11236 (67).
Flaming Youth—(A) RCA LPV-568 (69).
In my Solitude—(A) Harmony 11323.
North of the Border (In Canada)—(A) Decca DL-75069; MCA MCF2627.
Seventieth Birthday Concert (1969)—(A) Solid State SS-19000 (2); United Artists UAD60001/2.

Mercer Ellington

(b Washington, DC, March 11 1919)
Son of Duke Ellington and collaborator in Duke's music and orchestra. Took over the band after Duke's death in 1974. In the early part of his career he did not throw in with his father but forged his own way in the music business. He formed his first band in 1939, but joined Duke to gain experience in 1941. After service in World War II Mercer Ellington led his own band until 1950 when he briefly rejoined Duke and founded his own record company. From 1955 on was associated with Duke's band with various intervals for other work. Prominent arranger and composer.

Selected LP recordings

Continuum—Fantasy FT525 (76); (A) Fantasy 9481. *Jump for Joy; Black and Tan Fantasy; Warm Valley; Drop me off at Harlem; All Too Soon; Rock Skippin' at The Blue Note; Jeeps Blues; Ko-Ko; Carney; Blue Serge; Happy-go-lucky Local* (1975.)
Also:
Stepping into Swing Society—(A) Coral CRL-57225.
Colors in Rhythm—(A) Coral CRL-57293.

Gil Evans

(b Toronto, May 13 1912)
Best known as arranger who influenced modern style via the Claude Thornhill orchestra in the 1940s and later for Miles Davis, Evans began by leading a big band between 1933 and 1938 when it was taken over by Skinnay Ennis, with Evans as arranger. His work for Thornhill (qv) either side of World War II set new standards. Associated with the evolutionary 'Birth of the Cool' headed by Miles Davis, he later (late 1950s and early 1960s) arranged famous Davis albums such as *Miles Ahead, Porgy and Bess* and *Sketches of Spain*. Also arranged during 1940s for Benny Goodman, Jimmy and Tommy Dorsey, Peggy Lee and many others. He has continued in demand as arranger and ad hoc band leader up to the present.

Selected LP recordings

The Individualism of Gil Evans—Verve 2683 045 (2) (74); (A) Verve MGV-8555 (64). *The Barbara Song* (1964); *Las Vegas Tango* (1964); *Flute Song* (1963); *Hotel Me* (1964); *El Toreador* (1963); *Cheryl* (1963-64) (Quartet); *Spoonful* (1963-64); *Concorde* (1963-64); *The Underdog* (1963-64); *General Assembly* (1964).

Great Jazz Standards—Vogue LAE12234 (60) (d), Fontana 688000 (63) (d); (A) Pacific WP-1270. *Davenport Blues; Straight, no Chaser; Ballad of the Sad Young Men; Joy Spring; Django; Chant of the Weed; Theme* (1960.)

Svengali—Atlantic SD1643, (A) K40528 (74). *Thoroughbred; Blues in Orbit; Eleven; Cry of Hunger; Summertime; Zee Zee* (1973.)

Also:

Gil Evans Orchestra (1958)—Vogue LAE12173 (d); (A) Pacific WP-1246.

New Bottle, Old Wine—(A) Pacific WP-1246.

Big Stuff—Transatlantic XTRA5034; (A) Prestige PRLP-7120, (S) S-7756; NJ-8215.

Roots—Fontana 688003; (A)-Pacific Jazz 40 (d).

Out of the Cool—HMV CLP1456, (S) CSD1367 (61) (d); Impulse IMPL8040; (A) Impulse 4, (S) S-4.

Into the Hot—Impulse IMPL8016 (76); (A) Impulse 9, (S) S-9 (62).

Gil Evans plays the Music of Jimi Hendrix (1974)—RCA LSA-3197 (75) (d).

Gil Evans Live—RCA PL-25209 (79).

The Arranger's Touch—RCA Prestige PR24049 (2) (75) (d).

Pacific Standard Time—Blue Note BNLAD-461 (75); (A) BND-4024 (2) (79).

There comes Gil Evans—(A) RCA APL1-1057.

There Comes a Time—RCA LSA3197 (78).

Empathy—Polydor 2332 087 (79).

Little Wing—Circle RK23578/13 (79).

Parabola—Horo HDLP31/32 (79).

Porgy and Bess—CBS 62108.

Maynard Ferguson

(b Montreal, May 4 1928)

First brought into prominence with fantastic high-note trumpet style by Charlie Barnet (qv); also with Boyd Raeburn (qv) and Jimmy Dorsey. Youthful prodigy, he formed his first band with his brother at age 16. Worked with Stan Kenton in 1950 and again 1952-53. Sensational soloist who led a number of big bands through the 1950s and 1960s, largely as showcases for his own playing. Strong musician in modern style with excellent supporting bands likewise in contemporary hard hitting style.

Selected LP recordings

Big Band Sound—Polydor Roulette 2432 010. *Bye Bye Blackbird; Maria; Stompin' at the Savoy; 'Round about Midnight; Dancing in the Dark; That Old Feeling; Four; I'll Be Seeing You; Tenderly; They can't take that away from me; What's new; It's a pity to say goodnight; Almost like being in love; Mangos.* (1958-62.)

Freaky—Atlantic 2464 008. *The Rise and Fall of Seven; Light Green; Kundalini Woman; Sunny; Meet a Cheetah; Molecules; Wack-wack; Satan Speaks; Alfie.* (1967.)

The World of Maynard Ferguson—CBS (S) 64101; (A) Roulette 52110, (S) S-52110. *Chala Nata; If I thought you'd ever change your mind; L-Dopa; Eli's Comin'; A Ballad to Max; McArthur Park.* (1968-69.)

Alive and Well in London—CBS (S) 64432; (A) Columbia C-31117. *Move Over; Fire and Rain; Aquarius; The Serpent; My sweet Lord; Bridge Over Troubled Water; Your Song; Stoney End; Living in the Past.* (1972.)

Also:

Carnival—(A) Colubia (S) JC-35480.

SI SI M.F.—Columbia 33SX1503 (63); (A) Roulette 52084 & RE-122 (2).

Maynard '62—Columbia 33SX1439 (62); (A) Roulette 52083.

Around the Horn—(A) EmArcy MG36076.

Two's Company (with Chris Connor)—Columbia 33SX1377, (S) SCX3415 (61).

Double Exposure (with Chris Connor)—London LTZ-K15229, (S) SAH-K6190 (62).

Jazz for Dancing—Columbia 33SX1270, (S) SCX-3338 (60).

Boy with lots of Brass (1957)—Mercury MMC14050 (60); (A) EmArcy MG-36114.

Blues Roar—Fontana TL5274 (66) (d); (A) Mainstream 56045.

Message from Birdland—Columbia 33SX1210, (S) SCX3245 (60) (d); (A) Roulette 52027.

Message from Newport—Columbia 33SX1146; (A) Roulette 52012 (59) & RE-116 (2).

Maynard Ferguson—Columbia 33SX1173 (58) (d); (A) Roulette R-25058; CBS 64101 (d).

Maynard '63—(A) Roulette 52090.
Maynard '64—(A) Roulette 52107.
Hollywood Party—(A) EmArcy MG-36046.
Jam Session—(A) EmArcy MG-36009.
Dimensions—(A) EmArcy MG-36044 (d), MG-26024.
Maynard '61—(A) Roulette R-52064 (61).
Newport Suite—Columbia 33SX1301 (61); (A) Roulette 52047 & Re-116 (2).
Maynard 1969—(A) Prestige S-7636.
The Ballad Style of Maynard Ferguson—CBS 63514 (d).
Chameleon—CBS 80216 (74) (d).
Conquistador—CBS 81839 (77); (A) Columbia PC-34457.
Ridin' High—(A) Enterprise S-13-101.
Live at Jimmy's—CBS 65952 (74) (d).
MF Horn—(A) Columbia (S) C-30466 (71).
MF Horn Two—CBS 65027 (72) (d); (A) Columbia C-31709.
MF Horn Three—CBS 65598 (73) (d); (A) Columbia C-32403.
MF Horn Four & Five Live—(A) Columbia (S) PG-32732 (2).
New Vintage—CBS 82282 (77); (A) Columbia JC-34971.
Primal Scream—CBS 81150 (76); (A) Columbia PC-33953.
Screamin' Blues—Pye MSL1021 (74) (d); (A) Mainstream 316.
Trumpets Out Front—Vogue VJD-567 (2) (80).
Birdland Dream Band—(A) Vix LX-1070.
Birdland Dream Band, Vol.2—(A) Vix LX-1077.
Come Blow Your Horn—(A) Cameo CL-1066.
Color Him Wild—(A) Mainstream 56031, (S) S-6031.

Bert Firman

(b 1906)

Firman was one of the first to organize a dance band in England and one of the first to broadcast. He was musical director for the Zonophone Company before the amalgamation with Regal, and he gathered together some of the leading London musicians for recording under the name of Bert Firman's Dance Orchestra and the Cabaret Novelty Orchestra. Among those who appeared on the Zonophone records in the 1920s and subsequently played with the big 'name' bands were Ted Heath (tb) (qv) and Joe Brannelly (g).

Selected LP recordings

The Bert Firman Bands 1925-1931—World Records SHB30 (2). *Who Takes Care of the Caretaker's Daughter* (1925); *Headin' for Louisville* (1926); *You got 'em* (1926); *Spanish Shawl* (1926); *Five Foot Two, Eyes of Blue* (1926); *Stampede* (1927); *Up Jumped the Devil* (1926); *Sax Appeal* (1927); *Sugar Foot Stomp* (1927); *Milenberg Joys* (1927); *Slippery Elm* (1927); *Hangin' Around* (1927); *Sentimental Baby* (1929); *When I met Connie in the Cornfield* (1929); *Ain't Misbehavin'* (1929); *At the End of the Lonesome Trail* (1929); *Corn-fed* (1927); *I ain't got Nobody* (1928); *Mississippi Mud* (1928); *She's a Great, Great Girl* (1928); *Didn't I tell you* (1928); *Because my baby don't mean 'maybe' now* (1929); *Slow music* (1929); *This is the way the puff-puff goes* (1929); *Diga Diga Doo* (1929); *Kansas City Kitty* (1929); *Reaching for Someone* (1929); *I've got a Feeling I'm Falling* (1929); *Lovable and Sweet* (1929); *Painting the Clouds with Sunshine* (1929); *Tip-toe Through the Tulips* (1930); *Roll On, Mississippi, Roll On* (1931). (Record 2 by The Rhythmic Eight.)
Also:
My Baby loves to Charleston (with Rhythmic Eight)—Music for Pleasure MFP1158 (67) (d).

Roy Fox

(b Denver, Colorado, October 25 1901)

Although he was born in America and began his musical career there, Roy Fox gained his major reputation in London, notably during a long stay in the 1930s at the Monseigneur Restaurant. He began playing cornet with Abe Lyman, then led a band at the Club Royale, Culver City. Subsequently played at various spots in Los Angeles, Miami and New York, then became music director for 20th Century Fox studios in Hollywood. He was at one time engaged to 'blonde bombshell' Jean Harlow, but was then called to London to form a band at the Café de Paris, and when he went back to the States Harlow was dead. As well as the Monseigneur, Fox played in London at the Kit-Cat Club and the Café Anglais. He was also Musical Director for Decca records. Suffered from poor health which frequently interrupted his career. In 1932 Lew Stone (qv) took over the

Monseigneur band, which had Nat Gonella (t, vo) and top period vocalist Al Bowlly. Fox soon returned and continued with his own band until 1939. The next years, including the war, were spent first in Australia then in California, largely for health reasons. Although he formed a new band after the war, the dance band era was over and after trying the music halls Fox eventually found success as a theatrical agent.

Selected LP recordings

The Bands that Matter—Decca 'Eclipse' ECM2045. *Londonola* (1935); *Build a Little Home* (1934); *June in January* (1934); *May I?* (1934); *Lovable* (1932); *Jungle Drums* (1934); *Goodnight, Vienna* (1932); *Living in Clover* (1932); *Corrine Corrina* (1932); *Japanese Sandman* (1935); *Everything I Have is Yours* (1934); *Drowsy Blues* (1934); *What a Perfect Combination* (1933); *Goodnight, Lovely Little Lady* (1934). (Vocals by Denny Dennis, Al Bowlly & Nat Gonella.)

Roy Fox 1936-1938—World Records SHB33 (2) (75). *Love is a Dancing Thing* (1936); *Play, Orchestra, Play* (1936); *But where Are You* (1936); *Let's Face the Music and Dance* (1936); *Rose Marie* (1936); *Calling me Home* (1936); *South Sea Island Magic* (1936); *Hit Parade of 1936* (1936); *Did your mother come from Ireland?* (1936); *The Miller's Daughter Marianne* (1936); *When the Sun says 'Goodnight' to the Mountain* (1936); *Whispering* (1936); *You do the Darndest Things, Baby* (1937); *The night is young, and you're so beautiful* (1937); *What will I tell my heart* (1937); *I've got Beginner's Luck* (1937); *Where are you?* (1937); *I've got my love to keep me warm* (1937); *The Merry-go-round Broke Down* (1937); *Fifty Million Robins can't be Wrong* (1937); *Gone with the Wind* (1937); *Can I Forget You?* (1937); *Hit Songs 1928-1937* (1937); *Things are Looking Up* (1937); *Roses in December* (1937); *Dearest Love* (1938); *I Could Use a Dream* (1938); *I fall in love with you every day* (1938); *You Leave Me Breathless* (1938); *You Went to my Head* (1938); *If it Rains, Who Cares?* (1938). (Vocals by Denny Dennis, Bobby Joy, Mary Lee, Sid Buckman, Barry Gray, etc.)

The Golden Age of British Dance Bands—World Records SH118/9 (69). *Afraid to Dream; These Foolish Things; Let's Call the Whole Thing off; This Year's Kisses; Too Marvellous for Words; That Old Feeling; Harbour Lights; I let a song go out of my heart.* (Coupled with recordings by Harry Roy, Lew Stone and Ray Noble.)

Also:

At the Monseigneur Restaurant—Decca 'Ace of Clubs' ACL1172 (64).

Fox Favourites—Decca 'Ace of Clubs' ACL1240 (67).

Strictly Instrumental—Halcyon HAL1 (79).

This is Roy Fox, 1938—Halcyon HAL7 (74).

With Vocal Refrain (1938)—Halcyon HAL9 (75).

Let's Reminisce—Music for Pleasure MFP1179.

Geraldo (Gerald Bright)

(b London, 1904; d Vevey, Switzerland, May 4 1974)

After travelling extensively in his youth, during which he absorbed a good deal of national folk music of many countries, he formed a band and played at the Hotel Majestic, St Anne's, Lancs, for five years. Also directed various orchestras in England and Europe. In 1930 he appeared at London's Savoy Hotel with a new orchestra known as Geraldo and his Gaucho Tango Orchestra, having become a devotee of the tango and other Latin American dances. In 1933 he formed a straight dance band, also at the Savoy, and in both capacities became a top attraction throughout the 1930s. He continued actively during and after World War II, modernizing his style without losing his particular personal touch. Al Bowlly (vo) often recorded with Geraldo, and the bands appeared on many popular radio shows.

Selected LP recordings

Geraldo and his Orchestra—World Records SH215 (74). *Let the People Sing* (1940); *Jealousy* (1932); *You're as Pretty as a Picture* (1938); *Deep Purple* (1939); *It's D'lovely* (1938); *You're a Sweet Little Headache* (1939); *In the Blue of the Evening* (1943); *Sunday, Monday or Always* (1943); *I Want to be in Dixie* (1943); *Blues in the Night* (1942); *Russian Salad* (1941); *Don't Sit Under the Apple Tree* (1942); *I'm Old-Fashioned* (1943); *My Guy's Come Back* (1943); *Shoo-shoo Baby* (1944); *Moonlight Mood* (1943).

Also:

Geraldo at the Royal Festival Hall—Philips BBR8055 (55) (d); (A) Epic LN-3209.

Geraldo (The Decca Record Co).

Hello Again—Parlophone PMC7139 (71) (d).
Hello Again . . . Again—Transatlantic TRA332 (76).
50 Hits of the Naughty 40s—Pickwick 50DA.308 (2) (77).
Gerry's Music Shop—Decca Vintage RFL2 (80).
Dance, Dance, Dance—(A) Camden CAL-442.
Dance, Dance, Dance, Vol.2—(A) Camden CAL-555.
Dance, Dance, Dance, Vol.3—(A) Camden CAL-652.

Carroll Gibbons

(b Clinton, Massachussets, January 4 1903; d London, May 1954)
Famous as leader of top society dance band at the Savoy Hotel, London, known as The Savoy Orpheans (the original Savoy Orpheans (qv) was formed by Debroy Somers in 1923; Gibbons took over in 1927). Continued at the Savoy through the 1930s (except for two years 1929-31 when he was in America as staff composer at MGM studios in Hollywood) through World War II and after, playing high quality dance music with his own distinctive piano prominent. This band of the 1930s contained several musicians later to become famous in their own right [George Melachrino (as, bar, cl), Paul Fenoulet (tb), Eugene Pini (vln), Ian Stewart (p), Max Abrams (d)].

Selected LP recordings

The Carroll Gibbons Story—World Records SH167/8 (72). *Mama's Gone, Goodbye* (1925); *Where'd you get those eyes* (1926); *Garden in the Rain* (1928); *Can't we talk it over* (1932); *When We're Alone* (1932); *I'll Never be the Same* (1932); *Isn't it Romantic* (1932); *I Guess I'll have to Change My Plan* (1932) (solo); *Shuffle off to Buffalo* (1933); *On the Air* (1934) (piano duet); *Living in Dreams* (1934) (piano duet); *Easy come, easy go* (1934); *Judy* (1934); *The Piccolino* (1935); *Broadway Rhythm* (1935); *I've got a feelin' you're foolin'* (1935); *These Foolish Things* (1936); *Midnight in Mayfair* (1937) (solo); *Goodnight my Love* (1937); *There's a Lull in my Life* (1937); *So Rare* (1937); *High, Wide and Handsome*-selection (1937); *A Foggy Day* (1937); *Remember Me* (1937); *Sing my Heart* (1939); *F.D.R. Jones* (1939); *There Goes my Dream* (1940); *I don't want to walk without you* (1942); *I'll Get By* (1944); *Don't You Know I Care* (1944); *It was swell while it lasted* (1945); *The Moment I Saw You* (1945).

Carroll Gibbons (from a sheet music cover) (Campbell Connelly & Co).

(With various groups including The Savoy Hotel Orpheans, The Boy Friends and featuring Al Bowlly, Leslie Douglas, Johnny Green, Anne Lenner, George Melachrino, George Metaxa and Rita Williams.)
Carroll Gibbons & the Boy Friends—World Records SH360 (79). *Who?*; Smoke Gets in Your Eyes; Don't let it bother you*; I Saw Stars; Messengers*; Walking the Chalk Line*; I'll See You again*; Love is in the air again*; Coffee in the Morning*; Tea for Two*; The Continental*; Lost in a Fog*; Take a Number from One to Ten*; If the Moon Turns Green*; Straight from the Shoulder; You Turned Your Head; Other People's Babies; Dinah*; What a Difference a Day Made*; Pardon my Southern Accent*; Heat Wave.* (Commercial tracks made for *On the Air* for Hartley's Jam 1934 & *1935. Featuring Anne Lenner (vocals).)
Also:
The Magic Touch of Carroll Gibbons—Music for Pleasure MFP1230.

Terry Gibbs

(b Brooklyn, New York, October 13 1924)
A leading vibes player in the modern idiom following on from swing style of Lionel Hampton, Gibbs played drums first, then after World War II emerged as vibes specialist with Woody Herman (1948/9), Tommy Dorsey and Benny Goodman. Formed his own big band in 1959 to take over job at the Seville Club in Hollywood. His band contained several influential jazz soloists [Conte Candoli (t), Frank Rosolino (tb), Bill Perkins (ts), Lou Levy (p) and Mel Lewis (d)] and employed leading arrangers, including Marty Paich, Al Cohn, Shorty Rogers, and especially, Bill Holman who was a foremost influence in forming the band's style.

Selected LP recordings
The Big Band Sound of Terry Gibbs—Verve 2317 112 (76). *The Fat Man; My Reverie; Back Bay Shuffle; Day in, day out; Mainstem; Nose Cone; The Song is You; Bright Eyes; Softly, as in a Morning Sunrise; Evil Eyes; You don't know what love is; Limerick Waltz; T & S.* (1960 studio recording; 1961 live recording.)
Also:
Terry Gibbs and his Orchestra—(A) Mercury MG-20440.
Explosion!—(A) Mercury MG-20704.
Launching a New Sound in Music—Mercury MMC14018 (60) (d); (A) Mercury MG20440 (59); Trip 5545.
Take It From Me (1964)—(A) Impulse AS58.
Swing is Here (1959)—HMV CLP1394, (S) CSD1324 (60).
The exciting Terry Gibbs Big Band—HMV CLP1560, (S) CSD1439 (62).

Dizzy Gillespie

(b Cheraw, SC, October 21 1917)
With Charlie Parker, Bud Powell and Thelonious Monk, one of the founders of the 'bop' movement in the 1940s; and with Parker and Louis Armstrong one of the most influential instrumentalists in the history of jazz. Played with several big bands in youth, including those of Teddy Hill (qv), Cab Calloway (qv), Earl Hines and Billy Eckstine. Extremely talented arranger who worked with many important leaders before forming his own big band in second half of 1940s. Although he has led and worked with mostly small groups and combos, he has always had a strong penchant for the big band which he often persisted in running against the current taste and the economic tides. He has also had strong leanings towards Latin American and Afro-Cuban music, the idioms of which he has exploited with great skill and imagination. In 1947 he used the outstanding conga drummer Chano Pozo and later a number of other similar musicians. In 1956 he took a band to Pakistan, the Middle East, Greece and Yugoslavia and then to Latin America, both tours subsidized by the US government. At various times since Gillespie has fronted big bands for specific purposes, often to play his own compositions, in the early 1960s in association with Lalo Schifrin. He has also worked with Latin American bands of Machito (qv) and others. He has also worked from time to time with Benny Carter (qv). A brilliant and versatile musician with a continually probing and exploratory mind, Gillespie has been for 40 years one of the formative influences in modern jazz, both as a trumpet virtuoso with a style evolving originally from Louis Armstrong via Roy Eldridge, and as composer, arranger and leader. His compositions include many modern jazz standards, such as *A Night in Tunisia, Woody'n You, Manteca, Anthropology, Rumbola* and many others.

Dizzy Gillespie (EMI Records).

Selected LP recordings

In the Beginning—RCA Prestige PR24030 (2) (74) (79). *Things to come; Good Dues Blues; One Bass Hit; Our Delight; Ray's Idea; Emanon; He Beeped When He Shoulda Bopped; I Waited for You.* (The first Gillespie Orchestra tracks of 1946; the 1st record is made up of small group sessions 1945-46; 2nd record also includes 3 small group tracks from 1950.)

Dizzy Gillespie and his Orchestra—Queen-Disc Q-003 (74). *Guarchi Guaro (Rhumbop Concerto); Soulphony in Three Hearts; Oop-pop-pa-da; I'm Be-boppin' Too; Lover come back to me; Algo Bueno (Woody 'n' You); Good Bait; Ool-ya-koo.* (1949.)

When Be-bop Meets the Big Band (Dizzy Gillespie, Vol.1 1947-49)—RCA 741 095 (74) (d). *Ool-ya-koo* (1947); *Guarachi Guaro* (1948); *Duff Capers* (1948); *Lover, come back to me* (1948); *I'm Be-boppin' Too* (2 takes) (1948); *I Should Care* (1949); *St. Louis Blues* (1949); *That Old Black Magic* (1949); *Katy* (1949); *Jump did-le-ba* (1949); *Hey Pete, let's eat mo' meat* (1949); *Jumpin' with Symphony Sid* (1949); *If Love is Trouble* (1949); *In the Land of Oo-bla-dee* (1949).

Dizzy Gillespie and his Orchestra—Saga 6920 (74); Eros ER08017; (A) Savoy MG12020. *He Beeped When He Should Have Bopped* (1946); *Groovin' High* (Sextet) (1945); *Dizzy Atmosphere* (Sextet) (1945); *Oo bop sh'bam* (Sextet) (1946); *Our Delight* (1946); *Salt Peanuts* (1946); *Two Bass Hit* (1946); *All the Things You Are* (Sextet) (1945); *Hot House** (Quintet) (1945); *That's Earl, brother* (Sextet) (1946); *Things To Come* (1946); *Emanon* (1946). (*With Charlie Parker.)

Dizzy's Delight (The Big Bands)—Phoenix LP4 (74) (d). *Our Delight* (1946); *Good Dues Blues* (1946); *One Bass Hit, No.2* (1946); *Ray's Idea* (1946); *Things To Come* (1946); *He Beeped When He Should Have Bopped* (1946); *I Waited for You* (1946); *Jersey Bounce* (with Les Hite) (1942); *Night in Tunisia* (with Boyd Raeburn) (1945); *March of the Boyds* (with Boyd Raeburn) (1945); *In the Middle* (with Georgie Auld) (1945); *Co-pilot* (with Georgie Auld) (1945); *Who* (1946); *The Way You Look Tonight* (1946); *Why Do I Love You* (1946); *All the Things You are* (1946).

Dizzy Gillespie and his Orchestra, Vol.2—(F) RCA 731.068 (74) (d). *A Night in Tunisia; Ol' Man Rebop; Ow; Oop-pop-a-da; Two Bass Hit; Stay On It; Algo Bueno; Overtime; Manteca; Good Bait; Cool Breeze; Cubana Be; Cubana Bop; Minor Walk; Swedish Suite; Victory Ball; When Be-bop met the Big Band* (1945-49).

The Big Band Sound of Dizzy Gillespie—Verve 2317 080 (74). *Evening Sound* (1955); *'Bout to Wail* (1955); *Begin the Beguine* (1955); *The Shout by Rail* (1955); *Joogie Boogie* (1957); *Flamingo* (1957); *I remember Clifford* (1957); *Hob Nail Special* (1954); *Confusion* (1954); *Cool Eyes* (1954); *Pile Driver* (1954).

20th and 30th Anniversary—BASF BAP-5060 (75). *Things to Come; One Bass Hit; Frisco; Con Alma; The Things are Here; Theme-Birk's Works.* (1968.) (Recorded at the Berlin Jazz Days Festival with Reunion Big Band to celebrate first trip to Europe in 1938 and second in 1948.)

Also:

Gillespiana—HMV CLP1484, (S) CSD1392 (61); (A) Verve 8394, (S) 68394.

A Portrait of Duke Ellington—HMV CLP1431 (61); (A) Verve MGV-8386, (S) 68386.

World Statesman (1956) (music by Quincy

Jones)—Columbia 33CX10077 (d); (A) Verve 8174.
Dizzy in Greece (music by Quincy Jones) —Columbia 33CX10144 (d); (A) Verve 8017.
Dizzy Gillespie Orchestra (1945-46)—World Records R29 (d); (A) Savoy 12020.
Dizzy Gillespie (1946-47)—RCA RD-7827 (d); (A) RCA LPV-530.
Dizzy Gillespie Orchestra (1946-49)—HMV DLP1047 (d); (A) RCA LJM-1009.
The Greatest of Dizzy Gillespie (1947-49)—RCA RD2724 (62) (d); (A) RCA LPM-2398. (Alternative Victor recordings.)
Big Band in Concert—Vogue LAE-540 (d); (A) Gene Norman GNP-23; London ZGL119 (72) & VRL-3011 (63).
The Original D.G. Big Band in Concert —Phonogram GNP-23 (75); (A) GNP-23.
Dizzy Goes to College, Vol.1 (1947 live recordings)—(A) Jazz Showcase 5000 (76).
Dizzy Goes to College, Vol.2 (ditto)—(A) Jazz Showcase 5002 (76).

Jean Goldkette

(b Valenciennes, France, March 18 1899; d Santa Barbara, California, March 24 1962)
Though born in France, he received his first musical training in Russia before going to the US in 1911. Formed a big band for RCA-Victor in 1924 with Russ Morgan as arranger and agent from 1926. Best remembered for 'all-star' recordings with band containing most of the early white jazzmen [Bix Beiderbecke, Jimmy McPartland (ct), Sterling Bose, Andy Secrest (t), Bill Rank, (tb), Tommy Dorsey, Don Murray, Jimmy Dorsey, Danny Polo (cl), Joe Venuti (vln), Eddie Lang (g) etc]. Led bands at the Ivy Ballroom in Philadelphia and Graystone Ballroom, Detroit. He was also active as booking agent for various other bands, including McKinney's Cotton Pickers (qv) and the original Casa Loma Orchestra (qv). Latterly worked largely in classical field. Gave up regular band leading in 1927 but made occasional returns in 1940s and 1950s in and around Detroit.

Selected LP recordings
Dance Hits of the 20s—RCA Camden (S) SND5014 (60) (d); (A) Camden CAL-548. *My Pretty Girl; Dinah; Charleston; Always; Who; Put your Arms Around Me, Honey; Sweet Georgia Brown; The Varsity Drag; Blue Skies; It Had To Be You.* (1959.)
The Goldkette Bands 1924-1929—(G) RCA FXM 1 7136 (75). *In the Evening; Where the Lazy Daisies Grow; It's the Blues; I want to see my Tennessee; After I Say I'm Sorry; Dinah; Cover me up with Sunshine**; Just One More Kiss**; Look at the World and Smile**; Sunny Disposish**; My Ohio Home; So Tired; Here Comes the Showboat; Just Imagine; That's what puts the sweet in Home Sweet Home; Take a Good Look at Mine; 'Ya comin' up tonight, huh?* (*with Bix Beiderbecke: 1926.)
Also:
The Victorious Bix—(Sw) Divergent 301/2 (2) (includes tracks by Goldkette.)
The Bix Beiderbecke Legend (3 tracks)—RCA RD-27225; (A) LPM-2323.
Jean Goldkette—(A) 'X' LVA-3017.

Benny Goodman

(b Chicago, May 30 1909)
Youngest brother of three who all became musicians, he played in local bands from the age of 14. Joined Ben Pollack in 1927, aged 16, and stayed until 1931. Led the pit band for the Broadway musical *Hello Daddy* in 1928 and subsequently worked in other theatre orchestras and led his own recording groups as well as playing with other groups under Red Nichols, Rube Bloom, Jack Petits, Joe Venuti, Teddy Wilson etc. He formed a band in 1933 at the instigation of impresario John Hammond for recording sessions featuring Jack Teagarden (tb, vo) and in 1934 formed a big band to play at Billy Rose's Music Hall which had Claude Thornhill (p) and used arrangements by Benny Carter, Dean Kincaide and Will Hudson. Late in 1934 Goodman won a place in the three-band booking for the National Biscuit Co's *Let's Dance* Radio programme (the other bands were Xavier Cugat (qv) and Kel Murray). It was the turning point in big band history and inaugurated the 'Swing' era. Though the impact was not immediate and a tour proved initially disappointing, it took off suddenly with the famous sensation at the Palomar Ballroom in Los Angeles when the kids went wild and not only astonished but also terrified the band, whose reputation had reached Los Angeles via the broadcasts. The same thing happened again in Chicago and by 1936 Goodman was established as the 'King of Swing'. The 1935 band [Bunny Berigan (t), Joe Harris (tb), Arthur Rollini (ts), Jess Stacy (p), Gene Krupa (d) and Helen Ward (vo)] had a freshness and spontaneity never quite

recaptured, especially in the outstanding arrangements by Fletcher Henderson (qv), and also those of Jimmy Mundy, Glenn Miller and Edgar Sampson. Later bands of the 1930s continued to use top arrangers, including more scores by Henderson, and featured between 1937 and 1938 the famous trumpet section of Harry James, Ziggy Elman and Chris Griffin. At the same time Goodman organised and extensively used the Benny Goodman Trio (Goodman, Krupa, Teddy Wilson (p)), soon extended to the Quartet with the addition of Lionel Hampton (qv), and later again to the Quintet and Sextet, the latter featuring Cootie Williams (t) and Charlie Christian (g), which were landmarks in jazz history and helped open the way for the more sophisticated jazz of the 1940s. The Goodman orchestra also flirted with more modern idioms with musicians like Wardell Gray, Zoot Sims (ts), Mundell Lowe (g) as well as Christian and others who joined for short periods. Goodman continued leading good swing-type bands into the 1970s, and even if the early freshness was no longer there and they often sounded, as did his own playing, more like imitations than inspirations, the high standard of musicianship was never lost. Goodman himself was always an outstanding clarinet player, with a decidedly hot and gutsy tone in the early days: his playing became more refined and 'pure' later, partly due to his involvement in 'straight' music when he played and recorded music by Mozart, Bartók and Copland. The Goodman bands were widely featured in films during the 1930s and 1940s, including the 1955 'biog' *The Benny Goodman Story*. He also toured extensively in Europe, Russia, the Far East and South America. Whatever one may say about Goodman's music at particular stages of his career, he was undeniably one of the most important and formative influences on the evolution of jazz as the popular music of the 20th century.

Selected LP recordings

The Fletcher Henderson Arrangements (Benny Goodman, Vol.6)—(F) RCA 741.059. *Jingle Bells* (1935); *Sandman* (1935); *Between the Devil and the Deep Blue Sea* (1935); *Get Happy* (1936); *Stardust* (1936); *You Turned the Tables On Me* (1936); *Somebody Loves Me* (1936); *Rosetta* (1937); *When it's sleepy time down South* (1937); *Changes* (1937); *I can't give you anything but love* (1937); *Wrappin' it Up* (1938); *Bumble Bee Stomp* (1938); *Please Be Kind* (1938); *It Had To Be You* (1938); *Louise* (1938).

The Big Band Sound of Benny Goodman—Polydor Verve 2317 056. *Manhouse; Swing Low, Sweet Chariot; Dear old Southland; When Buddha Smiles; Camel Hop; Can't We Be Friends; Hallelujah; I've got my love to keep me warm; Big John's Special; Bach Goes to Town; Three Little Words; If Dreams Come True; Chicago; Honeysuckle Rose; When it's sleepy time down South; Chloe; You Forgot to Remember; I know that you know* (Broadcasts 1937/8).

The Best of Benny Goodman—RCA RD8001, (S) SF8001 (t), HY1020 (75); (A) RCA LPM-4005; (S) LSP-4005 (68). *Don't Be That Way* (1938); *One o'clock Jump* (1938); *Goodnight My Love* (1936); *After You've Gone* (Trio) (1935); *Sing, Sing, Sing* (1937); *Stompin' at the Savoy* (1936); *Loch Lomond* (1937); *King Porter Stomp* (1935); *Avalon* (Quartet) (1937); *And the Angels Sing* (1939); *Goodbye* (1935). [Reissued as Legendary Performer, RCA PL12470.]

Carnegie Hall Jazz Concert—Philips BBL7000/1 (34); BBL7441/2 (61) (d); CBS BPG66202/1-2; (A) Columbia CL814/5/6 (3); OSL-160 (2). *Don't Be That Way; One o'clock Jump; Sensation Rag; I'm Comin' Virginia; When my Baby Smiles at Me; Shine; Blue Reverie; Life goes to a Party; Honeysuckle Rose; Body and Soul; Avalon; The Man I Love; I got Rhythm; Blue Skies; Loch Lomond; Blue Room; Swingtime in the Rockies; Bei mir bist du schon; China Boy; Stompin' at the Savoy; Dizzy Spells; Big John Special; Sing, Sing, Sing.* (1938.)

Benny Goodman (1935-1948)—RCA FXM1 7083 (75). *Santa Claus came in the Spring* (1935); *Get Rhythm in your Feet* (1935); *Goody Goody* (1936); *Never Should Have Told You* (1936); *Afraid to Dream* (1937); *Pop Corn Man* (1937); *True Confessions* (1937); *Show your Linen, Miss Richardson* (1939); *Here's Love in your Eyes; Stompin' at the Savoy* (Quartet) (1936); *I'm a Ding Dong Daddy from Dumas* (Quartet) (1937); *Whispering* (1938); *Undecided; Pick-a-rib; A Song was Born* (1948) (From the film.)

Benny Goodman 1937-1941—(A) Jazum 41 & 42 (76). *Sing, Sing, Sing Parts 1 & 2; Ciribiribin; Estrellita; I didn't know what time it was; Love Never Went to College; It Never Entered my Mind; Devil May Care; Ev'ry Sunday Afternoon: The Sheik; Buds won't*

Benny Goodman (Verve Records).

Bud; I surrender, dear; I can't love you anymore; Once More; These Foolish Things; Henderson Stomp; I'm Always Chasing Rainbows; I Left my Heart in Your Hand; I Hear a Rhapsody; Gone With What Draft; This is New; I'm not Complainin'; My Sister and I; Good Evening, Good Looking; I found a Million Dollar Baby; Time on my Hands. (1937-41.)

The Benny Goodman Story, Vol.1—Brunswick LAT8102 (55) (d); Coral CP11. *Let's Dance; Down South Camp Meeting; King Porter Stomp; It's been so Long; Roll 'em; Bugle Call Rag; Don't Be That Way; You Turned the Tables On Me; Goody Goody; Slipped Disc; Stompin' at the Savoy; One o'clock Jump.* (1955.)

The Benny Goodman Story, Vol.2—Brunswick LAT8103 (55) (d); Coral CP17. (Trios & quartets) *Memories of You; China Boy; Moonglow; Avalon;* (Orchestra) *And the Angels Sing; Jersey Bounce; Sometimes I'm Happy; Shine; Sing, Sing, Sing.* (1955.)

Benny Goodman Today—Decca DDS3 (2) (71); (A) London SPB-21 (2) (71). *Let's Dance; Sweet Georgia Brown; If I Had You; Baubles, Bangles and Beads; Stealin' Apples; Don't Be That Way; Willow Weep for Me; Big John's Special; Body and Soul; A String of Pearls; Poor Butterfly; Dear Dave; Roll 'em; Blue Skies; One o'clock Jump; I would do most anything for you; Benus H.B.; Sing, Sing,*

Sing; Goodbye. (1970.)
Also:
Benny Goodman, Vol.1 (mainly small groups)—(F) RCA 730.629.
Benny Goodman, Vol.2 (mainly small groups)—(F) RCA 730.707.
Benny Goodman, Vol.3 (mainly small groups)—(F) RCA 731.041.
Benny Goodman, Vol.4 (mainly small groups)—(F) RCA 731.092.
Benny Goodman, Vol.5 (Henderson arranged)—(F) RCA 741.044.
Benny Goodman, Vol.6 (Henderson arranged)—(F) RCA 741.059.
Benny Goodman, Vol.7—(F) RCA 741.072.
Benny Goodman, Vol.8 (Sampson & Mundy)—(F) RCA 741.084.
Benny Goodman, Vol.9—(F) RCA 741.102.
Benny Goodman, Vol.10 (1935-48)—(F) RCA FXM1-7083.
Benny Goodman 1937-38—Jazz Concert No.2 (broadcasts)—(A) Columbia SL-180 (2).
Benny Goodman plays Solid Gold Hits (1940-45)—CBS 88130 (2) (75).
The Benny Goodman Treasure Chest (1937-38), Vol.1—MGM C-805 (60) (d); (A) MGM 3E9 (3).
The Benny Goodman Treasure Chest (1937-38), Vol.2—MGM C-807 (60) (d); (A) MGM 3E9 (3).
The Benny Goodman Treasure Chest (1937-38), Vol.3—MGM C-810 (60) (d); (A) MGM 3E9 (3).
All The Cats Join In (1939-46)—Fontana TFL5067 (60) (d).
Benny Goodman Swings Again (1960)—Philips BBL7449 (61).
Swing, Swing, Swing—RCA Camden CDN-148 (61); (A) Camden CAL-624 (60).
The Famous Benny Goodman Orchestra 1937-38—(G) Metro 2626 003 (2).
Collectors' Gems 1929-45 (previously unissued items)—(A) Nostalgia/Columbia CSM890/891 (2).
Benny Goodman and his Orchestra (1940 broadcasts)—(A) Aircheck 16 (76).
The War Years (1943-45)—(A) Jazz Society AA-510 (76).
The Forgotten Years (1943 broadcasts)—(A) Swing Treasury 103 (76).
Early Years (1947 orchestra & small groups)—Capitol VMPM-1002 (76).
In Hollywood (1949 live)—(A) Swing Treasury 100 (76).
Hall of Fame—Black Lion BLPS-20151 (77).
Legendary Performer—RCA PL12470 (78).
Clarinet à la King—(A) Epic EE-22025.
Fortieth Anniversary Concert—Decca DBC3/4 (78); (A) London 44182/3.
The Golden Age of Benny Goodman—(A) RCA LPM-1099.
Benny Goodman 1946-49—(A) First Heard 1974-1 (75).
Giants of Swing (1969)—(A) Prestige 7644 (69).
Take It (1936-58)—(A) Swing Era LP-1001.
Benny Goodman Vols.1-5—(A) Jazum 7 & 16/19.
Benny Goodman-Hotel Astor 1943—(A) Jazum 27.
Benny Goodman (1941-52), Vols. 1 & 2—(A) Jazum 35/36.
Benny Goodman (1958-61)—(A) Jazz Rarities 30 (76).
The Sound of Music—(A) MGM C-858 (61).
The King of Swing—(A) Columbia CL817/9 (3); OSO-1810; OSL-180 (2).
Benny Goodman Combos—(A) Columbia CL-500.
Goodman Presents Eddie Sauter Arrangements—(A) Columbia CL-523.
Goodman Presents Fletcher Henderson Arrangements—(A) Columbia CL-524.
The Golden Age of Swing—(A) RCA LPT-6703 (5).
Benny Goodman in Hi-Fi—(A) Capitol W-565.
The Benny Goodman Band—(A) Capitol H-409.
Swing with Benny Goodman—(A) Harmony HL-7190.
Benny Goodman's Greatest Hits—(A) Columbia CS-9283.
This is Benny Goodman—(A) RCA VPM-6040 (2).
Sing, Sing, Sing—(A) Harmony 11271 (68).
Benny Goodman and his Orchestra (1937 broadcasts)—Fanfare 13-113 (78).
The Hits of Benny Goodman (1954)—Capitol T-1514 (62).
Benny Goodman in Moscow, Vols. 1 & 2 (1962)—RCA RD7536/7, (S) SF7536/7 (63).
The Benny Goodman Story—(A) Capitol S-706.
The Goodman Touch—(A) Capitol T-441;

Capitol LC6620 (54) (d).
The Benny Goodman Orchestra—(A) Columbia CL-534.
Sauter Arrangements—(A) Columbia CL-523; Philips BBL7043 (55) (d).
This is Benny Goodman—(A) RCA LPM-1239.
Benny Goodman Hits—(A) Capitol TT-1514, (S) DTT-1514 (61).
The Essential Benny Goodman—(A) Verve 8582, (S) 68582 (64).
The Great Benny Goodman—(A) Columbia CL-820, (S) CS-8643 (62).
Easy Does It—Capitol LC6557 (53).
The Benny Goodman Band—Capitol LC6601 (53).
Benny Goodman Jazz Concert Vols. 1 & 2 (broadcasts 1937-38)—Philips BBL7009/10 (2) (55).
Benny Rides Again—Columbia 33SX1038 (55).
Benny Goodman Orchestra—Capitol LCT6012 (55).
Goodman with Strings—Philips BBR8064 (55).
Benny Goodman Orchestra—HMV DLP1116 (56).
Benny Goodman—Capitol LCT6104 (57).
Benny in Brussels, Vols. 1 & 2—Philips BBL7299/30 (2) (59); (S) SBBL536 (60).
Happy Session—Philips BBL7318 (59); (S) SBBL539 (60).

The Sunbeam series

A label devoted to all aspects of Benny Goodman.
'Let's Dance' Broadcasts 1934-1935—(A) Sunbeam SB-100.
Rhythm Makers-Vol.1 (1935)—(A) Sunbeam SB-101.
Rhythm Makers-Vol.2 (1935)—(A) Sunbeam SB-102.
Rhythm Makers—Vol.3 (1935)—(A) Sunbeam SB-103.
'Let's Dance' Broadcasts 1934-1935, Vol.2—(A) Sunbeam SB-104.
B.G. on the Air 1935-1936—(A) Sunbeam SB-105.
Benny Goodman in a Mellotone Manner 1930-31—(A) Sunbeam SB-106.
Benny Goodman on the Side 1929-1931—(A) Sunbeam SB-107.
Ben Selvin and his Orchestra featuring Benny Goodman, Vol.1 1929-1931—(A) Sunbeam SB-108.
Ben Selvin and his Orchestra featuring Benny Goodman, Vol.2 1931—(A) Sunbeam SB-109.
Ben Selvin and his Orchestra featuring Benny Goodman, Vol.3 1931-1933—(A) Sunbeam SB-110.
Benny Goodman Accompanies the Girls 1931-33—(A) Sunbeam SB-111.
The Rare B.G. 1927-1929—(A) Sunbeam SB-112.
Hotsy Totsy Gang with Benny Goodman 1928-1930—(A) Sunbeam SB-113.
Benny Goodman with the Whoopee Makers 1928-29—(A) Sunbeam SB-114.
Ted Lewis and his Band featuring Benny Goodman 1931-1932—(A) Sunbeam SB-115.
Benny Goodman at the Madhattan Room—(A) Sunbeam SB-116/126.
Benny Goodman at the Madhattan Room 1937/Carnegie Hall Encores—(A) Sunbeam SB-127.
Benny Goodman from the Congress Hotel 1936—(A) Sunbeam SB-128/132.
B.G. with Chick Bullock and Steve Washington (1933)—(A) Sunbeam SB-133.
B.G. with Adrian Rollini and his Orchestra (1933-1934)—(A) Sunbeam SB-134.
B.G. with Vincent Rose 1934/Jack Teagarden 1934/Reginald Foresythe 1935—(A) Sunbeam SB-135.
B.G. with Ben Pollack 1926-1931—(A) Sunbeam SB-136.
Red Nichols 1929-1931 featuring Benny Goodman—(A) Sunbeam SB-137.
Benny Goodman-The Early Years 1931-1933—(A) Sunbeam SB-138.
Benny Goodman-The Early Years 1933-1934—(A) Sunbeam SB-139.
Benny Goodman-The Early Years 1934-1935—(A) Sunbeam SB-140.
Benny Goodman's Boys 1928-1929—(A) Sunbeam SB-141.
Benny Goodman on V-Disc, Vol.1 1941-1945—(A) Sunbeam SB-142.
Benny Goodman on V-Disc, Vol.2 1945-1946—(A) Sunbeam SB-143.
Benny Goodman on V-Disc, Vol.2 1938-1948—(A) Sunbeam SB-144.

Henry Hall

(b Peckham, London, May 2 1898)
Musical training at Trinity College, subsequently studied for the Civil Service. He was for some time connected with the Salvation Army music department. Later

organized dance bands, notably at Gleneagles Hotel with which he has been associated ever since, beginning in 1924. In 1932 he joined the BBC and formed the BBC Dance Orchestra in succession to Jack Payne (qv). Remained with the BBC for many years, broadcasting regularly at 5.15 pm, presenting a varied programme of good dance music and 'novelty' numbers. The band played on a regular basis and contained a selection of good musicians of the period [Frankie Wilson (t), Bill Mulraney (tb), Bert Read (p), Len Bermon and George Elrick (d)]. Organised bands for the maiden voyage of the liner *Queen Mary* in 1936. Active throughout the war years presenting popular material in various contexts, and continued in similar capacities through 1950s, 1960s and 1970s.

Selected LP recordings

Henry Hall and the BBC Dance Orchestra—World Records SH140 (71). *The Music goes 'Round and Around* (1936); *Little man, you've had a busy day* (1934); *The Man on the Flying Trapeze* (1935); *Play to me, Gypsy* (1934); *Underneath the Arches* (1932); *I like Bananas* (1936); *Butterflies in the Rain* (1933); *Just an Echo in the Valley* (1932); *Music Hath Charms* (1935); *Wheezy Anna* (1933); *Did you ever see a Dream Walking* (1933); *Oh Johanna!* (1933); *Rusty and Dusty* (1936); *Somewhere at Sea* (1936); *It's a Sin To Tell A Lie* (1936); *Here's to the Next Time* (1932). (Vocals by George Elrick, Phyllis Robbins, Les Allan, Flanagan & Allen, Dan Donovan, Len Berman, Leslie Sarony, etc.)

Henry Hall (from a 1932 sheet music cover) (Victoria Music Publishing Co).

It's Five Fifteen and Time for Henry Hall and the BBC Dance Orchestra—World Records SH172 (73). *Five-Fifteen* (1933); *Have You Ever Been Lonely?* (1933); *Goody-Goody* (1936); *Wagon Wheels* (1934); *The Waltz in Swing Time* (1936); *Mine for Keeps* (1934); *The Sun Has Got His Hat On* (1932); *Wild Ride* (1934); *It's just the Time for Dancing* (1932); *An Elephant Never Forgets* (1934); *I'm putting all my eggs in one basket* (1936); *Teddy Bears' Picnic* (1932); *Life begins when you're in love* (1936); *I heard a Song in a Taxi* (1936); *One, Two, Button Your Shoe* (1937); *It's Time to Say Goodnight —Here's to the Next Time* (1933-34). (Vocals by Val Rosing, Les Allen, George Elrick, etc.)

This is Henry Hall—World Records SHB48 (2) (78). *Henry Hall Calling* (from Olympia) (1933); *Lullaby of the Leaves* (1932); *Leave the Pretty Girls Alone* (1933); *Keep it to Yourself* (1933); *It's the Talk of the Town* (1933); *Making conversation* (1933); *It's Time to say Goodnight* (1934); *East Wind* (1934); *I was in the mood* (1934); *The Three of Us* (1934); *Love Thy Neighbour* (1934); *Carolina* (1934); *Sweetmeat Joe the Candyman* (1934); *Olga Pullofski, the Beautiful Spy* (1935); *Many Happy Returns of the Day* (1935); *Just little Bits and Pieces* (1935); *Misty Island of the Highlands* (1935); *When the Guardsman started Crooning on Parade* (1935); *The Broken Record* (1936); *Buffoon* (1936); *Apple Blossoms* (1936); *Saddle your Blues to a Wild Mustang* (1936); *There's a Gold Mine in the Sky* (1938); *Under the Double-Eagle* (1938); *You Took the Words Right Out of my Heart* (1938); *Hall Marks* (1938); *Silver on the Sage* (1938); *The Highland Swing* (1938); *Blue Skies are Round the Corner* (1939); *One Man went to Blow* (1939); *If ever a Heart was in the Right Place* (1939). (Vocals by Val Rosing, Len Berman, Les Allen, Phyllis Robbins, Dan Donovan, Bob Mallin, Leslie Douglas, Anita Riddell, etc.)

Lionel Hampton

(b Louisville, Kentucky, April 12 1909)
Hampton shot to fame as founder member of the Benny Goodman Quartet in 1936, but he

had been active in jazz for many years before, first as a drummer, later on vibes, also as a typically forthright and simplistic pianist. After working around Chicago he ended a tour in California and, after a spell with Paul Howard, he worked as house musician at Sebastian's Cotton Club in Culver City, then joined Les Hite's band and began to work at the vibes. During 1935 and 1936 he led a band in California and sat in with Goodman and drummer Gene Krupa (qv) with the result that he joined the Goodman organisation and brought the Trio up to the Quartet. He stayed with Goodman until 1940, recording with small groups, and then formed his own band on the West Coast. The band reflected Hampton's outgoing, extrovert personality, innate showmanship and developing style through hard driving boogie based on early bop. He did not keep the full big band in being for long, returning to the smaller groups in which he always excelled. He went on government backed goodwill tours and appeared in several films, including *The Benny Goodman Story*. Irrepressible energy and persona in all contexts—a typical band example was the celebrated *Flying Home*. The Hampton band of the 1940s contained at various times many musicians who later became famous in other organisations, notably Ellington and Basie's, [Joe Newman, Al Killilan, Emmett Berry, Cat Anderson, Snooky Young, Wendell Culley, Kinney Dorham, Ed Mullens (t), Britt Woodman, Fred Beckett, Al Grey (tb), Dexter Gordon, Al Sears, Johnny Griffin (ts), Charlie Fowlkes (bar) and Charlie Mingus (b)].

Lionel Hampton.

Selected LP recordings

Hamp's Boogie Woogie (1942-46) (also septet & quartet tracks)—Brunswick LA8527; (A) Decca DL-5230.

All American Award Concert—Brunswick LAT8086 (d); (A) Decca 8088.

Hamp's Big Band—(A) Audio Fidelity AFLP-1913 (6), (S) AFSD-5913.

Apollo Hall Concert, 1954—Philips BBL7444 (61); (A) Epic LN-3190.

Hamp—Music for Pleasure MFP-1040; (A) Verve MGV-8019.

Lionel Hampton and his Orchestra—(A) Lion L-70064.

The Big Band Sound of Lionel Hampton—Polydor Verve 2317 079 (74) (d).

Lionel Hampton's Golden Favourites—(A) Decca DL-74296.

Steppin' Out (Hampton Vol.1) (1942-44)—(F) MCA 510.041.

Slide, Hamp, Slide (Hampton, Vol.2)—(1945-46)—(F) MCA 510.063.
Light my Fire—(A) Manhattan 5004 (80).
Easy Living—(A) Manhattan MAN-5030 (80).

Jack Harris

Jack Harris was one of several Americans who settled in London in the 1930s and helped to establish and perpetuate the dance band tradition. Others were the Starita brothers and Roy and Carroll Gibbons who both became well-known band leaders. Harris had directed bands in America at the Rector's Club, the Café Royal and Shubert's Century Roof in New York. He came to London in 1927 playing at the Embassy Club, Grosvenor House, the Café de Paris, and the Monseigneur, becoming a strong rival to the Ambrose band. In 1937 he went into partnership with Ambrose and took over Ciro's. Recorded prolifically between 1937 and 1939 and built up an orchestra at this time which frequently broadcast and contained such excellent jazzmen as Bill Amstell, Eric Breeze, Lew Davis, Max Goldberg, Alfie Noakes, Jock Cummings and used arrangements by Bill Sniderman, Jack Penn and Sid Phillips. Ciro's closed in 1939 and Jack Harris led an excellent band on stage at the London Palladium. Then went on a nation-wide tour. In April 1940 they were playing for the BBC at Bristol and appeared in a Jazz Jamboree at the Gaumont State, Kilburn. Returned to America in 1940 and found it difficult to come back, so he formed a band in America and worked there for the rest of his career.

Selected LP recordings

Jack Harris and his Orchestra—World Records SH219. *Amoresque* (1937); *Wake Up and Live* (1937); *Once in a While* (1938); *Toy Trumpet* (1937); *The Gypsy in my Soul* (1938); *How many Rhymes can you get* (1937); *Cry, Baby, Cry* (1938); *Caravan* (1937); *Swing Band* (1939); *I Can't Face the Music* (1938); *Back to Back* (1939); *Amazon goes A-wooing* (1937); *I'm Sorry for Myself* (1939); *It looks like Rain in Cherry Blossom Lane* (1937); *The Snake-charmer* (1938); *Mr. Reynard's Nightmare* (1939).

Coleman Hawkins

(b St Joseph, Missouri, November 12 1904; d New York, May 19 1969)

Although after his ten-year stay with Fletcher Henderson (qv) when he established the place of the tenor saxophone in jazz once and for all, Coleman Hawkins mostly played solo or led small groups, he did front a big band between 1939 and 1941 in New York. He had previously organized a nine-piece group with which he made, more or less as an afterthought, his most famous recording, the 1939 *Body and Soul.* His subsequent big band contained excellent musicians [Sandy Williams (tb) and J.C. Heard (d)] but was not a commercial success and did not last. Prior to World War II worked in London with Jack Hylton. Played an important part in the evolution of modern jazz and continued working until his death; but never again led a big band.

Selected LP recordings

Coleman Hawkins Memorial—Jazz Society AA504 (74) (d). *Chant of the Groove* (1940); *Georgia on my Mind* (with Benny Goodman Orchestra) (1941); *California, Here I Come* (1940); *King Porter Stomp* 1940); *Blue Room* (1940); *Body and Soul* (1944); *The Man I Love* (with Paul Baron Orchestra) (1944); *Mop Mop* (Quintet) (1944); *Sweet Adeline* (1940); *The Sheik of Araby* (1940); *I can't believe that you're in love with me* (Quintet) (1940).
Also:
Coleman Hawkins at the Savoy (1940)—(A) Sunbeam SB-204.
Stompin' at the Savoy (1940 broadcast) (also Count Basie)—(D) Collector's Classics CC8.
Hollywood Stampede (1945)—Capitol T20435 (63).
Coleman Hawkins with The Ramblers—Decca 'Ace of Clubs' ACL1247.

Erskine Hawkins

(b Birmingham, Alabama, July 26 1914)

Led a popular swing band in the 1930s and 1940s, having established reputation with a hard hitting version of *Tuxedo Junction.* Hawkins himself played trumpet in a somewhat flashy style with high note pyrotechnics, but the band had a hard swing and powerful ensemble. Played a good deal at the Savoy Ballroom, Harlem, also at the Ubangi Club. Pianist Avery Parrish was responsible for many of the arrangements, most notably for the piano feature *After Hours* which gave the band another popular hit. The band contained good jazz soloists [Dud Bascombe,

Bobby Johnson (t), Julian Dash (ts), Heywood Henry (cl) and Matthew Gee (tb)] and continued actively working through the 1950s. Hawkins himself subsequently led small groups in the 1960s and 1970s.

Selected LP recordings

Swingin' in Harlem (1936-38)—(Sw) Tax M8014 (74) (d). *Swingin' in Harlem* (1936); *Coquette* (1936); *Big John Special* (1936); *A Swingy Little Rhythm* (1936); *Dear old Southland* (1937); *Uproar Shout* (1937); *I'll see you in my dreams* (1937); *If You Leave Me* (1937); *Way down upon the Swanee River* (1937); *I found a New Baby* (1937); *Red Cap* (1937); *I'll get along somehow* (1937); *Let me Day Dream* (1938); *Lost in the Shuffle* (1938); *Who's Sorry Now* (1938); *Carry me back to old Virginny* (1938).

Erskine Hawkins and his Orchestra, Vol.2 (1938-40)—(F) RCA 741.116 (74) (d). *Rockin' Rollers Jubilee* (1938); *Miss Hallelujah Brown* (1938); *Swingin' on Lennox Avenue* (1939); *Hot Platter* (1939); *Weddin' Blues* (1939); *Baltimore Bounce* (1939); *Saboo* (1939); *Dolimite* (1940); *Gabriel meets the Duke* (1940); *Song of the Wanderer* (1940); *Junction Blues* (1940); *Sweet Georgia Brown* (1940); *Five o'clock Whistle* (1940); *Soft Winds* (1940); *Nola* (1940); *No use Squawkin'* (1940).

Erskine Hawkins and his Orchestra, Vol.3 (1941-46)—(F) RCA FPM1 7024 (75) (d). *Uncle Bud* (1941); *Black Out* (1941); *Shipyard Ramble* (1941); *Don't Cry, Baby* (1942); *Bicycle Bounce* (1942); *Lucky Seven* (1942); *Country Boy* (1942); *Tippin' In* (1945); *Hey, Doc* (1941); *Bear Mash Blues* (1942); *Caldonia* (1945); *Drifting Along* (1945); *Good Dip* (1945); *Holiday for Swing* (1945); *Sneakin' Out* (1946).

Also:

Erskine Hawkins and his Orchestra, Vol.1 (1928-38)—(F) RCA 730.708 (73).

Erskine Hawkins and his Orchestra, Vol.4 (1938-48)—(F) RCA FXM1-7126 (75).

Erskine Hawkins and his Orchestra, Vol.5 (1949-50)—(F) RCA FXM1-7232 (76).

One Night Stand (1946 broadcast)—(A) Joyce LP-1013 (75).

The Twentieth Century Gabriel (1939-49)—(A) Sounds of Swing LP-113.

After Hours—(A) Coral CRL-56061.

After Hours—(A) RCA LPM-2227 (60).

Hawk blows at Midnight—(A) Decca 4081, (S) 74081.

25 Golden Years—(A) Imperial 9191.97, (S) 12191.97.

Sneakin' Out—First Heard FH30 (79).

Ted Heath

(b Wandsworth, March 30 1900; d Surrey, November 18 1969)

Played trombone with leading British bands, Jack Hylton, Ambrose, Sydney Lipton and Geraldo. Formed his own band in 1945 and achieved success with jazz based modernistic arrangements brilliantly executed, especially in the later years. At various times band contained many top British jazzmen [Kenny Baker, Bobby Pratt (t), Don Lusher, John Keating (tb), Ronnie Scott (ts) and Jack Parnell (d)]. Heath's insistence on playing the same solos in the same arrangements all the time somewhat limited the band's potential jazz appeal; but it still maintained its place as one of the outstanding British units well into the 1960s. The Heath band recorded regularly for Decca and toured the US on several occasions with notable success. Used strong arrangements by Tadd Dameron, Bill

Ted Heath (The Decca Record Co).

Finnegan, John Keating etc.

Selected LP recordings

Swing is King—Decca LK4911, (S) PFS4135 (68); DGS6 (79); (A) London 44104 (68). *Flying Home; Cherokee; Begin the Beguine; One o'clock Jump; Song of India; The Woodchoppers' Ball; Elks' Parade; In the Mood; Two o'clock Jump; Contrasts; Take the 'A' Train; Sing, Sing, Sing.* (1968.)

21st Anniversary Album—Decca LK4903, (S) SKL4903 (68) (d); (A) London 535 (68). *Listen to my Music; Opus One; Swingin' Shepherd Blues; Holiday for Strings; Flying Home; Beaulieu Abbey; How High the Moon; Carioca; Bill; Johnny One Note; My Favourite Things; Camden Reunion.* (1967.) (Spoken tributes by Stan Kenton, Woody Herman, Johnny Mathis, Marlene Dietrich; with Count Basie & Ralph Dollimore.)

Big Band Blues—Decca LK4324, (S) SKL4074 (60) (d); SPA244 (72). *St. Louis Blues; Memphis Blues; Blues in the Night; Limehouse Blues; Basin Street Blues; The Jazz me Blues; St. James' Infirmary Blues; Tin Roof Blues; It's the Bluest Kind of Blues my Baby Sings; Honky Tonk Train Blues; A Blues Serenade; Royal Garden Blues.* (1959.)

The Big Band World of Ted Heath—Decca PA54, (S) SPA54 (70). *Opus 1* (1969); *The girl from Ipanema* (1966); *Hawaiian War Chant* (1964); *Michael Row the Boat Ashore* (1966); *More* (1966); *Flying Home* (1968); *My Favourite Things* (1965); *Fever* (1966); *Mirage* (1963); *Theme from 'A Summer Place'* (1966); *Bass in the Hole* (1964); *Sabre Dance* (1963).

My Very Good Friends The Bandleaders—Decca LK4344, (S) SKL4090 (60). *Sing, Sing, Sing; Sleepy time down South; Sorta Crazy; One o'clock Jump; I've got my love to keep me warm; Cherokee; Intermission Riff; Tuxedo Junction; Apple Honey; Take the 'A' Train; Dragnet; Night Train* (1960.)

The Years of Fame—Decca DPA3077/8 (79). *Listen to my Music/King's Cross Climax* (1956); *Blacksmith Blues* (1952); *Hot Toddy* (1953); *The Hawk Talks* (1953); *Lullaby of Birdland* (1953); *Lush Slide* (1954); *Send for Henry* (1955); *Stonehenge* (1956); *Cloudburst* (1955); *Malaguena* (1955); *The Faithful Hussar* (1956); *Hawaiian War Chant* (1956); *Walking Shoes* (1956); *Armen's Theme* (1956); *Lullaby of the Leaves* (1957); *Cool for Cats* (1957); *Swingin' Shepherd Blues* (1958); *Tequila* (1958); *Stardust* (1958); *The Champ* (1958); *Eloquence* (1958); *Sermonette* (1959); *I've got my love to keep me warm* (1959); *Cherokee* (1959); *Limehouse Blues* (1959); *Bags' Groove* (1959); *Doodlin'* (1959); *Beaulieu Abbey* (1959); *Bakerloo Non-stop* (1960); *Jubilation T. Cornpone* (1960); *Bombaby Duckling* (1964); *Johnny One Note* (1961).

Ted Heath salutes Tommy Dorsey—Decca (S) PFS4346 (76). *Marie; Chloe; Swanee River; I get a kick out of you; Well, git it; Song of India; Trombonology; On the Alamo; On the Sunny Side of the Street; Opus 1.*

Also:

Tempo for Dancers—Decca LF1037 (52) (d).

Listen to my Music—Decca LF1060 (53) (d).

Listen to my Music, No.2—Decca LF1064 (53) (d).

At the London Palladium—Decca LK4062 (54) (d); Decca 'Eclipse' ECS2164 (76) (A) London LL-802.

Strike up the Band—Decca LK4064 (54) (d).

Fats Waller Album—Decca LK4074 (54) (d); (A) London LL-978.

100th London Palladium Sunday Concert—Decca LK4075 (54) (d), Decca 'Eclipse' ECS2091 (71); (A) London LL-1000.

At the London Palladium, Vol.2—Decca LK4134 (55) (d); (A) London LL-1211.

At the London Palladium, Vol.3—Decca LK4097 (55) (d); (A) London LL-1379.

Gershwin for Moderns—Decca LK4098 (55) (d); (A) London LL-1217.

Kern for Moderns—Decca LK4121 (55) (d); (A) London LL-1279.

Rodgers for Moderns—Decca LK4148 (56); (A) London LL-1500.

Ted Heath's First American Tour—Decca LK4167 (56) (d); (A) London LL-1564.

Listen to my Music—Decca LK4165 (56) (d); (A) London LL-1475.

A Yank in Europe—Decca LK4191 (57) (d); (A) London LL-1676.

Spotlight on Sidemen—Decca LK4204 (57); (A) London LL-1721.

Ted Heath Showcase—Decca LK4210 (57) (d); (A) London LL-1737.

Ted Heath recalls The Fabulous Dorseys—Decca LK4224 (57) (d); Decca Eclipse ECM2004, (S) ECS2004 (70); (A) London LL-1743.

All Time Top Twelve—Decca LK4208

(58) (d); (S) SKL4054 (59); (A) London LL-1716, (S) 117 (58).
Al Jolson Classics—Decca LK4227 (58) (d); (A) London LL-1776.
Olde Englyshe—Decca LK4280 (58) (d); London 3058.
Hits I Missed—Decca LK4275 (58) (d); (A) London 3057, (S) 116 (58).
Shall we Dance?—Decca LK4299, (S) SKL4046 (59); (A) London 3062, (S) 148 (59).
Great Film Hits—Decca LK4307, (S) SKL4055 (59); (A) London LL-3106.
Pop Hits from the Classics—Decca LK4315, (S) SKL4066 (59).
Our Kind of Jazz—Decca LK4262 (59); (A) London 140.
Ted Heath in Concert—Decca LK4331, (S) SKL4079 (60) (d).
The Instruments of the Dance Orchestra—Decca LK4374, (S) SKL4117 (60) (d).
The Big Band Dixie Sound—Decca LK4076, (S) SKL4117 (61) (d).
Big Band Percussion—Decca (S) PFS4004 (62); (A) London 44002 (61).
Big Band Bash—Decca (S) PFS4018 (63); (A) London 44017.
Satin Saxes and Bouncing Brass—Decca (S) PFS4023 (63); (A) London 44023 (63).
Big Band Spirituals—Decca (S) PFS4031 (64); (A) London 44036 (64).
Coast to Coast—Decca (S) PFS4049 (64); (A) London 44284 (64).
The Palladium Revisited—Decca (S) PFS4046 (64).
The Sound of Music—Decca (S) PFS4065 (65); (A) London 44063 (65).
Fever—Decca (S) PFS4082 (66).
Pow—Decca (S) PFS4099 (66) (d); (A) London 44079 (66).
Swing is King, Vol.2—Decca (S) PFS4146 (69); DGS20 (80); (A) London 44113 (69).
Ted Heath recalls The Fabulous Dorseys—Decca 'Eclipse' ECM2004, (S) ECS2004 (70).
The Big Ones—Decca (S) PFS4182 (70).
Beatles, Bach and Bacharach—Decca (S) PFS4210 (71).
Those Were The Days—Decca (S) PFS4229 (71) (d).
World of the Big Band Blues—Decca (S) SPA244 (72).
Salute to Glenn Miller—Decca (S) PFS4259 (73).
Big Band Themes Remembered, Vol.1—Decca (S) PFS4303 (74).
Big Band Themes Remembered, Vol.2—Decca (S) PFS4304 (75).
Swing meets Latin—Decca (S) DS3210/2 (75); (A) London 44038.
Ted Heath salutes The Duke—Decca (S) PFS4328 (75).
Ted Heath salutes Benny Goodman—Decca (S) PFS4357 (76).
Ted Heath Years—Decca SPA497 (77).
Ted Heath Band In Concert—Decca (S) PFS4408 (77).
Swing is King—Decca (S) DS3198-1/2 (2) (78).
Focus on Ted Heath and his Orchestra—Decca (S) FOS29/30 (2) (78).
The Beginning—Decca DDV5015/6 (79).

Fletcher Henderson

(b Cuthbert, Georgia, December 18 1898; d New York, December 29 1952)
Originally studied at Atlanta to be a chemist; but soon turned to music along with his younger brother, Horace (qv). Acted as piano accompanist for many leading blues singers, including Bessie Smith, Ma Rainey, Trixie Smith, Ida Cox and Alberta Hunter. First led his own band in 1923 for the Roseland Ballroom, New York, where he remained for seven years and achieved nationwide reputation. The importance of the Henderson band lay not only in the music it styled but in the way it became a nursery or 'forcing ground' for many of the great black jazzmen. The young Louis Armstrong was with Henderson in 1924/25, and Coleman Hawkins gave the tenor saxophone its definitive voice in jazz during the 1920s which remained unchallenged until the advent of Lester Young a decade later. Over the years the muster of Henderson musicians was second to none [Tommy Ladnier, Joe Smith, Joe Thomas, Bobby Stark, Rex Stewart (t), Jimmy Harrison, Benny Morton, Sandy Williams, J.C. Higginbotham (tb), Don Redman (as), Buster Bailey, Benny Carter (as, cl), Ben Webster (ts), John Kirby (b); also at various times Henry Allen (t), Russell Procope (as, cl), Dicky Wells (tb) and many others]. Despite superb personnel and musical quality, the Henderson band had a somewhat uncertain existence, partly because Henderson himself was too easy going. Like a number of others it had a rough ride during the worst Depression years, but then it secured a good job at Connie's Inn, Harlem.

At the same time Henderson developed major talent as an arranger. He had residency at Chicago's Grand Terrace, but disbanded in 1939. When the 'swing' era opened in 1935, Henderson's music was of the right kind at the right time; but the accolade went to Benny Goodman and Henderson's main contribution was a series of brilliant arrangements for the Goodman band, using the 'call and response' style he had developed with his own. The best of these, *King Porter Stomp, Blue Skies, When Buddah Smiles, Honeysuckle Rose* etc remain classics of the 'swing' era and its best justification. During the 1940s, while continuing to arrange for Goodman, Henderson led occasional bands of his own, but without former success. A stroke ended his career late in 1950, leaving the memory of a man who achieved much but was ultimately disappointed, the major reward for his work being reaped by others. A set of his recordings (CBS) was aptly titled *A Study in Frustration.* Fletcher Henderson seems to have lacked the tough hard-headedness (and at times hard-heartedness) of the kind that enabled Benny Goodman to prosper using his fine work.

Selected LP recordings

Rare Fletcher Henderson Masterpieces —VJM VLP10 (66) (d). *31st Street Blues* (1924); *Old Black Joe's Blues* (1924); *Chicago Blues* (1924); *Why Put the Blame on Me* (1924); *Jiminy Gee* (1924); *Jealous* (1924); *I can't get the one I want* (1924); *Wait'll you see my gal* (1924); *Hard-hearted Hannah* (1924); *Charlie, my Boy* (1924); *One Of These Days* (1925); *Then I'll be happy* (1925); *Sleepy-time Gal* (1925); *Sorry* (1925).

Fletcher Henderson—Biograph BLPC-12 (74). *Shanghai Shuffle* (1924); *Naughty Man* (1924); *The Meanest Kind of Blues* (1924); *Naughty Man* (1924); *How come you do me like you do* (1924); *Everybody Loves my baby* (1924); *Memphis Bound* (1925); *When you do what you do* (1925); *Money Blues* (1925); *Carolina Stomp* (1925); *Casa Loma Stomp* (1932); *Great Caesar's Ghost* (1937); *Let's go Home* (1941).

Harlem Jazz 1921-1931—Classic Jazz Master CJM1 (74) (d). *Chicago Blues* (1924); *Why Put the Blame on Me* (1924). (With tracks by Mills Blue Rhythm, Cab Calloway and interesting smaller groups.)

Fletcher Henderson's Orchestra-1924-1926—VJM VLP36 (74) (d). *The Meanest Kind of Blues* (1924); *Naughty Man* (1924); *Bye and Bye* (1925); *Play me Slow* (1925); *Money Blues* (2 takes) (1925); *Sugar Foot Stomp* (1925); *What-cha-call-'em Blues* (1925); *T.N.T.* (1925); *Carolina Stomp* (1925); *Nobody's Rose* (1925); *Pensacola* (1925); *Stampede* (1926); *Jackass Blues* (1926); *Henderson Stomp* (1936).

Fletcher Henderson and his Orchestra, Vol.1—(Sw) Collector's Classics CC27. *Gulf Coast Blues* (1923); *Down-hearted Blues* (1923); *Dicty Blues* (1923); *Doo doodle oom* (1923); *Just Hot* (1923); *Down South Blues* (1923); *You've got to get hot* (1923); *Charleston Crazy* (1923); *Old Black Joe's Blues* (1923); *Potomac River Blues* (1923); *Cotton Pickers' Ball* (1924); *Lots o' Mama* (1924); *Chicago Blues* (1924); *Feelin' the Way I Do* (1924); *Tea Pot Dome Blues* (1924); *Mobile Blues* (1924).

Fletcher Henderson and his Orchestra, Vol.2—(Sw) Collector's Classics CC28. *I Don't Know and I Don't Care* (1924); *Strutter's Drag* (1924); *Do That Thing* (1924); *Those broken busted, can't be trusted blues* (1924); *The Gouge of Armour Avenue* (1924); *Hard-hearted Hannah* (1924); *A New Kind of Man* (1924); *The Meanest Kind of Blues* (1924); *Forsaken Blues* (1924); *Cold Mamas* (1924); *Words* (1924); *Copenhagen* (1924); *Shanghai Shuffle* (1924); *Naughty Man* (1924); *Memphis Bound* (1925); *When you do what you do* (1925).

The Immortal Fletcher Henderson—CBS 63737; (A) Mile 2005. *Chimes Blues* (1923) (solo); *Down hearted Blues* (1923); *Gulf Coast Blues* (1923); *When You Walked Out* (1923); *My Sweetie went Away* (1923); *Mandy, Make up your Mind* (1924); *I'll see you in my dreams* (1925); *Why couldn't it be poor little me* (1925); *Alabamy Bound* (1925); *Swamp Blues* (1927); *Off to Buffalo* (1927); *Hop Off* (1927); *Rough House Blues* (1927); *Star Dust* (1931).

Louis Armstrong with The Fletcher Henderson Orchestra (1924-5)—VJM VLP-60 (76). *Tell me, Dreamy Eyes; My Rose-Marie; Don't Forget you'll Regret; Shanghai Shuffle; One of These Days; My Dream Man; How come you do me like you do; Araby; Everybody loves my baby; Naughty Man; I'll see you in my dreams; Why couldn't it be poor little me; Alabamy Bound; Swanee Butterfly; Poplar Street Blues; 12th Street Blues; Me Neenyah (My Little One).* (1924-25.)

Fletcher Henderson and The Dixie Stompers—Parlophone PMC7109 (70). *Spanish Shawl* (1925); *Clap hands, here comes Charley* (1925); *Florida Stomp* (1925); *Get it Fixed* (1925); *Chinese Blues* (1925); *Panama* (1925); *I've found a New baby* (1926); *Nervous Charlie Stomp* (1926); *Black Horse Stomp* (1926); *Tampeekoe* (1926); *Hi-diddle-diddle* (1926); *Hard-to-get Gertie* (1926); *Dynamite* (1926); *Jackass Blues* (1926); *Static Strut* (1926); *Off to Buffalo* (1926); *Brotherly Love* (1926); *Alabama Stomp* (1926).

Fletcher Henderson and The Dixie Stompers—Parlophone PMC7059 (68). *Have it Ready* (1927); *Ain't She Sweet* (1927); *Snag it* (1927); *Wabash Blues* (1927); *The Wang Wang Blues* (1927); *St. Louis Shuffle* (1927); *Corn Fed* (1927); *Variety Stomp* (1927); *St. Louis Blues* (1927); *Black Maria* (1927); *Goose Pimples* (1927); *Baltimore* (1927); *Oh, Baby* (1928); *Feelin' Good* (1928); *I'm feelin' Devilish* (1928).

A Night at the Savoy—(Sw) Tax M-8006 (74). *Stampede* (1926); *Great Caesar's Ghost* (1937); *Stealing Apples* (1936); *A Pixie from Dixie.* (With tracks by Cab Calloway, Don Redman and Teddy Wilson.)

Ridin' in Rhythm—World Records SHB42 (2) (79). *Ol' Man River* (1933); *Minnie the Moocher's Wedding Day* (1933); *Ain'tcha glad* (1933); *I've got to sing a Torch Song* (1933); *Happy Feet* (1933); *I'm Rhythm Crazy Now* (1933); *Queer Notions* (1933); *It's the Talk of the Town* (1933); *Night Life* (1933); *Nagasaki* (1933). (Some tracks credited to Horace Henderson, coupled with tracks by Duke Ellington, Coleman Hawkins, Benny Carter, etc.)

Fletcher Henderson 1934—Decca 'Ace of Hearts' AH61 (63) (d). *Limehouse Blues; Shanghai Shuffle; Big John Special; Happy as the Day is Long; Tidal Wave; Down South Camp Meeting; Wrappin' it Up; Memphis Blues; Wild Party; Rug Cutter's Swing; Hotter than 'ell; Liza.* (1934.)

Fletcher Henderson with The Connie's Inn Orchestra (1926-31)—Decca 'Ace of Hearts' AH41 (63) (d); (A) Decca DL-9228. *Sugar Foot Stomp* (1931); *I'm crazy 'bout my baby* (1931); *Radio Rhythm* (1931); *Stockholm Stomp* (1927); *Have it Ready* (1927); *Hot Mustard* (1926); *Sensation* (1927); *Low down on the Bayou* (1931); *The House of David Blues* (1931); *You Rascal, You* (1931); *Singin' the Blues* (1931); *Just Blues* (1931.)

Also:

The Fletcher Henderson Story, Vols.1-4 (1923-41)—CBS BPG62001/2/3/4 (62) (d); (A) Columbia C4L-19 (4) (61).

Fletcher Henderson with The Connie's Inn Orchestra (1926-31)—Decca 'Ace of Hearts' AH41 (63) (d); (A) Decca DL-9228.

Fletcher Henderson, Vol.1 (1927-36)—(F) RCA 730.584.

Fletcher Henderson, Vol.2 (1927-34)—(F) RCA 741.071.

Fletcher Henderson, Vol.3 (1923-36)—(F) RCA FPM1.7011 (74).

The Immortal Fletcher Henderson—(A) Milestone MLP-2005.

Fletcher Henderson (featuring Louis Armstrong)—(Sw) Jazz Panorama JPLP-21.

Fletcher Henderson and his Connie's Inn Orchestra—HMV DLP1066 (54) (d).

Fletcher Henderson on Columbia, Vol.1 —Vintage Jazz VLP-24 (73).

Fletcher Henderson on Columbia, Vol.2 (1924-26)—Vintage Jazz VLP-36 (74).

A Study in Frustration—(A) Columbia C4L-19 (4) (74).

The Connie's Inn Orchestra—(A) 'X' LVA-3013.

1st Impressions (1924-31)—(F) MCA 510.035 (74).

In 'n' Out—(A) Blue Note BST-84166.

Swing's the Thing—(F) MCA 510.060 (74).

Fletcher Henderson Orchestra, Vol.1 (1923-24)—(A) Historical Jazz HLP-13 (67).

Fletcher Henderson Orchestra, Vol.2 (1923-25)—(A) Historical Jazz HLP-18 (67).

Fletcher Henderson Orchestra (1923-25) —(F) EMI FJ-112 (76).

Fletcher Henderson, Vols. 1/2—(2) Decca 79227/8 (2) (68).

Horace Henderson

(b Cuthbert, Georgia, November 22 1904)
Younger brother of Fletcher Henderson (qv) he led several bands of his own as well as working with his brother during the 1930s and 1940s. Gifted arranger who wrote for most of the top bands, including Benny Goodman, Don Redman, Tommy Dorsey, Charlie Barnet, Earl Hines and Jimmie Lunceford, as well as providing scores for Fletcher's band. Made a number of recordings under his own name: a 1940 selection with good band [Emmett Berry (t), Ray Nance (t, vln), Israel Crosby (b)] of arrangements by Fletcher, himself, and Sir

Charles Thompson is listed below.

Selected LP recordings

Horace Henderson: 1940—(Sw) Tax M8013 (74) (d). *Shufflin' Joe; Oh Boy, I'm in the Groove; Kitty on Toast; I got Rhythm; Sultan Serenade; Ginger Belle; Do Re Mi; When Dreams Come True; I still have my Dreams; Turkey Special; Flinging a Whing-ding; Coquette; You don't mean me no good; Smooth Sailing; Ain't Misbehavin'; I'll always be in love with you.* (1940.)

Woody Herman

(b Milwaukee, May 16 1913)

Boy prodigy on clarinet, Herman played with a number of bands, including Tom Gerun, Gus Arnheim (qv) and Isham Jones (qv). He formed his first band from the nucleus of the Isham Jones orchestra when Jones retired temporarily in 1936. Billed as 'The Band That Plays the Blues', major success came first in 1939 with *Woodchopper's Ball.* This early band was Dixieland based in style, but major changes in personnel [Pete Candoli, Conte Candoli (t), Bill Harris (tb), Flip Phillips (ts), Chubby Jackson (b), Dave Tough (d)] under the name 'The First Herd' won general recognition and established the style of the Herman band for more than a decade, with arrangements by Ralph Burns, Neal Hefti, etc. The First Herd was notable for splendid driving ensemble work. It broke up in 1946 and was replaced by the Second Herd which featured the saxophone quartet known as the Four Brothers [Stan Getz, Zoot Sims, Herbie Steward (ts) and Serge Chaloff (bar)]. Second Herd lasted into 1949, and the Third Herd was formed in 1950 after Herman had briefly led a small group. Herman continued to lead various bands up to the present, of varying quality and success but invariably with distinctive tone and style. Always a musician sensitive to the trends of the day, Herman has frequently employed young and rising stars, and has flirted, not always successfully, with jazz/rock and other passing fashions. Appeared in many movies, including *What's Cookin'?* (1942) and *Hit Parade of 1947.* Composer of many jazz feature numbers. Igor Stravinsky wrote *Ebony Concerto* for the Herman band, and Ralph Burns's *Summer Sequence* (1946) was a notable example of 'composed' jazz exploiting a particular band's potentialities.

Selected LP recordings

The Band that played the Blues—Decca 'Ace of Hearts' AH-156. *Blue Flame* (1941); *Peach Tree Street* (1940); *Bishop's Blues* (1941); *Blue Prelude* (1940); *Chip's Blues* (1940); *The Blues* (1940); *Bessie's Blues* (1940); *Casbah Blues* (1939); *River Bed Blues* (1938); *Dupree Blues* (1937); *Dallas Blues* (1939); *Farewell Blues.*

Woodchoppers' Ball—Brunswick LAT-8092; (A) Decca DL-8133. *Indian Boogie Woogie* (1938); *Woodchoppers' Ball* (1939); *Chip's Boogie Woogie* (1940); *The Golden Wedding* (1940); *Blue Flame* (1941); *Wood-sheddin' with Woody* (1941); *Yardbird Shuffle* (1941); *Las Chiapanecas* (1941); *Four or five times* (1942); *Down Under* (1942); *Who's dat up dere?* (1943); *Irresistible You* (1944).

The Turning Point (1943-44)—Coral CP2 (68) (d); (A) Decca DL-9229. *Basie's Basement; Do nothing till you hear from me; I get a kick out of you; Crying Sands; I'll Get By; I've got you Under My Skin; Noah; Cherry; Milkman keep those Bottles Quiet; It must be jelly 'cause jam don't shake like that; Ingie Speaks; Perdido; As Long as I Live; I ain't got nothin' but the blues.*

The Thundering Herds-Vol.1—CBS BPG62158 (63); (A) Columbia C3L25 (3) (63). *Laura; Apple Honey; I Wonder; Caldonia; Happiness is a Thing called Joe; Goosey Gander; Northwest Passage; A Kiss Goodnight; I've got the World on a String; The Good Earth; Put that Ring on my Finger; Bijou; Gee, but it's Good to Hold You; Your Father's Moustache; Wild Root; Blowin' up a Storm.* (1945.)

The Thundering Herds-Vol.2—CBS BPG62159 (63); (A) Columbia C3L25 (3). *Let it Snow, Let it Snow, Let it Snow* (1945); *Welcome to my Dreams; Panacea; Steps; Fan It; Igor; Nero's Conception; Lost Weekend; Pam; Sidewalks of Cuba; Lady McGowan's Dream; Romance in the Dark; Someday, Sweetheart; I surrender, dear; Woodchoppers' Ball.* (1946.)

The Thundering Herds-Vol.3—CBS BPG62160 (63); (A) Columbia C3L25 (3). *Summer Sequence Parts 1-3; Everywhere; With Someone New; Wrap your Troubles in Dreams; Back Talk; Non-alcoholic* (all 1946); *I told ya I love ya, now get out; I've got news for You; The Goof and I; Lazy Lullaby; Keen and Peachy; Four Brothers; Summer Sequence, Part 4; PS, I Love You.* (All 1947.)

Woody Herman at Carnegie Hall—Verve 2317 031 (72); (A) MGM-3043. *Red*

Woody Herman.

Top; Bijou; Mean to Me; Your Father's Moustache; Superman with a Horn; Heads Up; Hallelujah; Wild Root; The Good Earth; Four Men on a Horse; The man I Love; Blowin' up a Storm; Sweet and Lovely; Everywhere; Panacea. (1946.)
The Best of Woody Herman—CBS-Realm RM2551; (A). *Apple Honey* (1945); *The Good Earth* (1945); *Woodchopper's Ball* (1946); *Your Father's Moustache* (1946); *Blue Flame* (1946); *Northwest Passage* (1946); *Caldonia* (1946); *Summer Sequence, Part 4* (1947); *Bijou* (1947); *Four Brothers* (1947); *Wild Root* (1947); *Keen and Peachy* (1947).
The Great Big Bands-Vol.2—Capitol T20809. *That's Right; Music to Dance To; Keeper of the Flame; Early Autumn; Lemon Drop; Sonny Speaks; Lollipop; Not really the Blues; More Moon* (1949/50); *Opus De-Funk; Where or When; Captain Ahab; Sentimental Journey; I Remember Duke; Cool Cat on a Hot Tin Roof* (1955).
Pre-Herds—Ember SE8027 (74). *Natchel Blues; Don't get Around Much Anymore; Body and Soul; Ready, Get Set, Jump; At the Woodchoppers' Ball; Opus De-Funk; Park East; Saxy.* (1958.)
Jazz Hoot—CBS 80248 (74); (A) Columbia C-32530. *The Duck* (1967); *I can't get started* (1965); *Hallelujah Time* (1965); *The Black Opal* (1965); *Satin Doll* (1965); *Sidewinder* (1965); *Jazz Hoot* (1965); *Sumptuous* (1965); *Watermelon Man* (1965); *Boopsie* (1967); *Greasy Sack Blues* (1965.)
Light My Fire—Philips Chess 6310 127; (A) Cadet 819. *Pontieo: Here I am, baby; Hard to Keep my Mind on You; McArthur Park; Light my Fire; I Say a Little Prayer; Hush; For Love of Ivy; Impression of Strayhorn; Keep on keepin' on.* (1968.)
The Raven Speaks—Fantasy FT509 (74); (A) Fantasy 9416. *Fat Mama; Alone again (naturally); Sandia Chicano (Watermelon Man); It's Too Late; The Raven Speaks; Summer of '42; Reunion at Newport; Bill's Blues.* (1972.)
Thundering Herd—Fantasy FT-521 (74); (A) Fantasy 9452. *Lazy Bird; Blues for Poland; What are you doing the rest of your life; America Drinks and goes Home; Naima; Corazon; Come Saturday Morning; Bass Folk Song.* (1974.)
Also:
Golden Favourites—Decca 'Ace of Hearts' AH-78 (64) (d); (A) Decca DL-8133 or DL-74484 (64).

The Hits of Woody Herman (1948-55)—Regal-Starline SRS5055 (71) (d).
Men from Mars (1953)—London H-APB1018; (A) Verve 8216.
Woody Herman and The New Third Herd—London H-APB1014; (A) Verve 8216.
At the Monterey Jazz Festival (1959)—London LTZ-K15200, (S) SAH-K6100 (60); (A) Atlantic 1328 (60).
The Hits of Woody Herman (1948-55)—Capitol T-1554 (63); (A) ditto, (S) DTT-1554.
The New Swinging Herman Herd (1960)—Eros ERL50027, (S) ERLS50027 (62).
Woody Herman 1963—Philips 652025, (S) 852025 (63); (A) Trip 5547, Philips 200065, (S) 600065 (63).
Encore (1963)—Philips BL7574, (S) SBL7574 (63); (A) Philips 200092, (S) 600092 (63).
The Fourth Herd (1959)—(A) Jazzland JLP-17 (61).
Woody's Winners (1965)—CBS BPG62619, (S) SBPG62619 (d); (A) Columbia CL-2436, (S) CS-9236 (66).
The Swinging Herd-Recorded Live—Philips BL7649; (A) Philips PHM-200.
They heard The Herd—Verve VLP-9062; (A) Verve MGV-8216.
Brand New—(A) Fantasy 8414.
Woody Herman and his Orchestra (1937-42)—(A) Bandstand BS-7108.
Woody Herman and his Orchestra (1938-41)—(A) Bandstand BS-7122.
Woody Herman and his Orchestra (1936-41)—(A) Sunbeam SB-206.
Summer Sequence (1945-47)—Fontana TFR6012; (A) Harmony 7093.
Woody Herman (1948-50)—Capitol LC6560 (d); (A) Capitol T-324.
The Three Herds (1945-47, 1953-54)—Philips BBL7123; (A) Columbia CL-592.
Road Band (1955)—Capitol T-658; (A) ditto.
The Herd Rides Again (1958)—Top Rank 35/038 (60) (d); (A) Everest SDBR-1003.
Woody Herman and his Orchestra (1959)—Top Rank BUY*009 (60) (d).
Woody Herman (1936-40)—(G) Swingfan 1011.
The Great Herd 1946 (live)—(A) Swing Treasury 102 (76).
Boiled in Earl (1948)—(A) Swing Treasury 108 (76).
Bijou—(A) Harmony HL-7013.
Dance Parade—(A) Columbia CL-6049.
At Carnegie Hall 1946, Vol.2—(A) MGM E-159.
Woody Herman and The Third Herd—(A) MGM E-192.
Woody Herman at The London Palladium, 1948—(A) Hep HEP-7 (76).
Woody Herman: His Orchestra and The Woodchoppers, Vol.2 (1944-46 live and radio)—First Heard 10 (76).
The Herd at Montreux (1974)—Fantasy F9470; (A) ditto.
Hollywood Palladium, 1948—(A) Hep HEP-7 (76).
First Herd 1944 (broadcasts)—London HMP5058 (79).
40th Anniversary Carnegie Hall Concert—RCA PL02203 (2) (77); (A) BGL2-2203 (2).
Woody Herman and his Orchestra (1937) (broadcasts)—London HMP5048 (79).
Brand New—(A) Fantasy 8414.
The Best of Woody Herman—(F) MCA MCFM-2733 (75).
The Big Band Sound of Woody Herman—Polydor 2317 072 (72).
Children of Lima—Fantasy F9477 (75); (A) ditto.
Early Autumn—(G) Bovema 5C 052 80805 (72).
Giant Steps—Fantasy F-9432 (73) (d); (A) ditto.
Heavy Exposure—Phomogram Checker 6467 308 (73); (A) Cadet S-835.
In Disco Order, Vol.1—(F) Ajax 102 (77).
In Disco Order, Vol.2—(F) Ajax 109 (77).
Woody Live at Monterey (That's Jazz 6)—(A) Atlantic ATL-50236 (76).
One Night Stand with Woody Herman—(A) Joyce JLP-1021 (75).
The Big Bands—(F) CBS G-30009 (2).
Live at Basin Street West, Hollywood—(G) Sonic SON018 (76).
Woody Herman and his Orchestra—(G) MCA PCO-8221 (76).
Concerto for Herd—(A) Verve 68764 (68).
Light my Fire—(A) Cadet S-819 (69).
The Best of Woody Herman—(A) Everest 5222, (S) 1222 (64).
Big Band Goodies—(A) Philips 200171, (S) 600171 (65).
Featuring 'The Preacher'—(A) Verve 8255 (58).
First Herd—(A) VSP 1, (S) S-1 (66).
Hey!—(A) Verve 8558, (S) 68558 (63).

Moody Woody—(A) Everest 5032, (S) 1032.
My Kind of Broadway—(A) Columbia CL-2357, (S) CS-9157 (65).
Woody Herman 1964—(A) Philips 200118, (S) 600118 (64).
Recorded Live—(A) Philips 200131, (S) 600131 (64).
Woody Herman—(A) Metro 514, (S) S-514 (65).

Teddy Hill

(b Birmingham, Alabama, December 7 1906)
A forceful alto player who, in the 1930s, led an important band containing many outstanding jazzmen [Roy Eldridge, Dizzy Gillespie, Frankie Newton, Shad Collins, Bill Coleman, (t), Dicky Wells (tb), Russell Procope (as, cl) and Chu Berry, (ts)] which played first at the Ubango Club in Harlem and later at the Savoy Ballroom. The band undertook an important European tour in 1937, making a major impression in Paris, then at the New York World's Fair in 1939. Hill disbanded in 1940 and took over the management of Minton's Playhouse, New York, where he remained through the 1940s and into the 1950s and so saw the birth of 'bop' and the modernist movement.

Selected LP recordings
Teddy Hill and his Orchestra 1937 (with tracks by Willie Bryant, 1936)—(G) RCA LPM-10116.
Dizzy Gillespie, Vol.1—(F) RCA 730.676.
Teddy Hill and Orchestra—(A) 'X' LVA-3030.
Teddy Hill & The NBC Orchestra, 1937—(F) RCA FPMI-7035.
Teddy Hill 1935—Queen QU-021 (79).

Earl Hines

(b Duquesne, Pennsylvania, December 28 1905)
One of the greatest (many would say the greatest) of all jazz pianists, Hines also had a fairly brief but outstanding success as a band leader which began when he formed a band for the Grand Terrace club in Chicago in 1928 and remained until 1940. The Grand Terrace was generally thought to have been part owned by Al Capone (Hines maintains that Capone may have been a big racketeer but he also had a kind and generous side, ran a free restaurant in Chicago for the down and out and helped poor people who were dispossessed of their homes during the Depression years). The band at various times contained several major jazzmen [Walter Fuller (t), Trummy Young (tb), Omer Simeon, Darnell Howard (cl), Quinn Wilson, Budd Johnson (ts), Hayes Alvis (b), Alvin Burroughs and Walter Bishop (d)]. The Grand Terrace band peaked in 1939-40 which was Hines' high point as a leader. Later he organised other bands which included for occasional periods some of the men who were soon to create the modern movement in jazz [Dizzy Gillespie (t), Charlie Parker (as) and Wardell Gray (ts)]. The great jazz singer Sarah Vaughan made her debut with Hines, and led the band throughout the 1940s. Later joined Louis Armstrong's All-Stars (his work with Armstrong's second Hot Five in 1928 was hardly less important than Armstrong's own,

Earl Hines (Herve Derrien).

creating new standards for jazz piano) and has since usually played either with small groups or as guest with bigger bands. Though most highly esteemed as a pianist, Hines' work as band leader must not be under-rated, nor must his exceptional talent for spotting and encouraging rising stars among the junior generations. Also always featured high class arrangements by Budd Johnson, Jimmy Mundy, Edgar Battle etc.

Selected LP recordings

Earl Hines: 1929 Recordings—RCA FPM1 7023 (75). *Sweet Ella May* (2 takes); *Everybody loves my Baby* (3 takes); *Good little, bad little you* (2 takes); *Have you ever felt that way; Beau Koo Jack* (2 takes); *Sister Kate; Chicago Rhythm* (2 takes); *Glad Rag Doll* (2 takes); *Grand Piano Blues; Blue Nights.* (1929.)

Earl Hines and his Orchestra 1932-4, 1937—(A) Jazz Archives JA-2 (74). *Blue Drag* (1932); *I love you because I love you* (1932) (2 takes); *Sensational Mood* (1932); *Love me Tonight* (solo) (1932); *Down Among the Sheltering Palms* (solo) (1932); *Why Must we Part* (1933); *Maybe I'm to Blame* (1933); *Just to be in Caroline* (1934); *We found Romance* (1934); *Blue* (1934); *Julia* (1934); *Blue Skies* (1937); *Hines Rhythm* (1937); *A Mellow bit of Rhythm* (1937).

Earl Hines and his Orchestra (1934-48)—(A) Jazum 47 (76). *Blue* (1934); *We found Romance* (1934); *Just to be in Caroline* (1934); *You are the one of my dreams* (1934); *I can't believe that you're in love with me* (1937); *Tappin' at The Terrace* (1938); *Julia* (1941); *It Had to be You* (1941); *Sweet Honey Babe* (1942); *Midnight in New Orleans* (1942); *Keyboard Kapers; Lazy Morning; Louise; When I Dream of You* (1948.)

Swinging in Chicago—Coral CP-63 (71) (d); Decca 'Ace of Hearts' AH-159; (A) Decca DL-9221; Coral CRLM1045; etc. *That's a-plenty* (1934); *Fat Babes* (1934); *Maple Leaf Rag* (1934); *Sweet Georgia Brown* (1934); *Rosetta* (1934); *Copenhagen* (1934); *Angry* (1934); *Wolverine Blues* (1934); *Rock and Rye* (1934); *Cavernism* (1934); *Rhythm Lullaby* (1935); *Japanese Sandman* (1935); *Bubbling Over* (1935); *Blue* (1935.)

The Father Jumps—(A) Bandstand BS-7115. *In Swamp Lands* (1940); *I'm Fallin' for You* (1940); *Comin' in Home* (1940); *Jelly, Jelly* (1940); *Up Jumped the Devil* (1941); *South Side* (1941); *Windy City Jive* (1941); *Swingin' on C* (1941); *Yellow Fire* (1941); *Somehow* (1941); *The Father Jumps* (1941); *The Jitney Man* (1941); *The Earl* (1941); *You don't know what love is* (1941); *Second Balcony Jump* (1942); *Stormy Monday Blues* (1942.)

The Grand Terrace Band—RCA RD7720 (65); (A) RCA LPV-512 (65). *Piano Man* (1939); *Father Steps In* (1939); *G.T. Stomp* (1939); *Ridin' and Jivin'* (1939); *Indiana* (1939); *After all I've been to you* (1939); *'Gator Swing* (1939); *Grand Terrace Shuffle* (1939); *Deep Forest* (1940); *XYZ* (1939); *Riff Medley* (1939); *Boogie Woogie on St. Louis Blues* (1940); *Number 19* (1940); *You can Depend on Me* (1940); *Tantalizing a Cuban* (1940); *Call me Happy* (1940.)

The Indispensable Earl Hines, Vol.3—RCA FPM1-7000 (74). *In Swamp Lands* (1940); *Jelly, Jelly* (1940); *Comin' in Home* (1940); *Up jumped the Devil* (1941); *Jersey Bounce* (1941); *The Sunny Side of the Street* (2 takes) (1941); *My Melancholy Baby* (2 takes) (1941); *South Side* (1940); *Windy City Jive* (1941); *Swingin' on C* (1941); *Yellow Fire* (1941); *The Father Jumps* (1941); *The Earl* (1941); *The Jitney Man* (1941); *2nd Balcony Jump* (1942); *Stormy Monday Blues* (1942.)

Also:

The Indispensable Hines, Vol.1 (1929-39)—(F) RCA 731.065.

The Indispensable Earl Hines, Vol.2 (1939-40)—(F) RCA 741.041.

Hines Rhythm—(A) Epic EE-22021.

Earl Hines et son grand Orchestre—(F) Mode CMDINT-9733.

Earl Hines Orchestra (1950s)—(A) Tops L-1599.

Claude Hopkins

(b Alexandria, Virginia, August 24 1903)

Associated with Wilbur Sweatman in the 1920s, and also led band accompanying singer/dancer Josephine Baker. Formed his own band at the Roseland Ballroom, New York, in 1932. A talented pianist and arranger, Hopkins' band featured Edmond Hall (cl) and later Vic Dickenson (tb) and trumpeter Jabbo Smith. Subsequently led various bands after break-up of original group in 1940. Famous in his day (1930s) for excellent arrangements with genuine jazz content, a number of his recordings of the period are valued by jazz collectors.

Selected LP recordings

The Golden Swing Years—Polydor 423269 *Hodge Podge; Chasing my blues away;*

Swingin' and Jivin'; Just as long as the World goes round; Minor mania; Lazy bones; Washington Squabble; Farewell Blues; Truckin'; You stayed away too long; Put on your old grey bonnet. (c 1935, broadcast material.)

Unissued and Rare Sides 1932/33/40—(A) Jazz Archives JA-4 (74). *Three little words; (I would do) Anything for you; Hopkins Scream; Washington Squabble; Shake your Ashes; Mystic moan; Just you, Just me; Ain't misbehavin'; Honeysuckle Rose; Yacht Club Swing; Out to lunch; A little rain must fall; What's the matter with me.*

Also:

Crazy Fingers—(A) Chiaroscuro 114.

Claude Hopkins and his Cotton Club Orchestra (Singing in the Rain)—(A) Jazz Archive JA-27 (75).

Big Bands (1934-42) (with tracks by Carolina Cotton Pickers & Andy Kirk)—(G) Swingfan 1010.

Harlem 1935—(Sw) Jazz Panorama LP13; Jazz Anthology—JA 5156.

Safari Stomp (July 74)—(F) Black & Blue BB-33086.

Harlem 1934—Swing Classics ET2 (79).

Hudson-Delange Orchestra

Formed in 1935 under the auspices of Irving Mills (manager of many famous bands, including Duke Ellington) and under the joint leadership of Will Hudson (b March 8 1908) and Eddie DeLange (January 12 1904-July 13 1949). Mostly featured arrangements by Hudson who also contributed charts to other units. Hudson took over full leadership in 1938. The band broke up in 1941, but Hudson continued actively with arranging and composing. The Hudson-DeLange Orchestra had only a short life but achieved a high reputation through sound playing of good arrangements.

Selected LP recordings

The Hudson-DeLange Orchestra (1936-39)—(A) Bandstand BS-7105.

Easy Rocker (Will Hudson Orchestra) (1937-40) (A)—Sounds of Swing LP-120.

Spike Hughes

(b London, October 19 1908)

Active as composer and arranger for British bands during the late 1920s and 1930s, Spike Hughes is remembered in the popular music field principally for his innovation of the 'slap' style of string bass playing and the series of recordings he made in America with an all-star band in 1933. He played with several English orchestras and recorded with groups under his own leadership which contained most of the leading British musicians of the period [Max Goldberg, Jack Jackson (t), Lew Davis, Jock Fleming (tb), Harry Hayes (as, cl), Buddy Featherstonhaugh, Billy Amstell (ts, cl), Bill Harty, Ronnie Gubertini (d) and Elsie Carlisle (vo)]. The American band of 1933, brought together solely for recording and billed originally as 'Spike Hughes and His Negro Orchestra' (later because of racial squeamishness and linguistic evasion called 'All American Orchestra' then just 'Orchestra') playing Hughes' compositions and arrangements, contained a rollcall of distinguished jazz names [Henry 'Red' Allen (t), Dicky Wells, Wilbur de Paris (tb), Benny Carter (as), Coleman Hawkins, Chu Berry (ts), Ram Rodriguez, Luis Russell (p) and Sidney Catlett (d)]. The nucleus of this band was Benny Carter's (qv) playing, with additions by the leading soloists, notably Hawkins, Berry and Allen. These recordings, especially Hughes' *Donegal Cradle Song, Arabesque, Music at Midnight, Pastorale* etc caused a sensation at the time and have remained classics of their kind ever since. Hughes' subsequent career has been mostly in musical journalism (jazz and classical, predominantly opera in the latter).

Selected LP recordings

Spike Hughes and his All American Orchestra—Decca LK4173 (d); Decca Ace of Clubs ACL1153* (63); (A) London LL-1387. *Nocturne; Pastoral; Bugle Call Rag; Fanfare; Sweet Sorrow Blues; Arabesque; Music at Midnight; Sweet Sue, just you; Air in D flat; Donegal Cradle Song; Firebird; How come you do me like you do.* (1933*) plus: *Someone stole Gabriel's horn; Music at Sunrise.*

Jack Hylton

(b Great Lever, Lancs, July 2 1894; d London January 29 1965)

One of the leading and most influential band leaders of the British scene during the 1920s and 1930s. Led a band at The Queens, Langham Place, immediately after World War I, later played at the Piccadilly Hotel. Made a speciality of shows and stage appearances, and built up big reputation. Toured abroad with his band during the late

1920s and early 1930s, always with marked success. Numerous later famous dance band musicians passed through his ranks, and in 1934-35 Coleman Hawkins (ts) was featured with Hylton and returned for a brief spell in 1939 before returning to America. Hylton himself spent 1935-36 in the US leading a group of American musicians. In his later years Hylton was a highly successful agent, producer and impresario. Although Jack Hylton's band played largely smooth dance type music and novelties, he also featured jazz numbers from time to time, sometimes recording it with a group known as Hylton's Rhythmagicians, [Jack Jackson (t), Lew Davis (tb), Edward 'Poggy' Pogson (as, ts, cl), Chappie D'Amato (g), Hugo Rignold (vln) and Arthur Young (p) etc]. (At least one passage for three violins in a Hylton record is reputed to be played by Hugo Rignold, Jean Pougnet and Alfredo Campoli and arranged by William Walton.)

Selected LP recordings

Jack Hylton and his Orchestra (The Early Years)—World Records SH127 (70). *Tiger Rag* (1930); *Limehouse Blues* (1930); *High and low* (1929)* *Shepherd of the hills* (1927); *Rhymes* (1931); *Number 10* (1927); *I must have that man* (1929)*; *Oh, Miss Hannah!* (1926); *Diga diga doo* (1929); *That's my weakness now* (1928)* *The Varsity Drag* (1928); *Breakaway—Big City Blues* (1929)*; *A Broadway melody—You were meant for me* (1929)*; *I want to be bad* (1929); *Me and Jane in a plane* (1927); *Ain't that a grand and glorious feeling* (1927); (*Vocals by Sam Brown.)

A Programme of Light Orchestral Favourites—World Records SH269 (79). *The selfish giant* (1926); *Pas des echarpes* (1925); *Songs of the Fair* (1926); *Prelude in C sharp minor* (1930); *Bolero* (1936); *The Three Bears* (1926); *Grasshoppers' dance* (1931); *Prelude in G minor* (1930); *Nell Gwyn*—dances Nos 1-3 (1938); *Henry VIII*—dance No 1.

Good News! The Music of de Sylva, Brown & Henderson—World Records SH218 (74). *Button up your overcoat* (1929)*; *My lucky star* (1929); *If I had a talking picture of you* (1929); *Turn on the heat* (1929); *Come to me* (1931); *If you haven't got love* (1931); *Lucky day* (1927); *Here am I, broken-hearted* (1927); *Good News* (1928); *The best things in life are free* (1928); *Lucky in love* (1928); *Don't hold everything* (1929)*; *You wouldn't fool me, would you* (1929); *You're the cream in my coffee* (1929)*: *Without love* (1931); *Thank your Father* (1931). (*Vocals by Sam Browne.)

Hits from Berlin 1927-1931—World Records SH308 (79). *When day is done* (1927); *Heut' war ich bei der Frieda* (1928); *Wir wollen tun, als ob wir Freunde waren* (1928); *Ja, ja, di Frau'n sinf meine schwache Seite* (1928); *Passen Sie mal auf* (1928); *I kiss your hand, Madame* (1928); *When the white lilacs bloom again* (1928); *O maiden, My maiden* (1928); *Four words* (1929); *Handsome gigolo* (1930); *You are my heart's delight* (1930); *Falling in love again* (1930); *White Horse Inn*—selection (1931); *Mausie* (1931); *Today I feel so happy* (1931). (Vocals by Austin Egen and Sam Browne, Marcel Wittrisch & Pat O'Malley.)

Jack Hylton, Vol.2—Monmouth-Evergreen MES7055 (73). *She shall have music* (1936); *Limehouse Blues* (1930); *If the moon turns green* (1935); *When the white elder tree blooms again* (1928); *Tiger Rag* (1930); *I kiss your hand, Madame* (1928); *White Horse Inn*—selection (1931); *Your eyes* (1931); *It would be wonderful* (1931); *White Horse Inn*—foxtrot medley (1931); *Sweet Sue* (1936); *Grinzing* (1936). (Vocals by Sam Costa, Pat O'Malley and Sam Browne.)

The Bands that Matter—Decca 'Eclipse' ECM2046 (70). *Wear a great big smile* (1933); *Love is the sweetest thing* (1932); *Honeymoon Hotel* (1933); *We just couldn't say goodbye* (1932); *Paradise* (1932); *Mad about the Boy* (1932); *You're an old smoothie* (1933); *By a waterfall* (1933); *Waltzing in a dream* (1933); *Moonstruck* (1933); *Can't we meet again* (1933); *The younger generation* (1932); *This is the rhythm for me* (1933); *Auf wiedersehen, my dear* (1932). (Vocals by Pat O'Malley and Phyllis Robbins.)

The Band that Jack Built (1935-1939)—World Records SH190 (73). *Music, maestro, please* (1938); *Now it can be told* (1938); *One, two, button your shoe* (1937); *Don't let that moon get away* (1938); *Sing, baby, sing* (1936); *Have you met Miss Jones?* (1939); *Why doesn't somebody tell me these things* (1939); *Chinatown, my Chinatown* (1935); *She shall have music* (1936); *You turned the tables on me* (1936); *Get out of town* (1939); *Swing is in the air* (1937); *Free* (1936); *Why does my heart go boom* (1939); *Blue skies are around the corner* (1938); *Cole Porter medley* (1935). (Vocals by Sam Browne, Peggy Dell, Bruce Trent,

Alice Mann, June Malo, Sam Costa, Dolly Elsie, Pat O'Malley, Eve Becke, etc.)
Also:
Jack Hylton and his Orchestra—Decca 'Ace of Clubs' ACL1205 (66).
Jack's Back, Vol.1—Decca LF1130 (53) (d).
Jack's Back, Vol.2—Decca LF1143 (53) (d).
Jack's Back, Vol.3—Decca LF1146 (54) (d).
Jack's Back—EMI 'Encore' ENC-162.
Memories of Jack Hylton—(A) RCA LPT-1013.
Jack Hylton, Vol.1 (1929-31)—(A) Monmouth-Evergreen MES-7033 (73).
Jack Hylton and his Orchestra—Flapper PAST702 (80).

Jack Jackson

(b Barnsley, Yorks, 1907; d Jersey, January 15 1978)
Played trumpet with various leading British dance bands in the 1920s after working with military bands. Joined Bert Railton's band in 1926; then with Ambrose, Ronnie Monroe, Jack Hylton, Spike Hughes, and in 1931 with Jack Payne (qv). In the 1930s (beginning in 1933) and the 1940s Jack Jackson led a very successful and popular band at the Dorchester Hotel. Later work included successful career as a radio disc jockey.

Selected LP recordings

Jack Jackson and his Orchestra—World Records SH210. *Make those people sway* (1933); *I'm playing with fire* (1933)*; *Long may we love* (1934); *I travel alone* (1934); *Come on, be happy* (1933)*; *Miss Otis regrets* (1934)†; *I'm getting sentimental over you* (1933)**; *Two cigarettes in the dark* (1934)†; *Dixie Lee* (1934); *Two little flies on a lump of sugar* (1934); *Sittin' in the dark* (1933)*; *What a little moonlight can do* (1934); *Stars fell on Alabama* (1934); *Blue river, roll on* (1933); *Be still, my heart* (1934); *Let bygones be bygones* (1933)*. (Vocals by *Al Bowlly, †Alberta Hunter, **Denny Dennis.)

Harry James

(b Albany, Georgia, March 15, 1916)
Son of a circus bandmaster, he first came into prominence with the Benny Goodman orchestra in 1936-1938 both as star soloist and member of the outstanding trumpet trio

Harry James (MGM).

of James, Ziggy Elman and Chris Griffin. After he left Goodman in 1938 James formed his own band and has continued to front successful bands ever since. (Before joining Goodman he had worked briefly with Ben Pollack (qv).) Harry James won an easy popular acclaim with flashy styled trumpet solos and excursions into technical exhibitions of the order of *Flight of the bumble bee* and *Chiribiribin*. But he could play better music and better jazz than that, as his work with Goodman had already demonstrated; and although he was always tempted into the exhibitionist or sentimental veins, his later work with his own band showed a good deal more restraint. The band themselves often contained top class musicians besides himself [Willie Smith (as), Corky Corkoran (ts), Juan Tizol (v-tb), Louie Bellson and Buddy Rich (d)], as well as top arrangers, Ernie Wilkins and Neal Hefti especially providing admirable charts in the basic Basie idiom and style. Much of the James band's best work was always Basie-based. Vocalists included the young Frank Sinatra immediately before he joined Tommy Dorsey and achieved universal fame, Dick Haymes, Helen Forrest, and later Kitty Kallen. James was for many years married to film star and World War II pin-up girl Betty Grable, of the famous legs.

Selected LP recordings

Texas Chatter—(Swi) Tax M-8015 (75). *Jubilee* (2 takes) (1937); *When we're alone* (2 takes) (1937); *Can't I* (1937); *Life goes to a party* (1937); *Texas chatter* (2 takes) (1938); *Song of the wanderer* (1938); *It's the dreamer in me* (2 takes) (1938); *One o'clock Jump* (1938). (James' first two sessions as a leader.)

In the Beginning—(A) Big Band Archives LP-1206. *When we're alone* (1937); *Life goes to a party* (1937); *Headin' for Hallelujah* (1940); *Tuxedo Junction* (1940); *Alice blue gown* (1940); *Hodge podge* (1940); *Come and get it* (1940); *The Sheik of Araby* (1940); *Four or five times* (1940); *Superchief* (1940); *Maybe* (1940); *Swanee River* (1940); *Exactly like you* (1940); *Tempo de luxe* (1940); *Answer, man* (1941); *Duke's mixture* (1941.)

The Hits of Harry James—Regal-Starline SRS5049 (70); (A) Capitol TT-1515 (61). *The mole; You made me love you; I've heard that song before; Trumpet Blues; Cherry; I'm beginning to see the light; Sleepy lagoon; Two o'clock Jump; I cried for you; Music makers; Velvet Moon; Chiribiribin.* (1955.)

An Evening of Jazz with Harry James—Polydor 2682 029 (2) (72) (d). *Get off the stand; Kingsize Blues; Tweet Tweet; Time on my hands; Eyes; End of town Blues; Cottontail; Lester leaps in; Jones Beach; Ensemble; Spring can really hang you up the most; Mister Johnson; The Creeper; Harry, not Jesse; The Jazz connoisseur; Blues like; Koo Koo; Rockin' chair; Walkin'; Doodlin'; Connectin' the bones; Sweets' tooth; Harry's delight; Hot Pink; I cover the waterfront; A swinging serenade; Slats; Undecided.* (1959-64.) (Previously on Verve or MGM.)

Big Band Sound—Polydor Verve 2317 055 (74). *The opener; Confessin'; Too close for comfort; How deep is the ocean; Jersey Bounce; Satin doll; Rockin' in rhythm; Shiny stockings; Sentimental journey; King Porter Stomp; Deep purple; Take the 'A' train; Flying home; Cherokee.* (1959-64.)

The Third Big Band Sound—Polydor Verve 2317 110 (76). *Cornet Chop Suey; Tuxedo Junction; Serenade in blue; Chiarina; Two deuces; Harlem nocturne; I'm in the market for you; Two o'clock jump; Frenesi; Weather bird Rag; Man with the Blues; What a woman feels; Swingin' together; New life; Three's a crowd; Fontainbleu; The truth.* (1961-64.)

Also:

Rhythm Session—Columbia 33S1031; (A) Columbia CL-6088.

The Jazz Side of Harry James (1959-62)—Verve VLP-9128 (66) (d).

Big Band Favourites—MGM C-830 (60).

Harry's Choice (1959)—Capitol T1093, (S) ST1093 (60) (d); (A) same.

Harry James plays Neil Hefti (1961)—MGM C-881, (S) CS6052 (62).

Harry James Orchestra (1959)—MGM C-795 (60) (d); (A) MGM E-3778, (S) SE-3778.

The New Swinging Band—Capitol T1037, (S) ST1037; (A) same.

Harry James Classics—CBS 88145 (77).

At the Hollywood Palladium—Philips B.07691R; (A) Columbia CL-562 or CL-688.

The Golden Trumpet of Harry James—Decca (S) PFS4132 (68); (A) London 44109 (68).

Harry James and his Orchestra—Philips BBL7176; (A) Columbia CL-669.

The Greatest Hits of Harry James—CBS 52367; (A) Columbia CS-9430 (67).

Greatest Hits, Vol.2—CBS 52838.

Requests on the Road—MGM C908 (63) (d).

The Solid Gold Trumpet of Harry James—MGM C932 (63) (d); (A) MGM-4058, (S) S-4058 (62).

All the Way (1941-54)—(A) Big Band Archives LP-2202 (2) (74).

The Spectacular Sound of Harry James—MGM C862, (S) CS-6036 (61) (d).

One Night Stand—(A) Columbia CL-522.

Soft Lights, Sweet Trumpet—(A) Columbia CL-581.

Sharp as a Tack (1939-59)—(A) Swing Era LP-1004.

All-time Favorites—(A) Columbia CL-655.

Harry James Broadcasts (1940-41) (with

Dick Haymes)—(A) Sunbeam SB-203.
Live at the Riverboat—(A) Dot 25728 (66).
Harry James Today—(A) MGM E-3848, (S) S-3848 (60).
Harry James and his Music Makers (1945-49)—First Heard 9 (75).
New Versions of Down Beat Favorites—(A) MGM E-4265.
One Night Stand with Harry James (1946/1953)—(A) Joyce LP-1014 (75).
Harry James in Hi-Fi—(A) Capitol W-654.
More Harry James in Hi-Fi (1955-56)—Capitol LCT6107; (A) Capitol W-712.
Wild About Harry (1957)—Capitol LCT6146; (A) Capitol T874, (S) ST874.
Harry James and his Orchestra 1943/6 (broadcasts)—London HMP5038 (79).
Harry James and his Orchestra 1948/9 (broadcasts)—London HMP5060 (79), HMP5052 (79), HMA5067 (79).
One Night Stand with Harry James, Vol.2 (1939-44)—(A) Joyce LP-1024 (75).
Laura—(A) CBS Harmony 11326 (69).
Songs that Sold a Million—CBS Hallmark SHM523; (A) Harmony 7191 & 11245 (59).
The Harry James Big Band—Rediffusion 01.175.
Harry James and his Music Makers (1942-47)—First Heard FH-14.
Harry James and his Orchestra (1940-41)—(F) Musidisc JA-5150.
Harry James's Greatest Hits—Pye 'Golden Hour' GH817 (73).
The Second Big Band Sound—Polydor Verve 2317 083 (75).
Mr. Trumpet—(A) Pickwick S-3006.
The Shadow of your Smile—(A) Pickwick S-3126.
You made me Love you—(A) Pickwick S-3044.
San Antonio Rose—(A) Dot 25735 (66).
Ballads & Beat—(A) Dot 3669, (S) 25669 (66).
Double Dixie—(A) MGM 4137, (S) S-4137 (63).
Harry, not Jesse—(A) Metro 536, (S) S-536 (65).
Harry James—Giants of Jazz GOJ1009 (79).
Saturday Night Swing—Giants of Jazz GOJ1016 (79).
Harry James and his Orchestra (1948-49)—Solid Sender SOL501 (79).
Harry James in Texas—Joker SM3058 (79).
The Uncollected Harry James—Hindsight HRS135 (79).
One Night Stand—Queen QU026 (79).

Buddy Johnson

(b Darlington, SC, January 10 1915)

A gifted pianist and arranger Johnson went to New York in 1938 and at first worked with small groups, often featuring his sister Ella as vocalist. In 1944 he had a big band which was immensely popular at the Savoy Ballroom, Harlem, and on tours of the Southern States. The band did not contain many 'name' soloists but was notable for its fine ensemble and solid beat which particularly pleased the dancers. Vocalist Arthur Prysock was also well featured as well as sister Ella. In the 1950s Johnson was mostly involved in rhythm and blues, no less successfully, but by 1960 he had left music and worked thereafter as a minister with his own parish in the Bronx. Arrangements for the big band were mostly by Johnson himself, with some by Slide Hampton.

Selected LP recordings

Buddy Johnson at the Savoy Ballroom 1945-46—(A) Jazz Archives JA-25 (75). *Walk'em (theme); Opus 2; Since I fell for you; St. Louis Blues; Waitin' for the train to come in; Night shift; Jodi; One o'clock Boogie; The other side of the Rainbow; Exactly like you; One for a nickel; Gee, it's good to hold you; On there; Traffic jam; If you never return (theme).* (1945-46.)

Also:
Buddy Johnson and his Orchestra—(G) MCA PC08222.
Rockin' Time—(F) Vogue LDM30221 (75).
Arthur Prysock—Songs that made him Famous—(A) Decca DL-4628.
Rock 'n' Roll Stage Show—(A) Mercury-Wing MGW-12111.
Rock and Roll with Buddy Johnson—(A) Mercury-Wing MG-20209.
Go ahead and Rock—(A) Forum F-9022.

Charlie Johnson

(b Philadelphia, November 21 1891; d New York, December 13 1959)

Led a hot band at Small's Paradise Club in Harlem during the 1920s and 1930s, similar in style to the Fletcher Henderson orchestra. The group broke up in 1938 and Johnson continued as a session musician in the 1930s and 1940s until illness forced him to leave music. This fine band, which only recorded a handful of sides, included such players as Jabbo Smith, Sidney de Paris, Jimmy Harrison and Edgar Sampson, Benny Carter, Dicky Wells, Roy Eldridge and Frankie Newton.

Selected LP recordings

Charlie Johnson—(F) RCA 7410.065/6 (2). *Paradise Wobble; Birmingham Black Bottom; Don't you leave me here; You ain't the one; Charleston's the best dance after all; Hot-tempered Blues; The boy in the boat; Walk that thing.* (1927-29, various takes; plus tracks by the Lloyd Scott Orchestra and Cecil Scott and his Bright Boys.) (Fr. RCA issue (430.687) also included *Harlem drag; Hot bones and rice* (1929).)

Also:

Charlie Johnson's Paradise Band—(A) 'X' LVA-3026.

Isham Jones

(b Coalton, Ohio, January 31 1894; d Hollywood, October 19 1956)

After playing locally as a youth, Jones went to Chicago in 1915 and joined several bands as well as leading a small group of his own. He soon formed his own full band, first at the Green Mill then at the Hotel Sherman. After taking the band to the Automobile Association Club (later the Casa Lopez) in New York, Jones came to London in 1924. After returning to America he gained increasing fame until his retirement in 1936 and the band was taken over by Woody Herman (qv) and became 'The Band That Plays the Blues'. He reformed a band the following year and remained in business with it until 1941; thereafter he led various groups on the West Coast and did a certain amount of recording, arranging and composing. The Isham Jones Orchestra had an impressive reputation during its heyday, which came in the middle 1930s, doing many radio shows and playing all over the States, frequently with arrangements by Gordon Jenkins. Some records by Bing Crosby were accompanied by Jones.

Selected LP recordings

Isham Jones Orchestra featuring Louis Panico—Retrieval FG-404. *Sweet woman* (1920); *Wabash Blues* (1921); *Virginia Blues* (1922); *High brown Blues* (1922); *My Honey's lovin' arms* (1922); *Aunt Hagar's children Blues* (1922); *Farewell Blues* (1923); *Frankie and Johnny* (1923); *Memphis Blues* (1923); *Somebody's wrong* (1923); *Wop Blues* (1923); *Forgetful Blues* (1923); *Cotton Pickers' Ball* (1923); *Mama loves Papa* (1923); *Unfortunate Blues* (1924); *Hula Lou* (1924); *Never again* (1924).

Swingin' Down the Lane—Decca Ace of Hearts AH110 (66) (d). *Swingin' down the Lane; I'll be blue, just thinking of you; Stardust; I keep remembering; Lonesome lover; My ideal; There's a wah-wah girl in Agua Caliente; Miss Hannah; What's the use; Trees; Good evening; Goodnight, sweet dreams.* (1930-31.)

Isham Jones and his Famous Orchestra 1929-30—Sunbeam MFC8 (74) (d). *What's the use; A song without a name; Not a cloud in the sky; Trees; Stardust; Miss Hannah; There's a wah-wah gal in Caliente; Don't tell her; My baby just cares for me; Good evenin', sweet Jennie Lee; I'll be blue; In my heart it's you; Ideal; I'm so afraid of you; Goodnight, sweet dreams.* (1929-30.)

Also:

Isham Jones (Rare Broadcast Recordings of his Last Band Featuring Woody Herman) (1936)—(A) Sunbeam SB-306 (76).

The Great Isham Jones and his Orchestra—RCA RD-7643 (d); (A) RCA LPV-504.

Quincy Jones

(b Chicago, Illinois March 14 1933)

Moved to Seattle at the age of ten and began to study piano and trumpet. In 1950 had trumpet lessons with Clark Terry (then visiting Seattle with Basie). But the principal local influence on him was the blues singer and pianist, Ray Charles. In Boston for two years from 1951 on a Schillinger scholarship. Then toured briefly with Jay McShann before joining Lionel Hampton. Within the latter's band he met Clifford Brown, Gigi Gryce, Art Farmer, Jimmy Cleveland et al and for the first time began to make a name for himself as a composer/arranger. Hampton also took him to Europe, where he studied with Nadia Boulanger and became a staff writer for Barclay Records. In 1956/57 organised and served as musical director of Dizzy Gillespie's 'World Statesman' band which toured the Middle and Far East and also South America, then wrote for Count Basie. Led his own big bands on and off for festivals, overseas tours and records since 1960. However, in the 1970s, moving to California, has divided his time between band activities, serving as musical director for A & M Records and writing for TV and movies. Wrote the theme for *Ironside*; also film scores including *The Pawnbroker, The Anderson Tapes, Cactus Flower, Bob & Carol & Ted & Alice, In Cold Blood* and *In The Heat Of The Night.* In 1971 wrote *Black Requiem*, a major piece about the Negro's struggles against slavery and prejudice. It featured Ray Charles, the Houston Symphony Orchestra and 80 singers. *Body Heat* (included on the LP *I Heard That*) earned a gold disc for one million copies sold.

Selected LP recordings

The Great Wide World of Quincy Jones—Mercury MMC14046, (S) CMS18031 (60) (d).
I Dig Dancers—Mercury MMC14080, (S) CMS18055 (61) (d).
Around the World—Mercury MMC14098, (S) CMS18064 (62) (d).
The Quintessence—HMV CLP1581, (S) CSD1452 (62) (d); (A) Impulse AS-11 (62), (70).
Gula Matira—CBS A & M AMLS992; (A) A & M 3030.
Smackwater Jack—CBS A & M AMLS 63037; (A) A & M 3037.
Walking in Space—CBS A & M AMLS 68050, (A) A & M 3023.
You've got it bad, Girl—CBS A & M AMLS 63041 (73).
Ironside—CBS Hamlet AMLP 8005 (75).
Mellow Madness—CBS A & M AMLH 64526 (75).
The Quintessence—CBS Impulse IMPL 8042 (76).
We had a Ball—Sonic SON033 (76).
I Heard That!—CBS A & M AMLM 63075 (2) (76).
Mode—(A) ABC AB-782.
Quincy Jones and his Orchestra—Music for Pleasure MFP50441 (80).
This is how I feel about Jazz—ABC Paramount 149; (A) ditto.
Quincy's Home Again (with Harry Arnold's Swedish Radio Studio Orchestra)—Metronome MLP-15010.
The Birth of a Band—Mercury MMC14038, (A) MG-20444.
Sounds . . . and Stuff like that—CBS A & M AMLH64685.
NDEDA—(A) Mercury SRM-2-623 (2).

Hal Kemp

(b Marion, Alabama, March 27 1905; d Madera, California, December 21 1940)
After leading various college bands in the mid-1920s, he formed his first professional band in 1927. Soon achieved success as Carolina Club Orchestra and in 1930 toured Europe with Bunny Berigan (t) (qv) in brass section. During the 1930s Kemp evolved a smooth 'sweet' style of society dance music with emphasis on muted trumpets playing staccato against flowing reeds. Up to 1935 chief arranger was John Scott Trotter, who had been with Kemp in college band days; after Trotter left, Hal Mooney took over as principal arranger. Success continued until 1940 when difficulties over personnel and other matters, but these were being resolved when Kemp was fatally injured in a car crash. Band continued briefly under other members, but did not last beyond 1943.

Selected LP recordings

Workout—(A) Big Band Archive LP1213 (74).
Great Dance Bands—(A) RCA LPM-2041.
Bunny Berigan with Hal Kemp—(A) Shoestring SS110.
Hal Kemp Orchestra 1927-31—(A) The Old Masters TOM-24.
This is Hal Kemp—(A) RCA LPT-3016.
Hal Kemp and his Orchestra 1934 (broadcasts)—London HM-A5069 (80).

Stan Kenton

(b Wichita, Kansas, February 19 1912; d New York, August 28 1979)
After playing in various bands, including that of Gus Arnheim (qv) and developing his talents as pianist, arranger and composer, Kenton formed his first big band in 1941 and immediately showed himself a strong minded leader, with views of his own that he was able to put over. The Kenton band mixed at first hard driving, powerhouse music of some originality with commercial material, achieving 'hits' in both categories and became the apostle of 'progressive jazz' with complex scores and many technical experiments. His music tended to inhabit a kind of hinterland between jazz and concert music, much as Paul Whiteman's had a generation earlier. There is no doubting the Kenton influence on jazz and popular music generally from the 1940s on, but most of the

time he was assessed on untenable terms and only incidentally related to jazz. That does not in itself invalidate his work, and much that he did maintains at least a technical interest, though if one probes beneath the surface the content is found to be shallow. All the same he did in his own way spearhead the idea of modern jazz and in some respects made the path easier for those who followed him with genuinely 'progressive' music (the term is really meaningless; no one was more truly progressive through five decades than Duke Ellington, who never used the term and to whom it was never applied). The various Kenton bands contained excellent musicians, especially vocalists Anita O'Day and June Christy, and though improvisation was not a major feature of Kenton's music, good jazz soloists played with him [Conte Candoli, Shorty Rogers, Maynard Ferguson (t), Kai Winding, Eddie Bert, (tb) Art Pepper, Lee Konitz, Bud Shank, (as), Stan Getz (ts) and Shelly Manne (d) and a good many others]. Kenton's career was interrupted several times by poor health; but he remained active, continually evolving a style of music which, like the Whiteman and similar types before him, owed as much to European concert music as to indigenous American jazz and folk idioms. As well as Kenton himself, prominent arrangers included Pete Rugolo, Bill Holman, Johnny Richards and Bill Russo.

Selected LP recordings

The Formative Years—Brunswick LAT8122 (56) (d); Decca 'Ace of Hearts' AH-123 (69) (d); (A) Decca DL-8259. *The Tango* (1941); *Taboo* (1941); *This love of mine* (1941); *Adios* (1941); *El Choclo* (1942); *Lamento Gitano* (1942); *Gambler's Blues* (1942); *Reed rapture* (1942); *Concerto for Doghouse* (1942.)

Greatest Hits—Capitol T2327, (S) ST2327 (67) (d); (A) same; CAPS1002 (77). *Artistry in rhythm* (1943); *Tampico* (1945); *Interlude; Eager Beaver* (1943); *September Song; Unison riff* (1947); *Lover* (1947); *Painted rhythm* (1945); *And her tears flowed like wine* (1944); *Laura; The peanut vendor.*

Artistry in Jazz—EMI 'One Up' OU2001 (72). *Bues in Riffs (Hammersmith riffs); Riff rhapsody; Coop's solo; Riff raff; Of all things; Opus in beige; Artistry in Blues; Design for Blues; Wagon; Piece for soft brass, woodwinds and percussion.* (1951-65.)

Adventures in Blues—Capitol T1985, (S) ST1985 (67) (d); (A) ditto. *Reuben's Blues; Dragonwyck; Blue Ghost; Exit stage left; Night at The Gold Nugget; Formula SK-32; Aphrodisia; Fitz; The Blues Story.* (1961.)

Stan Kenton Today—Decca DKL3/1-2 (2); (A) London 44179/80. *What are you doing for the rest of your life; Chiapas; Opus in pastels; Malaguena; Artistry in percussion; Yesterdays; Fringe benefits; Bogota; Intermission Riff; Ambivalence; Interlude; Peanut vendor; Malaga; Walk softly; Take the 'A' train; Artistry in rhythm; God save the Queen.* (Fairfield Hall, Croydon, 1953.)

Also:

Milestones—Capitol LC6517 (53); (A) Capitol T-190.

Encores—Capitol LC6523 (53); (A) Capitol T-155.

Artistry in Rhythm—Capitol LC6545 (53); (A) Capitol DT-167; (A) DT-167.

Progressive Jazz—Capitol LC6546 (53); (A) Capitol T-172.

Stan Kenton in London (The Decca Record Co).

City of Glass—Capitol LC6577 (53); (A) Capitol W-738.
New Concepts—Capitol LC6595; (A) T-383.
Sketches on Standards—Capitol LC6602 (53); (A) T-426.
Innovations—Capitol LCT6006 (54); (A) Capitol W-189.
This Modern World—Capitol LC6667 (54); (A) Capitol W-738.
Stan Kenton Classics—Capitol LC6676 (54); (A) Capitol T-356.
Kenton Showcase—Capitol LCT6009 (55); (A) Capitol T-598.
Portraits on Standards—Capitol LC6697 (55); (A) T-462.
Stan Kenton in Hi-Fi—Capitol LCT6109 (55); (A) Capitol W-724.
Stan Kenton—Capitol LCT6118 (56); (A) Capitol T-2.
Kenton with Voices—Capitol LCT6138 (57); (A) Capitol T-810.
Rendezvous with Kenton—Capitol T932 (58); (S) ST932 (59); (A) ditto.
The Kenton Era, Vol.1—Capitol LCT6157 (58); (A) W-569 (4).
The Kenton Era, Vol.2—Capitol LCT6158 (58); (A) W-569 (4).
The Kenton Era, Vol.3—Capitol LCT6159 (58); (A) W-569 (4).
The Kenton Era, Vol.4—Capitol LCT6160 (58); (A) W-569 (4).
Back to Balboa—Capitol T995 (59); (A) T-995.
The Ballad Style of Stan Kenton—Capitol T1068 (59); (S) ST1068 (60); (A) Capitol T-1068.
Lush Interlude—Capitol T1130 (59); (A) ditto.
Artistry in Voices—(A) Capitol T-2132, (S) ST2132 (64).
Adventures in Time—(A) Capitol T-1844, (S) ST-1844 (63).
The Stage Door Swings (1958)—Capitol T1166, (S) ST1166; (A) ditto.
The Kenton Touch—Capitol T1276, (S) ST1276; (A) ditto.
Viva Kenton—Capitol W-1305, (S) SW-1305; (A) ditto.
Standards in Silhouette—Capitol T1394, (S) ST1394 (61); (A) ditto.
Kenton at The Tropicana (1959)—Capitol T1460, (S) ST1460 (61); (A) ditto.
Kenton Road Show, Vols. 1 & 2—Capitol T1327/8, (S) ST1237/8 (61); (A) STBO-1327 (2).
The Sophisticated Approach—Capitol ST-1674 (62); (A) ditto (62).
West Side Story—Capitol ST1609 (62).
Adventures in Jazz—Capitol T1796, (S) ST1796 (63); (A) ditto.
Stan Kenton Plays for Today—Capitol ST-2655 (64); (A) ditto.
The World we Know—Capitol ST-2810 (65); (A) ditto.
Stan Kenton De Luxe Set—Capitol STCL-2989 (3) (66); (A) ditto (68).
Stan Kenton—(A) Capitol STCL-575 (3).
Kenton Climax—World Records T109 (d).
Afro-Cuban Jazz Suite—Metro 2356 098.
The Aztec Suite—London LTZ-15198 (d); (A) Atlantic.
Cuban Fire—(A) Capitol T-731.
Hair—(G) Electrola 1C 062 80173.
Stan Kenton in Concert—(F) Pathé Marconi 2C 064 81043 (d).
One Night Stand with Kenton—(A) Joyce JLP1026.
Stan Kenton-1941 (broadcasts)—London HMP5049 (79).
Stan Kenton-1941, Vol.2 (broadcasts)—London HMP5055 (79).
Stan Kenton-1943-44 (broadcasts)—London HMP5061 (79).
Stan Kenton Live in Europe—Decca PFS4393 (77); (A) London 44276.
Artistry in Kenton—Decca KEN1 (79).
The Uncollected Stan Kenton—Hindsight HSR136 (79).

Creative World

Kenton organised his own direct mail label, 'Creative World', (drawn from Capitol material)—of which the following are a selection:
New Concepts in Artistry in Jazz (W or ST1002); **Kenton in Stereo** (W/ST1004); **Lush Interlude** (1005); **West Side Story** (1007); **Cuban Fire** (1008); **Innovations in Modern Music** (1009); **Adventures in Jazz** (1010); **Adventures in Time** (1011); **Adventures in Blues** (1012); **Live at Redlands** (2) (1015); **Sophisticated Approach** (1018); **Compositions of Dee Barton** (1022); **Kenton/Wagner** (1024); **Adventures in Standards** (1025); **Kenton Showcase** (1026); **Collectors Choice** (1027); **The Fabulous Alumni** (1028); **The Kenton Era** (1030); **Back to Balbao** (1031); **At Las Vegas Tropicana** (1032); **The Kenton Touch** (1033); **Stan Kenton Encores** (1034); **By Request, Vol.1** (1036); **A Concert in Progressive Jazz** (1037);

Artistry in Voices and Brass (1038); **Live at Brigham Young** (2) (1039); **The Stage Door Swings** (1044); **Artistry in Bossa Nova** (1045); **With Jean Turner** (1046); **Milestones** (1047); **Standards in Silhouette** (1049); **The Lighter Side** (1050); **Rendezvous** (1057); **Live at Butler University** (1058); **With Four Freshmen** (2) (1059); **By Request, Vol.3** (1062); **Viva Kenton** (1063); **By Request, Vol.4** (1064); **Birthday in Britain** (1065); **Too Much** (1067); **7.5 on the Richter Scale** (1070); **Solo** (1071); **Kenton plays Chicago** (1072); **Fire, Fury and Fun** (1073); **Hits in Concert** (1074); **Kenton '74** (1076); etc.

Wayne King

(b Savannah, Illinois, February 16 1901)
Known during the high noon of the big band era as The Waltz King. As sax player and vocalist, King favoured a somewhat wailing and desolate sound which attained notable popularity, especially in the Chicago area where he played in many hotels and ballrooms. Featured on radio shows, especially *Lady Esther Serenade* between 19311 and 1938. Reformed bands after military service in World War II and added television to radio appearances.

Selected LP recordings

Introducing Wayne King—One Up OU2145 (76).
Enchanted Evening—(A) Decca DL-8277 (58).
Smooth as Silk—(A) Decca DL-8353.
Dream Time—(A) Decca DL-8663 (58).
The Sound of Wayne King—(A) Decca DL-8823.
Orchids to my Lady—(A) Decca DL-8876.
Lady Esther Serenade—(A) Decca DL-8951.
The Songs of Irving Berlin—(A) RCA LPM-3057.
The Best of Wayne King—(A) RCA LSP-3742 (67).
Smoke Gets in Your Eyes—(A) Vocalion 73840 (68).
The Best of Wayne King—(A) Decca DXS-7189 (2) (65).

Andy Kirk

(b Newport, Kentucky, May 28 1898)
In the 1930s and up till 1948 Andy Kirk led an important band known as the (Twelve) Clouds of Joy. In the band's heyday the outstanding member was pianist, composer/arranger, Mary Lou Williams, who gave it its particular mark of distinction under Kirk's intelligent leadership. But the roots of the band's style were from Kansas City, where it rivalled that of Benny Moten. Sometimes there are distinct sounds of Ellington in the scoring and solo integration. It would be tempting to think this a result of Mary Lou's admiration for Duke; but in fact it was there before she joined. What it probably demonstrates yet again is the universal nature of Ellington's music, taking in as it did elements of virtually all forms of jazz. Kirk himself grew up in Denver, Colorado, where he worked with a band under violinist George Morrison and alongside an alto player named Jimmie Lunceford (qv). In 1925 he joined a Texas band of trumpet player Terrence Holder and four years later took over the band himself. Played in the Roseland and Savoy Ballrooms, New York, in 1930 and in Philadelphia in 1931, though the band's hometown was always Kansas City. Kirk's success continued until 1948, though in the later years, under pressure of trends of the day, he enlarged it to its detriment, as he himself later admitted. Later years were spent with occasional contacts with music, and in property and hotel business. During the 1940s, Howard McGhee (t) and Charlie Parker (as) played with Kirk; early recordings featured as well as Mary Lou Williams (p), a number of good soloists [Gene Prince (t), Allen Durham, Ted Donnelly (tb), John Harrington (cl), Dick Wilson (ts), June Richmond (vo) and Floyd Smith (g)].

Selected LP recordings

Andy Kirk and his 12 Clouds of Joy (March 1936)—Parlophone PMC7156 (73) (d). *Walkin' and swingin'; Moten Swing; Lotta sax appeal; Git; All the Jive is gone; Froggy Bottom; Bearcat Shuffle; Steppin' pretty; Christopher Columbus; Corky; I'se a muggin'; Until the real thing comes along; Puddin' head serenade* (1936). (Plus five tracks by the Mary Lou Williams Trio (1936).)
Kansas City Jazz—Coral CP39; Decca 'Ace of Hearts' AH-110; (A) Decca 8044. *The Count* (1940); *Twelfth Street Rag* (1940). (With tracks by Count Basie, Hot Lips Page, etc.)
Andy Kirk's 12 Clouds of Joy—Coral

56019 (d); Decca Ace of Hearts AH160 (67) (d). *Fifty-Second Street* (1936); *Wednesday Night Hop* (1937); *Bear down* (1937); *Little Joe from Chicago* (1938); *Mary's idea* (1938); *S'posin'* (1939); *Big Jim Blues* (1939); *Little Miss* (1940); *Twelfth Street Rag* (1940); *Ring dem bells* (1941); *47th Street Jive* (1941); *McGhee special* (1942).
Also:
Andy Kirk—Live from the Trianon Ballroom 1937—(Sw) Jazz Society AA-503 (74).
Live Session '37—Jazz Archives JA5133 (74).
Andy Kirk and his Clouds of Joy—Ace of Hearts AH106 (66) (d).
Instrumentally Speaking—(F) MCA 510.033 (74); (A) Decca DL-9232 (68).
Big Bands (1934-42), (with Claude Hopkins & Carolina Cotton Pickers)—(G) Swingfan 1010.
Souvenir Album—(A) Coral CRL-56019.
A Mellow Bit of Rhythm—(A) RCA LPM-1302.
Clouds of Joy—Decca 'Ace of Hearts' AH-110 (d).

Gene Krupa

(b Chicago, January 15 1909; d New York, October 16 1973)
Decided to become a drummer after hearing Ben Pollack. Made steady headway as jazz drummer, playing with Red McKenzie and Eddie Condon's Chicagoans, Red Nichols, Russ Colombo and Buddy Rogers. In 1934 he joined Benny Goodman and was a leading influence on the band's popularity and the birth of the 'swing' era. Notable for strong beat, brilliant technique and showmanship. He was important member of the Goodman Trio and Quartet, and made major impact when the Goodman band appeared at Carnegie Hall in January, 1938. Left Goodman to form his own big band later in 1938, with much publicity and a good deal of success. The band had good members including tenor stars Vido Musso and Sam Donahue; and in the early 1940s featured Roy Eldridge (t, vo) and singer Anita O'Day. Rejoined Goodman in 1943 and played later with Tommy Dorsey. Another band, with strings and things, was less successful, and Krupa began heading small groups with more success. Sometimes indulged in 'drum battles' with Buddy Rich (qv). Maintained loose association with Goodman, and appeared in a number of films, including *The Gene Krupa Story, The Benny Goodman*

Gene Krupa (left) and Cozy Cole (Universal International).

Story, The Glenn Miller Story and *Some Like It Hot*. Suffered from declining health during his later years, but continued playing although at the end he was mortally ill with leukemia.

Selected LP recordings

Drummin' Man—CBS BPG62289/90; (A) Columbia C2L29 (2) (63). *Apurksody* (1938); *Drummin' man* (1939); *Rhythm jam* (1938); *Quiet and roll 'em* (1939); *Tutti frutti* (1938); *Sweetheart, honey, darlin' dear* (1939); *Tuxedo Junction* (1940); *Drum Boogie* (1941); *Bolero at the Savoy* (1938); *Let me off Uptown* (1941); *Rockin' chair* (1941); *Massachusetts* (1942); *After you've gone* (1941); *Skylark* (1941); *Knock me a kiss* (1942); *That's what you think* (1942); Record 2: *Leave us leap* (1945); *What's this* (1945); *Dark eyes* (1945); *Body and soul* (1945); *Opus 1* (1945); *How high the Moon* (1945); *Boogie Blues* (1945); *Lover* (1945); *Starburst* (1946); *Gene's Boogie* (1947); *Disc Jockey Jump* (1947); *There is no breeze* (1946); *Calling Doctor Gillespie* (1947); *I should have kept on dreaming* (1948); *Up an atom* (1949); *Lemon drop* (1949).

Big Band Sound—Verve 2317 078 (74). *Let me off Uptown; Rockin' chair; Opus 1; Fifth fry; Drummin' man; Drum Boogie; Boogie Blues; Leave us leap; Slow down; Wire Brush Stomp; That's what you think; After you've gone.* (1956.)

Wire Brush Stomp (1938-1941)—(A) Bandstand BS-7117. *Jam on toast* (1938); *Wire Brush Stomp* (1938); *Meet the beat of my heart* (1938); *Nagasaki* (1938); *Bolero at the Savoy* (1938); *Murdy Purdy* (1938); *Some like it hot* (1939); *The madam swings it* (1939); *Symphony in Riffs* (1939); *Marcheta* (1940); *Manhattan transfer* (1940); *The big do* (1940); *Alreet* (1941); *Slow down* (1941); *Flamingo* (1941); *Watch the Birdie* (1941).

Second Big Band Sound—Verve 2317 113 (76). *Birdhouse; Margie; Mulligan Stew; Begin the Beguine; Sugar; The way of all flesh; Disc Jockey Jump; Birds of a feather; Sometimes I'm Happy; How high the Moon; If you were the only girl in the world; Yardbird Suite.* (1958, early Gerry Mulligan arrangements.)

Also:

Swingin' with Krupa—RCA INTS1072 (70) (d).

The Big Bands—(A) CBS G30009 (2).

Gene Krupa Orchestra 1946-47—Musidisc 30 JA 5115 (75).

Gene Krupa and his Orchestra 1945-49—First Heard FH7 (77).

King of the Drums—(F) CBS 52736.

Gene Krupa Orchestra 1945-46—Jazz Record Collectors 10 (74).

That Drummer's Band (1939-47)—(A) Sounds of Swing LP114.

To be or Not to Bop (1938-46)—(A) Sounds of Swing LP119.

Gene Krupa, Vols.1-14—Ajax 101/105/110/111/121/122/125/127/130/132/138/146/156 & 161 (79).

Kay Kyser

(b Rocky Mount, North Carolina, June 18 1906)

Leader of commercially successful dance band during 1930s and 1940s after fronting college bands in North Carolina. Featured on many radio shows and in movies between 1939 and 1944. Like most American dance bands of the period (and also some British) Kyser featured a certain amount of jazz-tinged material in the 'swing' idiom, featuring Herbie Haymer (ts). Kyser also had a gimmick of singing song titles and introducing singers with explanations of songs. Gave up music and show business in the early 1950s.

Selected LP recordings

Kay Kyser—(A) Big Band Archive LP1220 (75). *Deed I do; Come to baby, do; Put that ring on my finger; Two guitars; My darling; I don't want to do it alone; Parade of the wooden soldiers; Rio Rita; Yearning; Milkman, keep those bottles quiet; Five feet two; That's for me; Moon of Manakoura; They chopped down the apple tree; Angel; Great day.* (1939-44.)

Also:

Dance Parade—(A) Columbia CL-6061.

Kay Kyser—(A) Harmony HL-7041.

Campus Rally—(A) Harmony HL-7136 (58).

Kay Kyser's Greatest Hits—(A) Capitol T-1692.

Pushin' Sand—(A) Big Band Archives LP 1207 (74).

Elliot Lawrence

(b Philadelphia, February 14 1925)

From mid-1940s to mid-1950s led a fashionable dance band somewhat on the lines of Claude Thornhill (qv) and featuring solos and arrangement of Gerry Mulligan (qv). Band played at Hotel Pennsylvania, New York, from 1946 and won considerable recognition. Lawrence gave up band leading in the mid-1950s and subsequently concentrated on shows and television, becoming musical director of a number of major Broadway successes. He led a jazz group on his own CBS radio show after relinquishing band leadership.

Selected LP recordings

Sugar Beat (1945-1954)—(A) Big Band Archives LP1219 (75). *Lawrence leaps* (1945); *Chloe* (1945); *The song is you* (1945); *How high the Moon* (1945); *Elevation* (1949); *Between the Devil and the deep blue sea* (1945); *Cool days* (1954); *Box 155* (1946); *Listen to Lawrence* (1945); *The night is young and you're so beautiful* (1945); *March from Carmen* (1945); *Someone to watch over me* (1945); *Hand me five* (1945); *If you are but a dream* (1945); *The old night owl* (1945); *Sugar beat* (1947).

Also:

Elliot Lawrence Plays Gerry Mulligan Arrangements—Vogue LAE 12057 (58) (d) (A) Fantasy 3-206.

Elliot Lawrence Plays Tiny Kahn and Johnny Mandell Arrangements—Vogue LAE12101 (58); (A) Fantasy 3-219.

Dream—Vogue VA160110 (60) (d); (A) Fantasy 3-226.

Swinging at the Steel Pier—Vogue LAE12071 (58) (d); (A) Fantasy 3-236.

Elliot Lawrence Plays for Swinging Dancers—(A) Fantasy 3-246.

College Prom—(A) Decca DL-5274.

Elliot Lawrence—(A) Decca DL-5353.

Jazz Goes Broadway—(A) Vik LX-1113.

Hi-Fi-ing Winds—(A) Vik LX-1124.

One Night Stand (1947)—(A) Joyce JLP-1004 (74).

Prom Night—(A) Decca 8338.

Ted Lewis

(b Circleville, Ohio, June 6 1892; d New York, August 25 1971)

Worked in vaudeville during the 1910s, then led his own bands before running his own nightclub in New York. Played schmaltzy clarinet and sang in a mildly ghoulish half-talking, half-singing style which, together with battered top-hat routine and catch phrase 'Is everyone happy?' gained widespread popularity. Lewis' affection for jazz, though he had little idea how to play it himself, led him to employ several leading jazzmen in his band [Muggsy Spanier (ct), Benny Goodman, Tony Parenti (cl) Fats Waller (p) and George Brunies (tb), etc]. Lewis kept a band going intermittently in his later years, and appeared on radio and television. Lewis wrote a number of popular songs, including *When my Baby Smiles at Me* and *While we danced till dawn.*

Selected LP recordings

Ted Lewis Band (1931-32)—(A) Sunbeam SB-115 (74).

Ted Lewis Orchestra 1928-32 (Vol.2)—(F) Biograph BLPC-8 (74).

Everybody Happy (1927-31)—(A) Epic LN3170 (d).

Ted Lewis Souvenir, Vol.1—Brunswick LA8601 (53); (A) Decca DL-5114.

Ted Lewis Souvenir, Vol.2—Brunswick LA8608 (53); (A) Decca DL-5223.

Ted Lewis Band—(A) Decca DL-4905.

Is Everybody Happy—(A) Decca DL-8321.

Medicine Man for the Blues—(A) Decca DL-8322.

Me and my Shadow—(A) Unique RKO-180.

A Jazz Holiday (1925-28)—Academy AJA-5006 (81).

Million Memories—(A) Unique RKO-122.

Vic Lewis

(b London, July 29 1919)

Co-leader with Jack Parnell (qv) of excellent big band and small group music, with many recordings through five decades. He spent a time in America in 1938 and was active there on the jazz scene. After service in World War II, Lewis played with Buddy Featherstonhaugh, Stephane Grappelli and Ted Heath, and in the 1950s led various excellent bands, twice taking them on tours to the US. A first class musician and energetic leader, Lewis' bands invariably showed fine musical qualities and set high standards. A four-disc album of his recordings following his career through was issued in 1975.

Selected LP recordings

Big Band Explosion—Pye Ember SE8018 (74) (d).

My Life my Way—DJM SPECB103 (4) (75).

Vic's Riffs (Big Band Jazz from England) (1947-51)—Big Band International LP2701 (2) (74) (d).

Mulligan's Music—Decca LF1157 (54) (d).

Progressive Jazz—Decca LF1216 (55) (d).

Sydney Lipton

After playing the violin in several early bands of British leaders, including Ambrose and Billy Cotton, Lipton took his own band to Grosvenor House, Park Lane, in 1932 for a residency which lasted for the rest of the 1930s, through the war years and for more than two decades after, which must be a record for the course. Until 1935 Max Abrams (d) played with Lipton, and at the end of that year two of the stars of the Ambrose Orchestra, Max Goldberg (t) and Ted Heath (tb) joined him and were prominently featured. Subsequently, a number of leading British musicians were in the ranks. The Grosvenor House music was smooth, polished, eminently danceable, in which musicianship rather than show novelties were the order.

Selected LP recordings

Syd Lipton and his Grosvenor House Band—World Records SH257 (77). *For you, just you, my baby* (1932); *Ooh! that kiss* (1932); *A great big bunch of you* (1932); *Happy-go-lucky you* (1932); *Masquerade* (1932); *I'm positively in love* (1932); *We're a couple of soldiers, my baby and me* (1932); *I'll follow you* (1932); *Down on the Delta* (1932); *More beautiful than ever* (1932); *I can't write the words* (1932); *Hey! young fella* (1933); *The sister of the girl I love* (1933); *This is no dream* (1933); *In the moonlight* (1933); *What a perfect combination* (1933).

Guy Lombardo

(b London, Ontario, June 19 1902; d Houston, Texas, November 3 1977)

One of four brothers who formed a band known as Guy Lombardo and His Royal Canadians, among the most commercially successful in dance band history. First formed in the 1920s, it was high in the charts by 1925 and remained there for four decades, prolific in recording, on radio and later television, and playing in leading hotels and clubs throughout America. All three of Guy's brothers [Lebert (t), Carmen (as) and Victor (bar)] remained with the band until Lebert retired and Carmen died (1971), although Victor was absent between 1947 and 1951. The Lombardo style, sweet and luscious music for dancing, was formed chiefly by Carmen who led the saxes and contributed vocals as well as doing many of the typical arrangements. Sister Rose Marie also sang with the band at times. During the 1930s Lombardo was featured on the 'Burns and Allen' radio show, and in 1938 took over from Wayne King (qv) on the *Lady Esther Serenade.* He retained his popularity during the years of big band decline and latterly became associated with New Year celebrations on television. The Lombardo signature tune was *Coquette* written by Carmen. Among the (perhaps surprising) admirers of Guy Lombardo was Louis Armstrong. Lombardo was also a power boat racer and achieved many successes.

Selected LP recordings

The best of Guy Lombardo—(A) Capitol T-1461.

Guy Lombardo Plays—(A) Camden CAL-255.

An Evening with Guy Lombardo—(A) Camden CAL-445.

Your Guy Lombardo Medley—(A) Decca ST-1598.

Lombardo Land, U.S.A.—(A) Decca DL-8097.

Soft and Sweet—(A) Decca DL-8135.

The Sweetest Music this Side of Heaven—Decca 'Ace of Heart' AH-86 (65) (d); (A) Decca DXM-154 (4 records).

Lombardoland—(A) Decca DL-8249.

Every Night is New Year's Eve—Decca (S) PFS4283 (73).

Your Guy Lombardo Medley—(A) Capitol T-739; Capitol LCT6127 (55).

Guy Lombardo in Hi-Fi—Capitol T738.

The Lively Guy—(A) Capitol T-892.

Berlin by Lombardo—(A) Capitol T-1019.

At Harrah's Club—(A) Capitol T-1393.

Twin Piano Magic—Brunswick LA8685 (53) (d); (A) Decca 8251.

Guy Lombardo—Brunswick LAT8063 (55) (d).

Guy Lombardo—Capitol LCT6117 (55) (d).

Decade on Broadway (1935-45)—Capitol T-916 (55); (A) same.

Decade on Broadway (1946-56)—Capitol T-788 (58); (A) same.

Joe Loss

(b Liverpool, June 22 1910)

Formed his first band after studying music at Trinity College of Music and the London School of Music. Played vaudeville briefly before settling to permanent band leadership. In 1930 he went to the Astoria Ballroom in London's Charing Cross Road, then to the

Joe Loss (a 1939 sheet music cover) (Peter Maurice).

Kit-Cat for a short period before returning to the Astoria. Latterly became top society dance band much in demand for social occasions and specialising in strict ballroom dance music.

Selected LP recordings

Let's Dance at the Make Believe Ballroom (32 items 1934-40)—World Records SHB46 (2).

Also:

Numerous commercial dance records.

Jimmie Lunceford

(b Fulton, Missouri, June 6 1902; d Seaside, Oregon, July 13 1947)

After taking his BA at Frisk University and playing several instruments in local groups, Lunceford formed his own band in 1929 as a full-time unit with engagements in Lake and Buffalo. He had worked previously for short times with Wilbur Sweatman and Elmer Snowden in New York. Made great reputation at the Cotton Club in 1934 with powerful swinging hot style in arrangements by Will Hudson and, most important, trumpeter Sy Oliver who did much to form the band's style and identity. The band had a superb sound with brilliant soloists [Eddie Tomkins, Tommy Stevenson (t), Trummy Young (tb, vo), Willie Smith (as), Joe Thomas (ts) and Jimmy Crawford (d)]. Oliver left in 1939 when the arranging was taken over by his protégé Billy Moore. Willie Smith, a great section leader as well as soloist, left in 1942 and was followed out by Young and Crawford. Later Snooky Young and Paul Webster (t) did good work but, after the loss of the original stars, the band lost some of its quality. After Lunceford's sudden death from a heart attack, the band was led briefly by Joe Thomas and Ed Wilcox (p, arr), but it never regained stability and soon broke up. In its heyday the Lunceford band was equalled only by those of Duke Ellington and Count Basie (later) as a finely integrated and genuinely swinging hot band, revealing an exuberance and natural feeling unrivalled by any of the white bands that had the larger public's ear, although these admittedly played deliberately in a less relaxed, more overtly sophisticated style.

Selected LP recordings

Harlem Express—Coral CP21 (70) (d). *Mood indigo* (1934); *Black and Tan Fantasy* (1934); *Dream of you* (1934); *Rain* (1934); *Shake your head* (1934); *Sleepy time gal* (1935); *Bird of Paradise* (1935); *Rhapsody junior* (1935); *The best things in life are free* (1935); *Organ grinder's swing* (1936); *Me and the Moon* (1936); *On the beach at Bali-Bali* (1936).

Jimmie Lunceford and his Orchestra—DJM DJB26048 (76). *Battle axe* (1941); *Moonlight and music; etc.*

Lunceford Special—CBS Realm 52567; (A) Columbia CS9515 or CL-2715. *Flaming reeds and screaming brass* (1933); *While love lasts* (1933); *'Tain't what you do* (1939); *Cheatin' on me* (1939); *Time's a-wastin'* (1939); *Baby, won't you please come home* (1939); *Ain't she sweet* (1939); *Well all right then* (1939); *Belgium Stomp* (1939); *I'm alone with you* (1939); *I'm in an awful mood* (1939); *Uptown Blues* (1939); *Lunceford special* (1939); *Bugs Parade* (1940); *I wanna hear swing songs* (1940); *What's your story, morning glory?* (1940).

Rhythm is our Business—Decca Ace of Hearts AH155; (A) *Sophisticated lady* (1934); *Rose room* (1934); *Stomp it off* (1934); *Since my best gal turned me down* (1934); *Jealous*

(1934); *Rhythm is our business* (1934); *Hittin' the bottle* (1935); *Avalon* (1935); *Muddy water* (1936); *Harlem Shout* (1936); *Slummin' on Park Avenue* (1937); *He ain't got rhythm* (1937).
Takin' off with Jimmie—(Sw) Tax M8003 (74) (d). *Jazznocracy* (1940); *Swingin' on C* (1940); *I got it* (1940); *Monotony in four flats* (1940); *Blues in the groove* (1939); *Barefoot Blues* (1940); *Rock it for me* (1939); *Wham* (1939); *Le Jazz Hot* (1939); *Blue blazes* (1939); *Pavanne* (1940); *Minnie the Moocher* (1940); *Flight of the Jitterbug* (1940); *Okay for baby* (1940); *Dinah* (1940); *Mix-up* (1939).
Lunceford Special—Philips BBL7037 (55) (d); (A) Columbia CL634 (d). *Cheatin' on me* (1939); *'Tain't what you do* (1939); *Shoemaker's holiday* (1939); *Ain't she sweet* (1939); *What's your story, morning glory?* (1940); *White heat* (1939); *Well, all right then* (1939); *The lonesome road* (1939); *Uptown Blues* (1939); *Baby, won't you please come home* (1939); *Chopin's Prelude No.7* (1940); *Lunceford Special* (1939).
The Kings of Jazz Big Bands—Festival 146 (2) (74). *Hallelujah* (1942-43); *Yesterdays* (1942-43); *Bust out* (1946); *Meditation* (1946); *Little John* (1944); *Alone together* (1944); *Holiday for strings* (1944-45); *Estrellita* (1944-45); *Moonlight and music* (1942); *O.K. for baby* (1946); *Just you* (1942); *What a difference a day made* (1942). (With tracks by Chick Webb.)
Also:
Rhythm is our Business (1934-35 (Vol.1) —(F) MCA.510.012; (74); (A) Decca DL-79237.
Harlem Shout (Vol.2)—(F) MCA 510.018 (74); (A) Decca DL-79238.
For Dancers Only (1936-37) (Vol.3)—(F) MCA 510.032 (74); (A) Decca DL-79239.
Blues in the Night (1938-42) (Vol.4)—(F) MCA 510.040 (74); (A) Decca DL-79240.
Jimmie's Legacy (1934-37) (Vol.5)—(F) MCA 510.066 (74); (A) Decca DL-79241.
Last Sparks (1941-44) (Vol.6)—(F) MCA 510.067 (74); (A) Decca DL-79242.
Little John, etc (broadcasts) (1945)—(A) First Heard FH-15 (77).
Memphis to Harlem (with Mills Blue Rhythm)—(F) RCA 741.045.
Golden Swing Years (1946-47)—(A) Storyville SLP1935 & SLP828.
Original Sessions (1942-43)—(F) Musidisc 30 JA 5112 (75).
Jimmie Lunceford—(A) 'X' LX-3002.
Jimmie Lunceford in Hi-Fi—Capitol T924 (57); (S) ST924 (59); (A) TAO-924.

Billy May

(b Pittsburgh, November 10 1916)
Played trumpet and trombone in bands of Charlie Barnet, Glenn Miller and others before leading his own band modelled on Jimmie Lunceford style. A brilliant arranger, he did many arrangements for Barnet and Miller, and later for Woody Herman and Phil Harris. Worked with bands backing singers then made a hit with his own big band in 1951 which lasted until 1954 featuring originally styled arrangements and novel instrumental, especially section, effect. Latterly worked in radio and television with studio-type bands of high quality and continually challenging scores.

Selected LP recordings

Bill's Bag—(G) Electrola 1C 048 50713.
Skyliner (with Charlie Barnet)—Pye 'Golden Hour' GH868 (77).
The Great Jimmie Lunceford (1957)—Capitol T1581, (S) ST1581 (62); (A) Capitol T1581.
Billy May Orchestra—Capitol LC6571 (53); (A) Capitol H-237.
Big Band Bash—Capitol LC6623 (53); (A) Capitol T-329.
Bacchanalia—Capitol LC6644 (54; (A) Capitol H-349.
Naughty Operetta—Capitol LC6650 (54); (A) Capitol H-374.
Billy May Orchestra—Capitol LCT6015 (55).
Sorta Dixie—Capitol LC6819 (56); (A) Capitol H-487.
Fancy Dancing—Capitol T771 (57); (A) ditto.
Billy May's Big Fat Brass—Capitol T1043 (58); (A) ditto.
Cha Cha Billy May—Capitol T1329, (S) ST1329 (60); (A) ditto.
Billy May and his Orchestra—(A) Time S-2064.
Hey, it's May—(A) Pickwick S-3010.
Sorta-May—Capitol M562.

Ray McKinley

(b Fort Worth, Texas, June 18 1910)
Gifted drummer/vocalist who played with the Dorsey Brothers (qv) and after Dorsey split went with Jimmy. Later played with Will Bradley then formed his own band in

1942 [Dick Cathcart (t), Brad Gowans (tb) and Lou Stein (p)]. During World War II he was drummer with Glenn Miller's AAF Orchestra and took over leadership after Miller's death in 1944. After the war formed a progressive band featuring arrangements by Eddie Sauter and Deane Kincaide. In 1956 he lead the Glenn Miller Orchestra again under agreement with Miller's widow, playing US forces bases overseas. He continued to perpetuate the Miller sound and material until he left the music business in 1965. Returned for occasional stints of Miller-music into 1970s.

Selected LP recordings

Class of '49 (1949)—(A) Hep 4 (75).
Rock-a-Bye the Boogie (w Will Bradley)—(A) Bandstand BS-7112.
Ray McKinley and his Musicians (1946-49)—(A) First Heard FH11 (77).
Blue Skies—(A) Heard FH32 (79).
Ray McKinley Plays Sauter—(A) Allegro 4015.
Ray McKinley—(A) Camden CAL-295.
Dixieland Jazz Battle, Vol.2 (w Joe Marsala) (small group) (1936)—Brunswick LA8545; (A) Decca DL-5262.
The Swingin' Thirties—(A) GA 33-333.
See also with Glenn Miller.

McKinney's Cotton Pickers

Top jazz organisation formed by drummer William McKinney (1894-1926). McKinney previously led a smaller group, playing much comedy and vaudeville material; but the new band was booked into Detroit's Greystone Ballroom by Jean Goldkette (qv) in 1926 and under musical directorship of Don Redman (qv). Between 1927 and 1931 became leading black jazz band with outstanding, if changeable, personnel [Rex Stewart, Joe Smith, John Nesbitt, Doc Cheatham, Sidney de Paris (t), Quentin Jackson, Ed Cuffee, Claude Jones, (tb), Redman, Benny Carter, Hilton Jefferson (as), Coleman Hawkins, Prince Robinson (ts), Fats Waller, James P. Johnson (p), Billy Taylor (b), Cuba Austin and Kaiser Marshall (d)]. The band broke up in 1934 but was revived by Detroit musicians in the 1970s as the New McKinney's Cotton Pickers, playing the old book with considerable success at American and European jazz festivals.

Selected LP recordings

McKinney's Cotton Pickers, Vol.1-1928—RCA B & W 741 080 (73). *Four or five times; Put it there; Stop kidding; Crying and sighing; Nobody's sweetheart; Milenberg Joys; Shim-me-sha-wabble; Cherry; Some sweet day; It's tight like that; There's a rainbow 'round my shoulder.* (1928.)

McKinney's Cotton Pickers, Vol.2-1928-29—(F) RCA B & W 741 088 (73). *It's a precious little thing called love; Save it, pretty Mama; I found a new baby; Will you, won't you, be my baby; Do something; Beedle um bum; Sellin' that stuff; It feels so good; Plain dirt; Gee, ain't I good to you; I'd love it.* (1929.)

McKinney's Cotton Pickers, Vol.3-1929-1930—(F) RCA B & W 741 109 (74); (G) RCA LPM 10.020. *The way I feel today* (1929); *Miss Hannah* (1929); *Peggy* (1929); *Wherever there's a will there's a way* (2 takes) (1929); *I'll make fun for you; Words can't express; If I could be with you one hour tonight* (2 takes); *Then someone's in love; Honeysuckle; Zonky; Trav'lin' all alone; Just a shade corn; Baby, won't you please come home* (1930.)

McKinney's Cotton Pickers, Vol.4-1930—(F) RCA B & W FPM1 7007 (74). *Okay, baby; Blues sure have got me; Hullabaloo; I want a little girl* (3 takes); *Cotton picker's scat; Talk to me* (2 takes); *Rocky road; Laughing at life* (2 takes); *Never swat a fly* (2 takes); *I want your love* (2 takes). (1930.)

McKinney's Cotton Pickers, Vol.5-1930/3—(F) RCA B & W FXM1 7059 (75). *Hello; After all, you're all I'm after; I miss a little miss; To whom it may concern; You're driving me crazy; Come a little closer* (1930); *It's a lonesome old town; She's my secret passion; Come easy, go easy love; When I can't be with you; Do you believe in love at sight; Wrap your troubles in dreams* (1931.)

Also:
McKinney's Cotton Pickers—(Swi) Collector's 12-2.
McKinney's Cotton Pickers—(F) RCA 430.673.
McKinney's Cotton Pickers (1928-29)—F RCA DPM42407.
McKinney's Cotton Pickers (1929-31)—RCA RD7561 (63) (d).
McKinney's Cotton Pickers—(A) RCA LPT-24.
McKinney's Cotton Pickers—(A) 'X' LVA-3031.
Cotton Pickers, Vols.1-3—Bountiful 38000/1/3 (79).

Jay McShann

(b Muskagee, Oklahoma, January 12 1909)

A strong, incisive blues and boogie pianist, Jay McShann first played with a band led by Eddie Hill in New Mexico and Arizona, then went to Kansas City and in 1937 formed a small group which included Gene Ramey (b) and Gus Johnson (d) which he expanded into a full band two years later. Among the personnel of that band was Charlie Parker (as) who made his first recordings with it. In 1941 McShann took the band to New York, a move that was to have lasting consequences for the whole of jazz since it marked Parker's introduction to the New York scene where he soon found his way to Minton's Playhouse and consorted with Dizzy Gillespie, Thelonious Monk, Kenny Clarke and others who formed the new and then revolutionary 'bop' movement which inaugurated 'modern jazz'. McShann continued to play tough rugged music, often featuring Paul Quinichette (ts) and vocalist Al Hibbler. With the entry of America into the war, the band broke up and, after a period of military service, McShann himself formed a new band before settling to work with small groups in Kansas City and on the West Coast in the rhythm and blues idiom. He continued to record with singer Walter Brown and appeared several times in Europe. In McShann's peak period as band leader many of the arrangments were by Skip Hall.

Selected LP recordings

Spoon Calls Hootie (with Jimmy Witherspoon)—Polydor 545105. *Skidrow Blues; In the evening; Frog-i-more; McShann Bounce; How Long Blues; Money's getting cheaper; Spoon calls Hootie; Ain't nobody's business* (1 & 2); *Jumpin' with Louis; Backwater Blues; Destruction Blues* (1947-48.)

The Jumpin' Blues (1941-1943)—Coral CP4; (A) Decca DL-9236. (1941): *Swingmatism; Hootie Blues*; Dexter Blues; Confessin' the Blues*; One woman's man*; Red River Blues*; Hootie's ignorant oil*;* (1942): *The Jumpin' Blues*; Lonely Boy Blues*; Get me on your mind*; Sepian Bounce*;* (1943); *Wrong neighbourhood; Hometown Blues; Say forward I'll march* (with Charlie Parker*.)

The Band that Jumps the Blues—Polydor 2460 201. *Hot biscuits; Slow Drag Blues; M.R. Boogie; Buttermilk; Skidrow Blues; Soft winds; No Name Boogie; Thinking about my baby; Geronimo; Twelve o'clock whistle; Mellodrag; Eatin' watermelon* (1947-49.)

Also:

Kansas City Memories (1941-43)—Brunswick LA8735 (56) (d).

Big Apple—(A) Atlantic 8804.

The Last of Jay McShann—(A) Atlantic 8800.

Confessin' the Blues (1971)—(A) Class 128; (F) Barclay 33 022.

Glenn Miller

(b Clarinda, Iowa, March 1 1904; d (over English Channel) December 15-18, 1944)

A competent trombonist and gifted arranger, Miller's lasting fame rests on the fine civilian band he led between 1939 and 1942 and even more the AAF band he formed for the US military forces and led until his death in an air crash in 1944. This has some claim to be the most popular big band of all time, with innumberable 'recreations' ever since and a still vociferous 'fan' following. But Miller was active on the jazz and dance band scene long before that. He played with Boyd Senter (qv) as early as 1920, joined Ben Pollack (qv) 1926-28, freelanced and had irregular stints with Red Nichols, Benny Goodman and the Dorsey Brothers, and recruited Ray Noble's (qv) first American band in 1935. In 1935, too, he made his first records under his own name, with a remarkable line-up [Bunny Berigan, Charlie Spivak (t), Eddie Miller (ts), Claude Thornhill (p) and Ray Bauduc (d)]. His arranging talents were frequently in evidence, a notable example being the Red Nichols *The Sheik of Araby*, which has himself playing the melody on trombone and Jack Teagarden improvising, also on trombone, with a similar routine but different instrumentation later. This set a style for other arrangements for Nichols, the Dorseys and others. Formed a big band in 1937, but failed to make headway. Reformed in 1938, still without recognition; but made the breakthrough in 1939 with clarinet dominated reeds creating a 'new sound'. This band was a huge success which was only ended when Miller enlisted in the armed forces in 1942 and formed the famous AAF band. Though neither the civilian nor the AAF bands were jazz units, Miller always employed a quorum of jazz players [Bernie Privin, Johnny Best (t), Hal McIntyre (as), Ernie Caceres (as, cl, bar),

Peanuts Hucko (cl), Tex Beneke (ts), Mel Powell (p) Ray McKinley (d) and many others]. The arrangements were by Miller himself, Jerry Gray, Bill Finegan and in the later period of the civilian band, Billy May who also sat in on trumpet. Popular films *Sun Valley Serenade* (1941) and *Orchestra Wives* (1942) featured the civilian band, and *The Glenn Miller Story* with James Stewart came in 1954. Miller disappeared on an official flight from England to France and no trace of the plane or bodies was ever found. The plane took off on December 15 1944, and he was pronounced dead on December 18. After Miller's death the AAF band continued under leadership of Ray McKinley and Jerry Gray; and in the following decades the Miller style and sound has been faithfully recreated by a number of bands, including those of Tex Beneke (qv), Ralph Flanagan, Art Mooney and Ray Anthony, also by McKinley himself and later by Buddy de Franco. In England Syd Lawrence has made a corner in Miller recreation. Much of the Miller appeal is clearly linked to wartime nostalgia; on the other hand, the somewhat stylised sound and arrangements, though excellent in their field, make the task of 'recreation' comparatively easy. Whatever the reason, the phenomenon persists.

Glenn Miller (RCA Records).

Selected LP recordings

The Unforgettable Glenn Miller—RCA TVL1 (77); (A) RCA. *Moonlight Serenade; Little Brown Jug; Stairway to the stars; In the mood; Pennsylvania 6-5000; Don't sit under the apple tree; Sunrise serenade; Chattanooga choo-choo; Johnson Rag; Tuxedo Junction; American patrol; Londonderry air; Skylark; I've got a gal in Kalamazoo; Stardust; St. Louis Blues March; Serenade in blue; Perfidia; Juke box Saturday night; String of pearls.* (1939-42.)

Also:

Glenn Miller Concert, Vol.1—HMV DLP1012 (54) (d); (A) RCA LPM-1193.

Glenn Miller Concert, Vol.2—HMV DLP1013 (54) (d); (A) RCA LPM-1193.

Glenn Miller Concert, Vol.3—HMV DLP1021 (54) (d).

The Glenn Miller Story—HMV DLP1024 (54) (d).

Time for Melody—HMV DLP1049 (54) (d).

Orchestra Wives (film soundtrack)—HMV DLP1059 (54) (d).

Glenn Miller Limited Edition, 5 Vols—HMV CLPC1-5 (55) (d); (A) RCA LPT6700 (5).

Juke Box Saturday Night—(A) RCA LPT-1016.

The Nearness of You—(A) RCA LPT-1031; Camden S-2128 (67).

The Glenn Miller Orchestra—(A) RCA LPM-2080

Never Before on LP—(A) RCA LPM-3657.

The Glenn Miller Orchestra—Philips BBR8072 (55) (d).

The Glenn Miller Orchestra—HMV DLP1081, HMV DLP1104.

Glenn Miller Orchestra—Philips BBR8092 (56) (d).

The Glenn Miller Orchestra—HMV DLP1122 (55) (d).

Glenn Miller Limited Edition, Vol.2 (5) —HMV RLS1-5 (55) (d); (A) RCA LPT-6701 (5).
Polka Dots and Moonbeams—HMV DLP1145 (57).
Carnegie Hall Concert—RCA RD-27057 (58); RCA Starcall NL42010 (77); (A) RCA LPM-1506.
The Glenn Miller Story (originals)—RCA RD-27068 (58); (A) RCA LPM-1192, (5) LSP-1192.
Marvellous Miller Moods—TCA RD-27096 (58); (A) RCA LPM-1494.
Marvellous Miller Medleys—RCA RD-27090 (59); (A) RCA LOP-1005 (58), LPM1973 (60).
Glenn Miller Orchestra, Vol.1—Top Rank RX3004 (59).
The Miller Army Air Force Band, Vol.1 —RCA RD27135 (60).
The Miller Army Air Force Band, Vol.2 —Top Rank 35/023 (60).
This is Glenn Miller (soundtracks)—Ember EMB-3318 (60).
For the Very First Time-3 Vols (unissued material)—RCA RD27145/6/7 (61); SF8115/6/7 (70); (A) RCA LPM-6100 (3) (59).
Glenn Miller Limited Edition, Vol.3 (5)—(A) RCA LPT-6702 (5).

Army Air Force Band

Glenn Miller (1935-38)—Columbia 33SX1462 (62).
A Legendary Performer—RCA DPM2065 (2) (76).
A Legendary Performer, Vol.2—RCA PL12080 (77).

Glenn Miller and his Orchestra with George Montgomery in the 20th Century Fox film Orchestra Wives, *1942* (RCA Records).

A Memorial 1944-69—RCA GM1 (2); (A) RCA VPM-6019 (3).
Solo Hop—(A) Epic LN-3236.
The Best of Glenn Miller (3 Vols.)—(A) RCA LSP-3377 (65); LSP-3564 (66) or LSP-3564 (68); LSP-4125 (69).
Blue Moonlight—(A) RCA LSP-3657 (66).
On the Air—(A) RCA LPM-6101 (3) (S) LSP-6101 (3) (63), LPM-2767/9, (S) LSP-2767/9.
The Sound of Glenn Miller—(A) RCA LPM-1189.
This is Glenn Miller—(A) RCA LPM-1190.
The Chesterfield Broadcasts, Vol.1—RCA RD-7932 (68); (A) RCA LPM-3873, (S) LSP-3873.
The Chesterfield Broadcasts, Vol.2—RCA RD-7982 (69); (A) RCA LPM-3891.
A Memorial, (2 Vols.)—(F) RCA 730.661/2 (2).
A Memorial for Glenn Miller—(F) Musidisc CV-1317.
Glenn Miller Collection—Pickwick PDA 012 (2) (76).
The Glenn Miller Story (soundtrack) (studio orchestra)—Coral CP-41 (70); MCA CRLM1003 (75).
Golden Hour of Glenn Miller—Pye Golden Hour GH831 (75).
His Biggest Hits—(G) Teldec RCS3105 (75).
The Legendary Glenn Miller, Vols. 1-4 —(F) RCA LFM1.7500/1/2/3 (74).
The Legendary Glenn Miller, Vols. 5-9 —(F) RCA FFM1.7512/3/4/5/6 (74).
The Legendary Glenn Miller, Vols. 10-13—(F) RCA LSA.3237/8/9/40 (76).
The Legendary Glenn Miller, Vols. 14-17—(F) RCA PL 42016/7/8/9 (77).
Star Collection—(F) Warner 26014.
String of Pearls—(G) Teldec RCS-3220.
Swing Happy Years—Decca 'Ace of Hearts' AH-143 (67).
The Glenn Miller Story—(G) Teldec SRS560.
The Great Glenn Miller (soundtracks)—World Records ST984/5 (69); (A) 20th Century Fox TCF-100-2 (2).
This is Glenn Miller and the Army Air Force Band—(G) Teldec VPS6080.
Vintage Years—CBS Hallmark SHM691 (70).
A Memorial for Glenn Miller—(F) Musidisc Album 149 (75).
The Best of Glenn Miller—Ember EMB31015 (73) (d).
Best of the Glenn Miller Orchestra, (2 Vols)—CBS 22023 (2) (76).
Original Reunion-Live Concert—Pye PKL5543.
Glenn Miller Revival—(G) EMI 1C 148 93995/6/7 (3) (74).
Hits from the Glenn Miller Story—RCA LSA3274 (76).
The Original Recordings—Pickwick Camden CDS1004 (69); (A) Camden S-829 (64).
The Best of Glenn Miller—Pickwick Camden CDS1165 (78); (A) Camden S-751 (63).
Legendary Performer (Army Air Force Band)—RCA PL12495 (78) & PL12080 (77).
The Best of Glenn Miller—RCA INTS5015 (80).
The Unforgettable Glenn Miller—Reader's Digest (6).

Glenn Miller Band under Ray McKinley

The New Glenn Miller Orchestra in Hi-Fi—RCA RD27055, (S) SF5028; (A) RCA LPM-1522, (S) LSP-1522.
Something Old, New, Borrowed and Blue—RCA RD27079, (S) SF5032.

Lucky Millinder

(b Anniston, Alabama, August 8 1900; d New York, September 28 1966)
Took over leadership of Mills Blue Rhythm Band (qv) from 1934. From late 1930s the band operated exclusively under Millinder's own name. Changes in personnel and other difficulties sometimes prevented the groups from realising their full potential; but continued to play hard swinging jazz with top class musicians passing through the ranks [Dizzy Gillespie, Freddy Webster, Joe Guy (t), Sandy Williams (tb), Eddie 'Lockjaw' Davis, Lucky Thompson (ts), Ellis Larkins, Sir Charles Thompson, Bill Doggett (p), George Duvivier, Al McGibbon (b) and Panama Francis (d)] as well as some of the earlier members and the hot gospel/blues singing of Sister Rosetta Tharpe. The band continued just into the 1950s and were popular with dancers in Harlem, then Millinder gradually gave up band leadership on a regular basis. In later years he worked as a disc jockey and an agent.

Selected LP recordings

Awful Natural '49 (with Cab Calloway)—

(F) RCA PM32030.
Lucky Days 1941-45—(F) MCA 510.065.
With Mills' Blue Rhythm Band:
Keep the Rhythm Going—(A) Jazz Archives JA-10.

Mills' Blue Rhythm Band

Originally formed by Irving Mills, agent and promoter and President of Mills-Rockwell, Inc, in 1932. It made a number of excellent records under various names—Blue Rhythm Boys, Blue Racketeers, Baron Lee and the Blue Rhythm Band etc—and established a reputation for honest swinging jazz. The personnel included some good soloists [Shelton Hemphill (t), Charlie Holmes (as), Edgar Hayes (p, arr) and Hayes Alvis (b)]. Leadership was taken over in 1934 by Lucky Millinder (qv) and with expanded personnel [Henry Allen (t), George Washington, J.C. Higginbotham (tb), Tab Smith (as), Buster Bailey (cl), Billy Kyle (b) and John Kirby (b)].

Selected LP recordings

Keep Rhythm Going (1934-36)—(A) Jazz Archives JA10. *Swingin' in E-flat* (1934); *Let's have a Jubilee* (1934); *African lullaby* (1934); *Dancing dogs* (1934); *Keep rhythm going* (1934); *Harlem heat* (1935); *There's rhythm in Harlem* (1935); *Tallahassee* (1935); *Truckin'* (1935); *E-flat stride* (1935); *Yes! Yes!* (1935); *Merry-go-round* (1936); *Balloonacy* (1936); *Barrelhouse* (1936); *Big John's Special* (1936); *Callin' your bluff* (1936). (Led by Lucky Millinder.)
Big Bands—Polydor 2344 048 (75). *Blue Rhythm Jam; Blue Rhythm Blues; Blue Rhythm Swing; Blue Rhythm Bebop; Blue Rhythm Ramble; Blue Rhythm Bounce; Blue Rhythm Serenade; Blue Rhythm Chant* (1947). (Coupled with Louis Bellson.)
Ridin' in Rhythm—World Records SHB42 (2) (79). *Ridin' in rhythm* (1933); *Weary traveller* (1933); *Buddy's Wednesday outing* (1933). (Credited as by Baron Lee and The Blue Rhythm Band, coupled with tracks by Fletcher Henderson, Duke Ellington, Benny Carter, Coleman Hawkins, etc.)
Also:
Mills Blue Rhythm Band (with Don Redman)—(G) Swingfan 1019.
Mills Blue Rhythm Band—(Sw) Jazz Panorama LP-3.
Everybody Swing (also Carter, Henderson & Kirk)—Regal REG-1108.
Memphis to Harlem (with tracks by Jimmie Lunceford—(F) RCA 741.045.

Vaughn Monroe

(b Akron, Ohio, October 7 1911; d Stuart, Florida, May 21 1973)
Champion trumpet soloist at the age of 15, Monroe played with several dance bands during the 1930s and studied singing at the Carnegie Tech School of Music and then at the New England Conservatory before forming his own band in 1940. Based in the Boston area he soon achieved great popularity, notably on account of the way he used an operatically trained voice in popular songs. He and his band appeared on radio and records, with his own radio show during the 1940s and 1950s. Latterly became more renowned as a singer than as band leader; appeared with band in several films, and later worked in television and for RCA-Victor. Composer of a number of hit songs, mostly sentimental, which he featured in his own vocal style. Not much heard during the 1960s, but made occasional returns on television.

Selected LP recordings

Comin' on (1935-50s)—(A) Big Band Archives LP-1211.
The Monroe Doctrine (1935-50s)—(A) Swing Era LP-1014.
There I Sing/Swing it Again—(A) RCA LPM-1799 (58).
The Best of Vaughn Monroe—(A) RCA LSP-3817 (67).
Dreamland Special—(A) Camden CAL-354.
His Greatest Hits—(A) Dot DLP-3431 (62).
Great Themes of Famous Bands and Singers—(A) Dot DLP-3470.
Dance With Me—(A) Camden CAL-329.
House Party—(A) RCA LPM-1493.

Russ Morgan

(b Scranton, Pennsylvania, April 29 1904; d Las Vegas, August 8 1968)
After playing trombone in Scranton he went to New York in the early 1920s and began arranging for Victor Herbert and Sousa's band, then to Detroit where he joined Jean Goldkette (qv) and worked on radio. Back in New York he did arrangements for many of the top bands, including those of Fletcher

Henderson, Chick Webb, the Dorseys, and conducted theatre orchestras as well as acting as music director for Brunswick Records. Worked for a time with Freddy Martin and developed personal trombone style with 'wa-wa' effects which became famous. In 1935, as Musical Director of Columbia Records, Morgan organized a recording unit for recording purposes, using members of Ray Noble Orchestra (qv) with a number of ranking musicians [Toots Mandello (as), Arthur Rollini (ts), Joe Venuti (vln), Claude Thornhill (p) and Chauncey Moorehouse (d)]. Led his own band at the Baltmore Hotel, New York, and other venues, enhancing popularity with radio work, incuding Lever Brothers and Philip Morris shows. Composer of many good songs, some of which were hits in the 1940s and 1950s. Subsequent successes on television during the 1950s, and appeared in films.

Selected LP recordings

Tap Dancing for Pleasure—Brunswick LA8525 (53) (d); (A) Decca 8336.

Everybody Dance—Brunswick LA8564 (53) (d); (A) Decca 8337.

Moonlight Music—Brunswick LA8594 (53) (d); (A) Decca.

Viennese Waltz Favourites—Brunswick LA8654 (54) (d); (A) Decca 8582.

Everybody Dance, Vol.2—Brunswick LA8662 (54) (d).

Everybody Dance, Vol.3—Brunswick LA8707 (55) (d).

Does your Heart beat for Me—(A) Decca DL-8332, (S) 74503 (64).

Songs of Jimmy McHugh—(A) Decca DL-8423.

Songs of Harry Warren—(A) Decca DL-8581.

Music in the Morgan Manner—(A) Decca DL-5098.

Let's Dance—(A) Vocalion VL-3601.

There Goes That Song Again—(A) Pick SPC-3016.

Red Roses for a Blue Lady—(A) VJ 1139.

The Best of Russ Morgan—Crescendo GNP9015 (73).

His Greatest Hits—Joy JOY-114 (70).

Golden Favourites—Decca 'Ace of Hearts' AH-54 (63) (d); (A) Decca DL-4292 (63), (S) 74292.

The Best of Russ Morgan—(A) Decca DXS-7196 (2) (67).

Music in the Morgan Manner—(A) Vocalion 73792 (67).

Ferdinand 'Jelly Roll' Morton

(b New Orleans, September 20 1885; d Los Angeles, July 10 1941)

Whether or not he actually 'invented' jazz, as he claimed, Morton was unquestionably one of the most important of its early practitioners. He began playing guitar but soon switched to piano and started working in sporting houses and dives in New Orleans and around Louisiana. At the time, the early 1900s, ragtime and associated music was not respectable and those who played it were regarded as socially disreputable. There were conflicting views about him: some regarded him as a pool shark, a hustler, even a pimp, always after the easy money; others saw him as quite simply a genius. Both may have been right—or wrong. Morton was certainly a highly talented musician who, as composer, arranger, pianist and organiser, was the first in jazz history to bring a real sense of form and instrumental combination to support it into jazz. He led and recorded with many small groups; but his main contribution to band jazz lay in the outstanding series of recordings he made for Victor between 1926 and 1930 with his Red Hot Peppers. The personnel varied, but especially in the early period the band contained some of the finest jazz musicians [George Mitchell (cnt), Kid Ory (tb), Omer Simeon (cl) and John Lindsay (b)]. Henry Allen (t) and J.C. Higginbotham (tb) also worked with him. The later group had Ward Pinkett (t), Geechy Fields (tb), Albert Nicholas (cl) and others. Though the Peppers were never a 'big band' in the Ellington or Basie sense, they invariably worked and sounded like one. Morton was a difficult, conceited man, albeit of much charm when he wanted, and made many enemies. His decline was at least partly his own fault, but failing health also played its part. Not long before he died Alan Lomax recorded him in a long series for the Library of Congress archives, a series both historic and moving as Morton talked and played the piano through his own and jazz's history. But apart from his compositions, his major achievement remained the Red Hot Peppers recordings.

Selected LP recordings

New Orleans (Red Hot Peppers) (1926-30)—HMV DLP1016 (53), DLP1044 (54) & DLP1071 (55) (d).

King of New Orleans Jazz, Vol.1 (1926-

30)—RCA RD27113 (60) (d); (A) RCA LPM-1649 (59).

King of New Orleans Jazz, Vol.2 (1926-30)—RCA RD27184 (61) (d); (A) RCA LPM-508 (64).

Hot Jazz, Pop Jazz, Hokum and Hilarity —RCA RD-7807 (62) (d); (A) RCA LPV-524 (66).

Mr. Jelly Lord—RCA RD-7914 (63) (d); (A) RCA LPV-546 (67).

Integrale Jelly Roll Morton, Vols. 1-8—(F) RCA 730.559; 730.605; 731.069; 741.040; 741.054; 741.070; 741.081; 741.087.

Red Hot Peppers 1929-30—(A) Collector's Classics CC-1.

Transcriptions for Orchestra—CBS 61666 (75).

Bennie Moten

(b Kansas City, November 13 1896; d Kansas City, April 2 1935)

Pianist, composer and arranger, Moten led the band in the 1920s which virtually created the Kansas City style out of which, one way and another, evolved the bands of Count Basie (qv), Andy Kirk (qv) and Jay McShann (qv). The Moten band, which reached its peak around 1929, contained some excellent musicians (Lamar Wright, Ed Lewis (t), Thomas Hayes (tb), Harland Leonard (as, cl), Jack Washington (as, bar) and Vernon Page (b)] and played a rough riding, stomping style arising out of ragtime in which Moten himself as a pianist had grown up, mixed with the kind of 'novelty' numbers demanded by audiences of the period. Later the piano chair was taken over by the young Count Basie and a number of more famous jazzmen were featured [Oran 'Hot Lips' Page (t), Eddie Durham (tb, g), Eddie Barefield (cl), Ben Webster (ts), Walter Page (b) and Jimmy Rushing (vo)] played with the band. Moten took the band to New York in 1928, but turned down a regular job at Connie's Inn and returned to Kansas City. After Moten's death in 1935 (a victim, like the guitarist Eddie Lang of complications following a tonsilectomy), the band was led briefly by Count Basie and Moten's brother, Buster, before becoming the nucleus of the Basie outfit that caused a sensation in New York in 1936. Moten wrote a good deal of the material himself, and some of it was adapted from popular tunes of the day much in the way that the 'bop' innovators, a decade and more later, used current material for their own purposes. Moten and his band recorded regularly during the 1920s and 1930s and, although for a time it tended to be overlooked in the heat of new evolutions, it is now recognised as one of the formative influences in band jazz.

Selected LP recordings

Bennie Moten's Kansas City Orchestra, 1923-25—Parlophone PMC7119 (71). *Elephant's Wobble* (1923); *Crawdad Blues* (1923); *South* (1924); *Vine Street Blues* (1924); *Tulsa Blues* (1924); *Goofy dust* (1924); *Baby dear* (1924); *She's sweeter than sugar* (1925); *South Street Blues* (1925); *Sister Honky Tonk* (1925); *As I like it* (1925); *Things seem so blue to me* (1925); *18th Street Strut* (1925); *Kater Street Rag* (1925).

Kay-Cee Jazz (1926-28)—HMV DLP1057 (54) (d). *South* (1928); *Harmony Blues* (1926); *She's no trouble* (1928); *Get low down Blues* (1928); *Kansas City Shuffle* (1926); *The new Tulsa Blues* (1927); *Thick Lip Stomp* (1926); *Pass out lightly* (1927); *Ding-dong Blues* (1927); *Moten Stomp* (1927).

Bennie Moten and his Kansas City Orchestra (1926-29)—RCA RD7660 (d). *Yazoo Blues* (1926); *Midnight Mama* (1926); *Missouri Wobble* (1926); *Twelfth Street Rag* (1927); *Justrite* (1928); *Slow motion* (1928); *Kansas City breakdown* (1928); *Trouble in mind* (1928); *Hot Water Blues* (1928); *Kansas City squabble* (1929); *Rite tite* (1929); *Moten's Blues* (1929); *That certain motion* (1929); *New Goofy Dust Rag* (1929).

Moten's Blues (1929)—(F) RCA B & W 741.108 (74). *Moten's Blues* (1929); *That certain motion* (1929); *It won't be long* (1929); *When life seems so blue* (1929); *Loose like a goose* (1929); *Just say it's me* (1929); *New Goofy Dust Rag* (1929); *Rumba Negro* (1929); *The Jones Law Blues* (1929); *Band Box Shuffle* (1929); *Small back* (2 takes), (1929); *Every Day Blues* (1929); *Boot it* (1929); *Mary Lee* (1929); *Rit dit day* (1929).

Bennie Moten's Kansas City Orchestra (1929-30)—(F) RCA FPM1 7004 (74). *New Vine Street Blues; Sweethearts of yesterday; Won't you be my baby; I wish I could be blue; Oh! Eddie; That too, do; Mack's rhythm; You made me happy; Here comes Marjorie; The Count; Liza Lee; Get goin'; Professor Hot Stuff; When I'm alone; New Moten Stomp; As long as I love you.*

Moten's Swing (Vol.5-1929-32)—(F) RCA

FXM1 7062 (75). *The Jones Law Blues* (1929); *Somebody stole my gal* (1930); *Now that I need you* (1930); *Bouncin' around* (1930); *Ya got love* (1931); *I wanna be around my baby all the time* (1931); *Toby* (1932); *Moten's Swing* (1932); *Blue room* (1932); *Imagination* (1932); *New Orleans* (1932); *The only girl I ever loved* (1932); *Milenberg joys* (1932); *Lafayette* (1932); *Prince of Wails* (1932); *Two times* (1932). (All with Count Basie piano.)

Also:

Bennie Moten's Kansas City Orchestra, Vol.1 (1926-27)—(F) RCA 741.056 & DPM-42410 (2).

Vol.2 (1927-28)—(F) RCA 741.078 & DPM-42410 (2).

Count Basie in Kansas City (Bennie Moten's Great Band of 1930-32)—(A) RCA LPV-514.

Bennie Moten's Kansas City Jazz, Vol.1 —(A) 'X' LX-3004.

Bennie Moten's Kansas City Jazz, Vol.2 —(A) 'X' LXA-3025.

Bennie Moten's Kansas City Jazz, Vol.3 —(A) 'X' LVA-3038.

Kansas City Orchestra 1923-29—(A) Historical HLP-9 (66).

Gerry Mulligan

(b New York, April 6 1927)

Although his importance in the evolution of modern jazz, in the wake of the 'bop' innovations of the 1950s, cannot be over-estimated, most of the recordings under Gerry Mulligan's own name have been with small groups, beginning with the innovatory 'pianoless quartet' in the early 1950s. But he has always been active and influential as an arranger, and his work with his Concert Jazz band has special significance. He began his arranging as a teenager with Gene Krupa (qv), and was then deeply impressed by Gil Evans' (qv) work with the Claude Thornhill Orchestra (qv). He did some of the scores for Miles Davis' epoch-maching *Birth of the Cool* album with a nine-piece band in which he also played baritone saxophone. His strongly linear conceptions (the reason why the piano was dropped in the original quartet) were developed with the succeeding Sextet. In 1957 Mulligan and Bob Brookmeyer (v-tb) worked together on Phil Sunkel's *Jazz Concerto Grosso*. In 1957 Mulligan formed an All-Star Band for recording, but it did not last. Then in 1960 he formed the Concert Jazz Band which lasted, not without difficulty, until the end of 1962. It produced, however, a series of important recordings and appeared in Europe in 1960. As always with Mulligan, the line-up was unusual, and again there was no regular pianist, though as before Mulligan himself could play piano when required. Mulligan conceived the band as 'a framework for soloists and as a vehicle for writers, but not "far out" writers'. He did some of the writing himself; other charts were by Johnny Mandel, Bill Holman and Bob Brookmeyer. Mulligan himself was primary soloist, but not the only one; other notable names appeared in the ranks [Clark Terry, Conte Candoli, Nick Travis (t), Brookmeyer (v-tb), Gene Quill (as) and Zoot Sims (ts)]. Mulligan appeared in several films, including the important jazz film *Jazz on a Summer's Day* and led a group in Johnny Mandel's score for *I Want to Live* (1958) which remains one of the most successful of all jazz contributions to the cinema. He also wrote during the 1950s for Elliot-Lawrence (qv) and Stan Kenton (qv). His recorded 'meetings' with other jazz stars [Johnny Hodges, Paul Desmond (as), Ben Webster, Stan Getz (ts) and Thelonious Monk (p)] were also famous and successful.

Selected LP recordings

The Concert Jazz Band (1960)—HMV CLP1432, (S) CSD1351 (61); (A) Verve MGV-8388.

At the Village Vanguard (1960)—HMV CLP1488, (S) CSD1396 (62); (A) Verve MGV-8396 (61).

A Concert in Jazz (1961)—HMV CLP1549 (62); (A) Verve MGV-8515.

On Tour (1962)—HMV CLP1585 (62); (A) Verve.

Gerry Mulligan '63—Verve VLP-9037, (S) SVLP9037 (63); (A) Verve ditto.

Red Nichols

(b Ogden, Utah, May 8 1905; d Las Vegas, June 28 1965)

One of the early white jazzmen, Nichols is best known in that context for his small group work under the title the Five Pennies [originally Nichols (t), Miff Mole (tb), Jimmy Dorsey (cl), Arthur Schutt (p) and Victor Berton (tymp, d)] but later loosely formed in number while retaining the title. Nichols himself was a gifted cornet/trumpet player in the Bix Beiderbecke mould, and an energetic organiser. Most of the top white jazzmen played with him on records at one time or another, including Jack Teagarden (tb, vo) (qv), Gene Krupa (qv), Jimmy Dorsey (qv), Bud Freeman (ts), Pee Wee Russell (cl) and Frankie Trumbauer (C sax) (qv). Later Nichols organised big bands for touring and theatre work. He directed the bands for Broadway shows *Strike Up the Band* and *Crazy Girl* in 1930, and then led the bands in the Hollywood Hotel and the Park Central Hotel in New York. Subsequently he fronted various bands mixing large units and Dixieland groups in about equal proportion, and was associated with many leading entertainers, including Bing Crosby, Kay Starr and Phil Harris. The 1959 Hollywood 'biog' picture *The Five Pennies*, though typically corny, covered Nichols' career with Danny Kaye playing the lead.

Selected LP recordings

Red Nichols and his Orchestra 1934-1940—(A) Sounds of Swing LP124.

See also California Ramblers.

Ray Noble

(b Brighton, England, December 17 1907; d London, April 2 1978)

The son of a London neurologist and nephew of T. Terties Noble, organist of St Thomas's Episcopal Church in Manhattan, Ray Noble had a dual British and American musical career. After studying piano at the Royal Academy of Music in London, he went up to Cambridge and subsequently continued his musical studies. He took great pains to understand the dance band idiom from the bottom up and, when he entered the field, he had thoroughgoing knowledge. He was successively arranger for the Lawrence Wright Music Co, arranger for Jack Payne (qv), and Musical Director for The Gramophone Co when he organised recording bands for HMV, using some of the best British musicians [Nat Gonella, Max Goldberg (t), Lew Davis, Jock Flemming, Joe Ferrie (tb), Freddy Gardner, Danny Polo (as, cl), Harry Berly (ts), Leon Goossens (ob), Stanley Black, Monia Liter, Eddie Carroll (p), Tiny Winters (b), Bill Harty (d) and others] at various times between 1929 and 1934. The star of these recordings was Al Bowlly, often claimed to be the finest dance band singer of the pre-World War II era. In 1935 Noble went to New York and formed, with the assistance of Glenn Miller (qv), another outstanding band, this time with top ranking American musicians [Charlie Spivak, Sterling Bose (t), Miller (tb, arr), Bud Freeman (ts), Claude Thornhill (p) and George van Eps (g)], among the best known. Al Bowlly went with him, so did Bill Harty as drummer and manager. While in the US, Noble played at the Rainbow Room in New York and appeared on a number of high rating radio shows. Bowlly returned to England in 1936 and the next year the Noble band broke up; but he later reorganised and continued successful work. After his retirement in the mid-1950s Noble divided his time between England and America. He appeared with his band in a number of movies also regularly on the Milton Berle TV Show and was responsible for some of the best and most famous songs of the 1930s and 1940s, as well as fronting bands which many consider to be the ideal dance bands of the period.

Selected LP recordings

Ray Noble plays Ray Noble—World Records SH198 (76). *Brighter than the Sun* (1931); *I'll be good because of you* (1931); *By the fireside* (1932); *If you'll say 'yes', chérie* (1933); *I'll do my best to make you happy* (1932); *Love is the sweetest thing* (1932); *What more can I ask* (1932); *Goodnight, sweetheart* (1931); *The very thought of you* (1934); *Happy and contented* (1933); *Love locked out* (1933); *Spanish eyes* (1933); *That's what life is made of* (1933); *It's all forgotten now* (1936); *Ray Noble medley* (1933). (Vocals by Jack Plant, Al Bowlly.)

The Golden Age of British Dance Bands—World Records SH118/9 (69). *Maybe it's because; Lazy days* (1931); *You ought to see Sally on Sunday* (1933); *How could we be wrong* (1933); *Close your eyes* (1933); *Time on my hands* (1930); *Mad about the boy; One morning in May* (1934). (Vocals by Al Bowlly, coupled with recordings by Harry Roy, Lew Stone and Roy Fox.)

The Ray Noble Orchestra featuring Al Bowlly—World Records SM621/34 (79).

Vol.1 *I'm telling the world she's mine* (1930); *How could I be lonely* (1930); *Underneath the Spanish stars* (1930); *Sunny days* (1930); *Make yourself a Happiness Pie* (1930); *Time on my hands* (1930); *Makin' wickey wackey down in Waikiki* (1931); *Shout for happiness* (1931); *Goodnight, sweetheart* (1931); *I'm glad I waited* (1931); *Really mine* (1931); *Goodnight, sweetheart* (1930); *You're driving me crazy* (1931); *Pages of Radioland* (1931);

We two (1931); *Lady of Spain* (1931).

Vol.2 *Sunshine and shadows* (1931); *That's Somerset* (1931); *Fiesta* (1931); *You're twice as nice as the girl in my dreams* (1931); *On With the Show 1931* (1931); *Lights of Paris* (1931); *June time is love time* (1931); *Roll on, Mississippi, roll on* (1931); *Lazy day* (1931); *I'd rather be a beggar with you* (1931); *Miracle Melodies* (1931); *Holiday Hits* (1931); *Tunes of not so long ago* (1931); *Pagan Serenade* (1931).

Vol.3 *Belle of Barcelona* (1931); *There's something in your eyes* (1931); *Just a dancing sweetheart* (1931); *When it's sunset on the Nile* (1931); *Honeymoon Lane* (1931); *Hang out the stars in Indiana* (1931); *Down Sunnyside Lane* (1931); *This is the day of days* (1931); *Gotta date with an Angel* (1931); *Guilty* (1931); *Twentieth Century Blues* (1931); *Hold my hand* (1931); *Pied Piper of Hamelin* (1931); *I was true* (1931); *One little quarrel* (1931); *Put your little arms around me* (1932).

Vol.4 *Meet me tonight in the cowshed* (1932); *By the fireside* (1932); *Must it end like this* (1932); *Sweetheart in my dreams tonight* (1932); *It's great to be in love* (1932); *Blues in my heart* (1932); *There's a ring around the moon* (1932); *With love in my heart* (1932); *Goodnight, Vienna* (1932); *Give me a tune* (1932); *Living in clover* (1932); *With all my love and kisses* (1932); *We've got the moon and sixpence* (1932); *One Hour With You*-selection (1932); *Sailin' on the Robert E. Lee* (1932).

Vol.5 *Songs Everybody is Singing*-selection (1932); *Good evening* (1932); *The echo of a song* (1932); *Dreams that don't grow old* (1932); *Why be so unkind to me* (1932); *Please don't mention it* (1932); *Where are you* (1932); *Pagan Moon* (1932); *Looking on the bright side of life* (1932); *The younger generation* (1932); *You're more than all the world to me* (1932); *I'll do my best to make you happy* (1932); *Love is the sweetest thing* (1932); *Don't say goodbye* (1932); *Song of the bells* (1932).

Vol.6 *A bedtime story* (1932); *Marching along together* (1932); *You, just you* (1932); *Rock your cares away* (1932); *Here lies love* (1932); *Please* (1932); *What more can I ask* (1932); *Brighter than the Sun* (1932); *A little street where old friends meet* (1933); *Lying in the hay* (1933); *Wanderer* (1933); *Just an echo in the valley* (1933); *Butterflies in the rain* (1933); *A letter to my Mother* (1933); *Play, fiddle, play* (1933); *Look what you've done* (1933).

Vol.7 *Standing on the corner* (1933); *Poor me, poor you* (1933); *Have you ever been lonely* (1933); *Wheezy Anna* (1933); *Love tales* (1933); *Can't we meet again* (1933); *Sweetheart* (1933); *The moment I saw you* (1933); *My heart's to let* (1933); *When you've fallen in love* (1933); *Three wishes* (1933); *Let me give happiness to you* (1933); *Hustlin' and bustlin' for baby* (1933); *Stay on the right side of the road* (1933); *I'm one of the lads of Valencia* (1933); *The village band* (1933).

Vol.8 *Waltzing in a dream* (1933); *Maybe I love you too much* (1933); *It's within your power* (1933); *The old spinning wheel* (1933); *When my little Pomeranian meets your little Pekinese* (1933); *That's what life is made of* (1933); *Hiawatha's Lullaby* (1933); *I shall still keep smiling along* (1933); *Seven years with the wrong woman* (1933); *All over Italy* (1933); *You're mine you* (1933); *Gypsy fiddles* (1933); *Something came and got me in the Spring* (1933); *A couple of fools in love* (1933); *I only want one girl* (1933); *Shadow Waltz* (1933).

Vol.9 *Pettin' in the park* (1933); *I've got to sing a torch song* (1933); *Roll up the carpet* (1933); *It's Sunday down in Carolina* (1933); *Si petite* (1933); *If you'll say 'yes', chérie* (1933); *There's a cabin in the pines* (1933); *On the other side of Lover's Lane* (1933); *Mademoiselle* (1933); *How could we be wrong* (1933); *It's bad for me* (1933); *Trouble in Paradise* (1933); *Oh! Johanna!* (1933); *Snowball* (1933); *Dinner at eight* (1933); *Experiment* (1933).

Vol.10 *Weep no more, my baby* (1933); *Love locked out* (1933); *Happy and contented* (1933); *Goodnight, little girl of my dreams* (1933); *Thanks* (1933); *My hat's on the side of my head* (1933); *Hand in hand* (1933); *And so goodbye* (1933); *This is romance* (1933); *Song without words* (1933); *When you were the girl on the scooter* (1933); *My song goes around the world* (1933); *Oceans of time* (1933); *Close your eyes* (1933); *On a steamer coming over* (1933); *Did you ever see a dream walking* (1933).

Vol.11 *You ought to see Sally on Sunday* (1933); *Unless* (1934); *Have a heart* (1934); *Who walks in when I walk out* (1934); *It's time to say goodnight* (1934); *Midnight, the stars and you* (1934); *This little piggy went to market* (1934); *Over on the sunny side* (1934); *Wagon wheels* (1934); *Not bad* (1934); *What now* (1934); *You have taken my heart* (1934); *One morning in May* (1934); *You oughta be in pictures* (1934); *The old covered bridge* (1934).

Vol.12 *The little Dutch mill* (1934); *The very*

thought of you (1934); *She loves me not* (1934); *After all, you're all I'm after* (1934); *My sweet* (1934); *The show is over* (1934); *I love you truly* (1934); *Little man, you've had a busy day* (1934); *The beat o' my heart* (1934); *Night on the desert* (1934); *I'll string along with you* (1934); *Fair and warmer* (1934); *Hold my hand* (1934); *When you've got a little Springtime in your heart* (1934); *Moon country* (1934); *Happy!* (1934).

Vol.13 *It's all forgotten now* (1934); *All I do is dream of you* (1934); *Dreamy Serenade* (1934); *Remember me* (1934); *I never had a chance* (1934); *Lady of Madrid* (1934); *Little valley in the mountains* (1934); *Driftin' tide* (1934); *The Prize Waltz* (1934); *Grinzing* (1934); *Freckle face, you're beautiful* (1934); *Isle of Capri* (1934); *Love, wonderful love* (1934); *Dreaming a dream* (1934); *Sing as we go* (1934); *Ray Noble Medley* (1936).

Vol.14 *Copper Blues* (1929); *Terribly fond of you* (1929); *So the bluebirds and the blackbirds got together* (1929); *Baby, you've got the right idea* (1929); *Every day away from you* (1930); *What a perfect combination* (1933); *Tiger Rag* (1933); *The Japanese sandman* (1933); *Banditlied* (1930); *Die eensaam Weg* (1930); *Kleine Maat* (1930); *Sweet and lovely* (1931); *I can't get Mississippi off my mind* (1931); *Wonder Bar*-film selection (1934); *Ray Noble talks about Al Bowlly* (1956).

Ray Noble and his Orchestra—1935-1936 (broadcasts)—Decca London HMG5019 (76). *Rhythm is our business; California, here I come; Now; Little old lady; Let's spill the beans; In a little Gypsy tea room; El Relicario; Lullaby of Broadway; Sweet Sue, just you; Let's call a heart a heart; There's something in the air; Ray Noble Medley.*

Also:

The Swinging Briton (1938-40)—(A) Swing Era LP-1012.

The Radio Years, Vol.1 (1935-36)—London HMG-5019 (76).

The Radio Years, Vol.2—London HMG-5027 (78).

Ray Noble—RCA RD-7881 (d); (A) RCA LPV-536.

We Danced all Night—Camden CDN-5131 (d); (A) Camden CAL-536.

Al Bowlly, Vols.1-6—(A) Monmouth-Evergreen MES6816, MES7021, MES7027, MES7039, MES7040, MES7056.

Al Bowlly—World Records SH146 (70).

The Ray Noble Story, Vol.1—EMI 'Encore' ENC140 (d).

Ray Noble and his American Dance Orchestra, 1935—(A) Jazz Archives JA-22.

Ray Noble Encores—(A) Monmouth-Evergreen MES7070.

Mayfair and Ray Noble Rarities—(A) MFC MFC-6.

With all my Heart—RCA LSA3067 (d).

The Ray Noble Story, Vol.2—EMI 'Encore' ENC160 (d).

24 Distinguished Dance Arrangements by Ray Noble—(A) Capitol TBO-10312 (2).

Dance Parade—(A) Columbia CL-6065.

Red Norvo

(b Beardstown, Illinois, March 31 1908)

One of the pioneers of the jazz xylophone, Red Norvo subsequently led a progressive big band featuring arrangements by Eddie Sauter. Most of his early work was done with small groups, and he later played with the Benny Goodman Quintet and Sextet, but between 1935 and 1939 his band, which featured his wife singer Mildred Bailey (together they were known as 'Mr and Mrs Swing') contained excellent jazz musicians [Stew Pletcher (t), Hank D'Amico (cl), Herbie Hayward (ts), Eddie Sauter (mellophone, arr) and George Wettling (d)]. Played at Jack Dempsey's Supper Room, New York, in 1936. During the 1940s Norvo worked mostly freelance, with periods of work with Woody Herman and Benny Goodman (he had played with Paul Whiteman in the early 1930s). Featured on various radio and television shows through into the 1980s. Composer of a number of good jazz standards—*Knockin' on Wood, Blues in E-flat, Just a Mood, Hole in the Wall,* and many others.

Selected LP recordings

Red Norvo Featuring Mildred Bailey (1936-42)—(A) Sounds of Swing LP112.

Mildred Bailey — Her Greatest Performances—(A) Columbia C3L-22 (3).

Move—(A) Savoy 12088.

King Oliver

(b New Orleans, May 11 1885; d Savannah, Georgia, April 8 1938)

Oliver's Creole Jazz Band of the 1920s is still regarded as the apotheosis of the classic New Orleans style. Young Louis Armstrong joined Oliver in 1923 and learned, as he always claimed, much from the experience, especially in the matter of the essential duet form of the blues. The other members

[Oliver (cnt), Honore Dutrey (tb), Johnny Dodds (cl), Bill Johnson (bj) and Baby Dodds (d)] were top New Orleans players who integrated into an outstanding and influential band that played the Lincoln Gardens, Chicago, until it was burnt down in 1924. After that Oliver's great band broke up; he himself led a new band in 1925 at the Plantation Cafe. In 1927 Oliver turned down the offer to play at the Cotton Club, New York, an offer which Duke Ellington accepted. It was a momentous decision, both ways, for the jazz world: from that date Ellington's star rose while Oliver's declined. Oliver fronted several larger bands for recording, often in collaboration with his trumpet-playing nephew, Dave Nelson, showing a perhaps unexpected refinement and modernity of style. What it would have led to is hard to assess: certainly King Oliver was not a man to stand still or be content to repeat his former glories (surely a lesson for the so-called 'revivalists' of the 1940s). But after forming a band of young musicians with which he toured briefly, Oliver's health declined: he had trouble with his teeth, slowly lost his ability to play well, and was harrassed by financial problems. When he died in 1938 he had been out of music for several years and had declined into poverty.

Selected LP recordings

King Oliver and his Dixie Snycopators—Vogue LRA10020 (d); (A) Brunswick BL58020. *Too bad* (1926); *Sugar Foot Stomp* (1926); *Snag it (No.2)* (1926); *Someday, sweetheart* (1926); *Willie the Weeper* (1927); *Black Snake Blues* (1927); *Aunt Hagar's Blues* (1927); *Speakeasy Blues* (1927).

King Oliver's Dixie Syncopators, Vol.1—Decca Ace of Hearts AH34 (62) (d). *Deep Henderson* (1926); *Jackass Blues* (1926); *Wa-wa-wa* (1926); *Farewell Blues* (1927); *Every tub* (1927); *Show Boat Shuffle* (1927); *New Wang Wang Blues* (1926); *Sobbin' Blues* (1927); *Tack Annie* (1926); *Willie the Weeper* (1927); *Someday sweetheart* (1926); *Dead Man Blues* (1926).

King Oliver's Dixie Syncopators, Vol.2—Decca Ace of Hearts AH91 (65) (d). *Too bad* (1926); *Sugar Foot Stomp* (1926); *Snag it* (1926); *Black Snake Blues* (1927); *Tin Roof Blues* (1928); *West End Blues* (1928); *Sweet Emmalina* (1928); *Lazy Mama* (1928); *Speakeasy Blues* (1928); *Aunt Hagar's Blues* (1928); *I'm watchin' the clock* (1928); *Slow and steady* (1928).

King Oliver, Vol.1—(A) Classic Jazz Masters CJM19 (76). *Too bad* (2 takes) (1926); *Snag it* (2 takes) (1926); *Georgia man* (1926); *Deep Henderson* (1926); *Jackass Blues* (1926); *Home Town Blues* (1926); *Sorrow Valley Blues* (1926); *Sugar Foot Stomp* (1926); *Wa-wa-wa* (1926); *Tack Annie* (1926); *Someday sweetheart* (1926); *Dead Man Blues* (1926); *New Wang Wang Blues* (1926); *Snag it* (2 takes, 1926).

King Oliver and Dave Nelson, Vol.3 (1929-31)—RCA FXM1 7061 (75). *I've got that thing* (1929); *The trumpet's prayer* (1929); *Freakish Light Blues* (1929); *Can I tell you* (1929); *Everybody does it in Hawaii* (1929); *What's the use of living without love* (1930); *You were only passing time with me* (1930); *Nelson Stomp* (1930); *I ain't got nobody* (1931); *When day is done* (1931); *Some of these days* (1931); *Somebody stole my gal* (1931); *Rockin' chair* (1931); *Loveless love* (1931); *St. Louis Blues* (1931).

Also:

The Dixie Syncopators—(G) EMI COPS7396/1-2 (2) (75).

Papa Joe 1926-28—(F) MCA 510.034 (74).

King Oliver, Vol.1—(F) RCA 730.557.

King Oliver, Vol.2 (1929-30)—(F) RCA 741.055; (A) RCA LPV-529.

Jazz from New York 1928-32—(A) Historical Jazz HLP-33.

King Oliver in New York—(A) RCA LPV-529 (66).

Jack Parnell

(b London, August 6 1923)

Best known now as leader of high class orchestras for radio, television and theatrical shows, Jack Parnell began as a fine drummer with Buddy Featherstonhaugh in the 1940s and later with Ted Heath. Partnered Vic Lewis (qv) as co-leader of jazz groups playing in the modern style influenced by American bands. Still regular leader of high quality orchestras for television shows.

Selected LP recordings

Big Band Stereo—Music for Pleasure MFP1007 (2) (80). *Skyliner; Peanut vendor; Carnival; Sing, sing, sing; Tuxedo Junction; St. Louis Blues March; Brasil; Tristeza; Mood indigo; South Rampart Street Parade; Viramundo; Opus 1; Li'l darlin'; American patrol; etc.*

Also:

The Big Band Show—Music for Pleasure MFP50302 (76).

Braziliana—Music for Pleasure MFP50327 (77).
Jack Parnell Plays Music of the Giants—Sounds Superior SPR90082 (75).

Tony Pastor

(b Middletown, Connecticut, October 26 1907; d Old Lyme, Connecticut, October 31 1969)

Before joining Artie Shaw (qv) in 1936, Pastor had played and sung with a number of bands, including Irving Aaronson, Austin Wylie, Vincent Lopez and Joe Venuti (qv), and led his own band in Hartford. Shaw was the first to make original use of a string section and when Pastor joined as tenor saxist and singer, the band was strongly string oriented. Shaw subsequently formed several different bands without strings, and Pastor continued to be featured. He formed his own band in 1939 which perpetuated the Shaw style. Later bands under Pastor's leadership featured arrangements by Ralph Flanagan, Budd Johnson and other top writers, and included vocals by Rosemary Clooney and her sister Betty. Although Pastor was a good leader and singer who sometimes adopted a Louis Armstrong-like manner, he was much addicted to corn and 'novelty numbers'. He led bands during the 1950s, then concentrated mostly on solo appearances.

Selected LP recordings

Just for Kicks (1940-45)—(A) Big Band Archives LP-1210.
Ready, Get Set (1940-49)—(A) Bandstand BS-7114.
Dance Parade—(A) Columbia CL-6070.
Dance Date—(A) Columbia CL-6122.
Hey, Tony—(A) Harmony HL-7011.
Tony Pastor's Best—(A) 'X' LXA-3025.
Let's Dance with Tony Pastor—(A) Forum F-9009.
Pastor Plays and Sings Shaw—(A) Everest 5031.
Tony Pastor and his Orchestra (1945-49)—(A) FTR 1516.
Let's Dance—(A) Roulette 25024.
Guy Pastor and his Dad—(A) Roulette 25027.

Jack Payne

(b Leamington Spa, Warwicks, August 22 1899; d 1970)

First organised dance bands while serving in the RFC during World War I. In 1925 he took a small band to London's Hotel Cecil and enlarged it when broadcasting from the hotel began. In 1928 he was appointed Director of Dance Music for the BBC at Savoy Hill, and remained in that position until succeeded by Henry Hall (qv) in 1932. After leaving the BBC, Jack Payne appeared with his orchestra in stage shows, dances, and in the films *Say it With Music* (1932) and *Sunshine Ahead* (1933). Following World War II, Payne continued in the music business, latterly as an agent. Highly successful in his heyday, his career ended sadly with poor health and bankruptcy. Over the years several top ranking British musicians played in the Payne ranks [Tommy McQuater, Jack Jackson (t), Sid Millward (as, cl), Billy Thorburn (p) and Billy Scott-Coomber (vo)]. Bert Read was the pianist in the first Hotel Cecil band.

Jack Payne (from a 1943 sheet music cover) (Campbell, Connelly & Co).

Selected LP recordings

Jack Payne with his BBC Dance Orchestra—World Records SH143 (70). *Say it with music* (1931); *Choo Choo* (1931); *Wrap your troubles in dreams* (1931); *The man from the South* (1930); *Lazy day* (1931); *Hot and heavy* (1928); *Ain't that the way it goes* (1931); *My brother makes the noises for the talkies* (1931); *Happy days are here again* (1930); *Underneath the Spanish stars* (1930);

Harmonica Harry (1930); *Twentieth Century Blues* (1931); *The peanut vendor* (1931); *Hot bricks* (1928); *Fire, fire, fire* (1930); *Entrance of the little fauns* (1931). (Vocals by Jack Payne, Billy Scott-Coomber, etc.)

Say it with Music—Decca 'Eclipse' ECM2111 (72). *Now's the time to fall in love* (1932); *There's a home in Wyomin'* (1933); *By a waterfall* (1933); *Miss What's Her Name* (1934); *Just another dream of you* (1932); *What more can I ask?* (1933); *How'm I doin'?* (1932); *The argument song* (1933); *Kid from Spain*-medley (1933); *Seven years with the wrong woman* (1933); *Dinner at eight* (1933); *Good morning Mr. Sun* (1932); *In the dim, dim dawning* (1932); *Happy ending* (1933). (Vocals by Billy Scott-Coomber, Leslie Sarony & Jack Payne.)

Ben Pollack

(b Chicago, June 22 1903; d (suicide) Palm Springs, June 7 1971)

Began by playing drums in various jazz groups, notably the New Orleans Rhythm Kings at Friars Inn, also Red Nichols and the Charleston Chasers. Formed his own band in 1925 and began recording using top white jazz musicians for several years and into the 1930s [Jimmy McPartland, Charlie Spivak, Yank Lawson (t), Jack Teagarden (tb, vo), Glenn Miller (tb), Benny Goodman (cl), Bud Freeman, Fud Livingston (ts), Harry Goodman (b) and Ray Bauduc (d)]. In 1928 he conducted the band for the Broadway musical *Hello Daddy*. Back in Chicago he led another fine white band featuring more top jazzmen [Charlie Teagarden, Sterling Bose (t), Joe Harris (tb), Matty Matlock (cl), Eddie Miller, Babe Russin (ts) and Nappy Lamare (g), as well as some former associates]. Later again featured still more [Harry James (t), Muggsy Spanier (cnt) and Irving Fazola (cl)]. He led a band for comedian Chico Marx in 1942, but his band leading work dropped off during the 1940s when he worked as an agent. Returned briefly during the Dixieland 'revival' and appeared in the film *The Benny Goodman Story* (1956). Subsequently he was little involved with music, running a restaurant in Palm Springs. Ben Pollack's importance lies in the recordings he made with star-studded bands in the 1920s and 1930s, when he had the reputation as the best white leader of the period. (*Note:* In 1935 the Ben Pollack band was taken over by Bob Crosby (qv), after which Pollack formed the new unit with Harry James etc.)

Selected LP recordings

Ben Pollack 1926-1931—(A) Sunbeam SB-316. *He's the last word* (1926); *Waitin' for Katie* (1927); *Memphis Blues* (1927); *Singapore sorrows* (1928); *Buy, buy for baby* (1928); *Wang Wang Blues* (1929); *Yellow Dog Blues* (1929); *Bashful baby* (1929); *Sing-song girl* (1931); *I'm a ding dong Daddy* (1931); *I've got five dollars* (1931); *Sweet and hot* (1931); *Beale Street Blues* (1931). (With Benny Goodman & Jack Teagarden.)

Ben Pollack and his Orchestra 1933-1934—VJM VLP43 (75.) *Got the jitters* (1933); *Deep jungle* (1933); *Swing out* (1933); *I'm full of the Devil* (1933); *My little grass shack in Kealakekua Hawaii* (1934); *Goin' to Heaven on a mule* (1934); *Dancing in the moonlight* (1934); *The voodoo* (1934); *Ole Mammy ain't gonna sing no more* (1934); *Here goes* (1934); *The beat o' my heart* (1934); *Alone on the range* (1934); *Night on the desert* (1934); *Sleepy head* (1934); *Freckle face, you're beautiful* (1934); *I've got a warm spot for you* (1934).

Also:

Ben Pollack and his Orchestra 1928-1929—(A) Old Masters TOM-22 (d).

Ben Pollack and his Orchestra—(Arg) Collectors OFC-40.

Jack Teagarden (2 tracks)—RCA RD-7826, (A) LPV-528.

Ben Pollack—(A) 'X' LX-3003.

The Pick-A-Rib Boys—(A) Coral BL-58025.

Dixieland (with Teagarden)—(A) Savoy MG-12090.

Radio Rarities 1926-27—Broadway BR103 (79).

Boyd Raeburn

(b Faith, San Diego, October 27 1913; d August 2 1966)

While studying medicine at Chicago University he was already leading bands, one of which won a competition in 1933 and led to engagements. He led a society type dance band in mid-1930s and switched to a swing style in later 30s. Played at the Chez Paree club in 1940 at the instigation of Paul Whiteman (qv), and again in 1942 after being injured in a road smash. Began a 'progressive jazz' policy at Chicago's new Band Box club, employing a number of top class jazzmen [Dizzy Gillespie, Benny Harris (t), Trummy Young, Earl Swope (tb), Johnny Bothwell, Hal McKusik (as), Buddy de Franco (cl), Dodo Marmarosa (p), Oscar Pettiford (b) and Don Lamond (d)] in outstanding modernist arrangements by Johnny Richards, Ed Finckel and George Handy. With Stan Kenton (qv), Lennie Tristano, Claude Thornhill (qv) and sometimes Woody Herman (qv) became prominently associated with the 'progressive' band style which drew heavily on European 'straight' music, at times somewhat selfconsciously. Continued to lead and play this kind of music through the 1940s and into the 1950s, though not on a regular basis. He later concentrated on arranging and returned to band leading with the emphasis more on dance music than the 'far out' material of the prime years.

Selected LP recordings

On the Air, Volume 2—(A) Hep 3 (74). *Boyd meets Stravinsky* (1945); *Where you at* (1945-46); *Tea for two* (1945-46); *Caravan* (1946); *High tide* (1945); *Bagdad* (1945); *Hep Boyds* (1945); *Two spoos in an igloo* (1946); *There's no you* (1946); *Duck waddle* (1946); *How high the moon* (1947); *St. Louis Blues* (1947); *Begin the beguine* (1945-46); *Tonsillectomy* (1945-46).

Also:

Hep Boyds (1945-47-broadcasts)—Golden Era LP-15014 (75).

Boyd Raeburn (1943-48)—First Heard 8 (76).

Out of this World—(A) Sounds of Swing LP-115.

Man with the Horns—(A) Savoy MG-12025.

Innovations, Vol.1—(A) Savoy MG-15010.

Innovations, Vol.2—(A) Savoy MG-15011.

Innovations, Vo.3—(A) Savoy MG-15012.

Dance Spectacular—(A) Columbia CL-889.

Fraternity Rush—(A) Columbia CL-957.

Boyd Raeburn and his Orchestra (1944-46)—(A) First Time FTR-1515.

On the Air (1946)—(A) Hep 1 (73).

Boyd meets Stravinsky—(A) Savoy MG-12040.

Teen Rock—(A) Columbia CL-1073 (58).

Boyd Raeburn 1945—Aircheck 20 (79).

The Ramblers

Formed in 1929 by Theodore Uden Massman, The Ramblers soon became one of the top Dutch bands, and one of the best in Europe. They played for a number of years at the Hamdorff Hotel and Casino in Laren and at the Carlton Hotel, Amsterdam. They were twice in London, in 1932 and 1933 for concerts and recording. In 1934 they backed Coleman Hawkins (qv) in a number of recordings, all for Decca except for a few titles made for HMV in 1929 by a smaller group known as the Original Ramblers. (See Coleman Hawkins.)

Selected LP recordings

Coleman Hawkins with The Ramblers Decca 'Ace of Clubs' ACL1247.

The Original Ramblers—EMI Bovema 5C 052 24332.

Don Redman

(b Piedmont, West Vancouver, July 29 1900; d New York, November 30 1964)

Played most instruments but mostly heard on alto sax, on which he often went solo. But he is best remembered as an arranger and leader who led McKinney's Cotton Pickers (qv) for five years and for later bands of his own. After playing with Billy Paige in Pittsburgh he went to New York and joined Fletcher Henderson (qv) and during 1923-24, Redman virtually created big band scoring. His work in that department remained prominent and influential; he arranged for Paul Whiteman, who commissioned work from him, and in 1931 took a band of his own to Connie's Inn, New York, after his stint with the Cotton Pickers. From then until 1940 he led various bands, featuring many leading jazzmen [Renauld Jones, Sidney de Paris, Henry Allen, Harold Baker (t), Quentin Jackson, Claude Jones, Benny Morton (tb), Eddie Barefield (cl), Gene Sedric (ts), Horace Henderson (p, arr) and Sid Catlett (d)]. After 1940 Redman concentrated on arranging, writing scores for Paul Whiteman, Louis Armstrong, Jimmy Dorsey, Count Basie, Jimmie Lunceford and others. In 1946 he took a band [Tyree Glenn (tb, vib), Don Byas (ts), Billy Taylor (p), etc] to Europe and, from 1951 until his death in 1964, he was musical director for the singer, Pearl Bailey. Don Redman was greatly admired both as man and musician, and his impression on the evolution of big band jazz cannot be exaggerated. He composed a number of first class tunes, including *Chant of the Weed* which, in his own recording made in December 1938, is a jazz classic.

Selected LP recordings

Don Redman and his Orchestra—CBS Realm RM52539. *How'm I doin'; Hey, hey* (1932); *I heard* (1932); *Reefer man* (1932); *Tea for two* (1932); *I got rhythm* (1932); *Nagasaki* (1932); *Hot and anxious* (1932); *Sophisticated lady* (1933); *That blue-eyed baby from Memphis* (1933); *That Dallas man* (1933); *Got the jitters* (1934); *Bugle Call Rag* (1936); *Sweet Sue* (1936); *Exactly like you* (1936); *On the sunny side of the street* (1936); *Swingin' with the fat man* (1937).

Don Redman and his Orchestra 1932-1933—(A) Jazz Archives JA-5 (74). *Chant of the weed* (as Harlan Lattimore and his Connie's Inn Orchestra, 1932); *Got the South in my soul* (ditto, 1932); *Try gettin' a good night's sleep* (1932); *It's a great world after all* (1932); *Two-time man* (1932); *Underneath the Harlem moon* (1932); *How ya feelin'* (1933); *Shuffle your feet* (1933); *Bandana Babies* (1933); *I found a new way to go home* (1933); *She's not bad* (1933); *Our big love scene* (1933); *After sundown* (1933); *Puddin' Head Jones* (1933); *My old man* (1933); *Tired of it all* (1933); *Keep on doin' what you're doin'* (1933).

Don Redman and his Orchestra—(Swi) Collector's 12-5 (75). *Trouble, why pick on me* (1931); *Chant of the weed* (1931); *Shakin' the African* (1931); *I heard* (1931); *How'm I doin'* (1932); *Hot and anxious* (1932); *I got rhythm* (1932); *Two time man* (1932); *How can I hi-de-hi* (1933); *Sophisticated lady* (1933); *Got the jitters* (1934); *A little bit later on* (1936); *Down home rag* (1938); *Margie* (1938).

Also:

Don Redman (1932-39, with Mills' Blue Rhythm Band)—(G) Swingfan 1019.

Don Redman-the Little Giant of Jazz (1938-40)—(F) RCA 741.061.

Master of the Big Band (with McKinney's Cotton Pickers & own band)—(A) RCA LPV-520.

Park Avenue Patter—(A) Golden Crest 3017.

Buddy Rich

(b Brooklyn, New York, September 30 1917)

An outstanding jazz drummer, he began playing as a child and was recognised as a prodigy. He worked freelance for some years, then with Joe Marsala in 1937 and Bunny Berigan (qv) in 1938. Made a big impression with Artie Shaw in 1939, and confirmed it with Tommy Dorsey in two stints either side of World War II; with Jazz at the Philharmonic in 1947, then for a short time with Les Brown (qv). He was again with JATP in the early 1950s, staging drum 'battles' with Gene Krupa. Rich joined Harry James (qv) in 1953, then went back to Tommy Dorsey in 1954, and rejoined James in 1956 and again in 1961 for five years. Also played with some 'bop' groups in the 1940s. In intervals of permanent jobs, Rich led bands and small groups, but formed a regular band in 1966 to play hard driving modern arrangements. Always in the van as a drummer with a fine sense of showmanship as well as musical ability, the various Buddy Rich bands have provided excitement and sensitivity proportionately mixed. Poor health (heart) sometimes baulked his more ambitious excursions; but he has continued to play exciting music with fine bands, appearing often in England and on the Continent. Prolific recording star.

Selected LP recordings

Buddy Rich and his Greatest Band 1946-47—First Heard FH-5 (2) (75). *Rags to riches; You've got me crying again; Quiet riot; The wonder of you; Aren't you glad you're you; Route 66; A little handicap; Just a-sittin' and a-rockin'; Frim fram sauce; Great moments; Daily double; Nellie's nightmare.* (1946-47).

Buddy Rich plays Count Basie—Polydor Verve 2317 058. *Down for double; Blue and sentimental; Shorty George; Jumpin' at the Woodside; Ain't it the truth; 9:20 Special; Blues for Basie; Jump for me.* (1956.)

Swingin' new Big Band—Fontana LBL83090, (S) LBLS83090; Liberty LBS83107; (A) PJ(S) 20113. *Readymix; Basically Blues; The critics' choice; My man's gone now; Up tight; Sister Sadie; More soul; West Side Story*-medley. (1966.)

Big swing face—Fontana TL5435, (S) STL5435 (67); Sunset SLS50174 (71); (A) PJ(S) 10117. *Norwegian Wood; Big swing face; Monitor theme; Wack wack; Love for sale; Mexicali rose; Willowcrest; The beat goes on; Bugle Call Rag.* (1966.)

A different drummer—RCA SF-8229; (A) RCA ANL1-1090. *Superstar; Domino; Chelsea Bridge; Paul's Tune; Straight, no chaser; Heaven on their minds; A Piece of the Road Suite.* (1971.)

Also:

Superstar—RCA INTS1475 (74).

The New One—(A) PJ (S) 20126.

Take it Away—Liberty LBL83090, (S) LBLS83090.

Very Alive at Ronnie Scott's—RCA DPS2031 (2) (72); (A) RCA LSP-4666, AFL1-4666; INTS-5012 (80).
The Buddy Rich Collection—Sunset SLD505/6 (2) (77).
The Monster (1955-57)—Verve 2352 100 (75).
Great Moments (1946-48)—Golden Era LP-15021 (76).
Buddy and Soul—(A) PJ(S) 20158; Liberty LBS83269.
Class of '78 (1977)—RCA PL25164 (78); (A) Gryphon 781.
Both Sides of Buddy Rich—(A) Ember 402 (2).
Mr. Drums—(A) Quintessence 25051.
Buddy Rich Plays and Plays and Plays (1977)—RCA PL12273; (A) RCA CPL1-2273.
Stick It (1972)—RCA LSP-4802; (A) RCA AFL1-4802.
Superpak—(A) United Artists UXS-86 (2).
Speak no Evil—RCA RS1073 (76); (A) RCA AFL1-1503.
The best of Buddy Rich—United Artists UAS29187 (71).
Big Band/Small Combos 1947-48—(A) Hep HEP-12 (77).
Conversations/Drum Spectacle—Parlophone PCS7151 (72).
Keep the Customers Satisfied—Liberty LBS-83334 (70).
Mercy, Mercy, Mercy—Liberty LBS-83168 (69).
Are You Ready for This (with Louis Bellson)—Roulette 2432 003.
One Night Stand—(A) Joyce JLP-1007 (74).
The Roar of '74—Moon CREST-7 (74).
Strike it Rich—Verve 2683 035 (2).
The Driver—Philips 6336 232 (75).
The Monster—Polydor 2352 100 (75).
Drum Battle (with Gene Krupa)—Verve 2317 116 (76).
Anatomy of a Jam Session (with Charlie Shavers)—Black Lion BLP301-04 (75).
The Man From Planet Jazz—Pye NSPL-18620 (81).

Nelson Riddle

(b Oradell, New Jersey, June 1 1921)
Famous latterly for arranging and conducting studio and recording orchestras, usually behind top popular singers. Earlier he played trombone and did arrangements for a number of bands, including those of Charlie Spivak (qv) and Tommy Dorsey (qv), either side of World War II, before becoming staff arranger for NBC radio. He won particular fame for work with Frank Sinatra, and developed further his talent as arranger/conductor for various singers. Riddle had many appearances on television during the 1960s, and was strongly involved in films, being responsible for music for a whole sequence between 1957 *(Pal Joey)* and 1967 *(How to Succeed in Business Without Really Trying)*. He continues actively involved in all forms of musical entertainment as arranger and conductor in the top flight.

Selected LP recordings

Love Letters—Capitol T-753; (A) Capitol T-753.
Hey, Let Yourself Go—Capitol T-814; (A) Capitol T-814.
The Joy of Living—Capitol T-1148, (S) ST-1148; (A) Capitol T-1148.
More Hit TV Themes—Capitol T-1869; (A) Capitol T-1869.
C'mon . . . Get Happy—Capitol T-893; (A) Capitol T-893.
Sea of Dreams—Capitol T-915; (A) Capitol T-915.
The Sound of Nelson Riddle Today—Sunset SLS50166.
The Special Magic of Nelson Riddle (with Oscar Peterson)—Polydor 2317 071.
Ella Swings with Nelson Riddle—Polydor 2682 035 (2).
Golden Hour of Nelson Riddle—Pye (Golden Hour) GH823 (73).
Vive Legrand—Pye 'Daybreak' DAL2004 (73).
A Perfect Mix (with Frank Sinatra)—EMI 1C 054 81582.
Changing Colours—BASF BAP5022 (74).
Communications—BASF BAP5023 (74).
The Best of Nelson Riddle—(A) Capitol DT-1990 (63).

Harry Roy

(b London, January 12 1900; d London 1969)
Originally intended for a business career, he formed his first band with his brother Sydney immediately after World War I, in which the family firm had suffered heavy losses. The band played in a number of London venues and then toured South Africa in 1928 and Germany in 1930. In 1931 Harry Roy and his RKOlians played at the Leicester Square Theatre, then at the

Harry Roy (from a 1935 sheet music cover) (Herman Darewski).

London Pavilion and the Café Anglais. In 1934 they opened for a celebrated run at the Mayfair Hotel, succeeding Ambrose (qv) in this prestigious residency. The features of the band, apart from its general spirit and accomplishment, were Roy's characteristic high pitched singing and the two-piano work of Ivor Morton and Dave Kaye (succeeded in 1936 by Stanley Black and Norman Yarlett). Harry Roy always had a penchant for 'hot' numbers and from time to time recorded with a small group; also with another group featuring the two pianos of Morton and Kaye under the title of Harry Roy and His Tiger-Ragamuffins. In 1935 he caused a mild social furore when he married Elizabeth Brooke, daughter of the Rajah of Sarawak. After World War II, Roy like most other band leaders of the 1930s, found the going hard, but kept active in various fields. He died at some pecuniary disadvantage, having been an inveterate gambler all his life.

Selected LP recordings

Are You Listening—World Records SH187/8 (73). *Bugle Call Rag/I can't give you anything but love* (1933); *Sentimental gentleman from Georgia* (1933); *Waiting for tomorrow and you* (1933); *Wah-de-dah* (1933); *Mood indigo* (1933); *Nasty man* (1934); *Emaline* (1934); *Temperamental Blues* (1934); *Sarawaki* (1934); *No word—nor anything* (1934); *It's the animal in me* (1934); *I'm somebody's sweetheart now* (1934); *Jubilation Rag* (1935); *Campansina* (1935); *Okay Toots* (1935); *Heart of gold* (1936); *Sky high honeymoon* (1936); *Down Home Rag* (1937); *Heatwave* (1934); *What a difference a day made* (1934); *San Sue Strut* (1937); *Cheerful Blues* (1936); *You're a sweetheart* (1938); *Old mammy mine* (1935); *Swinging with Rig* (1942); *I've got a gal in Kalamazoo* (1942); *Missouri scrambler* (1940); *Dear old lady, London Town* (1941); *A man and his drum* (1941); *Keep an eye on your heart* (1943); *Light Cavalry* (1942); *Infatuation* (1942). (Vocals by Harry Roy, Bill Currie, Ivor Moreton.)

Bands on Film—World Records SH197 (76). Soundtrack of *Everything is Rhythm* (1936)—*You're the last word in love* (2 versions); *Cheerful Blues; Black Minnie's got the Blues; Make some music; Life is empty without love; The Internationale;* also *Man of my dreams.* (Vocals by Harry Roy, Mrs Harry Roy, Phyllis Thackery, Ivor Moreton, Mabel Mercer. Coupled with soundtrack of 'Nat Gonella and his Georgians' (1935).)

The World of Harry Roy—Decca (S) SPA141 (71). *Leicester Square Rag; Blues in Mayfair; Piano madness; Mammy Bong; Guilty; That mysterious Rag; I've found a new baby; Park Lane Blues; Darktown Strutters' Ball; Piccadilly Rag; There ought to be a society; Bugle Call Rag.* (Vocals by Eve Lombard, Harry Roy & Joy Nichols. Recordings made between 1944 and 1950, electronically processed.)

The Golden Age of British Dance Bands—World Records SH118/9 (69). *South American Joe; Avalon; Build a little home; Limehouse Blues; Spanish shawl; Margie; Music, maestro, please; Piano madness.* (Vocalist Harry Roy. Recordings from 1933-1935. Coupled with recordings by Lew Stone, Roy Fix and Ray Noble.)

Also:

Hotcha-ma-cha-cha—Music for Pleasure MFP1135 (d).

The King of Hotcha—Regal-Starline MRS5068 (d).

Harry Roy and his Orchestra—Music for Pleasure MFP50334 (77).

Harry Roy and his Band—President 'Joy' JOY131.

Luis Russell

(b Panama, August 6 1902; d New York, December 11 1963)

He gained his first experience playing in local cinemas in Panama; then in 1919 he won $5000 in a lottery and went to the US, first to New York then to New Orleans where he stayed. He played with Albert Nicholas for a while in 1923, then went to Chicago in 1924. He played for two years with King Oliver at the Plantation Club and toured with Oliver until he quit in New York in 1927. He made his major mark with his own orchestra in 1929-30 in a number of outstanding recordings featuring some of the greatest jazz musicians [Henry Allen (t), J.C. Higginbotham (tn), Charlie Holmes (as), Albert Nicholas (cl), Pops Foster (b) and Paul Barbarin (d)]. He achieved a big reputation in New York at the Roseland, Connie's Inn, the Savoy Ballroom and other haunts of fine jazz. From 1935 Louis Armstrong fronted the band which had small changes in personnel [James Archey (tb) and Greely Walton (ts)]. Russell himself left in 1944 and formed a new band which lasted until 1948, when he virtually gave up music, apart from some teaching, and work as an agent. Many of the early Russell recordings were made under the names of Henry Allen or J.C. Higginbotham, and the later ones were billed as by Louis Armstrong and His Orchestra.

Selected LP recordings

Henry 'Red' Allen and his New York Orchestra—RCA FXM1 7060 (75); (A) RCA LPV-556. *It should be you* (3 takes, 1929); *Biffly's Blues* (2 takes, 1929); *Feeling drowsy* (3 takes, 1929); *Swing out* (3 takes, 1929); *Doggin' that thing* (1929); *Yo-yo* (1929); *Make a country bird fly wild* (2 takes, 1929); *Funny Feathers Blues* (1929). (Vocals by Red Allen.)

The Luis Russell Story—Parlophone PMC7025 (d). *Savoy Shout* (1929); *Call of the freaks* (1929); *It's tight like that* (1929); *The new call of the freaks* (1929); *Feelin' the spirit* (1929); *Jersey lightning* (1929); *Doctor Blues* (1929); *Saratoga shout* (1930); *Song of the Swanee* (1930); *Louisiana Swing* (1930); *Poor L'il me* (1930); *On Revival Day* (1930); *Muggin' lightly* (1930); *High tension* (1930).

Also:

Do You Like Jazz? Vol.22—(F) CBS 63721.

Satchmo Style—Parlophone PMC7045 (d).

Luis Russell and his Orchestra—(D) Collector's Classics CC-34.

Luis Russell and his Louisiana Swing Orchestra—(A) Columbia KG-32338 (2).

Riding' with Red Allen—(A) 'X' LVA-3033.

Sauter-Finegan Orchestra

Between 1952 and 1957 this orchestra was co-led by Eddie Sauter (born December 2 1914) and Bill Finegan (born April 3 1917), two outstandingly original arrangers whose combined talents made the unit a memorable contribution to the popular music of the 1950s. Sauter worked first for Charlie Barnet (qv) then did most of the arrangements for Red Norvo (qv) between 1936 and 1938. Later Sauter did major arranging series for Benny Goodman, Artie Shaw, Tommy Dorsey and many other leading bands. Finegan did a no less notable series for Tommy Dorsey and Glenn Miller in 1939-42, then, after World War II, for Dorsey again. The Sauter-Finegan Orchestra featured scores of exceptional quality which made particular use of instruments from the 'straight' field, including various wind and brass plus original percussion effects, as well as the normal jazz constitution. Despite the non-commercial approach, the band lasted for five years and was highly regarded, offering music that owed virtually nothing either to the old 'symphonic jazz' of Paul Whiteman (qv) or the 'progressive jazz' of Stan Kenton (qv), either in conception or execution. After the break up of the band, both Sauter and Finegan concentrated mostly on radio and television work, though Finegan did some more arranging for the New Glenn Miller Orchestra which Buddy de Franco led in 1973.

Selected LP recordings

Sauter-Finegan—RCA DPM2025 (2). *Doodletown Fifers; Nina never knew; The moon is blue; Moonlight on the Ganges; A foggy day; Doodletown Races; Azure te (Paris Blues); Love is a simple thing; April in Paris; Rain; Tweedle Dee and Tweedle Dum; When hearts are young; Yankee Doodletown; Where or when; Midnight sleigh-ride; Hit the road to Dreamland; Stop beating around the mulberry bush; Autumn leaves; Clarinet à la King; Swing low, sweet chariot; Mobile; Sunshine girl; Now that I'm in love; What is this thing called love?* (1952-54.)

Also:
Sleigh Ride —EMI Sunset SLS50253 (71).
Inside Sauter-Finegan—HMV CLP1027 (d); (A) RCA LPM-1003.
The Sound—(A) RCA LPM-1009.
Concert Jazz—(A) RCA LPM-1051.
Adventure in Time—(A) RCA LPM-1240.
Memories of Goodman and Miller—RCA RD27093, (S) SF-5029; (A) RCA LPM-1634.
Inside Sauter-Finegan—(A) RCA LPM-2474.
New Directions in Music—(A) RCA LPM-1227 & LPM-3115.
Straight Down the Middle—RCA RD-27030 (58) (d) (S) SF-5042; (A) RCA LPM-1497.

Jan Savitt

(b Petrograd, September 4 1913; d Sacramento, California, October 4 1948)
Though he died of a cerebral haemorrhage at the age of 35, Savitt made a distinctive impression on the popular music scene during his short career. He was brought to the US in the first year of his life, and grew up in Philadelphia where he later studied at the Curtis Institute. Showed remarkable musical gifts, especially with the violin and, while still very young, was associated with the Philadelphia Orchestra, but turned to popular music in 1934 and became director of music on radio, still in Philadelphia. He formed a dance band for the first time in 1937 and created a strong impression on the *Music for Moderns* show with adventurous modernistic arrangements. He began touring in 1938 with an excellent band featuring an individual ballad style and 'shuffle rhythm' on up-tempo numbers. From 1942 he began to feature a string section, and appeared in a number of minor films.

Selected LP recordings

One Night Stand—(A) Joyce LP-1002 (75). *Theme; Tuxedo Junction; They say it's wonderful; If you were the only girl in the world; I don't know why; Opus No.1; Begin the beguine; Where or when; Surrender; Kansas City moods.*
Also:
The Swinging Mr. Savitt (1938-41)—(A) Sounds of Swing LP-104.
Swinging the Classics—(A) Coral BL-58028.
And the Angels Sing (1937-41)—(A) Swing Era LP-1016.
Futuristic Shuffle (1938-41)—(A) Bandstand BS-7113.
The Top-Hatters (1939-41)—(A) Decca DL-79243 (69).
Jan Savitt and his Orchestra (1938-39)—(A) First Time FTR-1505.
Souvenirs—Brunswick LA8605 (53) (d).
In Disco Order, Vols.1-3—(A) Ajax 113/152/162 (79).
Swing Happy Years—Decca 'Ace of Hearts' AH-143 (67) (d).

Savoy Orpheans & Savoy Havana Band

These two organisations were closely associated at the Savoy Hotel during the 1920s. Both were formed in 1923, the Orpheans by Debroy Somers, the Havana Band by Reginald Batten when Bert Ralton (qv) took his band to Australia. The Orpheans was the larger group, and gave concerts of symphonic proportions, but still in association with the Havana Band [Max Goldberg (t), Jock Fleming (tb) and Van Phillips (as, cl)]. The relationship between the two bands is complicated by changes in leadership. In 1926 Cyril Ramon took over the Havana Band from Reginald Batten who was deputy leader of the Orpheans; then Newton took over the Orpheans and Batten went back to the Havana. In 1927 the Havana Band was dissolved and leadership of the Orpheans passed to Carroll Gibbons (qv). When Gibbons went to America in 1928, the Orpheans were also disbanded; but on his return were reformed under his permanent leadership. The original Savoy Orpheans recorded prolifically and were frequently heard on the radio.

Selected LP recordings

The Savoy Bands—World Records SH165/6 (7). *Eccentric* (1924); *Oh, Eva (ain't you coming out tonight)* (1925); *Copenhagen* (1925); *Hard-hearted Hannah* (1925); *Oh! that sweet in Suite 16* (1925); *Blue Evening Blues* (1925); *Dinah* (1925); *It ain't gonna rain no mo'* (1925); *Charleston* (1925); *Baby face* (1926); *Let's all go to Mary's house* (1926); *Five foot two, eyes of blue* (1926); *Vladivostock* (1927); *When Erastus plays his old kazoo* (1927); *Ain't that too bad* (1927); *Then I'll be happy* (1927); *Pasadena* (1924); *Sister Kate* (1923); *Farewell Blues* (1923); *Sahara* (1924); *Hen Pecked Blues* (1923); *My sweetie went away* (1923); *Everybody Stomp*

(1925); *Show me the way to go home* (1925); *Crazy words, crazy tune* (1927); *I'm a little blackbird looking for a bluebird* (1926); *Masculine women and feminine men* (1926); *Take your pick* (1926); *I never see Maggie alone* (1926); *There ain't no maybe in my baby's eyes* (1927); *I'm knee deep in daisies* (1926); *Side by side* (1927).
Also:
Light Music at The Savoy—Flapper PAST701 (80).

Raymond Scott

(b Brooklyn, New York, September 10 1910)
A composer and arranger of individual talent, Scott became famous as leader of a Quintette playing semi-novelty numbers in the 1930s, the most famous of which, *In an Eighteenth Century Drawing Room* and *War Dance for Wooden Indians*, gained him a considerable cachet later. He was a staff musician for CBS from 1934 and played in various radio bands, including that of Andre Kostalanetz. He led a big band from 1939 to 1941, playing more of his curiously titled numbers. In 1942 he became music director for CBS and fronted a band which contained many top ranking jazzmen [Charlie Shavers, Emmett Berry (t), Benny Morton (tb), Ben Webster (ts), Johnny Guarnieri, Mel Powell (p), Israel Crosby (b) and Cozy Cole (d), etc] on his own radio show. During the later 1940s Scott led and toured with several small groups and big bands and directed music on the 'Lucky Strike Hit Parade' on radio and television before going into business with Raymond Scott Enterprises specialising in electronic instruments. He is remembered chiefly for his uniquely-styled instrumental pieces, many of which became major hits.

Selected LP recordings
On the Swinging Side (1940-41)—(A) Sounds of Swing LP107.
Get Happy (1937-42)—(A) Swing Era LP-1013.
Raymond Scott's Drawing Room—(A) Columbia CL-6083.
Raymond Scott—(A) MGM E-549.
The Unexpected—(A) Top Rank RM-335.

Artie Shaw

(b New York, May 23 1910)
At one time during the swing era, Shaw rivalled Benny Goodman in the popularity polls as clarinet playing band leader. After working in various jobs he joined Irving Aaronson's band in 1929, at the instigation of Tony Pastor (qv). He stayed on in New York after Aaronson left for further touring and played briefly with a number of bands, including Vincent Lopez, Roger Wolfe Kahn (qv), Andre Kostelanetz and Paul Whiteman. He left music for a short period then returned to lead a band featuring strong section, but was not successful with this idea until the 1940s when he became perhaps the first jazz musician to make really effective use of strings rather than simply having a few violins around. From 1937 Shaw led a major swing band with top rate musicians with good arrangements by himself and Jerry Gray. During 1938 the great singer Billie Holiday was prominently featured with Shaw. The following year the vocalist was Helen Forrest and the band achieved tremendous drive through the presence of drummer, Buddy Rich (qv). Shaw seldom led the same band for long; he was in the habit of frequently disbanding and re-grouping; but he continued with undiminished success. He was clever enough

Artie Shaw (RCA Records).

not to challenge Benny Goodman direct on the clarinet, but evolved a style of his own which achieved great popularity in its own right, although he took a period of rest from band leading for a while at the end of 1939 before returning the next year with an even more successful unit. Likc the other big band leaders, Shaw also featured a small group playing straight jazz, the 'Grammercy Five' which also had major following. Bands of the 1940s included more leading jazz players [Billy Butterfield, Roy Eldridge, 'Hot Lips' Page (t), Jack Jenny (tb), George Auld (ts) and Dave Tough (d)], at one time or another. With America's entry into the war, Shaw joined the navy in 1942 and led the US Navy band [John Best, Max Kaminsky (t), Sam Donahue (ts), Claude Thornhill (p), etc] until given medical discharge in 1944 when the band was taken on by Donahue (qv). After this show he was less active, though continuing with bands occasionally, then he went into theatrical and film production. Eight times married to notable ladies, including film stars Lana Turner and Ava Gardner (also novelist Kathleen Winsor), Shaw often made the headlines for other than purely musical reasons.

Selected LP recordings

Artie Shaw and his Orchestra, Vol.2—RCA DPM2041 (2) (74). *Comin' on* (1938); *I can't believe that you're in love with me* (1938); *Indian love call* (1938); *Non-stop flight* (1938); *Softly, as in a morning sunrise* (1938); *A room with a view* (1938); *Jungle drums* (1938); *Lover, come back to me* (1939); *Vilia* (1939); *Donkey Serenade* (1939); *Serenade to a savage* (1939); *Zigeuner* (1939); *All the things you are* (1939); *Out of nowhere* (1939); *Rose room* (1939); *I didn't know what time it was* (1939); *Temptation* (1940); *Gloomy Sunday* (1940); *King for a day* (1940); *Marinella* (1940); *What is there to say* (1940); *Dancing in the dark* (1941); *If I had you* (1941); *Moonglow* (1941); *St. James' Infirmary* (1941); *I'll never be the same* (1945); *Don't take your love from me* (1945); *S'wonderful* (1945); *Tea for two* (1945); *These foolish things* (1945); *I can't get started* (1945).

The Beat of the Big Bands—Embassy 31017 (74). *Night and day* (1937); *Fee fi fo fum* (1937); *I concentrate on you* (1937); *I'm yours* (1936); *I surrender, dear* (1937); *Non-stop flight* (1937); *Nightmare* (1937); *Free wheeling* (1937); *Blue skies* (1937); *The man I love.* (Previously available as *Free For All*—CBS 52636 (16 tracks).)

Spotlight on Artie Shaw-1945—(A) Joyce LP1003 (74) (d). *Theme (Nightmare); Tabu; Little Jazz; Summit Ridge Drive; Lucky number; Begin the beguine; My heart stood still; On the Atcheson, Topeka and the Santa Fe; Scuttlebut; Got be this or that; Just floating along; Blue skies; On the sunny side of the street; Hop, skip and jump; Jumpin' on the merry-go-round.* (1945.)

The Big Band Years—(A) Sounds of Swing LP101 (74). *I want my share of love; You're so indifferent; Melancholy mood; Without a dream to my name; To a Broadway rose; Deuces wild; Kasbah; Lament; Tabu; My lucky number; Thrill of a lifetime; No one but you; Just floating along; I can't escape from you; Jumpin' on the merry-go-round.* (1939-45).

Dance to Artie Shaw—Coral CP103; Decca Ace of Hearts AH76; Coral CRLM 1064; (A) Decca DL-4462. *I get a kick out of you; Love walked in; I'm forever blowing bubbles; Foggy foggy dew; Crumbum; Love is the sweetest thing; Where or when; The Continental; The Shekomeko Shuffle; I'll remember April; You're mine you; So easy.* (1950.)

The Best of Artie Shaw—RCA Starcall NL-11089 (77). *Frenesi* (1940); *Stardust* (1940); *Moonglow* (1941); *Oh, lady be good* (1939); *All the things you are* (1939); *Temptation* (1940); *Begin the beguine* (1938); *Serenade to a savage* (1939); *Indian love call* (1938); *Traffic jam* (1939); *Nightmare* (1938); *Dancing in the dark* (1941).

Also:

Concerto for Clarinet (1938-45)—RCA DPM2028 (2).

The Great Artie Shaw (1938-45)—Camden CDN-127; (A) Camden CAL-465, (S) S-465.

Artie Shaw Swings Show Tunes (1938-45)—Camden CDN-137; (A) Camden CAL-515.

The Dancing Years (1938-49)—(A) Sounds of Swing LP-118 (74).

The String Years (1939-45)—(A) Sounds of Swing LP-102.

The Ballad Years (1939-40)—(A) Sounds of Swing LP-116.

The Vocal Years (1939-49)—(A) Sounds of Swing LP-117.

The Sideman Years (1938-45)—(A) Sounds of Swing LP-122.

Artie Shaw and his Musicians (1949)—

First Heard 6 (75).
Free For All—CBS Realm 52636; (A) Epic EE-22023.
The Helen Forrest Years—(A) Sounds of Swing LP-123.
The Jazz Years—(A) Sounds of Swing LP-125.
The Broadcast Years—(A) Sounds of Swing LP-126.
Artie Shaw with Strings (1936)—(A) Epic LN-3112.
Artie Shaw and his Orchestra (1937)—(A) Epic LN-3150.
Any Old Time (1938-45)—RCA RD-27065 (d); (A) RCA LPM-1570.
Both Feet in the Groove (1938-45)—(A) RCA LPM-1201 (d).
Melody and Madness, Vols.1 & 2 (1938-39)—(C) Jazz Guild 100 & 1003.
Artie Shaw and his Orchestra, 1938 (broadcasts)—London HM-A5065 (80).
Artie Shaw and his Orchestra, 1938, Vol.2 (broadcasts)—London HM-A5066 (80).
One Night Stand (1939-41)—Camden CDN-5107.
Featuring Roy Eldridge—(A) RCA LPV-582.
Moonglow—(A) RCA LPM-1244.
In the Blue Room/In the Café Rouge (1938-39) (broadcasts)—(A) RCA LPT-6000-1 (2).
Swing with Artie Shaw—(A) Reader's Digest (4).
This is Artie Shaw—(A) RCA VPM-6039 (2).
An Hour with Artie Shaw—(A) Roy 1405.
Artie Shaw Hour—(A) Roy 1466.
September Song—(A) Camden S-908 (65).
Artie Shaw, Vol.1—(F) RCA FXM1-7336.
Did Someone Say a Party—Coral CRLM-1065.
Artie Shaw Re-creates His '38 Band—Capitol ST-2992; (A) ditto.
The Swinging 30s—CBS EPC80094.

Noble Sissle

(b Indianapolis, July 10 1889; d Florida, December 17 1975)
He worked, mostly as lyricist, with the ragtime pianist, Eubie Blake, and sang regularly, either side of World War I. Blake and Sissle toured both Europe and the US. During the 1920s he composed scores for a number of musical shows. After parting with Blake in 1928, Sissle formed a band and, during the 1930s, led a fine group which featured the great jazz star, Sidney Bechet (ss, cl), also Buster Bailey (cl) and for a time in the mid-1930s, singer Lena Horne. He continued to lead a band through World War II and afterwards again toured Europe, with Eubie Blake an occasional participant. Later ran his own publishing company and a club with occasional returns to band leading.

Selected LP recordings

Noble Sissle Orchestra (1931-36)—(with tracks by Cab Calloway)—(G) Swingfan 1023.

Freddie Slack

(b LaCrosse, Wisconsin, August 7 1910; d Hollywood, August 10 1965)
Studied at the American Conservatory of Music in Chicago, then played piano with Ben Pollack (qv), Jimmy Dorsey (qv) during the 1930s, and with Will Bradley in 1939-41, for whom he wrote successful arrangements and made a speciality of boogie-woogie numbers which achieved huge popularity. He formed his own band in 1941, continuing the boogie policy with great success. He was featured in a number of movies during the 1940s, then for the rest of his life was heard mostly on his own or with a trio. Composer of a number of boogie type jazz standards, including *Mr Freddie's Boogie* and *Cuban Sugar Mill.*

Selected LP recordings

Riffette (1941-49)—(A) Big Band Archives ULP-1202.
The Hits of Ella Mae Morse and Freddie Slack—(A) Capitol T-1802.
Boogie Woogie on the Eighty-Eight—(A) EmArcy MG-36094.
Boogie Woogie—Capitol LC6559 (54) (d).

Charlie Spivak

(b New Haven, Connecticut, February 17 1906)
Outstanding lead trumpet, Charlie Spivak played with most leading bands—Ben Pollack (qv), Dorsey Brothers (qv), Ray Noble (qv), Glenn Miller (qv), and Jack Teagarden (qv)—before fronting his own bands which played in a predominantly sweet, though jazz inflected, style and sometimes featured leading jazzmen [Willie Smith (as) and Dave Tough (d)] in arrangements by himself, Sonny Burke, Nelson Riddle (qv), and Jimmy Mundy, through the 1940s and 1950s. Gave up at the end of the 1950s when

big bands went out and worked intermittently thereafter, mostly with small groups.

Selected LP recordings

Bulldozer-Charlie Spivak and his Orchestra (1941-47)–(A) Big Band Archives LP1214.
Stomping Room Only (1941-50)–(A) Swing Era LP-1017.
Charlie Spivak and his Orchestra (1943-46) (radio)—London HMP5044 (79).
Dance to Sweet Trumpet in Soft Moonlight–(A) Decca DL-4355.
One Way Passage—First Heard FH28 (79).

The Squadronaires

In 1940 during World War II the Royal Air Force asked various members of well-known British dance bands to join up and form a Service dance orchestra, the first to be formed by any of the services. From the Ambrose band came eight musicians—Tommy McQuater, George Chisholm, Eric Breeze, Harry Lewis, Andy McDevitt, Jock Cummings, Sid Colin and Archie Craig. These, plus those from other bands, led by Ronnie Aldrich, formed what was to become one of the most exciting 'hot' dance bands of the period, a respectable rival to the similar orchestra formed in America by Glenn Miller. They, in fact, set new standards in swing styling that were carried on in the post-war era.

Selected LP recordings

There's Something in the Air—Decca Eclipse ECM2112 (72); (S) ECS2112 (t). *There's something in the air* (1941); *South Rampart Street Parade* (1942); *C jam Blues* (1945); *Pompton Turnpike* (1946); *Ringle dingle* (1942); *Anchors a-weigh* (1943); *Commando patrol* (1943); *Boston bounce* (1945); *Ring dem bells* (1947); *Cow-cow Boogie* (1943); *High society* (1947); *Mistakes* (1952); *Mission to Moscow* (1945); *That's a-plenty* (1941).
Also:
Contrasts in Jazz—Decca LF-1141 (d).

The Starita Brothers

The bands in the Piccadilly Hotel in London had been, until the mid-20s in the light music tradition, led by the violinist, Van de Groot. In 1925, however, the growing demand for jazz-orientated styling caused Jack Hylton, who organised the music for various London venues as well as leading his own band, to send to America for the Starita brothers. Al Starita led the Kit-Cat Band from 1925 and Ray Starita led the Piccadilly Revels Band. Later Al led the Picadilly Players. In 1926, younger brother Rudy Starita came and joined them. These bands maintained a strong 'hot' tradition with many good jazzmen in the band, besides the Staritas. They recorded regularly between 1926 and 1929 and became a popular part of the London dance band scene. Al and Ray both returned to America in the early 1930s.

Selected LP recordings

The Kit-Cat-Band Play 'Hot' Dance Music 1925-7—World Records SH333 (79). *Can't your friend find a friend for me* (1925); *Milenberg joys* (1925); *My sugar* (1925); *Riverboat Shuffle* (1925); *If you hadn't gone away* (1925); *Headin' for home* (1925); *The Camel Walk* (1925); *Piccadilly Strut* (1925); *Breezin' along with the breeze* (1926); *I've got some lovin' to do* (1926); *I wonder what's become of Joe* (1926); *Sunday* (1926); *Brown sugar* (1927); *Ain't she sweet* (1927); *Sam the old accordeon man* (1927); *Muddy water* (1927); *Lily* (1927); *From now on* (1925).
The Piccadilly Hotel Bands—World Records SH250 (77). *The Piccadilly Revels: My cutie's due at two-to-two today* (1927); *Brown sugar* (1927); *Positively, absolutely* (1927); *Back beats* (1927); *Tapping the time* (1927); *Deep River Blues* (1927); *Is she my girl friend?* (1927); *Mary (what are you waiting for)* (1928); *The Piccadilly Players: How long has this been going on* (1928); *It don't do nothing but rain* (1928); *Do the sugar step with me* (1928); *I'm afraid of you* (1928); *What a wonderful wedding that will be* (1928); *Blues grass* (1929); *He's a good man to have around* (1929); *I've never seen a smile like yours* (1929).

Lew Stone

(b London, June 11 1898; d London, February 13 1969)

One of the best and most successful jazz-inflected bands of the 'Golden Age' of dance music was led by Lew Stone who played first for Bert Ralton (qv) and later did some arranging for Ambrose (qv) before joining Roy Fox (qv) at the Monseigneur Restaurant in London's Piccadilly. When Fox became ill, Stone took over the leadership and later formed his own band in 1932. Whereas Ambrose's jazz style was based on Duke

Ellington, that of Lew Stone drew on the Casa Loma (qv), some of their major successes being Gene Gifford numbers—*White Jazz, Blue Jazz*—from the Casa Loma book, though both bands developed recognisably British styles of their own. The Stone band featured many of the best English musicians [Nat Gonella (t, vo), Tommy McQuater (t), Lew Davis (tb), Joe Crossman (as, cl), Harry Berly (ts), Eddie Carrol (p), Tiny Winters (b), Bill Harty (d) and Al Bowlly (vo)]. Stone's weekly broadcasts were high spots of the listening routine: of course he purveyed 'novelties' and other gimmickry, as was required in those days; but the band's musicianship and teamwork was remarkable and gave it a distinction shared by only the very best among the others. Stone continued working in music, leading bands and organising others, on radio and television, as well as 'on the boards', until well into the 1960s.

Selected LP recordings

Presenting Lew Stone 1934-1935—World Records SH177/8 (73). *Oh! Susannah* (1935); *Oh Suzanna (dust off that old pianna)* (1935); *Stay as sweet as you are* (1934); *The gentleman obviously doesn't believe* (1935); *East of the sun* (1935); *The wheel of the wagon is broken* (1935); *Sidewalks of Cuba* (1935); *Maybe I'm wrong again* (1935); *The girl with the dreamy eyes* (1935); *My old dog* (1935); *Isn't this a lovely day* (1935); *Vilia* (1934); *Yes suh!* (1935); *I get a kick out of you* (1935); *Rain* (1935); *Here comes cookie* (1935); *Anything goes* (1935); *The bouncing ball* (1935); *Stars fell on Alabama* (1934); *I won't dance* (1935); *Caranga* (1934); *I was lucky* (1935); *Two Trumpet Toot* (1935); *Zing! went the strings of my heart* (1935); *Solitude* (1934); *Winter wonderland* (1934); *The general's fast asleep* (1935); *The leech* (1935); *Algernon Wifflesnoop John* (1935); *It's easy to remember* (1935); *(Where were you) On the night of June the Third* (1935); *I'll B.B.C.-ing you* (1935).

The bands that Matter—Decca 'Eclipse' ECM2047 (70). *Look what I've got* (1933); *The glory of love* (1936); *With my eyes wide open I'm dreaming* (1934); *Canadian Pacific* (1939); *(I've got) Beginner's luck* (1937); *Lazy rhythm* (1933); *As long as I live* (1934); *Mama, I wanna make rhythm* (1938); *Dinner*

The Lew Stone Band (The Decca Record Co).

and dance (1938); *Louisiana hayride* (1934); *Sing me a swing song* (1936); *The Down and Out Blues* (1938); *Plastered in Paris* (1938); *Let's put out the lights and go to sleep* (1932).
10.30 Tuesday Night—Decca 'Ace of Clubs' ACL1147 (63). *Oh! Susannah* (1934); *Goodbye Blues* (1934); *That's a plenty* (1934); *I'll never be the same* (1932)*; *Isle of Capri* (1934)†; *Eadie was a lady* (1933)*; *Lazybones* (1933); *White Jazz* (1933); *Ja-da* (1941); *I never had a chance* (1934)*; *Miss Otis regrets* (1934); *Ebony shadows* (1937); *A Brivella der Mama* (1933)*; *Lying in the hay* (1932)*†; *Canadian Capers* (1934). (Featuring Al Bowlly* and Nat Gonella†.)
The Golden Age of British Dance Bands—World Records SH118/9 (69). *I ain't got nobody; Red sails in the sunset; Dinner for one, please, James; She's a Latin from Manhattan; Thank you so much, Mrs. Lowsborough-Goodbye; She wore a little jacket of blue; The continental; Cheek to cheek.* (Vocals by Tiny Winters, Joe Ferrie, Sam Browne, Al Hoffman, Lew Stone and Nat Gonella. Coupled with recordings by Harry Roy, Roy Fox and Ray Noble.)
Also:
Al Bowlly with Lew Stone and his Band—Decca 'Ace of Clubs' ACL1178 (64).
London Jazz Scene—The 30s (with Ambrose)—Decca 'Ace of Clubs' ACL1103 (62).
My Kind of Music—Decca 'Ace of Clubs' ACL1231 (67).
Lew Stone and his Band—Decca DDV5005/6 (77).
The Echo of a Song (1932)—Halcyon HAL-12 (79).
By the Fireside—Halcyon HAL-2 (68).

Jack Teagarden

(b Vernon, Texas, August 20 1905; d New Orleans, January 15 1964)
One of the greatest of all white jazz musicians with his flexible, rich toned trombone and characteristically 'lazy' singing, both strongly blues intonated, Jack Teagarden was senior member of a talented musical family. His sister, Norma, was an excellent pianist, his brother, Charlie, a trumpet player who never quite achieved the recognition that was his due, and another brother, 'Cubby', was a drummer. He was born in Texas and retained a species of 'Texas drawl' in his music all his life. He played trombone first with Peck Kelly in Houston, then joined Ben Pollack (qv). Most of his best work was done with small groups, with Red Nichols, Red McKenzie, Eddie Condon and others, and sometimes with groups under his own name. But after a five-year stint spent, not too happily, with the Paul Whiteman (qv) organisation, he set out on a course of band leading on his own account. It was a disaster—not because the bands and the music were not good, but because Teagarden had virtually every quality as a musician except that of natural leadership. His business acumen was terrible; his judgement all too fallible. (An example of the latter: he gave the important drum chair in his first bands to his little brother, 'Cubby', out of family loyalty, until forced to acknowledge his mistake and bring in Dave Tough to give the band its necessary lift). All the same, his bands were good and if they had not driven him into bankruptcy they would have established themselves better in the busy market place. They had good musicians [Charlie Spivak, Charlie Teagarden, Jimmy McPartland (t), Ernie Cacares (bar, cl), Hub Lytle (ts), Kitty Kallen (vo), etc] and Teagarden's own contributions were never less than admirable. After the failure of his band leading adventure, Teagarden joined Louis Armstrong's All-Stars, then from 1951 formed groups for playing round the US and touring (including a famous Far East tour). Unfortunately, his private life was not better organised than his bands: his marriages broke up, heavy drinking took its toll and his health began to fail. He was loved and admired by everyone; but he just could not put his life and his bands properly together. But the legacy he left was, and will remain, permanent.

Selected LP recordings

Jack Teagarden, Vol.2—RCA 741 101 (74). *Futuristic Rhythm* (with Ben Pollack Orchestra, 1928); *Futuristic Rhythm* (part take with Benny Goodman, 1928); *I'm gonna stomp, Mr Henry Lee* (Eddie's Hot Shots) (1929); *That's a serious thing* (Eddie's Hot Shots) (1929); *Song of the Blues* (with Ben Pollack, 1929); *Keep your undershirt on* (with Ben Pollack) (1929); *Fare thee well to Harlem* (with Paul Whiteman Orchestra, 1934); *Christmas night in Harlem* (with Paul Whiteman, 1934); *Darktown Strutters' Ball* (with Paul Whiteman, 1934); *Blue Lou* (with All-Star Band, 1939); *Prince of Wails* (with

Bud Freeman's Summa Cum Laude, 1957); *Jack hits the road* (with Bud Freeman, 1957); *Forty-Seventh and State* (with Freeman, 1957); *At the Jazz Band Ball* (with Freeman, 1957); *There'll be some changes made* (with Freeman, 1957).

Sincerely, Jack Teagarden—(A) International Association of Jazz Record Collectors 19 (75). *Persian rug; The Sheik of Araby; Class will tell; If it's good; Cinderella, stay in my arms; I gotta right to sing the Blues; That's right, I'm wrong; Yankee Doodle; White sails; Octoroon; Especially for you; You're the moment in my life; You know; The little man who wasn't there; Puttin' and takin'; Blues to the dole.* (1939.)

Jack Teagarden; Big Band 1939—(Swi) Tax M-8024 (76). *Persian rug; The Sheik of Araby; I gotta right to sing the Blues; Yankee Doodle; White sails; Octoroon; Pickin' for Patsy; Undertwo; Especially for you; You're the moment in my life; I swung the election; Aunt Hagar's Blues; Muddy Water Blues; Red wing; United we swing; Somewhere a voice is calling.* (1939—first Teagarden big band sessions, variously chosen on two above records.)

Also:

Jazz Teagarden, Vol.1—Storyville Code O SLP700 (76).

The Unforgettable Jack Teagarden—Halcyon HAL-4.

It's time for Teagarden (1939-1945)—(A) Sounds of Swing LP111.

Standard Library of Jazz—Storyville SLP704 (78).

Rompin' and Stompin' (1939-44)—(A) Swing Era LP-1020.

Big T's Jazz—Decca's Ace of Hearts AH28 (62) (d).

King of the Blues Trombone—Columbia 33SX1573.

Claude Thornhill

(b Terre Haute, Indiana, August 10 1909; d Caldwell, New Jersey, July 1 1965)

Studied at the Cincinnati Conservatory; played piano with Austin Wylie and Hal Kemp (qv) and began arranging. He played with other bands and made an increasing name for himself as an arranger with Ray Noble. Worked with Maxine Sullivan and Benny Goodman (qv) and was musical director for Skinnay Ennis and on radio shows. He formed his first major band in 1940 and won recognition in 1941 with arrangements by Gil Evans (qv) which set new trends and standards in orchestration. Evans' arrangements, which included French horns and other novel features, greatly influenced the young Gerry Mulligan (qv). Irving Fazola (cl) prominently featured as a soloist. In 1942 Thornhill joined Artie Shaw's Navy Band. After the end of war, Thornhill formed a new band (1946) using arrangements by Evans, Mulligan and Ralph Aldridge. Thornhill continued as musical director for Tony Bennet, then gradually dropped out of band leadership. The importance of the 1941 band is especially far reaching.

Selected LP recordings

The Real Birth of the Cool—(J) CBS SOPC57104. *Snowfall* (1941); *Arab Dance* (1946); *I get the Blues when it rains* (1946); *A Sunday kind of love* (1946); *We knew it all the time* (1947); *Early Autumn* (1947); *La paloma* (1947); *Anthropology* (1947); *Sorta kinda* (1947); *The old castle* (1947); *Robbin's nest* (1947); *Lover man* (1947); *Polka dots and moonbeams* (1947); *Happy stranger* (1947); *Donna Lee* (1947); *Yardbird Suite* (1947); *Let's call it a day* (1947).

Also:

Claude Thornhill Goes Modern (1953)—London H-APB1019 (58) (d); (A).

Dream Music (1953)—London H-APB1021 (58) (d); (A).

The Early Cool: Claud Thornhill-on stage '46-47'—Ember CJS828 (72) (d).

Claude Thornhill and his Orchestra 1947 (broadcasts)—London HMP5040 (79).

The Thornhill Sound—(A) Harmony HL-7088.

Dancing After Midnight—(A) Columbia CL-709.

Piano Reflections—(A) Columbia CL-6035.

Dance Parade—(A) Columbia CL-6050.

Encores—(A) Columbia CL-6164.

Dinner for Two—(A) Camden CAL-307.

Dream Stuff—(A) Trend 1001.

Claude Thornhill plays the Arrangements of Mulligan and Aldridge—(A) Trend 1002.

Snowfall—A Memory of Claude—(A) Monmouth-Evergreen MES-6606.

At Glen Island Casino—(A) Monmouth-Evergreen MES-7024.

On Stage—(A) Monmouth-Evergreen MES-7025.

Two Sides—(A) Kapp 1058.

Claude on a Cloud—(A) Decca DL-8722.

Frankie Trumbauer

(b Carbondale, Illinois, May 30 1900; d Kansas City, June 11 1956)

In his youth he led various dance bands and played a while with the US Navy Band in 1918. In 1923 he worked with the Benson Orchestra in Chicago and in 1925 began his legendary association with cornetist Bix Beiderbecke. Between 1927 and 1931 (when Bix died) they were both members of the Paul Whiteman (qv) orchestra and from this period date the famous recordings made with contingents from the Whiteman band—*Singin' the Blues, Crying All Day, I'm Coming Virginia* etc—[Bill Rank (tb), Jimmy Dorsey, Don Murray (cl), Arthur Schutt (p), Eddie Lang (g), Joe Venuti (vln) etc]. Previously (1926) Bix and Trumbauer had spent time with Jean Goldkette (qv). After Bix's death Trumbauer stayed for some time with Whiteman, with an excursion into band leading in 1933 then, in 1937, teamed with Manny Klein in a joint band leadership venture, and later led a band on his own. A flying enthusiast, he became a test pilot in World War II and never returned to music. His particular style, using the unfamiliar C-melody saxophone, was modernistic in approach, as were the arrangements he favoured. He was a major influence on the development of tenor saxist, Lester Young.

Selected LP recordings

Bix-Tram 1927—Parlophone PMC7064 (68). *Clarinet marmalade; Singin' the Blues; Ostrich Walk; Riverboat Shuffle; I'm coming, Virginia; 'Way down yonder in New Orleans; Three blind Mice; Blue river; There's a cradle in Carolina; Humpty Dumpty; Krazy Kat; Baltimore; Just an hour of love; I'm wondering who; Cryin' all day; A good man is hard to find.* (1927.)

Bix-Tram 1928—Parlophone PMC7100 (70). *There'll come a time; Jubilee; Mississippi mud; Our bungalow of dreams; Lila; Borneo; My pet; Bless you, sister; Dusky stevedore; Take your tomorrow; Love affairs; The love nest; Japanese sandman; High up on a hill-top; Sentimental baby.* (Featuring Bix Beiderbecke (cornet); vocals by Bing Crosby, Frankie Trumbauer, Martin Hurt, etc, 1928.)

Bix-Tram 1929 Plus—Parlophone PMC7113 (70). *Futuristic Rhythm* (1929); *Raisin' the roof* (1929); *Louise* (1929); *Wait till you see me, chérie* (1929); *Baby, won't you please come home* (1929); *No one can take your place* (1929); *I like that* (1929); *Trumbology* (1927); *For no reason at all in C* (1927); *Wringin' and twistin'* (1927); *There ain't no land like Dixieland to me* (1927); *There's a cradle in Carolina* (1927); *Sugar* (1927)*; *Manhattan Rag* (1927). (Featuring Bix Beiderbecke (* a doubtful item); vocals by Frankie Trumbauer, Irving Kaufman, etc.)

Also:

Frankie Trumbauer and his Orchestra (1937-38)—(A) I.A.J.R.C. 13.

Frankie Trumbauer—(A) The Old Masters TOM-26.

The Bix Beiderbecke Legend (Goldkette, Whiteman, etc)—(A) RCA LPM-2323.

Joe Venuti

(b Lecco (Como), September 1 1894; d Seattle, August 14 1978)

His date of birth is still usually given as

Joe Venuti.

1904; but it has been established that the date was deliberately falsified in order to facilitate his naturalisation as a US citizen, a practice by no means unusual in the days of high Italian immigration. Venuti learnt the rudiments of the violin from his grandfather and in America studied in Philadelphia. He soon became a notable jazz violinist, and with Eddie Lang (g), another Italo-American born Salvatore Massaro, formed a lasting partnership which was one of the most famous in jazz. Together they played with many top bands, including Jean Goldkette (qv), Roger Wolfe Kahn (qv), and Paul Whiteman, as well as making many records under their own names (sometimes one, sometimes the other, sometimes both) or with other jazz groups. After Lang's premature death in 1933, Venuti marked time for a while then formed his own big band which he led for the rest of the 1930s and up to 1943. He formed another band in 1945, and was featured on radio, especially on the Bing Crosby show. He went on playing mostly on the west coast through the 1950s and 1960s, and caused astonishment by his undiminished virtuosity well into the 1970s, despite the habit of knocking ten years off his age. He played and was loved and admired in Europe as well as US and recorded latterly in Italy.

Selected LP recordings

Joe Venuti Big Band—(A) Big Band Archive LP1215 (74) (d).

Daddy of the Violin—BASF BAP5050 (74) (d).

Nothing But Notes 1931-39—EMI PCO7838 (75).

Joe Venuti and his Orchestra 1934—London HMG5023 (76).

Chick Webb

(b Baltimore, February 10 1907; d Baltimore, June 16 1939)

Despite appalling health and a deformed body (he was a hunchback) Chick Webb was a superb jazz drummer and a highly successful band leader. As a boy he played on riverboats and freelanced in New York, then towards the end of the 1920s he led a fine band at the Savoy Ballroom, Harlem, after other New York engagements. The Webb band comprised Taft Jordan, Bobby Stark (t), Sandy Williams (tb), Hilton Jefferson, Chancy Haughton (as, cl), Wayman Carver (ts, fl), John Kirby (b) and Ella Fitzgerald (vo). Webb's earlier group had included Benny Carter (as, cl), Johnny Hodges (as, ss) and Jimmy Harrison (tb). The tremendous drive and swing of the band came principally from its diminutive drummer/leader, and the excellent arrangements were headed by those of Edgar Sampson. After Webb's death (from tuberculosis of the spine) the band continued for a couple of years under Ella Fitzgerald, who first came to the fore with Webb. The band finally broke up in 1942, when Ella set out on her permanent solo career. In its heyday, the Webb band challenged for popularity and acclaim, especially among black dancers, those of Ellington, Lunceford and Basie.

Selected LP recordings

Spinning the Webb—Coral CP3; CRLM1021 (74). *That rhythm man* (1934); *It's over because we're through* (1934); *Down Home Rag* (1935); *Facts and figures* (1935); *A little bit later on* (1936); *That naughty Waltz* (1937); *I got rhythm* (1937); *Harlem Congo* (1937); *The Dipsy Doodle* (1937); *Hallelujah* (1937); *A-tisket, a-tasket* (1938); *Spinning the Webb* (1938); *Who ya hunchin'* (1938); *Undecided* (1939).

Stompin' at the Savoy—CBS Realm 52537; (A) Columbia CL2639 (67). *Let's get together* (1933); *Blue minor* (1934); *On the sunny side of the street* (1933); *If it ain't love* (1934); *True* (1934); *Stompin' at the Savoy* (1934); *When dreams come true* (1934); *Why should I beg for love* (1934); *I can't dance, I've got ants in my pants* (1934); *Imagination* (1934); *Lonesome moments* (1934); *Darktown Strutters' Ball* (1934).

Five Feet of Swing—Brunswick LAT8037; (G) 87.525. *I want to be happy* (1937); *Hallelujah* (1937) (with Ella Fitzgerald.) (Other tracks by Bob Crosby, Dorsey Brothers, Jimmy Dorsey, Glenn Gray.)

The Kings of Jazz Big Bands—Festival 146 (2) (74). *Tea for two; How am I to know; One O'Clock Jump; Blue room; Crazy Rhythm; Grand Terrace Rhythm; Sugar Foot Stomp; Blue skies; By heck; Dinah; Poor little rich girl; Break 'em down; My wild Irish rose; The Stars and Stripes for ever.* (1939, with Jimmie Lunceford.)

Also:

Chick Webb, Vol.1-A Legend—(A) Decca 9222.

Chick Webb, Vol.2-King of the Savoy—(A) Decca 9223.

A Legend 1929-36—(F) MCA 510 014 (74)

(d); (A) Decca DL-9222.
Ella Swings the Band 1936-9—(F) MCA 510 087 (74).
The King of the Savoy 1937-9—(F) MCA 510 020 (74) (d); (A) Decca DL-9223.
Midnite in Harlem—Decca Ace of Hearts AH32 (62) (d).
Strictly Jive—(F) MCA 510 068 (74) (d).
Swing from Southland Café, Boston—(D) Collectors Classics CC11.
Original Sessions 1937-39—Musidisc 30 JA 5113 (75).
Silver Star Swing Series—EMI PCO7994 (75).
Stompin' at the Savoy—Collectors Classics CC17.
Chick Webb with Ella Fitzgerald (1936-39)—Jazz Anthology JA5139 (77); (G) Swingfan 1006.
Swing Music from the Southland Café, Boston (1939 (with tracks by Basie)—(D) Collector's Classics CC11 (75).
The Golden Swing Years—Polydor 423 428.
Ella Fitzgerald with Chick Webb—Decca Ace of Hearts AH36 (62) (d).
King of the Savoy, Vol.2—(A) Decca DL-9223.

Paul Whiteman

(b Denver Colorado, March 28 1890; d Daylestown, Pennsylvania, December 29 1967)

Once optimistically known as 'The King of Jazz', Whiteman's contribution to 20th century popular music was somewhat different. His real connections with jazz were tenuous, though he did employ (and generously employ) a number of prominent jazzmen in the ranks of his engorged orchestras [Bix Beiderbecke (cnt), Bunny Berigan (t), Jack Teagarden (tb, vo), Tommy Dorsey, Bill Rank, Miff Mole (tb), Jimmy Dorsey (as, cl), Fud Livingston (ts, cl), Joe Venuti (vln), Eddie Lang (g), Steve Brown (b), etc] and was not unwilling to give them their heads. But he was really more interested in 'symphonic jazz', that strange hybrid that did no one a lot of good but deceived audiences of the 1920s that they were listening to 'real music'. In fact, Whiteman's activities in this field did open up a small area of American music that did not survive, but looked forward to later excursions in the blending of jazz and elements of European music in the very different hands of men, as different and disparate as Stan Kenton (qv) and John Lewis, and instrumentally to the work of Gil Evans with Claude Thornhill (qv) and the Sauter-Finegan (qv) experiments. Whiteman's band was exceptionally successful; he himself was a shrewd man of business and an adroit musical operator who knew which way things were going and not only went with them but, more important, helped create them. It was at a famous concert at the Aeolian Hall, New York, that he premiered George Gershwin's *Rhapsody in Blue* in 1924; and that set the tenor for much of his subsequent work. It was also with Paul Whiteman's Rhythm Boys that Bing Crosby made his entry into the popular music scene. Whiteman's fame and prestige reached their peak around 1930, the year of the movie *King of Jazz* which featured him and the band. Frequent appearances on important radio shows (including his own with singer Al Jolson in 1934) and work on Broadway kept his name constantly before the public. Inevitably, his fame declined during the later years, and there is no doubt that his great era of success was up to 1930, though it continued into the next decade. He appeared in more movies between 1935 and 1945, and at times on television, then gradually faded out.

Selected LP recordings

Paul Whiteman, Vol.1—RCA RD7954 (68); (A) LPV-555. *Whispering* (1920); *The Japanese sandman* (1920); *Anytime, anyday, anywhere* (1920); *My man* (1921); *Song of India* (1926); *Hot lips* (1922); *Three o'clock in the morning* (1926); *I'll build a stairway to Paradise* (1922); *Rhapsody in Blue* (1927) (with George Gershwin (pno)); *When day is done* (1927); *What'll I do* (1924); *Love nest* (1928); *Anything Goes*—medley (1934).
Paul Whiteman's 50th Anniversary Record—Music for Pleasure MFP1183; (A) Grand Award GA33-901. *Jeepers creepers; Basin Street Blues; It's the dreamer in me; Washboard Blues; The night is young and you're so beautiful; How high the moon; My romance; Lazy river; Christmas night in Harlem; Lover; Mississippi mud.* (With Johnny Mercer, Jack Teagarden, Jimmy Dorsey, Hoagy Carmichael, Tommy Dorsey, Joe Venuti, Bing Crosby, Harry Barris & Al Rinker.)
Also:
Paul Whiteman and Bing Crosby—CBS

OL2830; (A) Columbia CL-2830.
Rhapsody in Blue—Electrola 1C 062 80797 (74).
Paul Whiteman, Vol.2—RCA RD-8090 (70); (A) LPV-570 [Vols. 1 & 2 issued as DPM2027 (2) (1920-35)].
Paul Whiteman and his Orchestra—(A) Columbia CL-2830.
Pops Remembers—Coral CPS-60; (A) Coral COPS-3871.
The Victorious Bix (various tracks)—(Sw) Divergent 301/2.
The Bix Beiderbecke Legend (7 tracks)—RCA RD-27225; (A) RCA LPM-2323.
Featuring Bix Beiderbecke—(A) RCA LVA-3040.
Featuring Bing Crosby—(A) Columbia CL-2830.
The night I Played 666 Fifth Avenue—(A) GA 33-409.
Cavalcade of Music—(A) GA 33-412.
The Bix Beiderbecke Story, Vol.3—(A) Columbia CL-846.

Cootie Williams

(b Mobile, Alabama, July 24 1908)
For a dozen years (1929-40), Cootie Williams was a major star of the Duke Ellington orchestra. When he left to join Benny Goodman, it caused a considerable furore and Raymond Scott (qv) was moved to write a lament about it, *When Cootie Left Duke*. Cootie stayed with Goodman a year, then left to form his own band. Before joining Duke he had played around the South before sitting in briefly with Fletcher Henderson and Chick Webb in New York. He then joined Ellington, where he soon became famous for his work with the plunger mute. (Incidentally, Cootie's resort to this style had no sinister, social, racial or Freudian connotations as has sometimes been suggested: it was purely practical. As he himself put it: 'I was hired to take Bubber Miley's place. Duke said growl—so I growled'.) The band he formed in 1941 featured, besides his own trumpet and vocals, the work of Eddie 'Cleanhead' Vincent (as, vo). He also had Charlie Parker (as) and Bud Powell (p) briefly through his ranks. The band was successful but ran into the recording ban of the early 1940s, as did a number of others whose work was consequently not well documented. After playing at the Savoy Ballroom, Cootie made the group smaller and in the 1950s was more associated with rhythm and blues than jazz proper. He returned to the Ellington fold in 1962 and spent another dozen years there until Duke's death in 1974, then continued on and off when Mercer Ellington (qv) took over.

Selected LP recordings

Cootie Williams and the Boys from Harlem 1937-40—(Sw) Tax M8005 (74).
Cootie Williams and his Orchestra—Storyville SLP803 (76).
Cootie Williams and his Rug Cutters 1937-40—(Sw) Tax M8011 (74) (d).
Big Band Bounce—Bovema 5C 052 80850.
Echoes of Harlem—(A) Big Band Archives LP1208 (74).
Sextet & Big Band, New York '44—Jazz Anthology JA5144 (77).
Cootie Williams (1941-47, with Hot Lips Page tracks)—(G) Swingfan 1022.
Cootie Williams/Hot Lips Page—(F) RCA 730.675.

Sam Wooding

(b Philadelphia, June 17 1895)
Wooding led one of the first black American jazz bands to tour overseas. He recorded in Berlin in 1924, went to Russia in 1926 and played in Copenhagen in 1931; he toured South America in 1927. The Wooding band at this time contained a number of celebrated jazz musicians [Tommy Ladnier (t), Herb Flemming (tb) and Garvin Bushell (as, cl)] and did a great deal to spread the gospel of jazz across the world, especially in Europe. When the Wooding combination broke up in 1931 it was partly reformed by Willie Lewis. Wooding himself returned to education later and took diplomas in science and education at the University of Pennsylvania. But he didn't give up music and was still active in the year of the American Bicentennial when, aged 80, he recorded with a ten-piece band in partnership with his protégé, singer Rae Robertson.

Selected LP recordings

Chocolate Dandies 1925-9—(A) Biograph BLP12025.
Bicentenial Jazz Vistas (1976)—(A) Twin Signs TS-1001 (77).

More bandleaders

Van Alexander (b 1915)
The Home of Happy Feet (The Savoy)—(A) Capitol T-1243.

Swing! Staged for Sound—(A) Capitol T-1635.

George Auld (b 1910)
Blue and Sentimental—EMI COPS6300 (75).
George Auld 1945, Vol.1—Musicraft MVS501 (79).
George Auld and his Orchestra—World Records WRC15 (d).
Dancing in the Land of Hi-Fi—(A) EmArcy MG-36090.
That's Auld—(A) Brunswick BL-54034.
That's Auld—(A) Dis DL-3007.
Sax Gone Latin—(A) Capitol T-1045.
(Records with Artie Shaw, Benny Goodman, Bunny Berigan and Maynard Ferguson.)

Les Baxter (b 1922)
Brazil Now—GNP GNP2036 (74).
Arthur Murray Favourites—(A) Capitol T-263.
Tamboo!—(A) Capitol T-655.
Caribbean Moonlight—(A) Capitol T-733.
Baxter's Best—(A) Capitol T-1388.

Tex Beneke (b 1914)
With no Strings (1949-51)—(A) Hep HEP-8.
Star Dust—(A) Camden CAL-316.
Tex Beneke and his Orchestra (1946)—FTR 1510.

Ben Bernie (1891-1943)
Curtain Call, Vol.4 (2 tracks)—Brunswick LA8709; (A) Decca DL-7021.

Will Bradley (b 1912)
Will Bradley and his Orchestra (1939-41)—(A) Bandstand BS-7101.
Will Bradley and his Orchestra, Vol.2 (1941-42)—(A) Bandstand BS-7110.
Boogie Woogie—(A) Epic LN-3115.
Rock-a-bye the Boogie (& Ray McKinley) (1940-41)—(A) Bandstand BS-7112.
Will Bradley Vols.1-8 (1939-46)—(Sw) Ajax 112/115/119/131/136/142/150 & 158 (79).
Big Band Boogie (with Johnny Guarnieri)—RCA LSA-3214; (A) RCA LSP-2098.
The House of Bradley—(A) Epic LN-3199.

Randy Brooks (1917-1967)
Trumpet Moods—(A) Decca DL-8201.
Randy Brooks and his Orchestra—(A) FTR 1511.

Henry Busse (1894-1955)
Henry Busse and his Orchestra, 1935 (broadcasts)—London HMP5051 (79).

Henry Busse (MCA).

Curtain call, Vol.5—Brunswick LA8650 (54).

Billy Butterfield (b 1917, led big band 1945-47)
That Butterfield Bounce—(A) Westminster WL-3020.
All-Star Jazz Concert, Vols.1 & 2 (1954)—Brunswick LAT8087 & 8089 (d); (A) Decca 8151/2.
Stardusting—(A) Capitol H-201.
New Dance Sound—Joy JOY108 (76).

Bobby Byrne (b 1918)
Tribute to The Dorseys—(A) GA 206, 33-382.
Big Band—(A) GA 33-336 (58).
Great Hit Songs of Miller—(A) GA 33-381 (58).

Frankie Carle (b 1903)
30 hits of the Tuneful 20s—(A) RCA LPM-2592, (S) LSP-2592 (63).

Bob Chester (b 1908)
Bob Chester and his Orchestra (1939-42)—(A) Bandstand BS-7103.

Al Cooper
Jumpin' at the Savoy—Decca 'Ace of

Hearts' AH-80; (A) Decca 4444, (S) 74444 (64).

Eddy Duchin (1910-1951)
The Eddy Duchin Story—(A) Columbia CL-790.
Eddy Duchin Reminisces—(A) Columbia CL-6010.
The Fabulous Eddie Duchin—(A) RCA LX-1043.
The Magic Fingers of Radio—(A) Big Band Archives LP-1205.
The Eddy Duchin Story (played by Carmen Cavallaro)—Coral CPS-18.

Roy Eldridge (b 1911)
Little Jazz (1937)—CBS80089 (74).
Little Jazz-Big Band (1943-46)—(A) Sounds of Swing LP-108.
Heckler's Hop 1935-1940 (also small groups)—(Sw) Tax M-8020.
Roy Eldridge at the Arcadia Ballroom 1939—(A) Jazz Archives JA-14.

Les Elgart (b 1918)
Sophisticated Swing—(A) Columbia CL-536.
Just One More Dance—(A) Columbia CL-594.
The Band of the Year—(A) Columbia CL-619.
The Dancing Sound—(A) Columbia CL-684.
For Dancers Only—(A) Columbia CL-803.
The Elgart Touch—(A) Columbia CL-875.
The Most Happy Fella—(A) Columbia CL-904.
For Dancers Also—(A) Columbia CL-1008.
The Greatest Dance Band in the Land—(A) Halcyon HL-7374.
Les and Larry Elgart and their Orchestra—(A) Columbia CL-1052.
Sound Ideas—(A) Columbia CL-1123, (S) CS-8002.
Les and Larry Elgart—(A) Columbia (S) CS-8092.

Ziggy Elman (1914-1968)
Zaggin' with Zig—(A) Swing Era LP-1015.
Ziggy Elman 1938-1939—(A) Sunbeam SB-202.
Sentimental Trumpet—(A) MGM 11197, 3389.
(Recordings with Goodman, Hampton, T. Dorsey, Stacy and Weston.)

Skinnay Ennis (1909-1963)
Got a Date with an Angel—(A) MGM E-3531.
Skinnay Ennis Salutes Hal Kemp—(A) Philips 200002.

Jim Europe (1881-1919)
Too Much Mustard (tracks)—Saydisc SDL221.

Shep Fields (b 1910)
One Man-Two Bands—(A) Camden CAL-388.
Designed for Dancing—(A) Lion E-70008.
Rippling Rhythm in Hi-Fi—(A) Golden Crest CR-3037.

Jan Garber (b 1897)
Jan Garber and his Orchestra 1939-41 (broadcasts)—London HMP5053 (79).
The Swinging Sweet Bands, Vol.2—(A) Swing Era LP-1007.
Jan Garber—(A) Camden CAL-297.
Among my Souvenirs—(A) Coral CRL-56007.
Music from the Blue Room—(A) Decca DL-8793.
Jan Garber—(A) Decca DL-4730.
Jan Garber—(A) Vogue 3694.
Satin Touch—(A) Ridgeway RLP-500.
The Shadow of your Smile—(A) Decca 74841.
Mello Medleys—(A) Decca 74971.

Jimmy Grier (1902-1959)
Jimmy Grier from the Cocoanut Grove, 1932—(A) Sunbeam SB-303.

Phil Harris (b 1904)
Phil Harris from the Cocoanut Grove, 1932—(A) Sunbeam SB-302.
That's What I Like About the South—(A) Camden CAL-456.
The South Shall Rise Again—(A) RCA LPM-1985.
You're Blasé—(A) RCA LPM-3203.

Edgar Hayes (b 1905)
Edgar Hayes and his Orchestra (1937-38)—(G) Swingfan 1003.
Edgar Hayes and his Orchestra—(G) MCA PCO-8224.

Jack Jenney (1910-1945)
Jack Jenney—(A) Columbia ML-4803.
Jack Jenney and his Orchestra (1938-40)—(A) Big Band Archives LP-1218 (74).

Louis Jordan (1908-1975)

Greatest Hits—(A) Decca DL-75035 (68).
Somebody up there Digs Me—(A) Mercury MG-20242.
Let the Good Times Roll—Decca 'Ace of Hearts' AH-85; Coral CP-50; CRLM1042 (74); (A) Decca DL-8551.
Louis Jordan and his Orchestra—(G) MCA PCO-8223.

Dick Jurgens (b 1911)

Dick Jurgens and his Orchestra 1937-39 (broadcasts)—London HMP5046 (79).
Dancing in person with Dick Jurgens—(A) Columbia CL-563.
Dance Parade—(A) Columbia CL-6072.
Dance Date with Dick Jurgens—(A) Harmony HL-7004.
The Uncollected Dick Jurgens—(A) Fanfare 31-13 (79).

Art Kassel (1896-1965)

Art Kassel—(A) Mercury MG-25038.

Sammy Kaye (b 1910)

Swing and sway with Sammy Kaye—(A) Columbia CL-561.
Music for Dancing—(A) Camden CAL-261.
Music, Maestro, Please—(A) Columbia CL-668.
Midnight Serenade—(A) Columbia CL-1107.
Swing and Sway—(A) Camden CAL-355.
Swing and Sway—(A) Decca DL-4306.
Come Dance with Me—(A) Decca DL-4357.
Dancing with Sammy Kaye in Hi-Fi—Fontana Z4005 (60).
The best of Sammy Kaye—(A) RCA LSP-3966.

Sam Lanin

Sam Lanin (1928-30)—(A) The Old Masters TOM-28.
Sam Lanin with Red Nichols (1925-28)—Broadway BR105.

Syd Lawrence

Syd Lawrence with the Glenn Miller Sound—Fontana SFL-131178.
More Miller and Big Band Music—Philips 6499 100/1 (2).
Spotlight on Syd Lawrence—Philips 6625 029 (2) (77).

Syd Lawrence and his Orchestra (Phonogram).

Harlan Leonard (b 1904)
Harlan Leonard and his Rockets—(A) RCA LPV-531.

Johnny Long (1916-1972)
Shanty in Old Shanty Town—(A) Vocalion VL-73746.
Johnny Long Plays for Saturday Night Dance Date—(A) Tops L-1575.
Sing and Dance Along—(A) Audio Lab 1503.

Vincent Lopez (b 1898)
The Swinging Sweet Bands (with Abe Lyman)—(A) Swing Era LP-1007.
The Vincent Lopez Show—(A) Coral CRL-57168.
Dance Along with Lopez—(A) MGM E-4055.
Moments to Remember—(A) Waldorf 33-1214.
A Tribute to Eddie Duchin—(A) Hollywood LPH-130.

Bert Lown (1903-1962)
Bert Lown and his Orchestra (1929-32)—(A) The Old Masters TOM-18.

Abe Lyman (1897-1957)
The Swinging Sweet Bands, Vol.1 (with Vincent Lopez)—(A) Swing Era LP-1007.
Waltz Time—(A) Columbia CL-6093.

Machito (b 1912)
Mucho Mucho Machito—Pablo 2625 714 (2) (78).
Afro-Cuban Jazz (with Dizzy Gillespie)—Pablo 2310 771 (76).

Percival Mackey
Percival Mackey's Band 1925-31—World Records SH356 (80).

Freddy Martin (b 1906)
Shall We Dance?—(A) RCA LPM-1160.
Most Requested—(A) Decca DL-4839.
Greatest Hits—(A) Decca DL-4908.
Concerto!—(A) Capitol SW-1066.
Salute to the Smooth Bands—(A) Capitol T-1116.
C'mon Let's Dance—(A) Capitol T-1269.
As Times Goes By—(A) Capitol T-2347.

Leo Mathiesen
Take it Easy—(D) Odeon MOCK-1003.

Clyde McCoy (b 1903)
Curtain Call, Vol.5 (54)—Brunswick LA8650 (with Ted Weems, Clyde McCoy & Johnny Long).
The Blues—(A) Mercury MG-20110.
Really McCoy—(A) Mercury MG-20677.
Sugar Blues—(A) Capitol T-311.
The Golden Era of the Sugar Blues—(A) Design 28.

Hal McIntyre (1914-1959)
Jumpin' Jubilee (1944-46)—(A) Big Band Archives LP-1218.
Hall McIntyre (broadcasts)—(A) Joyce LP-1006 (76).
Hal McIntyre and his Orchestra (1942-47)—First Heard FH-13.
Dance Date with Hal McIntyre—(A) Columbia CL-6142.
Hal McIntyre's Best—(A) Camden CAL-302.
Hal McIntyre—(A) Roulette R-25079.
It Seems Like Only Yesterday—(A) Forum SF-9018.
Hal McIntyre and his Orchestra—(A) FTR 1518.

Art Mooney
Art Mooney and his Orchestra in Hi-Fi Play for Dancing—(A) MGM E-3649.
Banjo Bonanza—(A) MGM E-206.
The Best of Art Mooney—(A) RCA LPM-3739.
Dance and Dream—(A) Coronet CX-220.

James Mundy (b 1907)
On a Mundy Flight—(A) Epic LN-3475.
Swing with Jimmy Mundy—(A) Epic LN-3557.
Bob Haymes-Jimmy Mundy Orchestra—(A) 20th Century Fox TFM-3142.

Ozzie Nelson (b 1906)
Riff Interlude—(A) Big Band Archives LP-1212.
Ozzie Nelson and his Orchestra (1936-41)—(A) Bandstand BS-7119.
Ozzie Nelson and his Orchestra (1940-42) (broadcasts)—London HMP5041 (79).
Afro-American Sketches—Esquire 36-162 (62).

George Olsen (1893-1971)
George Olsen and his Music—RCA RD-7925; (A) RCA LPV-549.

Sy Oliver (b 1910)
Dance to the Music of Sy Oliver—Brunswick LA8586 (54) (d).

Yes Indeed—(F) Black & Blue 33048.
Jimmie Lunceford Arrangements in Hi-Fi (new recordings)—(A) Decca DL-8636.
Sentimental Sy—(A) Dot DLP-3132.
The Big Sound—(A) Design DLP-174.

Hot Lips Page (1908-1954, led big band 1937-41)
Feelin' High and Happy—(A) RCA LPV-576.
Hot Lips Page Plays the Blues in B—(A) Jazz Archives JA-17.
After Hours in Harlem (1940-41)—(A) Onyx 207.

Van Phillips
Van Phillips and his Band (1928-34)—World Records SH277 (78).

Teddy Powell (b 1906)
Tapestry in Blue—(A) Sounds of Swing LP-110.
Teddy Powell Orchestra (1942-3)—(A) First Time FTR-1509.

Louis Prima (b 1911)
Louis Prima 1934-6—(A) The Old Masters TOM-37/8/9 (3).
The Wildest—(A) Capitol T-755.
The Wildest Show at Tahoe—(A) Capitol T-908.
His Greatest Hits—(A) Dot DLP-3262; EMI 2C 048 50754.
Wonderland by Night—(A) Dot DLP-3352.

Louis Prima with Keely Smith (Capitol Records).

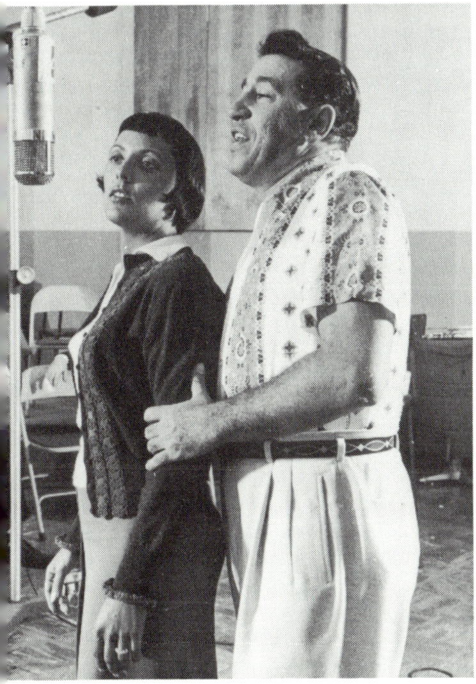

Leo Reisman (1897-1961)
Leo Reisman—(A) RCA LPV-565.
Three Little Words—(A) Decca DL-5160.
Dance Music—(A) Camden CAL-267.

Alvino Rey (b 1911)
Swingin' Fling—(A) Capitol ST-1085.
Alvino Rey and his Orchestra—1946 (broadcasts)—London HMP5057 (79).

Tommy Reynolds (b 1915)
Your Band of Tomorrow—(A) Swing Era LP-1005.
Jazz for Happy Feet—(A) King 395-510.
Tommy Reynolds (with Bon Bon Tunnell)—(A) Roy 18117.

Fred Rich (1898-1956)
Fred Rich and his Orchestra (1930-39)—(A) The Old Masters TOM-27.
Bands Across the Sea (2 tracks)—World Records SM327.

Arthur Rosebery
Arthur Rosebery (1930-38)—World Records SH310 (79).

Ben Selvin (b 1898)
Ben Selvin, Vol.1—(A) The Old Masters TOM-16.
Ben Selvin, Vol.2—(A) The Old Masters TOM-17.
Ben Selvin, Vols.1-3—(A) Sunbeam HB108/9/10.
Bands across the Sea (1 track)—World Records SM327.

Bobby Sherwood (b 1914)
Classics in Jazz—Capitol T-320; (KA) ditto.
Sherwood's Forest—(A) Big Band Archives LP-1201.
Bobby Sherwood—Capitol LC6632 (54) (d).
Politely—(A) Golden Era GE15018 (75).

Elmer Snowden (1900-1973)
Elmer Snowden—(Sw) I.A.J.R.C. 12.

Harry Sosnik (b 1906)
Jerome Kern Selections—(A) Roy VLP-6051.

Jess Stacy (b 1904, led big-bands 1945-46, 1947-48)
Tribute to Benny Goodman—London LTZ-K15012; (A).

Erskine Tate (b 1895)
Freddie Keppard with Doc Cook & Erskine Tate—(A) Jazz Treasury JT-1002.
(See also under Armstrong).

Orrin Tucker (b 1911)
Oh, Johnny!—(A) Harmony HL-7146.
I Remember Orrin Tucker—(A) Tops L-1684.

Tommy Tucker (b 1908)
Designed for Dancing—(A) Lion 70011.

Jerry Wald (1918-1973)
Jerry Wald—(A) Sounds of Swing LP-105.
Listen to the Music of Jerry Wald—(A) Kapp KL-1043.

Fred Waring (b 1900)
Listening Time—Brunswick LAT8011 (A).
Waring's Pennsylvanians—(A) RCA LPV-554.
Fred Waring Showcase—(A) Decca DL-4753.

Ted Weems (1901-1963)
Ted Weems—(A) The Old Masters TOM-23.
Golden Favorites—(A) Decca DL-4435.
Golden Hits (modern recordings)—(A) Mercury MG-20708.
Remember When—(A) Strand SL-1045.

Gerald Wilson (b 1918)
Gerald Wilson and his Orchestra (1945-47)—(A) Sounds of Swing LP-121.

Teddy Wilson (b 1912)
Teddy Wilson and his Orchestra (1939-40)—(A) Swing Era LP-1010.
Teddy Wilson and his Big Band (1939-40)—(Sw) Tax M-8018.

Maurice Winnick
The Sweetest Music this Side Heaven—World Records SH225 (75).
Maurice Winnick and his Sweet Music—Decca DVL1 (77).

Collections

Kings of Swing; (A) *The Great Dance Band Era*—Reader's Digest *In the Groove*—(six records, electronic stereo).
Vol.1 *A string of pearls* (Miller); *Muskrat ramble* (Dukes of Dixieland); *Backstage at Stuff's* (Basie); *Honeysuckle Rose* (All-Stars); *My melancholy baby* (Nichols); *Roll 'em* (Goodman); *Night and day* (Barnet); *Yes indeed* (Tommy Dorsey); *Ain't misbehavin'* (Armstrong); *Traffic jam* (Shaw); *Carolina shout* (Waller); *Bye, bye, blackbird* (Kelly).
Vol.2 *Life goes to a party* (Goodman); *St. Louis Boogie* (Basie); *12th Street Rag* (Bechet); *Sobbin' Blues* (Berigan); *On the sunny side of the street* (Hampton); *When the Saints come marching in* (Dukes of Dixieland) *I'm forever blowing bubbles* (Krupa); *Blue Lou* (Metronome All-Stars); *I never know* (Basie); *Limehouse Blues* (Manone); *It's all right with me* (Jonah Jones); *Well, git it* (Tommy Dorsey).
Vol.3 *Wrappin' it up* (Goodman); *Original Dixieland One-Step* (Dukes of Dixieland); *Boogie woogie cocktail* (Kirk); *Hard-hearted Hannah* (Kelly); *Special Delivery Stomp* (Shaw); *Cotton tail* (Ellington); *Poor butterfly* (Nichols); *Opus 1* (Goodman); *One O'Clock Jump* (Metronome All-Stars); *Learnin' the Blues* (Jonah Jones); *Boogie woogie maxixe* (Bradley/Guarnieri); *China boy* (Freeman).
Vol.4 *Bugle Call Rag* (Metronome All-Stars); *At sundown* (Spanier); *Quaker City Jazz* (Savitt); *Body and soul* (Hawkins); *Cow Cow Blues* (Zurke); *King Porter Stomp* (Goodman); *Honky tonk train* (Bradley/Guarnieri); *St. Louis Blues* (Kirby); *I've got the world on a string* (Armstrong); *That's a-plenty* (Dukes of Dixieland); *Second Balcony Jump* (Hines); *No Name Jive* (Barnet).
Vol.5 *C-Jam Blues* (Ellington); *I know that you know* (Goodman); *Mister Roberts' roost* (Basie); *At the Jazz Band Ball* (Spanier); *Loose lid special* (Tommy Dorsey); *The eel* (Freeman); *Redskin Rumba* (Barnet); *Erroll's Bounce* (Garner); *Gabriel's heater* (Erskine Hawkins); *Close shave* (Kirby); *St. James Infirmary Blues* (Shaw); *Not so quiet, please* (Tommy Dorsey).
Vol.6 *Camel Hop* (Goodman); *Yancey special* (Bradley/Guarnieri); *My blue heaven* (Shaw); *Johnson Rag* (Miller); *Hot mallets* (Hampton); *Zaggin' with Zig* (Elman); *Smiles* (Kelly); *S'wonderful* (Shaw); *Lulu's back in town* (Waller); *Long tall Mama* (Miller); *Ring dem bells* (Hampton); *One O'Clock Boogie* (Basie).

Swing in Europe—1936-1942—Telefunken DP6 28312 (2). *Milenberg joys* (Fud

Candrix); *Aunt Hagar's Blues* (Heinz Wehner); *Nice people* (Kurt Hohenberger); *Gay shuffle* (Schwedisches Tanzquintett); *One night stand* (Thore Ehrling); *Mein herz hat heut' premier* (Teddy Keindin); *Christopher Columbus* (Teddy Stauffer); *Lambeth Walk* (Heinz Wehner); *Well all right* (Stan Brenders); *Minnie from Trinidad* (Arne Hulphers); *Ti-pi-tin* (Kurt Hohenberger); *Studio 24* (Fud Candrix); *Swingtime in the Rockies* (Teddy Stauffer); *Eskapaden* (Heinz Wehner); *Teasing the piano* (Fud Candrix); *Jungle Swing* (Fud Candrix); *When you're smiling* (Jean Omer); *Melodie in G* (Swedisches Tanzquintett); *Bye Bye Blues* (Heinz Wehner); *Melodie in Schwarz* (Stan Brenders); *Melodie in moll* (Schwedisches Tanzquintett); *720 in the book* (Fud Candrix); *Pampas* (Heinz Wehner); *Ich hab' dich und du hast mich* (Teddy Kleindin).

The World of Swing—CBS 88134 (2) (75). *The growl* (Blue Rhythm Band); *I got rhythm* (Don Redman); *Three little words* (Claud Hopkins); *Stompin' at the Savoy* (Chick Webb); *Passionette* (Teddy Hill); *Here comes the man with the jive* (Stuff Smith); *Swinging in Harlem* (Erskine Hawkins); *Where are you* (Mildred Bailey); *Rose room* (Fletcher Henderson); *The wail of the Scromph* (Gene Sedric); *Effervescent Blues* (John Kirby); *Blue blazes* (Jimmie Lunceford); *Sleep* (Benny Carter); *Passin' it around* (Coleman Hawkins); *Ebony silhouette* (Cab Calloway); *Scarecrow* (Benny Goodman); *Who's sorry now* (Harry James); *Beulah's Boogie* (Lionel Hampton); *One more once* (Duke Ellington & Count Basie); *Opus de funk* (Woody Herman). (1932-1965.)

This is the Big Band Era—RCA DPS2019 (2). **Vol.1** *South* (Moten); *Song of India* (Tommy Dorsey); *Sing, sing, sing* (Goodman); *I can't get started* (Berigan); *Don't be that way* (Goodman); *Begin the beguine* (Shaw); *And the angels sing* (Elman); *12th Street Rag* (Hampton); *Cherokee* (Barnet); *In the mood* (Miller).

Vol.2 *Boogie woogie on St. Louis Blues* (Hines); *Frenesi* (Shaw); *After hours* (Erskine Hawkins); *Pompton Turnpike* (Barnet); *Take the 'A' train* (Ellington); *A string of pearls* (Miller); *Opus One* (Tommy Dorsey); *Tippin' in* (Erskine Hawkins); *Mister Roberts' Roost* (Basie); *Study in brown* (Clinton).

Those Dance Band Years 1925-1927—World Records SH361. *Paddlin' Madelin' home* (New Princes Toronto Band); *Everybody Stomp* (Savoy Havana Band); *Charleston Charley* (Carlton Hotel Dance Orchestra); *Valencia* (Savoy Orpheans); *You've got those wanna-go-back-again Blues* (Jay Whidden); *Hello, Alohoa, how are you* (Ronnie Munro); *Up and at 'em* (Jay Whidden); *Crazy quilt* (Jack Hylton); *Jig Walk* (Devonshire Restaurant Dance Band); *Brainstorm* (Debroy Somers); *Ain't she sweet* (Piccadilly Revels Band); *I need lovin'* (The Sylvians); *At sundown* (Savoy Havana Band); *Just the same* (Piccadilly Revels); *Vo-do-do-de-o Blues* (Savoy Orpheans); *The Devil is afraid of music* (London Radio Dance Band). (1925-27.)

Those Dance Band Years 1927-1931—World Records SH362. *Mississippi mud* (The Sylvians); *Nebraska* (Ronnie Munro); *Kiss and make up* (Piccadilly Players); *Blue butterfly* (The Rhythm Band); *Virginia* (Arthur Roseberry); *You went away once too often* (Charlie Kunz); *Wake up, chillun, wake up* (Ray Starita); *Do something* (Jack Payne); *Broadway Melody* (Arthur Roseberry); *You wouldn't fool me, would you* (Piccadilly Players); *Every day away from you* (Four Bright Sparks); *'Leven-thirty Saturday night* (Arcadians Dance Orchestra); *Tap your feet* (Jack Hylton); *If I could be with you one hour tonight* (Ambrose); *Time on my hands* (Percival Mackey); *Holiday Hits* (New Mayfair Orchestra). (1927-31.)

Those Dance Band Years 1931-1934—World Records SH363. *Holiday Hits* (New Mayfair Dance Orchestra); *Down Sunnyside Lane* (Jack Payne); *Me* (Sidney Kyte); *That's my desire* (John Firman); *All of me* (Blue Lyres); *You rascal, you* (Blue Lyres); *The clouds will soon roll by* (Ambrose); *Mean music* (Phillip Brown); *Sadie the Shaker* (Sydney Lipton); *You're an old smoothie* (Debroy Somers); *I like to go back in the evening* (Jack Jackson); *The Japanese sandman* (Ray Noble); *April in Paris* (BBC Dance Orchestra/Henry Hall); *We'll make hay while the sun shines* (Billy Merrin); *Annie doesn't live here anymore* (Billy Cotton); *Better think twice* (Carroll Gibbons). (1931-34.)

Those Dance Band Years 1934-1936—World Records SH364. *The Carioca* (Geraldo); *Deep forest* (Reginald Foresythe); *Tina* (Lew Stone); *What a little moonlight can do* (Gaumont British Dance Band/Louis Levy); *June in January* (Teddy Joyce);

Buchanan Stomp (Harry Perritt); *Holiday Express* (Teddy Joyce); *Roy Medley* (Harry Roy); *Pop goes your heart* (Lew Stone); *Footloose and fancy free* (Jack Hylton); *St. Louis Blues* (Joe Daniels); *Roll along, prairie moon* (Jack Jackson); *From the top of your head* (Carroll Gibbons); *Love is a dancing thing* (Maurice Winnick); *My sweetie went away* (Harry Leader). (1934-36.)

Those Dance Band Years 1936-1938—World Records SH365. *Moon over Miami* (Maurice Winnick); *Woe is me* (Oscar Rabin): *Oh! by jingo! Oh, by gee!* (The Krakajax); *A pretty girl is like a melody* (Roy Fox); *Free* (Billy Cotton); *When my dreamboat comes home* (Bram Martin); *West End Blues* (Bram Martin); *Boo-hoo* (Nat Gonella); *Swing high, swing low* (Bert Firman); *Never in a million years* (Billy Bissett); *Love is good for anything that ails you* (Orlando); *Swing session in Siberia* (George Elrick); *Getting some fun out of life* (Howard Jacobs); *Chinese Laundry Blues* (Syd Seymour); *You started something* (Billy Ternent); *She's the daughter of the old grey mare* (Dan Donovan). (1936-38.)

Those Dance Band Years 1938-1939—World Records SH366. *Someday, sweetheart* (Sid Millward); *Sweet as a song* (Jack White); *Mama, I wanna make rhythm* (Jack Harris); *How'd ja like to love me?* (Roy Fox); *Love makes the world go round* (Henry Hall); *Penny Serenade* (Geraldo); *My own* (Eddie Carroll); *There's a new apple tree* (Billy Thorburn); *You must have been a beautiful baby* (Hugo Rignold); *I'm madly in love with you* (Reginald Williams); *Heaven can wait* (Billy Thorburn); *Plain Jane* (Jack Harris); *South of the border* (Joe Loss); *The lady's in love with you* (Van Straten); *Begin the beguine* (Joe Loss); *Wishing* (Herman Darewski). (1938-39.)

Those Dance Band Years—Bands Across the Sea 1923-36—World Records SM327. *Tell me with a melody* (Paul Whiteman); *Just one more chance* (Paul Whiteman); *Clap hands, here comes Charlie* (Paul Specht); *Calling me home* (Fred Rich); *Baltimore* (Fred Rich); *You can't get to Heaven that way* (Noble Sissle); *Confessin'* (Noble Sissle); *Old Man Harlem* (Rudy Vallee); *Here is my heart* (Rudy Vallee); *Hiawatha's lullaby* (Joe Venuti); *Sweetheart darlin'* (Ben Selvin); *Lights out* (Jack Hylton); *The music goes 'round and around* (Jack Hylton); *Eeny meeny miney mo* (Jack Hylton); *A little bit independent* (Jack Hylton); *Cloudy* (Andy Kirk). (1923-36.)

Hits of the Forties—Decca Vintage RFLD4 (2) (80). (Oscar Rabin, Squadronaires, Lew Stone, Roy Fox, Nat Gonella & Ambrose.)

Hits of the 60s and 70s—Great British Dance Bands 1927-1945—World Records SH390 (80). (Jack Hylton, Joe Loss, Lew Stone, Ken Johnson, Harry Roy, Scott Wood, Eric Winstone, Percival Mackay, Henry Hall, Debroy Somers, Ambrose and Carroll Gibbons.)

And the Bands Played On—Decca DDV 5001/2 (77). *Memories of The Mayfair* (Ambrose) (1933); *Did you ever see a dream walking* (Bertini) (1934); *Somebody stole my gal* (Billy Cotton) (1940); *If I had you* (Fred Elizalde) (1928); *Whispering* (Roy Fox) (1933); *A foggy day* (Geraldo) (1937); *Georgia on my mind* (Nat Gonella) (1934); *Home* (Henry Hall) (1932); *On the sunny side of the street* (Jack Harris) (1930); *How do you do, Honolulu* (Jack Hylton) (1933); *Horsey, Horsey* (Jack Jackson) (1937); *Snakehips swing* (Ken 'Snakehips' Johnson) (1938); *I've got my fingers crossed* (Tommy Kinsman) (1936); *Where were you on the night of June 3rd* (Charlie Kunz) (1935); *Without a word of warning* (Sydney Kyte) (1935); *Toodle-oo* (Brian Lawrence) (1937); *Robins and roses* (Sidney Lipton) (1936); *Let's fall in love* (Joe Loss) (1934); *Begin the beguine* (Mantovani) (1943); *The girl in the upstairs flat* (Felix Mendelssohn) (1938); *The rose in her hair* (Billy Merrin) (1935); *The glory of love* (Lou Preager) (1936); *Lullaby of Broadway* (Rinaldo) (1935); *Jack Payne's Memories* (Jack Payne) (1933); *No words, nor anything* (Harry Roy) (1935); *The flat foot floogie* (Lew Stone) (1938); *I'll take the South* (1935); *We'll all go riding on a rainbow* (Maurice Winnick) (1934); *A little love song* (Marius B. Winter) (1931); *Chattanooga choo choo* (Squadronaires) (1942).

The Big Eighteen—RCA DPS2058 (2) (75); PJL28003. *Tuxedo Junction; Easy does it; Hors d'oeuvre: Blues on parade; Liza; Five O'Clock Drag; March of the Toys; I'm prayin' humble; The Campbells are swinging; Summit Ridge drive; Parade of the milk bottle tops; Swingtime in the Rockies; Feet Draggin' Blues; Okay for baby; Quaker City jazz; Celery stalks at midnight; Skyliner; Organ Grinder's Swing; Ton O'Rock Bump.* (1958.) Charlie Shavers, Buck Clayton, Billy Butterfield, Rex Stewart, Yak Lawson (trumpets); Dicky

Wells, Vic Dickenson; Lou McGarity, Lawrence Brown (trombones); Peanuts Hucko (clarinet); Hymie Scherzer, Sam Donahue, Boomie Richman, Ernie Carceres (reeds); Johnny Guarnieri (piano); Barry Galbraith (guitar); Milt Hinton (bass) and Jimmy Crawford (drums).

The Swinging Sweet Bands, Vol.3—(A) Swing Era LP-1009. Art Mooney; Sammy Kaye; Gray Gordan & Jimmy Grier.)

Themes of the Big Bands—(A) Swing Era LP-1011. Van Alexander; Raymond Scott; Ziggy Elman; Art Mooney; Vincent Lopez; Artie Shaw; Mal Hallett; Tony Pastor; Jan Savitt; Charlie Spivak; Gene Krupa; Bob Crosby; Jimmy Dorsey; Tommy Tucker; Bobby Sherwood; Jerry Wald; Shep Fields; Jimmie Lunceford; Jack Jenney; Earl Hines.

Screwballs of Swingtime—The Great Spoof Records (1934-51)—(A) Bandstand BS-7106. Dorsey Brothers; Jimmy Dorsey; Tommy Dorsey; Richard Himber; Raymond Scott; Freddie Fisher; Will Bradley; Horace Heidt; Bud Freeman; Kay Kyser; Charlie Barnet; Teddy Powell; Hollywood Hucksters and Sten Kenton.

Big Band Boogie—(A) Bandstand BS-7107. Larry Clinton; Artie Shaw; Erskine Hawkins; Bob Zurke; Red Nichols; Woody Herman; Count Basie; Teddy Powell; Gene Krupa; Will Bradley; Bob Crosby; Raymond Scott; Freddie Slack; Ray McKinley and Abe Lyman.

Musical Madness—The Great Spoof Records, Vol.2—(A) Bandstand BS-7118. Charlie Barnet; Spike Jones; Bud Freeman; Peter Cavanaugh; Red Ingle; Oscar Peterson; Woody Herman; Bill Harris; Chubby Jackson; The Three Ts; Tommy Dorsey; Kay Kyser; Will Bradley; Johnny Mercer and Slim Galliard.

Shake That Thing: America's Top Bands of the 20s—Academy AJA5002 (81): Broadway Nitelites, Ben Selvin, Al Lentz, Fred Waring, Ted Weems, Howard Lanin, Guy Lombardo, Abe Lyman, Vincent-Lopez, Charleston Chasers, Paul Whiteman, Irving Aaronson, Nat Shilkret, Ted Lewis, Rudy Vallee, Ben Bernie.

1926—RCA RD8000 (69); (A) RCA LPV557. Jean Goldkette, Coon-Sanders, Roger Wolfe Kahn, Irving Aaronson, Fred Waring, Original Memphis Five, Nat Shilkret, Paul Whiteman, etc.

1927—RCA RD7903 (68); (A) RCA LPV545. George Olsen, Irving Aaronson, Jean Goldkette, Nat Shilkret, Roger Wolfe Kahn, Fred Waring, Paul Whiteman, etc.

The following records are in the Great British Dance Bands Series:

Irving Berlin 1921-1931—World Records SH353.

Irving Berlin 1931-1939—World Records SHB35(2).

George Gershwin 1920-1928—World Records SHB45 (2) (77).

The Music of Arthur Schwartz (1930-36) —World Records SH274.

I'll String Along With You (The Music of Harry Warren)—World Records SH299.

Easy to Remember (Rodgers and Hart) —World Records SH355 (80).

Makin' Whoopee (Walter Donaldson)—World Records SH229 (75).

A Cheerful Little Earful (Harry Warren) —World Records SH298 (78).

The Music of Naceo Herb Brown—World Records SH267 (78).

Cole Porter—World Records SHB66 (2) (80).

Pennies from Heaven—World Records SH266.

More Pennies from Heaven—World Records SH276.

Roll Along Prairie Moon—World Records SH304.

Also:

Kings of Swing—Regal REG-1037.

Kings of Swing, Vol.2—Verve 2863 067 (76).

Kings of Swing—Verve 2863 055 (75).

Kings of Swing—K-Tel NE-960 (77).

Big Band Spectacular—Verve 2352 099 (75).

Big Band Blast—Sunset SLS-50249 (71).

Big Bands—Fontana STFL293 (74).

Big Bands—(A) CBS G30009 (2).

Big Bands Greatest Hits—CBS 66268 (72).

Big Bands Greatest Hits, Vol.2—CBS 67292 (73).

Big Bands in Hi-Fi Stereo—Polydor 2482 289 (76).

Big Bands Uptown (1931-40)—(F) MCA 510.070 (74); (A) Decca DL-79242 (69).

Golden Book of Classic Swing—(G) Brunswick 87097/8/9 (3).

Golden Book of Classic Swing, Vol.2—(G) Brunswick 87094/5/6 (3).

Territory Bands 1929-1933—(A) Historical HLP-24.
Territory Bands, Vol.2—(A) Historical HLP-26.
The Territory Bands—(Sw) Classic Jazz Masters CJM-10.
The Territory Bands 1926-1929—Parlophone PMC-7082.
The Territory Bands—(Sw) Tax M-8009.
Big Bands 1934-42—(G) Swingfan 1010.
Nights at the Savoy—(Sw) Tax M-8006.
Sounds of Chicago—(A) Columbia C3L-32 (3).
Sounds of Harlem—(A) Columbia C3L-33 (3).
Treasury of Golden Swing—Polydor 236.523/4/5 (3).
Swing Classics, Vol.1 (1944-45)—Storyville SLP-818 (75).
Swing Classics, Vol.2 (1944-45)—Storyville SLP-819 (75).
The Greatest of the Big Bands, Vol.8—(F) RCA FXM1 7228 (76).
The Golden Age of Berlin Dance Bands, Vols. 1 & 2—(G) HMV OXLP7544/5 (2) (72).
The Golden Era of Swing—(G) EMI COPS6222/1-2 (2).
The Greatest of the Big Bands—(F) RCA FXM1 7186 (76).
The Best of the Big Bands—(A) Columbia 5193 (3).
The Big Bands—(A) Capitol STFL293 (6) (69).
Big Bands Revisited—(A) Columbia DS-177 (8).
In the Groove—(A) Reader's Digest.
This is the Big Band Era—(A) RCA VPM-6043.

Re-creations

Hotter Than Hades (The Midnite Follies Orchestra)—EMI Odeon ODN1001 (78). *Old Man Blues; No strings; Midnite follies; Minnie the Moocher; Three little words; When the folks high up do the mean lowdown; Hot and anxious; Stormy weather; Krazy kat; Double Check Stomp; I've got the world on a string; Hotter than Hades; The man from Harlem; Jazznochracy.*

Jungle Nights in Harlem (The Midnite Follies Orchestra)—Academy ALA3001 (81). *Shakin' the African; Jungle Nights in Harlem; Happy as the day is long; The Mooche; Okay baby; Alligator Crawl; Blue skies; He's the viper; Kicking the gong around; Snake hips; Sophisticated lady; Ring dem bells; Truckin'; Black beauty; Let's do it; Stomp de luxe.*

New Paul Whiteman Orchestra—Argo ZDA167 (75). *Runnin' wild; Reaching for someone; China boy; You took advantage of me; I've found a new baby; Singin' the Blues; Back in your own backyard; 'Tain't so, honey, 'tain't so; When; There ain't no sweet man; Louisiana; Nobody's sweetheart.*

The Swing Era 1930-1936—Time-Life STL-340 (3).
The Swing Era 1936-1937—Time-Life STL-341 (3).
The Swing Era 1937-1938—Time-Life STL-342 (3).
The Swing Era 1938-1939—Time-Life STL-343 (3).
The Swing Era 1939-1940—Time-Life STL-344 (3).
The Swing Era 1940-1941—Time-Life STL-345 (3).
The Swing Era 1941-1942—Time-Life STL-346 (3).
The Swing Era 1942-1944—Time-Life STL-347 (3).
The Swing Era 1944-1945—Time-Life STL-348 (3).
The Swing Era 1945-1948—Time-Life STL-349 (3).
The Swing Era—Into the 50s—Time-Life STL-350 (3).
The Swing Era—Encore!—Time-Life STL-351 (3).
The Swing Era—Curtain Call—Time-Life STL-352 (3).
The Swing Era—One More Time—Time-Life STL-353 (3).
The Swing Era—Benny Goodman—Into the 70s—Time-Life STL-354 (3).
Each of the above with a 64-page bound book—see bibliography.

'Man, it's hard!': The Big Band life

by Raymond Horricks

'One-nighters were very tough. Many times there were halls with no windows and inside there were thousands of people shouting and fighting. And it was very rough when you had to go over mountains to make another town and you'd skid on ice. Man, there were some long hauls between states.'

— *Gene 'Honey Bear' Sedric*

'One thing you can be sure of, as long as I'm in America, I'll never in my life work with a white band again! Man, when you're on the stage, you're great, but as soon as you come off, you're nothing. It's not worth the glory, not worth the money, not worth anything!'

— *Roy 'Little Jazz' Eldridge*

'Man, it's hard!' is how most musicians who have acutally worked within big bands would describe the life. Their regional accents might vary, perhaps also their national language, and the words will often come out interspersed with expletives, but it all adds up to the same thing. Behind the glamour and the sentiment, after hit records, the praise of critics and applause from the fans, there remains one simple, stark fact. If you like, call it the basic necessity of coping with the day-to-day difficulties, of maintaining musical standards of expected excellence and, at the same time, having to take the thousand and one pinpricks of going away on tour, year in, year out . . . ..

Money alone is not a sufficient reason why such men have lived in this way or why some of them continue to do so. Nor is fame in most cases a sufficient spur. For every Benny Goodman, rich now and able to pick and choose his gigs, there are hundreds of tombstones over the bands that never did make it, or were a success with the critics and not with the public. And yet, and here is another simple fact, sidemen from these departed bands have moved on and continued to tour under other leaders, if the work has been available, but often well into their sixties and even their seventies. Guitarist Freddie Greene has been touring with Count Basie since 1937 and the band would not sound the same without him. To put up with this kind of life-style—or, in the lesser bands often a complete lack of one—a man must be enthusiastic and dedicated as well as in receipt of a weekly pay cheque. 'I've seen the insides of more old go-hungry hash houses, more bad hotels and greasy spoons that I thought could possibly exist', the late Jimmy Rushing, Basie's great blues shouter, once said to me. To which Quincy Jones later added tersely: 'In Pakistan the band [Dizzy Gillespie's] did everything we could to put on a good concert in spite of half the guys being in agonies with Karachi tummy'. Yes, even the highly-paid international circuit can be a hazard.

The first gramophone record I saved up to buy was one by a big band. A good, swinging, no-nonsense effort by Harry James called *Trumpet Blues and Cantabile* and it cost me four shillings and eight pence in 1948 when I had my first part-time job. The second record I acquired in those heady, pre-decimal days was Coleman

Hawkins' *Body and soul*, which taught me something of what a jazz master can do when improvising at length upon a chosen chord-sequence. Both purchases proved crucial, and ever since I've remained well and truly hooked on the things they have come to represent, the classic forms in America's modern music.

But my actual awareness of the big band life did not start until a few years later when I became a record producer for Ted Heath. It was then added to when I was finishing off my biography of Count Basie and travelled around a lot with his band, often rooming with Thad Jones, Bill Hughes and other sidemen, again, too, when I was writing some pieces for Peter Gammond's *Duke Ellington* book and travelled a lot with that band. (Britt Woodman, Duke's lead trombone and now my daughter's godfather, became a human Ministry of Information.) More information flowed from a longstanding friendship with Quincy Jones, and from correspondence with a host of American musicians, while my continuing work as a record producer has taken me in and out of more identikit bedrooms than I care to remember. (But unfortunately I do. Stockton was really bad, although a palace by comparison with that one with the broken windows and the red-rust running water in Leeds.) As for the great, grey, greasy British Rail breakfasts, well, I still get indigestion just thinking about them . . . .

A number of the attendant problems of a band are exclusively the leader's. The times I've sat in Ted Heath's London office and witnessed him trying to clinch a single additional engagement, the difference between being in the red or covering costs in that particular month. Then he's done it and a smile of Micawberish relief and satisfaction would come up on his face! To start a band has always required a great deal of money; to keep one going nearly as much. The original financial backers have to be repaid, there's a high ongoing payroll if you have good sidemen, then there are transport costs, the commissioning of new arangements, copying, various public relations exercises and even keeping the music-stands in decent repair.

The most upset I ever saw Ted Heath was when a provincial journalist and would-be critic, instead of assessing the band's performance in a responsible way, made some snide comments to the effect that the band's uniforms would benefit from a trip to the dry-cleaners. Ted was both angry and visibly hurt. The uniforms were not dirty, maybe a little creased after a punishing round of one-nighters. He was a proud man, proud of his music, proud of his musicians. Such slurs as this he took very personally. He also worried a lot. He cared about getting things right, and he was prepared to shoulder almost all the responsibility if need be—which took a terrible toll of his health in the later years. At the same time though I found him a good businessman. He paid his men well and was relentless in searching out the best possible musicians to play in the band. (Those who passed through his ranks are still the nucleus of British TV, radio and record session work at the beginning of the 1980s.)

He rightly regarded records as a shop-window for the band's normal bread-and-butter work. I say 'rightly' because this definitely proved to be the case. If we had a disc kicking around in the singles charts then the regional bookings would come rolling in; which in turn put more money in the band's coffers than the accumulated earnings in record royalties. Moreover, it was via records that Ted's name for high-quality big band music spread around the world. With recordings like the Fats Waller *London Suite* he gained big air-play in Canada, Australasia and, of course, the United States, leading on to full-scale tours and, eventually, the top honour of appearing at Carnegie Hall.

Consequently every recording session became an important affair, with each new arrangement an adventure and Ted worrying more than anyone else about the eventual outcome. He always took over the baton for the serious, likely-to-beimmortalised 'takes'. Before that he'd let the arranger put the band through its paces. The sessions were also very exciting affairs, and there was rarely any show of temper. They were team-efforts and afterwards we were all grateful to have been present at the creation. The only occasion I can recall Ted overreacting towards a session was when I invited Quincy Jones and Bobby Tucker, Billy Eckstine's accompanist, along to listen. It was then doubly, even trebly, important for his men to make a good showing. Needless to say they did. (Johnny Keating was the only obvious fall-guy. He was torn off a strip for turning up late with the second arrangement!)

Band leaders come in all shapes and sizes, with only music and idiosyncrasies of the life linking them together as a human phenomenon. Benny Goodman in his heyday could freeze a guy with a look, or 'the ray' as his see-through glance became known to the band's sidemen. He never did have to sack anyone in a heated exchange. If it was either for musical reasons or for discipline, and 'the ray' didn't do the trick, then BG just totally ignored the guy until he got the message and left. Even Goodman though had his other, more generous side. Perfection he expected; perfection he rewarded. As Popsie Randolph, his long-suffering road manager recalls: 'When a guy got in trouble or something Benny'd take an interest and help out with emergency money. He'd always lend the guys money and things like that. Sure, some of the guys didn't appreciate it—said he was buttin' in, but I didn't know of another leader in the business who took as much interest in the men as Benny—except Woody, maybe. Why, I can remember once he sent me over . . . to buy the guys wallets for Christmas, and he put a fifty-dollar bill in each. And on Christmas Day, I was feelin' kinda low 'cause I didn't get one. Benny and I were in Philly and we were ridin' back to the hotel on the trolley car when he says to me, 'You got my wallet, Pops?'. I had a couple of blank cheques with me and he wrote me a cheque for five hundred dollars. He told me, 'Now, that's better'n a wallet, ain't it?'.

Tommy Dorsey averaged a row a night with someone or other in the band. Temperamentally he seemed to need it. But he just as quickly simmered down, then apologised and afterwards confided in his former opponent: 'At least I don't quarrel with you as much as I do with my own brother!'. He, too, paid his men well and, once on the success trail, refused to tolerate the colour bar. Trumpeter Charlie Shavers, Dizzy Gillespie's elder cousin and the first black musician TD ever hired, recalled him as 'one of the most gentlemanly men I ever worked for'.

Another disciplinarian leader and perfectionist, Artie Shaw, is credited with using his liquorice-stick as a javelin against a drummer who missed a vital beat in one performance. But Shaw, volatile, emotional, brilliant, in turn had his freak outs. In 1939 he abandoned a band! 'By the time we got to New York and the Lincoln Hotel, our opening night there was like a mad-house. From then on I couldn't think straight. My life wasn't my own. *Life* magazine, autograph hunters, everything all at once, plus all kinds of disagreeable pressures being put on me. The bigger our success, the more dissatisfaction there seemed to be in the band. Billie Holiday, who had gotten along fine with Helen Forrest, began to resent her. Georgie Auld came in for a hundred and twenty-five dollars while the rest of the band, getting scale, objected. Buddy Rich joined us and the older guys didn't like it when he got so much applause. Instead of a bunch of guys who were happy struggling towards a common objective, we became a bunch of cliques, and I became gradually estranged from the men. When we went into the Strand Theatre, it was even worse. People jumping up on the stage, cops, riots—things that were almost impossible to live through. I was making more money than I had ever thought existed, and I guess I got carried away by it'.

That night he flew to Mexico and left Georgie Auld to carry on with the band as best he could. Twenty years later a much more mature and reflective Shaw had this to say (to George T. Simon) about the incident: 'I just got up . . . and left, leaving all the debris behind and letting anybody who wanted to scrabble for what was left do so. Looking back at it now, I'd have made arrangements. What I really *should* have done would have been to present my agents and lawyers with a much more viable set of alternatives. As it was, I kept saying, *I need a vacation*! But, like a little kid who argues with Daddy and gets frightened and hysterical and nervous, I overreacted. They were killing the goose with the golden egg kind of thing, getting their commissions and selling ninety-nine bands like tails to my kite. And I kept saying "Fellows, I can't go on at this pace anymore". Well, what I should have done was said, "Look fellows, goodbye. I'm going to take a vacation. Now, you make your own arrangements. Either that, or I'm going to walk out". Well, that was a kind of stupid thing to do without any thought of the future. But, you see, when you're twenty-eight and you're making umpteen thousand dollars a week anytime you want to work, it never occurs to you that the future is going to be any kind of problem. It's like young kids. They don't believe they're ever going to grow old'. However, he concluded: 'I don't think I'd have done much different, because I think the music I played was the best I could continue to play, given all circumstances, given what audiences would accept, given the length of the records you had to make'.

Whether the band leader is an ultra-disciplinarian (Goodman, T. Dorsey, Shaw, Glenn Miller), more free and easy (Woody Herman, Count Basie) or even lackadaisical (Duke Ellington letting Johnny Hodges and others wander on and off the stand), certain basic problems of a big band remain the same. Are the dates in the book, is the music ready and will the boys be there on the night?

Getting the music ready for the people. Rehearsing is as important to a band as a good heart to a fit body. The public only hears the end product, whether on record or in person. People pay over their money and they receive back the glamour aspects: the excitement, the sound of the band and the solos, but the performance they hear is the result of much meticulous work behind the scenes. Rehearsals are not just for familiarising the sidemen with new arrangements or settling in new personnel. First and foremost a band rehearses in order to set, then to maintain, its style and direction; also to keep its standards of musicianship high. The odd wrong note or sour harmonisation in a brand-new arrangement is easy enough to put right, but the actual sound of a band has to be worked on all the time, otherwise deterioration very rapidly becomes obvious. This is why a band will find time to rehearse even during a difficult sequence of one-nighters. The old chestnut 'it'll be alright on the night' just doesn't apply. Only work works. That, and the determination to excel. I well remember being backstage before Count Basie's first-ever Royal Festival Hall concert in London. There was a particular passage in one arrangement that had been bugging lead-alto Marshall Royal, and he kept on running it with the band's two tenors, Frank Wess and Foster, even after they'd changed and right up to the moment for going on-stage. There wasn't a single murmur of complaint from the younger players. They shared their section leader's wilful need to squeeze the musical maximum from the passage.

Even so, band rehearsals can be fascinatingly different. Ted Heath, for instance, personally supervised every one of his band's rehearsals that I attended. If there were new scores, then he'd let the arranger run them through for wrong notes or copying errors. But then Ted took over. The sound of the band was his, he set the tempo and he finalised the playing of the ensemble. He never interfered with solos. 'But I hire the best men to play them!' he added. In contrast, Count Basie rarely showed up for the earlier stages of a rehearsal. He liked Marshall Royal to get a lot of the donkey-work out of the way, the drilling of the sections and so on. Then he'd come in and put the finishing touches to it from the piano, working out his introductory cue (which the players had to memorise, because the Count seldom makes announcements) and perhaps marginally re-adjusting the rhythmic feeling. He trusted Marshall implicitly and the latter responded by becoming the perfect custodian of the band's sound and style.

Duke Ellington's rehearsals were more spur-of-the-moment affairs, and superficially appeared quite chaotic, until one realised how, in his own inimitable manner, this genius was carefully probing and exploring his musicians' strengths and weaknesses, often rewriting as he went along and finally pulling off something quite unique with them. (John Williams, the *Star Wars* composer, not the guitarist, told me that Gil Evans works in much the same way. At one point the music will sound totally disorganised. Then just another run-through later it becomes magically right.)

Another notable feature of Ellington rehearsals was the lack of band parts, the dilapidated state of those which did exist and the frequently surprising things they were written on—restaurant menus, pages torn from notebooks, even the back of an old train time-table. Because Duke was a composer who never ceased touring with his band, much of his writing was achieved while on the move and in moments of inspiration he would scribble it down on whatever came to hand, which was rarely lined manuscript paper.

Duke relied heavily on the personal identity and creative memories of his sidemen, often with some startling results. Britt Woodman's entry into the band was positively hair-raising. He had been working in California with the Charles Mingus workshop when Duke called long-distance and asked him to take over as lead trombone from Lawrence Brown. They agreed terms, but Britt insisted on having two weeks to understudy his famous predecessor. He then arranged to join the band in Las Vegas, along with Louis Bellson, Juan Tizol and Willie Smith from the Harry James orchestra. At the end of the first night, noting the lack of parts on the stand, Britt's only observation was: 'Thank God I've got a fortnight to learn the book'. 'To hell with that', Brown retorted, 'I'm taking off in the morning!' And he did. Once the music is right though, everyone involved can face the extra hassles of performing and going out on tour. Perhaps not with complete equanimity or a Trappist's tolerance, but at least with self-confidence and a belief that the show must go on.

Unfortunately, for every Willard Alexander and every Sol Hurok there are one hundred booking-agents and two thousand self-styled impresarios who can give a band a hard time. More often than not this is due to ignorance or incompetence rather than actual crookedness—giving the musicians almost impossibly long hauls between nightly engagements, forgetting to confirm hotel reservations and even, as sometimes happens, getting the dates confused. Ernie Wilkins, the Count Basie arranger and for several years an alto-saxophone player with the band, told me of one occasion—following a long bus journey—when the band reached the dance-hall only to find all the people standing about outside. 'There were police in front of the place, and the door was padlocked. It didn't take us long to find out that the local promoter didn't have a licence to give a dance—and so there was *no* dance. We all crawled back into the bus and made for the next town. There must have been a thousand people standing out there! Basie cried as we pulled away. He had a fifth of Scotch whisky with him so we all got drunk as we rolled down the highway to the next town . . .'.

Often as well it becomes a question of greed—trying to cash in too heavily on a band's success and working its musicians so hard that they get fed up and leave. Willard Alexander, Benny Goodman's and later Count Basie's agent, began by working out of the Music Corporation of America's office; and he quickly proved himself, everyone has agreed, a very fair and understanding man. But other, less scrupulous bookers at MCA gave the organisation such a bad name that at one point it became known as the 'Star-Spangled Octopus'. To quote George T. Simon again: 'In their plush, handsomely furnished, distressingly formal offices, MCA's approach was strictly business—cold, dry, hard, although tremendously efficient business. For band leaders like Guy Lombardo, Eddy Duchin, Horace Heidt, Xavier Cugat, Sammy Kaye, Wayne King and those less interested in musical notes than in bank notes, the agency performed magnificently well—especially its charming and tremendously convincing salesman, Sonny Werblin'. Willard Alexander eventually left MCA to start up on his own, and other band leaders never could get on with them, Tommy Dorsey for one. He only signed with them in the first place because his brother had gone to their main rivals, Tom Rockwell and Cork O'Keefe's General Artists Corporation, after which, for Tommy, it was arguments all the way. In the end he refused to set foot in their offices, and when his contract ran out, he published a huge trade ad which read: 'Whew . . . I'm finally out of the clutches of you-know-who!'.

Even for the most successful bands the continual travelling about never becomes easy. When the gifted British vibes-player and percussionist, Victor Feldman, first emigrated to the United States he was thrilled to be taken into the Woody Herman orchestra. Within a year though he'd been forced to drop out. 'Yes, it was the touring', he told me. 'I just couldn't take it any longer. At first I couldn't understand why I felt so tired. After all, a guy like trombonist Bill Harris was a lot older than I was, and he'd been coping with it for years. Then the penny dropped. He was a big, strong guy, big built with powerful shoulders—and he was hardened to the life. I'm shorter, with a light frame and I wasn't used to it.' He went on to detail the overcrowded dressing-rooms, lack of washing facilities, anti-social hours and often extremely disagreeable local managements. 'I still have to tour', he added, 'but now I only do it in short bursts'.

Duke Ellington found he couldn't guarantee his men sleep and a degree of relaxation without going to the additional expense of a Pullman coach. While Alice Goodman, John Hammond's sister who married Benny in 1942, estimated that in the first four months of their marriage they slept under no fewer than 73 different roofs. In fact, as she told the writer, Stanley Baron, on the honeymoon night they set off from Las Vegas, and Benny was so exhausted that he turned the wheel over to her and went to sleep in the back of the car. At the Californian border, around midnight, state police stopped the car and asked Alice what she was carrying. 'My husband', she replied, not without an edge of sarcasm.

As Benny himself says: 'Travelling with a band on tour is the next thing I can think of to moving a circus. There's music to be taken care of, the instruments to be checked, the trunks and other baggage to keep in line, all of which was in the care of a general handyman, porter and looker-outer. In our organisation he was an efficient fellow by the name of Pee Wee Monte, who had made a career out of nursing bands. Later it was Popsie Randolph.'

Goodman goes on with his story in his autobiography, *The Kingdom of Swing*: 'On a typical one-nighter around the New York territory, we travelled in a Greyhound bus that stayed with us throughout the entire tour. Generally it rolled up to the place late in the afternoon, and if we hadn't been there before, we had to find out about the P.A. (the public address system) and hook up the one we carried along, if the permanent installation wasn't any good. Then the stands had to be set up and the music laid out—and in most places, some kind of rope or guard rail put around the stand so that we could work without stepping on the fingers of the kids that hung around the band.

'By this time, Hymie Schertzer's nose for corn-beef had led him, without fail, to the best place in town for his favourite food, and a few of the boys went along with him. The rest of us picked out some likely-looking place for the kind of food we wanted, and got through the meal just in time to change our clothes and get on the bandstand. The crowd started coming in, the requests started piling up, and another job was under way. We played right through until about one o'clock, with the trio and quartet coming out for a session around midnight. What happened after that depended on the distance to the next booking. If the jump was a fairly short one, say two hundred miles or so, we spent the night at a hotel in the same town, and made the trip the following day. If it was closer to three hundred or anything up to four hundred, we piled into the bus when the job was finished, and made the jump at night, when we could make better time, and allow for any incidents that might come up on the trip. That brought us into the next town around nine or ten o'clock in the morning—and after eight hours bumping around in a bus, trying to catch a few winks of sleep, the only thing you wanted to do was crawl into bed at the hotel, and get some sleep before it was time to go to work again. There are more towns in America that I have only seen after dark than I would care to think about.'

But at least if the Goodman bus made it on time BG could check into a decent hotel. For the darker-skinned members of the big band, fraternity life wasn't quite so straightforward. Benny was the first important band leader to hit back against the colour-bar, but in certain Southern states the barriers are only now beginning to come down. The great trumpeter, Clark Terry, told me that he would rather be unemployed than go back below the Mason-Dixon line again. 'Once', he said, 'there was this rough-neck, Stetson-type sheriff. He was sort of running me out of town and at the same time ordering me to fix him up with a black chick. Fix him up! I felt I wanted to hit him with a house-brick!' For an all-black band playing to all-black audiences it wasn't quite so complicated, provided they settled for second-rate transport and fifth-rate accommodation. But when Goodman and Krupa and Charlie Barnet began to mix talented Negro players with white musicians, then the real trouble started.

Probably it has been best summed up in Roy Eldridge's celebrated outburst. 'It goes all the way back to when I joined Gene Krupa's band', he remembers. 'Until that time no coloured musicians had worked with a white band except as a separate attraction, like Teddy (Wilson) and Lionel (Hampton) with Benny Goodman. That was how I worked with Gene at first. But very soon I started sharing Shorty Sherock's book, and when he left I took over. All the guys in the band were nice, and Gene was especially wonderful. That was at the Pennsylvania Hotel. Then we headed west for some one-nighters, winding up in California. That was when it began. We arrived in one town and the rest of the band checks in. I can't get into their hotel, so I keep my bags and start riding around looking for another place, where someone's supposed to have made a reservation for me. I get there and move all my bags in. At least a dozen pieces of baggage. Then the clerk, when he sees that I'm the Mr. Eldridge the reservation was made for, suddenly discovers that one of their regular tenants just arrived and took the last available room. I lug that baggage back into the street and start looking around again.

'By the time that kind of thing has happened night after night, it begins to work on my mind; I can't think right, can't play right. When we finally got to the Palladium in Hollywood, I had to watch who I could sit at tables with. If they were movie stars who wanted me to come over, that was all right, if they were just the jitterbugs, no dice. And all the time the bouncer with his eye on me, just watching for a chance.

'Then it happened. One night the tension got so bad I flipped. I could feel it right up to my neck while I was playing *Rockin' chair*; I started trembling, ran off the stand, and threw up. They carried me to the doctor's. I had a hundred-and-five fever; my nerves were shot. When I went back a few nights later I heard that people were asking for their money back because they couldn't hear *Let me off uptown*. This time they let me sit at the bar' *(Down Beat)*.

Quincy Jones, a younger man than Eldridge, is rather more sanguine about it. He thinks things are improving, but admits that in certain areas the progress persists in being slow. 'I grew up in Seattle', he told me, 'where the Negro population is comparatively small. We had full integration in the schools. I'd never experienced racial prejudice until in my late 'teens when I set off on the road with Jay McShann's band. Then it hit me! We went down South and suddenly I couldn't eat here, I couldn't stay there; and the garage-attendant wouldn't let me use the lavatory because it was whites-only. Jesus, man: I didn't need that!' Quincy believes that the opening up of music internationally has helped, but he adds: 'The travelling bit is hard anyway, without having prejudice piled on top of it.'

Which brings me to the final point I want to make about the life. Followers of the big bands and discographers are always intensely interested in their continuing changes of personnel. Players leave or are replaced for a wide variety of reasons, and not necessarily musical ones. In fact, all things considered, it's amazing that the bands manage to hang together for as long as they do. Means of transport have been improved, but the human factor is still the same. Try to imagine what it's like in the modern, air-conditioned bus for 15 or 16 gifted, but often very varied, people thrown together day in, day out and at nights as well. They play cards, they do crosswords, they read, tell jokes, show each other family photographs, and they start to be bored with each other, to get on each other's nerves. Then any small, silly incident can cause a flare-up. Perhaps the leader will succeed in defusing the affair, but perhaps also one of the soloists will make a private resolution to leave the band at the end of its tour.

In his earlier years, for example, Buddy Rich was described as a swinger with his fists as well as his drumsticks. According to Bob Bach of *Metronome,* 'It used to be that you almost had to stand in line to be able to get a sock at him. He was cocky, rashly outspoken and brutally sarcastic.' But Buddy is also a perfectionist and the world's greatest drummer, so others had to learn to put up with his tongue. (I once heard him suggest to an inebriated fan who requested 'something swinging': 'How about a rope?'.) Often their music is all the members of a band have in common. They are individuals from different backgrounds and with different tastes and needs, and this itself can lead to abrasiveness. The Australian flautist and saxophone-player, Ray Swinfield, toured with a number of bands including Ted Heath's when he first moved to Europe. He instanced just one of the things that can bring on trouble. 'Say a couple of guys are bigger drinkers than the rest of the band. After the job they've found a bar that stays open and they stay there too long. Everyone else is tired and wants to get home, but they have to sit around in the coach waiting for the ones who are still in there drinking. Sometimes I've waited up to two hours before we could drive off.'

So why do they carry on, the Woody Hermans and the Count Basies? It surely can't be for the life. Woody says he can't resist standing in front of a good band and hearing it swing. Modestly he doesn't add that he's been a lifelong champion of youth. The list of talented younger musicians who've gained their first experience within his ranks is truly enormous. Count Basie told me many years ago that he wouldn't know what to do with himself if he didn't have his music. However, he also furnished me with the most cautionary tale I know of the big band life. 'I nearly didn't have a career at all', he said, smiling a little. 'Back in the Kansas City days I made some slighting remarks about one of the local gangsters. The hood offered me a simple alternative. I could go outside and be shot there and then, or I worked the next two weeks in the club without any pay!' Fortunately Mister Basie is an exceedingly practical and sensible man . . ..

Bibliography

Individual Bands

Bert Ambrose
Bert Ambrose: a Discography by Brian Rust in *Recorded Sound* (Jan 1966).
Louis Armstrong
Louis: the Louis Armstrong Story by Max Jones & John Milton (November Books, London, 1971; Little, Brown, New York, 1971; Mayflower, London, 1975).
Charlie Barnet
Charlie Barnet and his Orchestra by Ernie Edwards, George Hall & Bill Korst (Jazz Discographies, Whittier, 1965; repr 1967 & 1971).
Count Basie
Count Basie and his Orchestra, its Music and Musicians edited by Raymond Horricks (Gollancz, London, 1957; Citadel Press, New York, 1957; Jazz Book Club, London, 1958; Greenwood Press, New York, 1971).
A Discography of Count Basie-Vol.1 (1929-1950) by Bo Scherman & Carl A. Haellstrom (Knudson, Copenhagen, 1969).
A Discography of Count Basie-Vol.2 (1951-1968) by Jørgen Grunnet Jepsen (Knudson, Copenhagen, 1969).
The World of Count Basie edited by Stanley Dance (Scribner, New York, 1980; Sidgwick & Jackson, London, 1980).
Tex Beneke
Tex Beneke Discography by Ernie Edwards, George Hall & Bill Korst (Erngeobil, Whittier, 1969).
Will Bradley
Will Bradley Discography by Ernie Edwards (Erngeobil, Whittier, 1966).
Les Brown
Les Brown and his Band of Renown by Ernie Edwards, George Hall & Bill Korst (Erngeobil, Whittier, 1966).
Les Brown Discography 1936-1964 by Ernie Edwards, George Hall & Bill Korst (Erngeobil, Whittier, 1965).
Coon-Sanders Orchestra
'Coon-Sanders Discography' by H. Rettburg in *Second Line* (xiii, 1962).
Billy Cotton
I Did it My Way: the Life Story of Billy Cotton by Billy Cotton (Harrap, London, 1970).
Bob Crosby
Discography of Bob Crosby by Willem Frederik van Eyle (Van Eyle, Zaandam, 1966).
Johnny Dankworth
'A Johnny Dankworth Discography' in *Jazz Monthly* (Feb 1964).

Jimmy Dorsey
Jimmy Dorsey and his Orchestra: a Complete Discography 1953-1957 by Ernie Edwards, George Hall & Bill Korst (Erngeobil, Whittier, 1966).
Jimmy Dorsey & Tommy Dorsey
Tommy and Jimmy: the Dorsey Years by Herb Sanford (Arlington House, New York, 1972; Allan, Shepperton, 1973).
Duke Ellington
The 'Wax Works' of Duke Ellington: an up-to-date Discography by Benny H. Aasland (Aasland, Stockholm, 1954).
Duke Ellington on Microgroove, 1923-1942 by Dick M. Bakker (Micrography, Alphen aan den Rijn, 1974).
Twenty Years of the Duke. Part 1: 1933-1953 by Donald Russell Connor & others (Pope's Records, Carnegie, 1966).
The World of Duke Ellington by Stanley Dance (Scribner, New York, 1970; Macmillan, London, 1971).
Music is My Mistress by Duke Ellington (Doubleday, New York, 1973; Allen, London, 1974; Da Capo Press, New York, 1976; Quartet Books, London, 1977).
Duke Ellington in Person: an Intimate Memoir by Mercer Ellington & Stanley Dance (Houghton Mifflin, Boston, 1978).
'Discografia (Duke Ellington)' by E. Fresia in *Musica Jazz* XIX, Oct 1963.
Duke Ellington: his Life and Music edited by Peter Gammond (Phoenix House, London, 1958; Roy Publishers, New York, 1958; Jazz Book Club, London, 1959; Nymphenburger, Munich, 1961; Da Capo Press, New York, 1977).
Celebrating the Duke by Ralph Gleason (Little Brown, Boston, 1975).
Discography of Duke Ellington (3 Volumes) by Jørgen Grunnet Jepsen (Debut Records, Brande, 1959-60).
Duke: a Portrait of Duke Ellington by Derek Jewell (Elm Tree Press, London, 1977; Sphere Books, 1978).
Duke Ellington by G.E. Lambert (Cassell, London, 1961; Barnes, New York, 1961).
'Microgroove Re-issues of Rare Early Ellington Recordings' by G.E. Lambert in *Jazz Monthly*, XIII (Nov 1967).
Duke Ellington's Story on Records (6 Volumes) by Luciano Massagli, Liborio Pusateri & Giovanni M. Volonté (Musica Jazz, Milan, 1966-68; Seago, London, 1966-71).
Duke Ellington, King of Jazz by Elizabeth Rider Montgomery (Gerrard, Illinois, 1972).
Mood Indigo by Dennis Preston (Citizens Press, Egham, 1946).
Duke Ellington Discography (Pope's Records, Carnegie, Penn, 1967).
Duke Ellington Discography on Victor and Bluebird Records by John D. Reid (USA).
General Catalog of Duke Ellington's Recorded Music by Luigi Sanfilippo (New Jazz Society, Palermo, 1964; 2nd ed 1966).
Duke Ellington: Harlem Aristocrat of Jazz by Jean de Trazegnies (Hot Club de Belgique, Brussels, 1946).
Duke Ellington by Barry Ulanov (Creative Age Press, New York, 1946; Musicians Press, London, 1947; Da Capo Press, New York, 1975).
Roy Fox
Hollywood, Mayfair and All That Jazz: the Roy Fox Story by Roy Fox (Frewin, London, 1975).
Benny Goodman
BG—On the Record: a Bio-Discography of Benny Goodman by Donald Russell Connor & Warren W. Hicks (Arlington House, New Rochelle, 1969).
The Kingdom of Swing by Benny Goodman & Irving Kolodin (Stackpole, New York,

1939; Allen, London, 1939; Ungar, New York, 1961; Constable, London, 1962).
Benny: King of Swing: a Pictorial Biography by Benny Goodman. Introduced by Stanley Baron. (New York, 1980; Thames & Hudson, London, 1980).

Henry Hall

Here's to the Next Time: Autobiography by Henry Hall (Odhams, London, 1955).

Lionel Hampton

Discography of Lionel Hampton Orchestra 1954-1958 by Bertrand Demeusy & Otto Flückiger (Jazz Publications, Basel, 1963).
Discography of Lionel Hampton Orchestra 1951-1953 by Otto Flückiger (Jazz Publications, Reinach, 1961).
Lionel Hampton 1947-1957 by Jørgen Grunnet Jepsen (Jepsen, Copenhagen, 1957).

Coleman Hawkins

Discography of Coleman Hawkins by Willem Frederik van Eyle (Van Eyle, Zaandam, 1966).
Coleman Hawkins 1947-1957 by Jørgen Grunnet Jepsen (Jepsen, Copenhagen, 1957).
Coleman Hawkins by Albert McCarthy (Cassell, London, 1960; Barnes, New York, 1961).

Erskine Hawkins (and Horace Henderson)

Erskine Hawkins—Horace Henderson Discography by Ernie Edwards, George Hall & Bill Korst (Erngeobil, Whittier, 1965).

Ted Heath

Listen to My Music: an Autobiography by Ted Heath (Muller, London, 1957).

Fletcher Henderson

Hendersonia: the Music of Fletcher Henderson and his Musicians: a Bio-Discography by Walter C. Allen (Allen, Highland Park, NJ, 1973).
'Hendersonia' by W.C. Allen in *Record Research* (Sept 1963).

Woody Herman

Woody Herman Discography (2 Volumes) by Ernie Edwards (Debut Records, Brande, 1959/61).
Woody Herman Discography (3 Volumes) by Ernie Edwards, George Hall & Bill Korst (Erngeobil, Whittier, 1965/9).
Woody Herman 1947-1957 by Jørgen Grunnet Jepsen (Jepsen, Copenhagen, 1957).

Earl Hines

The World of Earl Hines by Stanley Dance (New York, 1980).

Spike Hughes

Opening Bars by Spike Hughes (Pilot Press, London, 1946).

Harry James

Harry James and his Orchestra, Vol.1—1937-50 by George I. Hall (Jazz Discographies, Laurel MD, 1971).

Stan Kenton

Straight Ahead: the Story of Stan Kenton by Carol Easton (Morrow, New York, 1973).
Discography of Stan Kenton and his Orchestra (2 Volumes) by Ernie Edwards (Debut Records, Brande, 1959/61).
Discography of Stan Kenton (2 Volumes) by Jørgen Grunnet Jepsen (Debut Records, Brande, 1962).
Artistry in Kenton: the Bio-Discography of Stan Kenton and his Music, Vol.1 by Christopher A. Pirie & Siegfried Müller (Müller, Vienna, 1969; rev 1969 & 1971).
Stan Kenton: ein Porträt by Dietrich Schulz-Köhn (Pegasus, Wetzlar, 1961).
The Great Kenton Arrangers by Michael Spark (Erngeobil, Whittier, 1968).
Kenton on Capitol: a Discography by Michael Sparke, Pete Venudor & Jack Hartley

(Hounslow, 1966).
Stan Kenton Discographie by Klaus Teubig (Teubig, Hamburg, 1963).
The Standard Kenton Directory, Vol.1, 1937-1949 by Pete Venudor & Michael Sparke (Venudor & Sparke, Amsterdam, 1968).

Gene Krupa

Gene Krupa and his Orchestra 1938-51 by Ernie Edwards, George Hall & Bill Korst (Erngeobil, Whittier, 1968).

Jimmie Lunceford

The Jimmie Lunceford Band by Ernie Edwards, George Hall & Bill Korst (Erngeobil, Whittier, 1965).
'Jimmie Lunceford' by E. Fresia in *Musica Jazz* XVIII (July-Aug 1962).

Ray McKinley

Ray McKinley Orchestra by Ernie Edwards (Erngeobil, Whittier, 1967).

William McKinney, (and his Cotton Pickers)

'McKinney's' by John Chilton & others in *Storyville,* No 33 (Feb 1971).

Jay McShann

'Jay McShann ou la légende de K.C.' by B. Niquet in *Jazz Hot*, No 235 (Oct 1967).

Glenn Miller

A Glenn Miller Discography and Biography by Stephen F. Bedwell (Glenn Miller Appreciation Society, London, 1955; rev 1956).
Glenn Miller Alumni (2 Vols) by Ernie Edwards & Mike H. Morris (Erngeobil, Whittier, 1965/9).
Moonlight Serenade: a Bio-Discography of the Glenn Miller Civilian Band by John Flower (Arlington House, New Rochelle, 1972).
Glenn Miller and the Age of Swing by Jonathan Green (Dempsey & Squires, London, 1976).
Glenn Miller and his Orchestra by George T. Simon (Crowell, New York, 1974; Allen, London, 1974).

Lucky Millinder

Discography of Lucky Millinder 1941-1960 by Bertrand Demeusy, Otto Flückiger, Jørgen Grunnet Jepsen & Kurt Mohr (Jazz Publications, Basel, 1962).

Jelly Roll Morton

Mister Jelly Roll by Alan Lomax (Duell, Sloane & Pearce, New York, 1950; Cassell, London, 1952; etc).

Ray Noble

The Ray Noble Orchestra featuring Al Bowlly—The HMV Sessions 1930-4 by Brian Rust & others; booklet to World Record set of 12 records.

King Oliver

King Joe Oliver by Walter C. Allen & Brian Rust (Allen, Belleville, 1955; Sidgwick & Jackson, London, 1958; etc).
King Oliver by Martin Williams (Cassell, London, 1960; Barnes, New York, 1961).

Jack Payne

Signature Tune by Jack Payne (Paul, London).
This is Jack Payne by Jack Payne (London, 1932).

Don Redman

Don Redman by Emanuel Ugge (Gramoklub, Prague, 1947).

Buddy Rich

Super Drummer: a Profile of Buddy Rich by Whitney Balliett (Bobs-Merrill, Indianapolis, 1968).

Jan Savitt

Jan Savitt and his Top Hatters by George I. Hall (Erngeobil, Whittier, 1965).

Savoy Orpheans etc
'A Discography of the Savoy Bands of the Twenties' by Brian Rust in *Recorded Sound* No 25 (Jan 1967).
Artie Shaw
Artie Shaw: a Bio-Discography by Edmund L. Blandford (Castle Books, Hastings, 1973).
Discography of Artie Shaw by Willem Frederik van Eyle (Van Eyle, Zaandam, 1966).
Artie Shaw '36-55' by A. Robertson (Robertson, London, 1971).
The Trouble with Cinderella: an Outline of Identity by Artie Shaw (Farrar, Straus & Young, New York, 1952; Jarrolds, London, 1955; Collier, New York, 1963).
Noble Sissle
Reminiscing with Sissle and Blake by William Bolcom & Robert Kimball (Viking Press, New York, 1973).
Freddie Slack
Freddie Slack by Ernie Edwards, George Hall & Bill Korst (Erngeobil, Whittier, 1965).
Lew Stone
Lew Stone—Career in Music by Keith Trodd (Stone, London, 1971).
Jack Teagarden
Jack Teagarden: the Story of a Jazz Maverick by Len Guttridge & Jay D. Smith (Cassell, London, 1960; Jazz Book Club, London, 1962; Da Capo Press, New York, 1976).
Jack Teagarden's Music: his Career and Recordings by Howard J. Waters (Allen, Stanhope, 1960).
'Teagarden and his Times—the Early Days Documented' by J.S. Wilson in *High Fidelity* XIII (June 1963).
Claude Thornhill
Claude Thornhill and his Orchestra (Discographies Unlimited, Maryland, 1971).
Paul Whiteman
'Paul Whiteman: a Discography' by Brian Rust in *Recorded Sound* No 28 (Oct 1967).

General

Stars of Swing by Stuart S. Allen (British Yearbooks, London, 1947).
Paul Whiteman, Jimmy Dorsey, etc, Give Their Secrets of Dance Band Success edited by Doron K. Antrim (Famous Stars, New York, 1936).
This Swing Business by Paul Arundel (Unwin, London, 1947).
And the Bands Played On: an Informal History of British Dance Bands by Sid Colin (Elm Tree Books, London, 1977).
The World of Swing by Stanley Dance (Scribner, New York, 1974).
'Swing: aux USA en 1946' by Charles Delaunay in *Le Point du Jazz* No 5 (Sept 1971).
Big Bands Discography (7 Volumes) by Ernie Edwards, George Hall & Bill Korst (Erngeobil, Whittier, 1965/9).
A Thousand Golden Horns: the Exciting Age of America's Greatest Dance Bands by Gene Fernett (Pendell, Midland, Michigan, 1966).
Swing Out: Great Negro Dance Bands by Gene Fernett (Pendell, Midland, Michigan, 1970).
78 rpm Swing Label Discography by Iwan Frésart (Frésart, Brussels, 1965).

The Kingdom of Swing by Benny Goodman & Irving Kolodin (Stackpole, New York, 1939; Ungar, New York, 1961; Constable, London, 1962).
21 Years of Swing on Brunswick Records by Leonard Hibbs (White, London, 1937).
Encyclopaedia of Swing Decca-Brunswick-Vocalion by Leonard Hibbs & Edgar Jackson (Decca, London, 1941).
The World of Big Bands by Arthur Jackson (David & Charles, Newton Abbot, 1977).
Jam: an Annual of Swing Music edited by Frank Johnson & Ron Wills (Tempo, Sydney, 1938).
The Dance Band Era: the Dancing Decades from Ragtime to Swing: 1910-1950 by Albert McCarthy (Studio Vista, London, 1971; Chilton, Philadelphia, 1972).
Big Band Jazz by Albert McCarthy (Barrie & Jenkins, London, 1974; Putnam, New York, 1974).
Down Beat's Yearbook of Swing, 1939 edited by Paul Eduard Miller (Down Beat, Chicago, 1939).
La Musique de Jazz et le Swing by Hugues Panassié (Correa, Paris, 1945).
Enciclopedia de Swing by Gene Poole (Academia Americana, Buenos Aires, 1939).
Swing Photo Album 1939 by Timme Rosenkrantz (Rosenkrantz, Copenhagen, 1939; Scorpion, Lowestoft, 1964).
The Dance Bands by Brian Rust (Ian Allan, Shepperton, 1972; Arlington House, New Rochelle, 1974).
British Dance Bands: a Discography 1912-1939 by Brian Rust (Rust, London).
American Dance Band Discography 1917-1942 (2 Volumes) by Brian Rust (Arlington House, New Rochelle, 1975).
Swing Discographie by A. Schwanniger & A. Gerwitsch (Grasset, Geneva, 1945).
The Big Bands by George T. Simon (Macmillan, New York 1967; Collier-Macmillan, London, 1967; new ed 1971 & 1975).
Simon Says: the Sights and Sounds of the Swing Era 1935-1955 by George T. Simon (Arlington House, New Rochelle, 1971).
How They Became Name Bands by Paul L. Specht (Fine Arts, New York, 1941).
Big Book of Swing by Bill Treadwell (Cambridge House, New York, 1946).
Swing et Moeurs by Henri Vemane (Editions de Marchenelles, Lille, 1943).
Band Leaders by Julian Vedey (Rockliff, London, 1950).
The Wonderful Era of the Great Dance Bands by Leo Walker (Howell-North, Berkeley, 1964; Doubleday, New York, 1972).

The following 64-page books were issued in conjunction with the various volumes of the Time-Life Swing Era sets (3 LPs each):
Vol 1—*Wonderful Times: Making a Lot Out of Little.* Vol 2—*The Movies: Between Vitaphone and Video.* Vol 3—*Vintage Years of Humor.* Vol 4—*Where Swing Came From.* Vol 5—*1939: a Real Dream of a Year.* Vol 6—*How It Was to be Young Then.* Vol 7—*Swing as a Way of Life.* Vol 8—*When Sport was Mighty Sporty.* Vol 9—*The Golden Age of Network Radio.* Vol 10—*How Sex Was Invented.* Vol 11—*The Day of the Great Entertainers.* Vol 12—*The Sounds of Swing.* Vol 13—*Swing Lives!* Vol 14—The King in Person (Benny Goodman).